PRISON NATION

PRISON NATION

THE WAREHOUSING OF AMERICA'S POOR

EDITED BY

TARA HERIVEL AND PAUL WRIGHT

Routledge
NEW YORK AND LONDON

Published in 2003 by
Routledge
29 West 35th Street
New York, NY 10001
www.routledge-ny.com

Published in Great Britain by
Routledge
11 New Fetter Lane
London EC4P 4EE
www.routledge.co.uk

10 9 8 7 6 5 4 3 2 1

Library of Congress Cataloging-in-Publication Data

  Prison nation : the warehousing of America's poor / edited by Tara Herivel
and Paul Wright.
     p.   cm.
Includes bibliographical references and index.
  ISBN 0-415-93537-7 (hardcover) — ISBN 0-415-93538-5 (pbk.)
  1. Prisons—United States. 2. Prisoners—United States. 3. Corrections—
United States. 4. Discrimination in criminal justice administration—United States.
5. Poor—Government policy—United States. I. Title: Warehousing of America's poor.
II. Herivel, Tara. III. Wright, Paul, 1965–
  HV9471 .W36 2002
  365' .973—dc21
                                         2002009260

This book is dedicated to all who struggle against, and live with the impact of prison and to the memory of Seiichi Michael Yasutake, 1920–2001, an inspiration to all who knew him.

"While there is a lower class, I am in it; while there is a criminal element, I am of it; while there is a soul in prison, I am not free."

—Eugene V. Debs, 1918: *to the court that sentenced him as guilty of violating the Espionage Act.*

Contents

Acknowledgments

We are grateful to all authors in the book, as well as all *Prison Legal News* contributors, both present and past. Much thanks to all publications that allowed article reprints.

To the folks who have gone the extra mile to ensure *PLN*'s survival: thanks to Don Miniken, Sandy Judd, Hans Sherrer, Ellen Spertus, Rollin and Zuraya Wright, Dan Axtell, Allen Parmelee, Daniel Burton Rose, Alex Friedman, Linda Novenski, Martin and Rebecca Chaney, Elizabeth Howard, Walter Tillow, Josephine Wigginton, Matt Esget, Bob Fischer, Thomas Sellman, Barbara Dority, the Humanists of Washington, and the folks at Prompt Press and Common Courage Press.

We would also like to thank the lawyers who have helped *PLN* challenge prison and jail censorship policies across the country. Without their help, *PLN* would have been barred from prisons and jails. In no particular order, thank you to David Fathi, David Zuckerman, Joseph Bringman, Janet Stanton, Brian Barnard, Marc Blackman, Tim Ford, Bruce Plenk, Alison Hardy, Shelly Hall, Andy Mar and David Bowman, Alison Howard, Frank Cuthbertson, Darrel Cochran and Jongwon Yi, Rhonda Brownstein of the Southern Poverty Law Center, Dan Manville, Don Evans, Mike Kipling, Donald Specter, Heather McKay, Anne Brick, Meridith Martin Rountree, Sam Stiltner, Mickey Gendler, Bob Kaplan, Bob Cumbow, Aaron Kornfield, Tim Scott and Julya Hampton, the Washington ACLU and Jesse Wing.

For research assistance, *grazie* to Terry Allen and Tom Sowa for their help with "Boeing Makes Slave Labor Fly."

For editorial assistance when it got ugly, big thanks to Lisa Hasselman. Raoul Schonemann: without your patience and skill we would not have had this stellar piece by Stephen Bright. David Fathi: your eagle-eyed editing continues to influence. Also thanks to David Jarman and thank you to Marcia Herivel, who supports the heart-felt passions.

Introduction

KEN SILVERSTEIN

When Paul Wright, a prisoner at the Monroe Correctional Complex in Washington state and co-editor of this rich volume, calls this country's system of mass incarceration "the most thoroughly implemented social experiment in American history," some readers might believe him to be guilty of exaggeration. But consider that during the past two decades, the American prison population has climbed from 300,000 to more than two million—roughly equal to the combined population of Austin, Denver, Nashville, and Washington, D.C. Largely because of racially biased drug sentencing laws, about half of America's prison population is African-American and one-quarter of all black men are likely to be imprisoned at some point during their lifetimes. One-and-a-half million children currently have a parent behind bars.

The huge swell in prisoner ranks does not reflect a nationwide crime wave. Indeed, the rate for most serious crimes has dropped or remained stagnant for close to two decades. Today, the vast majority of people entering state prisons are convicted of a nonviolent crime—often a drug charge that in many countries would bring a fine or a sentence of community service.

The soaring lock-up rate has produced a corresponding boom in prison construction. In California, where spending on prisons exceed outlays for higher education, passage of the infamous "three strikes" law a decade back has led to the construction of almost a score of new jails and prisons. According to the writer Eric Schlosser, California alone holds more inmates in its jails and prisons than do France, Great Britain, Germany, Japan, Singapore, and the Netherlands combined.

Schlosser calls this state of affairs a prison-industrial complex, which he defines as "a set of bureaucratic, political, and economic interests that encourage increased spending on imprisonment, regardless of the actual need." The prison-industrial complex is not a conspiracy, but a confluence of special interests that include politicians who exploit crime to win votes, private companies that make millions by running or supplying prisons, and small town officials who have turned to prisons as a method of economic development.

Prison Nation: The Warehousing of America's Poor—which Wright co-edited with Tara Herivel—goes beyond the numbers to show the complex, interwoven reasons that have produced the prison-industrial complex. In every section of the book—there are seven, which cover everything from the causes behind the prison explosion to jailhouse economics to the shoddy state of prison medicine—readers will find solid reporting, gripping writing and political revelation.

As the title of the book suggests, most prisoners are poor. An overwhelming number are minority and illiterate while huge numbers, perhaps a quarter-million, are mentally ill. Given this population it's no surprise that about 80 percent of people who go to prison weren't able to afford to pay for an attorney and were forced to rely on underpaid and often uninspired public defenders.

In the first essay of this book, Stephen Bright, the renowned anti-death penalty lawyer, writes about three Georgia lawyers, all from the same family, who handled the cases of 776 poor people in 2002. The average cost of defense was $49.86 per case—"less than the cost of a couple of tickets to a baseball game." In Virginia, fees for court appointed attorneys are limited to $305 for defending a felony if the punishment is less than twenty years, and $845 if the penalty exceeds that. As Bright shows, "the Supreme Court ruled in *Gideon v. Wainright* that lawyers are 'necessities, not luxuries,' [but] the reality is that representation by a capable attorney is a luxury, one few of those accused of a crime can afford."

Prosecutorial power and abuse are another factor that explains the growing number of people behind bars. One little noted issue, discussed here in a contribution from Robert Owen, is overcharging—when prosecutors seek the harshest possible charge for a given crime (for example, seeking the death sentence for any homicide that can conceivably be considered a capital crime). The result is to dissuade defendants from going to trial and instead accept a plea bargain that nominally reduces the punishment. As Owen explains, the reduced charge may be all the prosecutor can expect to win at trial, but many defendants, especially poor ones with inadequate counsel, aren't prepared to run the risk of having a jury convict him of the greater charges.

In an especially fine essay, Kelly Virella tells the story of Joseph Bostic to show how the parole system puts so many released prisoners back behind bars. After serving a seven-year term for manslaughter in a New York prison, Bostic moved to Georgia where he found a job with a construction company. Bostic stayed clean, other than committing the crime of overdrawing his checking account by $341. Unfortunately for Bostic, due process for ex-offenders is virtually suspended; as a result, he was sent back to prison for three years. In some cases, parole rules are so strict, Virella writes, that chronic unemployment can be considered grounds for re-incarceration. No wonder that 70 percent of incoming prisoners in some states are parole violators.

Another theme of this collection is the political economy of prisons. Take, for example, the reemergence of private prisons. These were a familiar feature of American life a hundred years ago, with disastrous consequences. Convicts were farmed out as slave labor. They were routinely beaten and abused, fed slops, and kept in horribly overcrowded cells. By the early-1930s, private prisons were out of business across the country.

But during the past two decades, the number of private prisons has grown from five to 150, while beds have climbed during that time from about 2,000 to around 95,000 (a number constantly in flux). The private prison upsurge was spawned by post-1980s free market ideological fervor, large budget deficits for the federal and state governments, and the discovery and creation of vast new reserves of "raw materials"—prisoners. While the stock market crash of the past few years has hit private prison stocks hard, until quite recently those companies were the darlings of Wall Street. "Everybody's doin' the jailhouse stock," read the headline in a *USA Today* story on the topic. A 1996 conference sponsored by World Research Group, a New York-based investment firm, informed investors, "While arrests and convictions are steadily on the rise, profits are to be made—profits from crime. Get in on the ground floor of this booming industry now!"

Prisoners also mean profits for certain well-known multinational corporations who employ prisoners for little or no pay. As Paul Wright shows, those companies include Boeing, Nintendo, Starbucks, and Trans World Airlines. Meanwhile, many of those same firms are laying off their own workers or moving abroad in order to cut costs.

The essays cited here are just a few of the many eye-opening contributions in *Prison Nation*. By the time readers are finished, Wright's description of the prison system as a gigantic social experiment won't seem hyperbolic at all.

SECTION 1

THE WAREHOUSING
OF AMERICA'S POOR

The Accused Get What the System Doesn't Pay For

Poor Legal Representation
for People Who Can't Afford Lawyers

STEPHEN B. BRIGHT

Many of the men, women, and children sent to prison in the United States every day are processed through courts without the legal representation that is indispensable to a fair trial, a reliable verdict, and a just sentence. Eighty percent of people accused of crimes are unable to afford a lawyer to defend them. While public defender offices or dedicated lawyers capably defend some of the accused, far more are assigned lawyers who work under crushing caseloads, are paid so little that they devote little time to the cases, and lack the time, knowledge, resources, and often even the inclination to defend a case properly. The result is coerced guilty pleas or unfair trials, unreliable verdicts, and sentences that do not fit the crime or the person convicted.

A poor person arrested by the police may languish in jail for days, weeks, or months before seeing a lawyer for the first time. Sometimes, they first meet their lawyers when they are brought to court. Their "representation" consists of hurried, whispered conversations with their lawyers outside the courtroom or even in court, before entering guilty pleas and being sentenced in courts that resemble fast-food restaurants. People who insist on trial often find that their court-appointed lawyers have done no investigation, are unprepared, and thus are unable to present a defense. Although the U.S. Supreme Court has ruled that states must provide lawyers to people facing serious charges, some people accused of crimes receive no representation at all and are forced to fend for themselves—even, on occasion, in cases where they face the prospect of many years in prison. Once convicted, a poor person may face years in prison, or even execution, without a lawyer to pursue avenues of post-conviction review. While in prison, he or she may endure human rights abuses, but have no access to a lawyer to seek remedies for those violations.

This article was written in May 2002.

In contrast, the person with adequate resources may secure a lawyer who will make a case for, and perhaps obtain release on bail, work closely with the client in conducting an immediate and thorough investigation, present a vigorous defense at trial, pursue all available avenues of post-conviction relief, and challenge any constitutional violations that occur in prison. When she was Attorney General, Janet Reno observed that if justice is available only to those who can pay for a lawyer, "That's not justice, and that does not give people confidence in the justice system."[1]

Nonetheless, many state and local governments make no pretense of complying with the constitutional requirement of providing lawyers to poor people accused of crimes. They are unwilling to allocate adequate resources for the representatives of indigent criminal defendants. Yet it is the defendant who pays with his or her life or liberty for the lawyer's ignorance of the law or failure to present critical evidence.

A Constitutional Promise Unfulfilled

The Supreme Court held in 1963 that a poor person facing felony charges "cannot be assured a fair trial unless counsel is provided for him."[2] Implementing the Court's decision, however, has proven to be an immense challenge. Although presumed innocent by the law, they are assumed to be guilty by much of the public. They are unpopular and have no political power. These and other factors have caused state and local governments to strive not toward the much-celebrated constitutional command of equal justice, but, rather, as observed by Chief Justice Harold Clarke of the Georgia Supreme Court in his 1993 address to the legislature, toward "the embarrassing target of mediocrity."[3]

Most state and local governments have been more concerned with keeping costs low than with providing quality defense services or ensuring fair trials. When they have examined factors other than costs, many evaluate indigent defense programs not from the standpoint of ensuring fair trials, but with an eye to increasing administrative convenience in moving dockets and securing convictions. In the pursuit of saving money, governments increasingly award contracts for representing indigent defendants to the lawyer who submits the lowest bid. Many states pay lawyers appointed to defend the poor such low rates that in some cases the attorneys make less than the minimum wage. Many jurisdictions have either refused outright to establish public defender programs or they have established programs but underfunded them, leaving the lawyers in those programs with staggering caseloads.

Many jurisdictions aim to process the maximum number of cases at the lowest possible cost without regard to justice. For example, three lawyers—all members of the same family—handled the cases of 776 poor people in five Georgia counties in 2002 for an average cost of $49.86 per case, less that the cost of a couple of tickets to a baseball game. As a result of placing a greater priority on economy than fairness, many poor people—even those charged with serious crimes—are still subject to the kind of "assembly line justice" the United States Supreme Court condemned 30 years ago.[4] Many localities have become accustomed to systems and practices that simply do not measure up to what the United States Constitution requires. For example:

- Some adults and children who cannot afford a lawyer plead guilty—even to felony charges—and are sentenced to prison or jail without the assistance of an attorney.
- In some municipal and state courts, there are no lawyers available to represent indigent defendants. Virtually all the poor people are processed through those courts without a lawyer.
- Indigent people may languish in jail for weeks or months before meeting with a lawyer, despite professional and ethical standards that require attorneys to meet promptly with their clients after appointment.
- In some courts, the determination of whether an accused can or cannot afford a lawyer is based on factors such as ability to make bail.
- Even after a lawyer has been appointed, some indigent people cannot communicate with their lawyer because their lawyer does not visit the jail, accept telephone calls from clients, or reply to letters and family inquiries, despite professional and ethical standards and guidelines which require a lawyer to meet with his or her client promptly after appointment.
- Many appointed lawyers rarely hire investigators and expert witnesses. Many lawyers do not seek funds for investigators or experts because they do not think that there is any chance the judge will order that funds be provided.
- Because many of the lawyers appointed to defend the poor do not specialize in criminal law, they may be unaware of important developments in the law as well as in areas such as forensic sciences and mental health.
- Important legal issues are not raised by motion or otherwise in many cases. Motions practice is virtually nonexistent in some counties; in others, the same boilerplate motions are filed in virtually every case.
- Despite their poverty, those convicted are often fined and required to pay court costs and various fees and surcharges they cannot afford.

These practices affect the lives of the thousands of people who are hurriedly processed through the courts, instead of being represented by competent, zealous, and independent counsel as required by the Constitution and the ethical and professional standards of the legal profession.

A former president of the Arkansas Association of Criminal Defense Lawyers, who was also involved in the defense of many capital cases in Arkansas, has described the plight of lawyers in that state. Lawyers there are, in effect, either forced to spend their own money or to perform "a sort of uninformed legal triage," ignoring some issues, lines of investigation, and defenses because of the lack of adequate compensation and resources. But the attorneys do not bear the greatest costs of this approach. "The lawyer pays some—in reputation, perhaps—but it is his client who may pay with his liberty or his life."[5]

Factors Contributing to Deficient Representation

While there are numerous reasons, varying from one jurisdiction to the next, which contribute to failures to comply with the constitutional requirements regarding representation of the poor, the primary reasons are no secret. Nor are they isolated factors unique to a particular state or region of the country. Deficient representation is the unavoidable result of several interrelated factors: the failure of the states to provide sufficient funding, the lack of independence of attorneys assigned to defend the poor, the absence of meaningful enforcement of the right to effective assistance of counsel, and the powerlessness of the accused.

Inadequate Funding

The most fundamental reason for the poor quality or absence of legal services for the poor in the criminal justice system is the refusal of governments to allocate sufficient funds for indigent defense programs. An American Bar Association report in 1993 found that "long-term neglect and underfunding of indigent defense have created a crisis of extraordinary proportions in many states throughout the country."[6]

Legislatures in many states have failed adequately to fund public defender programs, leaving public defenders with overwhelming caseloads, and the immense pressure of being responsible for the lives and liberty of too many fellow human beings. While public defender offices attract some of the most dedicated and conscientious young lawyers, those lawyers find it exhausting and enormously difficult to provide adequate representation when saddled with huge caseloads and lacking the necessary investigative assistance.

A public defender in New Orleans represented 418 defendants during the first seven months of 1991. During this time, he entered 130 guilty pleas at arraignment and had at least one serious case set for trial on every single trial date during the period. In "routine cases," he received no investigative support because the three investigators in the public defender's office were responsible for more than 7,000 cases per year. Additionally, no funds were available for expert witnesses.[7]

Even though funding for indigent defense programs has long been recognized as inadequate, some jurisdictions have reduced funding. In Pittsburgh, for example, the county commission slashed funds and job positions at the public defender's office in 1996, leaving the office with forty-five lawyers, twelve less than the fifty-seven who were there previously. Eight full-time investigators were also fired. The attorneys were paid between $24,000 and $32,000 and are permitted to have part-time legal practice on the side.[8] An independent study the year before had concluded that the public defender's office was in crisis because of chronic underfunding and "years of neglect."[9] Judge David S. Cercone, head of the court's Criminal Division, had expressed similar concern, saying that, "[w]e do not think there is any fat to be cut from the public defender's office."[10] The county commissioners responded to the study by cutting $1 million from the $3.9 million budget. Nonetheless, the commissioners somehow found a way to move two of their supporters into positions that paid $50,000 each, which is double the starting salary of a new public defender.[11]

In Wisconsin, then-Governor Tommy Thompson proposed cuts to the state public defender's budget, more flat rate payments to appointed counsel, increases in public defender caseloads, and limits on how much public defenders and appointed attorneys can spend on court documents and investigative services.[12] When the 1996–97 budget ultimately was passed, $3.85 million was cut from the allocation for indigent defense.

Many jurisdictions have no public defender programs. Cases are assigned to individual lawyers or lawyers who have contracted to handle the cases of indigent defendants. Many states and localities compensate lawyers so poorly that it is impossible to attract capable lawyers and impossible for the lawyers to survive in practice if they devote the time required to defend cases properly.

In Virginia, for example, attorneys for indigent defendants are limited to $100 for defending someone in a misdemeanor case in district court, $132 for defending a misdemeanor case in circuit court, $305 for defending a felony case where the punishment is less than 20 years, and $845 where the punishment is more than 20 years. When one attorney challenged the limit in felony cases, arguing that once the attorney exceeds the limit and is forced to work uncompensated, it creates a conflict between the lawyer's pecuniary interests and zealous representation of the client, the circuit judge removed him from the case. One circuit judge announced at calendar call that any attorney raising the conflict of interest issue would be removed from the list of appointed counsel. As each case was called, the judge asked the attorney whether he or she intended to raise the issue.[13]

The result is that these lawyers often earn less than the minimum wage for defending someone in a serious felony case or even a capital case. For example, a Mississippi lawyer who spends 500 hours preparing for a death penalty trial will be paid $2 an hour. Imagine what kind of legal representation a poor person accused of a capital crime gets for $2 an hour. Unfortunately, the old adage, "you get what you pay for," applies with special force in the law. Most good lawyers do not work for $2 an hour or

THE ACCUSED GET WHAT THE SYSTEM DOESN'T PAY FOR   11

even $20, $50, or $100 an hour. Lawyers paid so little cannot afford to spend the time required to conduct interviews, investigations and negotiations, and defend cases at trials. As one Virginia prosecutor observed:

> What it boils down to is, you get what you pay for. Look who's on a court-appointed list anywhere. Very few experienced attorneys are on those lists, and the reason is, they can't afford to be on them. So you either have very inexperienced attorneys right out of law school for whom any money is better than no money. Or you have people who are really bad lawyers who can't make a living except off the court appointed list. The prosecutor said that such a system "doesn't give me any satisfaction as a prosecutor, and I don't think it serves justice."[14]

In addition, lawyers appointed to defend indigent defendants are often not paid for months or years after they provide the representation. Often, their applications for compensation are arbitrarily reduced by judges and bureaucrats. This discourages lawyers from taking the cases of indigent defendants.

Frequently, lawyers are denied the investigative and expert assistance essential to providing adequate representation. The courts have constructed a Catch-22 by requiring the lawyer to demonstrate an extensive need for expert or investigative assistance, a showing that frequently cannot be made without the very expert assistance that is sought.

The burdens on already overtaxed and inadequate indigent defense systems are growing. With the passage of each new crime bill, Congress and state legislatures create scores of new crimes, increase penalties for existing crimes, and appropriate millions of dollars for law enforcement and prosecution.[15] These measures increase the number of arrests and prosecutions and the severity of the sentences that may be imposed. Despite the fact that the legislation creates a greater need for adequate defense counsel, such legislation usually does not include a single dollar for indigent defense.

The Lack of Independence of Indigent Defense Programs

In jurisdictions where judges appoint lawyers to defend cases, it is no secret that judges do not always appoint capable lawyers to defend the poor. Clarence Darrow made an observation that is as true today as it was when he made it in 1924: "[N]o court ever interferes with a good lawyer's business by calling him in and compelling him to give his time" in defense of an indigent defendant.[16] Many judges prefer to appoint lawyers who try cases rapidly, instead of zealously, in order to move their dockets.

For more than forty years, judges in Houston, Texas, repeatedly appointed Joe Frank Cannon, known for hurrying through trials like "greased lightning," to defend indigent defendants despite his tendency to doze off during trial.[17] Ten of Cannon's clients were sentenced to death, one of the largest numbers among Texas attorneys. While representing Calvin Burdine at a capital trial, Cannon "dozed and actually fell asleep" during trial, "in particular during the guilt-innocence phase when the State's solo prosecutor was questioning witnesses and presenting evidence."[18] The clerk of the court testified that "defense counsel was asleep on several occasions on several days over the course of the proceedings."[19] Cannon's file on the case contained only three pages of notes.[20] A law professor who later represented Carl Johnson, a previous Cannon client, in post-conviction proceedings found that Cannon's "ineptitude . . . jumps off the printed page" and that Cannon slept during the proceedings.[21] Nevertheless, the death sentences in both cases were upheld by the Texas courts. Carl Johnson has been executed.

Judges in Long Beach, California, assigned the representation of numerous indigent defendants to a lawyer who tried cases in very little time, not even obtaining discovery in some of them. According to a former supervisor at the local public defender's office, judges liked the lawyer, Ron Slick, "because he was always ready to go to trial, even when it seemed he had inadequate time to prepare." A substantial number of his clients asked judges to appoint someone else to defend them, but their motions were denied. At one time, Slick had the distinction of having more of his clients sentenced to death—eight—than any other attorney in California.[22]

Many judges may be more interested in docket control or avoiding reversal than in ensuring an earnest defense for poor defendants. Judges also use appointments as a patronage system for lawyers who need the business because they cannot get other legal work. A study of homicide cases in Philadelphia revealed that judges there appointed attorneys to defend cases based on political connections, not on legal ability.[23] The study disclosed that "Philadelphia's poor defendants often find themselves being represented by ward leaders, ward committeemen, failed politicians, the sons of judges and party leaders, and contributors to the judges' election campaigns."[24] As might be expected, treating the assignment of criminal cases as part of a judicial patronage system does not always result in the best legal representation. The study found that "even officials in charge of the system say they wouldn't want to be represented in Traffic Court by some of the people appointed to defend poor people accused of murder."[25] There is the appearance—and in many cases the reality—that many of the lawyers who depend upon appointments from judges are reluctant to provide zealous representation for fear of alienating the judge and jeopardizing future business. An experienced criminal defense lawyer in Houston described the attitude of many lawyers there who get appointed to defend indigents:

The mindset of a lot of court-appointed lawyers is to please the judge, to curry favor with the judge by getting a quick guilty plea from the client. Then everybody's happy. The judge has the case off the docket. The prosecutor doesn't have to mess with it. The defendant is off to wherever he's going. And the lawyer has made a relatively decent fee: about $150 for basically an hour of his time. That's much more economical for a lawyer who's earning a living off of court appointments than to reset the case, go out and investigate, probably not get paid for his time, have to do a bunch of work, and maybe aggravate the judge by keeping the case on the docket.[26]

The appointed lawyers also stay in the good graces of the judges by contributing to their campaigns for office.[27]

The problem is not limited to the state courts. The appointment of public defenders in many judicial districts by federal judges "creates a serious problem of perception and provides the opportunity for occasional abuse," a committee of judges and lawyers appointed by Chief Justice Rehnquist reported.[28] One example is the refusal in 1992 by the United States Court of Appeals for the Fourth Circuit to renew the appointment of highly respected federal defender Fred Bennett, after eleven years in office. The judges apparently did not like the aggressive advocacy of Bennett and his assistants, but it may be fairly questioned whether this action promoted the best interests of the clients served by the federal defender or whether the judges disagreed with the zealous representation of poor people.

In addition, many indigent defense programs are not independent of the people trying to imprison or execute the clients served by those programs. In some states, governors who sign death warrants also appoint the state defenders who are to defend the very people the governor has ordered killed. Legislatures have reduced or eliminated funding of programs that have been effective in the past or have restructured them. Judges control the appointment and compensation of defense counsel in many states and often assign cases to lawyers clearly incapable of providing competent representation. The lack of independence in many cases has a substantial adverse impact on the quality of legal services provided. Indeed, when judges and executives control programs that continually provide deficient representation to the accused, it can fairly be said that lawyers are being provided to the poor only to create an appearance of legitimacy to a system that lacks fairness.

Politicians who compete with one another to show who is the toughest on crime often control funding and even the appointment of personnel for indigent defense programs. For example, upon becoming the new governor of Kentucky, Paul Patton signed five execution warrants on his second day in office to show that he was tough on crime. The Public Advocate, Allison Connelly, noted the inappropriateness of signing the warrants because the cases of all five of the condemned were pending before courts.[29] Lawyers from her office secured stays of execution.

But the same governor who signed the death warrants appoints the public defender. When the time came to renew Connelly's appointment, Patton refused to reappoint her, even though the Public Advocacy Commission had unanimously recommended her reappointment and judges and lawyers had praised the job she had done.[30] Regardless of why Patton refused to reappoint Connelly, there was an appearance that it may have been related to the discharge of her duties in defending indigent clients.

In Florida, legislators attacked the office of the Capital Collateral Representative (CCR) for its representation of condemned prisoners in that state, saying that it needlessly delayed executions.[31] Stephen Hanlon, who oversees the Holland & Knight law firm's pro bono division and has worked with CCR attorneys, responded that, "I am firmly convinced that the criticism CCR received was not because it was frivolous but because it was effective."[32]

The legislature split CCR into three separate offices and provided that the governor, who signs the death warrants setting executions, would appoint the director of each new office.[33] The legislature also provided that the Judicial Nominating Commission would now submit nominees for the positions to the governor, instead of the state's public defenders, who had previously recommended three nominees to the governor for the position of Capital Collateral Representative.

The Judicial Nominating Commission gave the governor eight nominees: four lawyers who had experience in representing persons facing the death penalty and four with no such experience. Governor Lawton Chiles appointed only from the second group, choosing a lawyer in private practice and two former prosecutors, one of whom had worked in the governor's office for twelve years, and before that, represented the state in twelve capital cases during five and a half years as an assistant attorney general.[34]

It is neither unusual nor undesirable for a lawyer with prosecution experience to become a defense lawyer. A new convert, however, is usually not made Pope on the day of his conversion. These circumstances put together—the governor's role in signing death warrants, the enormous political benefits that Florida governors have reaped from signing death warrants, and the appointment of two prosecutors with no defense experience over nominees with experience in defending capital cases—would cause any objective observer to question whether the goal of the appointments was to frustrate zealous representation instead of ensuring it.

The representation provided by the offices created raises even graver questions. The most experienced attorney assigned to defend Judi Buenoaño when the governor signed a warrant for her execution was not qualified to work in federal court. Experienced attorneys were fired or left for new agencies. The office in Tampa, run by a former prosecutor and unsuccessful candidate for State Attorney, hired lawyers with no experience in capital litigation, including one lawyer who had spent three years managing Hogtown Bar-B-Q restaurants.[35] A circuit judge described the office as a "disorganized, chaotic place where, at times, interns/trainees file motions and pleadings in cases carrying society's most severe penalty;" the judge found the attorneys for one death row inmate "incompetent," and replaced them with a private lawyer.[36] The office in Tallahassee could not find lead attorneys for half of its cases.[37]

Ohio Attorney General Betty Montgomery attacked the state public defender's office, saying its death penalty attorneys were "gaming the system and making it a mockery" by maneuvering for delays to stop executions.[38] She introduced a proposal to prohibit public defenders from receiving tax funds for representing condemned inmates if they win appeals alleging ineffective assistance of counsel.[39] In February 1996, following Montgomery's statement and proposal, Ohio Public Defender David Bodiker fired two top staff members, including a twelve-year veteran. Bodiker stated "there's always been widespread optimism that we could prevent executions. I don't share that."[40]

Bodiker claimed his actions were unrelated to the Attorney General's criticism. The fired attorneys filed a complaint with the Ohio Public Defender Commission, claiming Bodiker prevents attorneys from zealously defending death-row clients and that he "has politicized the office to reflect the pro-death penalty views of" Governor George Voinovich and Attorney General Montgomery.[41]

A state's chief law enforcement officer who has responsibility for obtaining convictions should not be appointing the person responsible for the defense. Management of the defense is not a proper judicial function. Judges should be fair and impartial, and independent of both prosecution and defense. Instead, independent boards should operate indigent defense programs. Those programs should assign lawyers to cases based upon the lawyer's ability to provide effective representation, not speed, administrative convenience, political connections, or other factors unrelated to the lawyer's ability to represent the accused.

A Standard of Effective Assistance that Denies Equal Justice

The Supreme Court correctly observed in 1942 that "[t]he right to have the assistance of counsel is too fundamental and absolute to allow courts to indulge in nice calculations as to the amount of prejudice resulting from its denial."[42] In 1984, however, the Court decided that prejudice to a defendant could be based on a rough calculation of whether counsel's deficient performance affected the outcome. In *Strickland v. Washington*, the Court not only adopted this standard of prejudice; it went one step further in putting the burden of proof on the defendant to make the showing.[43] The Court also required that, in order to prevail on a claim of ineffective assistance, a defendant must overcome "a strong presumption

that counsel's conduct falls within the wide range of reasonable professional assistance," and show that the attorney's representation "fell
below an objective standard of reasonableness."[44] This standard has
proven to be so malleable that the mere presence of a lawyer at counsel
table is often found to be sufficient representation.[45]

Judge Alvin Rubin of the Fifth Circuit put it bluntly:

> The Constitution, as interpreted by the courts, does not require that the
> accused, even in a capital case, be represented by able or effective
> counsel. . . . Consequently, accused persons who are represented by "not-
> legally-ineffective" lawyers may be condemned to die when the same
> accused, if represented by effective counsel, would receive at least the
> clemency of a life sentence.[46]

There is ample support for this frank admission that, under the standard established in *Strickland*, the courts do not deliver on the promise of
equal justice for rich and poor. Stark examples of just how bad a lawyer
can be and still be found effective under *Strickland* are provided by three
Texas capital cases in which defense lawyers slept during trial. The
Houston Chronicle described the following spectacle in one of the cases:

> Seated beside his client—a convicted capital murderer—defense attorney
> John Benn spent much of Thursday afternoon's trial in apparent deep sleep.
> His mouth kept falling open and his head lolled back on his shoulders, and
> then he awakened just long enough to catch himself and sit upright. Then
> it happened again. And again. And again. And again. Every time he opened his eyes, a
> different prosecution witness was on the stand describing another aspect of
> the Nov. 19, 1991, arrest of George McFarland in the robbery-killing of gro-
> cer Kenneth Kwan.
>
> When state District Judge Doug Shaver finally called a recess, Benn was
> asked if he truly had fallen asleep during a capital murder trial. "It's bor-
> ing," the 72-year-old longtime Houston lawyer explained. . . . Court
> observers said Benn seems to have slept his way through virtually the entire
> trial.[47]

Attorney Benn's sleeping did not offend the Sixth Amendment, the
trial judge explained, because, "[t]he Constitution doesn't say the lawyer
has to be awake."[48] The Texas Court of Criminal Appeals apparently
agreed. It rejected McFarland's claim of ineffective assistance of counsel,
applying the standard established in *Strickland*;[49] the dissent, however,
argued that "[a] sleeping counsel is unprepared to present evidence, to
cross-examine witnesses, and to present any coordinated effort to evaluate evidence and present a defense."[50]

The Texas Court of Criminal Appeals also found that a sleeping
attorney was sufficient "counsel" under *Strickland* in the case of Calvin

Burdine.[51] And both the Texas Court of Criminal Appeals and the United States Court of Appeals for the Fifth Circuit held Carl Johnson did not satisfy *Strickland* even though his attorney slept during parts of the trial.[52] Neither court published its opinion. Carl Johnson was executed on September 19, 1995.

Wallace Fugate was sentenced to death after a two-day trial in Georgia, in which he was represented by a lawyer who had never heard of *Gregg v. Georgia*,[53] the case that upheld the current death penalty law in Georgia, *Furman v. Georgia*,[54] the decision that declared the death penalty unconstitutional in 1972, or any other relevant case.[55] Not surprisingly, given his complete ignorance of the law, the lawyer did not make a single objection during the entire two-day capital trial.

Being defended by such a lawyer is much like being treated by a doctor who has never heard of penicillin. Such a doctor likely never heard of tetracycline or of heart bypass surgery, either. If a doctor failed to treat a patient properly due to such a gross lack of knowledge, courts would not hesitate to find malpractice. But under *Strickland*, such ignorance on the part of a lawyer does not violate the Sixth Amendment. The following question was presented to the Georgia Supreme Court in seeking review of the representation provided to Wallace Fugate:

> Whether the standard of "counsel" is now so low in capital trials in this state that it is satisfied by the mere presence of individuals with bar cards at counsel table with the accused, who act primarily as spectators and are completely ignorant of the law—even to the point of being unaware of the Supreme Court's opinion in the seminal capital case of *Gregg v. Georgia*, 428 U.S. 153 (1976), make no objections, give closing arguments which contradict each other, and fail completely to make the trial an adversarial testing process?

The court denied a certificate of probable cause even to review the case.

The Supreme Court has adopted strict "procedural default" doctrines that bar review of any issue not properly raised and preserved by counsel. *Strickland*, however, allows defendants to be represented by lawyers who are ignorant of the law, who do no investigation, and who are thus completely incapable of complying with the strict procedural requirements the Court has adopted. As a result, states have no incentive to provide adequate representation to poor people. By assigning the indigent accused inadequate counsel, the state increases its chances of obtaining a conviction and reduces the scope of appellate and post-conviction review. So long as the lawyer's performance meets the *Strickland* standard, those cases in which the accused received the poorest legal representation will receive the least scrutiny on appeal and in post-conviction review because of the lawyer's failure to preserve issues, assert the right legal grounds for objections, and put on evidence to provide a factual basis for relief.

The Supreme Court stated as one basis for requiring the defendant to prove prejudice, "[t]he government is not responsible for, and hence not able to prevent, attorney errors."[56] That is simply not true in cases involving poor people who have court-appointed lawyers. A poor person accused of a crime does not choose an attorney; a judge or some other government official assigns a lawyer to represent the defendant. Thus, the government is responsible for deficient representation when it provides a lawyer who lacks the experience and skill to handle the case, or when it denies the lawyer the resources necessary to investigate the case and present a defense. *Strickland* allows the government to get away with it.

The Powerlessness of the Accused

People accused of crime depend upon their lawyers to assert and enforce their rights. But people assigned incompetent lawyers have no way to enforce their most fundamental right, the right to a competent lawyer. Gregory Wilson, an African-American man who faced the death penalty in Covington, Kentucky, sought to secure competent counsel, but was repeatedly rebuffed by the judge who presided over this case. Wilson had no lawyer because the state public defender program would not handle the case and the local indigent defense program could not find a lawyer because compensation for defense counsel in capital cases at that time was limited by statute to $2,500.

When the head of the local indigent defense program urged the judge to order compensation beyond the statutory limit in order to secure a lawyer qualified for such a serious case, the judge refused and suggested that the indigent defense program rent a river boat and sponsor a cruise down the Ohio river to raise money for the defense. The judge eventually obtained counsel by posting a letter in the courthouse asking any member of the bar to take the case with the plea "PLEASE HELP. DESPERATE." The notice said nothing about qualifications to handle a capital case. The judge appointed three lawyers who responded, but one later withdrew.

Not surprisingly, this method of selecting counsel did not produce a "dream team." The lead counsel, William Hagedorn, can charitably be described as well past his prime. He did not have an office or support staff, but practiced out of his home, where a large flashing Budweiser beer sign was prominently displayed. He had never previously handled a death penalty case. The other lawyer who responded to the judge's plea for help had never before handled a felony case. That lawyer found that Hagedorn "manifested all the signs of a burned-out alcoholic. . . . [H]e would ramble and digress. At times he appeared disoriented. He did not make sense. . . . He seemed incapable of having any meaningful discussion about the case." The attorney who administered the county's indigent defense system strongly objected to the appointments, saying that they were "unworkable" and the two lawyers could not provide "the quality of representation that is needed in this the most serious of all cases."

Wilson became concerned. Almost any consumer of legal services, even one who wanted a lawyer only to prepare a will or an uncontested divorce, would be concerned if he or she found that one lawyer who was to provide those services did not have a law office and had never provided the services before.

Wilson became even more concerned upon learning that the police had recently executed a search warrant and recovered stolen property in garbage bags from beneath Hagedorn's floor; that Hagedorn had engaged in unethical conduct, including forging a client's name to a check; and that Hagedorn was a "heavy drinker," who had appeared in court drunk on occasion, and was consistently to be found at a bar known as "Kelly's Keg." Mr. Hagedorn had even given the name and telephone number of Kelly's Keg as his business address and telephone number. It is hard to fault Wilson for his concern. Most people would be reluctant to trust even a minor legal matter to such a lawyer.

But, unlike those with resources, Wilson could not afford another lawyer. Wilson repeatedly objected to being represented by the lawyers appointed by the court. He asked the judge that he be provided with a lawyer who was capable of defending a capital case. The judge refused and proceeded to conduct a trial that was a travesty of justice. Hagedorn was not even present for parts of the trial. He cross-examined only a few witnesses, including one witness whose direct testimony he missed because he was out of the courtroom. Wilson was sentenced to death.

What more could Gregory Wilson have done to enforce his constitutional right to counsel? He objected. He complained about the lawyers appointed by the judge, who were clearly incapable of defending a capital case. He asked for a real lawyer. Wilson did far more to assert his right to a lawyer than most poor people who are assigned incompetent lawyers. Even these efforts were insufficient to enforce the right to counsel. On appeal, the Kentucky Supreme Court attributed Hagedorn's performance to Wilson's supposed lack of cooperation.

Conclusion

Although the Supreme Court stated in *Gideon v. Wainwright* that lawyers are "necessities, not luxuries," the reality is that representation by a capable attorney is a luxury, one few of those accused of a crime can afford. Many states are not meeting their constitutional, ethical, and professional obligations to provide fair and equal treatment to poor people accused of crimes.

One does not need to look far for an example of a structure for the delivery of legal services in criminal cases. The prosecution of criminal cases is generally state-funded and efficiently structured to ensure that the State is competently represented in criminal cases. The district attorneys recruit, train, and supervise lawyers who prosecute cases on a full-time basis. The lawyers hired by these offices specialize in the prosecution of cases, attend continuing legal education programs on their responsibilities, learn both the law and new approaches to dealing with their duties, and stay current on developments in forensic sciences and other areas of importance to their practice. The offices of district attorneys share information with one another, avoiding unnecessary and costly duplication of effort.

Public defender offices that employ full-time attorneys who specialize in the defense of criminal cases benefit from economies of scale that are not available in contract and appointed-counsel programs. Of course, no office and no lawyer can provide adequate representation without adequate resources so that attorneys carry reasonable caseloads and have the investigative and expert assistance necessary to provide competent representation.

But the poor person accused of a crime has no lobby, no political action committee. There is no constituency for adequate representation for the poor. As a result, there is little likelihood that the scandalous representation provided in many courts will improve. However, unless those accused of crimes are provided with adequate representation, "equal justice" will remain an aspiration, not a reality, and poor lawyering—along with misguided policies, excessive sentences, and other factors described in other chapters of this book—will continue to be a major factor in the lottery that sends so many people to prisons and jails each year.

Notes

1. Janet Reno, Address to the American Bar Association Criminal Justice Section 6 (Aug. 2, 1997).
2. *Gideon v. Wainwright,* 372 U.S. 335 (1963); see also Anthony Lewis, *Gideon's Trumpet* (1964).
3. Hon. Harold G. Clarke, State of the Judiciary Address to the Georgia General Assembly (Jan. 13, 1994), in *Fulton County Daily Report,* Jan. 14, 1993, at 5.
4. *Argersinger v. Hamlin,* 407 U.S. 25, 34 (1972).
5. Jeff Rosenzweig, *The Crisis in Indigent Defense: An Arkansas Commentary,* 44 *Ark. L. Rev.* 409, 413 (1991).
6. Richard Klein and Robert Spangenberg, *The Indigent Defense Crisis* 25 (1993) (prepared for the American Bar Association Section of Criminal Justice Ad Hoc Committee on the Indigent Defense Crisis).
7. See *State v. Peart,* 621 So.2d 780, 784 (La. 1993).
8. See Jan Ackerman, "Public Defenders Feel Betrayed by Heavy-Handed County Axing," *Pittsburgh Post-Gazette,* Feb. 27, 1996, at B1.
9. Jan Ackerman, "Justice on a Tight Budget; Commissioners Are Courting Disaster by Cutting Budget of Overworked Public Defenders," *Pittsburgh Post-Gazette,* Feb. 4, 1996, at A1.
10. Id.
11. See Ackerman, *supra* note 8, at B1.

12. Dave Daley, "Defense Attorney Fears Poor Clients Will be Hurt by Cuts," *Milwaukee Journal*, Mar. 16, 1995, at A18; Daniel Bice, "Lawyers May Boycott Public Cases," *Milwaukee Journal*, Apr. 7, 1995, at B5.

13. Laura LaFay, "Virginia's Poor Receive Justice on the Cheap," *Virginian-Pilot*, Feb. 15, 1998, at A1.

14. Id.

15. See Pierre Thomas, "First Fruit of Crime Bill is Marketed; Reno: $200 Million to Police in October," *Washington Post*, Sept. 9, 1994 at A25.

16. Clarence Darrow on Capital Punishment 34 (Chicago Historical Bookworks 1991) (1924).

17. Paul M. Barrett, "Lawyer's Fast Work on Death Cases Raises Doubts About System," *Wall Street Journal*, Sept. 7, 1994, at A1.

18. *Ex parte Burdine*, 901 S.W.2d 456, 457 (Tex. Crim. App. 1995) (Maloney, J., dissenting).

19. Id.

20. See Barrett, *supra* note 17, at A1.

21. David R. Dow, "The State, The Death Penalty, and Carl Johnson," 37 *Boston College Law Review* 691, 694–95 (1996).

22. See Ted Rohrlick, The Case of the Speedy Attorney, *Los Angeles Times*, Sept. 26, 1991, at A1.

23. Frederic N. Tulsky, "Big-Time Trials, Small Time Defenses," *Philadelphia Inquirer*, Sept. 14, 1992, at A1.

24. Id.

25. Id.

26. Andrew Hammel, "Discrimination and Death in Dallas: A Case Study in Systematic Racial Exclusion," *Texas Forum on Civil Liberties & Civil Rights*, Summer 1998, at 225–26.

27. Id.

28. Alison Frankel, "Too Independent," *American Law*, Jan.–Feb. 1993, at 67, 68.

29. Gil Lawson, "Patton Sets Execution Date in 5 Death-Row Cases; Order Issued to Speed Appeals," *Louisville Courier Journal*, Jan. 4, 1996, at 1B.

30. Gil Lawson, "Patton Picks Lewis to Replace Connelly as Public Advocate; Appointee is 20-Year Veteran of Defender Systems," *Louisville Courier Journal*, Sept. 18, 1996, at 1B.

31. Robin Blumner, "Killing Agency Won't Speed Up Executions," *St. Petersburg Times*, Feb. 16, 1997, at 4D.

32. "Inexperience Defines Chiles' Death Row Staff," *Florida Today*, Oct. 5, 1997, at 8B.

33. *Florida Statutes Annotated* §27.701 (West Supp. 1998).

34. Jackie Hallifax, "New Death Row Lawyers Have No Background in Capital Appeals," *Tallahassee Democrat*, Sept. 30, 1997, at 1B; Jackie Hallifax, "Chiles Appoints 2 New Death Row Attorneys," *Miami Herald*, Aug. 9, 1997, at 6B.

35. Jenny Staletovich, "Office That Defends Death Row Inmates Near Collapse," *Palm Beach Post*, May 4, 1998, at 1A.

36. William R. Levesque, "Death Row Inmate Gets New Attorneys," *St. Petersburg Times*, Oct. 27, 1998, at 3B.

37. Jackie Hallifax, "One Death Row Appeals Office is Struggling With its Caseload," *Tallahassee Democrat*, Oct. 1, 1998.

38. Alan Johnson, "2 Fired Public Defenders Take Fight to Higher Level," *Columbus Dispatch*, Feb. 29, 1996, at 7C.

39. "Attorney General is Keeping the Death Penalty Argument Alive," *Cincinnati Post*, Apr. 8, 1996, at 6A.

40. Alan Johnson, "Public Defender Signals New Tack on Capital Cases," *Columbus Dispatch*, Feb. 20, 1996, at 1A.

41. Mary Beth Lane, "Lawyers File Job-Loss Actions; Complaints Name Public Defender," *Plain Dealer*, Feb. 29, 1996, at 6B.

42. *Glasser v. United States*, 315 U.S. 60, 76 (1942).

43. 466 U.S. 668, 694 (1984).

44. Id. at 688–89.

45. See William S. Geimer, "A Decade of Strickland's Tin Horn: Doctrinal and Practical Undermining of the Right to Counsel," 4 *William & Mary Bill of Rights Journal* 91 (1995).

46. *Riles v. McCotter*, 799 F.2d 947, 955 (5th Cir. 1986) (Rubin, J., concurring).

47. John Makeig, "Asleep on the Job; Slaying Trial Boring, Lawyer Says," *Houston Chronicle*, Aug. 14, 1992, at A35.

48. Id.

49. *McFarland v. State*, 928 S.W.2d 482 (Tex. Crim. App. 1996).

50. Id. at 527 (Baird, J., dissenting).

51. *Ex parte Burdine*, 901 S.W.2d 456 (Tex. Crim. App. 1995).

52. *Johnson v. Scott*, 68 F.3d 470 (5th Cir. 1995).

53. 428 U.S. 153 (1976).

54. 408 U.S. 238 (1972).

55. See "A Lawyer Without Precedent," *Harper's Magazine*, June 1, 1997, at 24, 26.

56. *Strickland v. Washington*, 466 U.S. 668, 693 (1984).

Absolute Power, Absolute Corruption

ROBERT OWEN

American society conventionally regards public prosecutors not just as lawyers out to win cases but as representatives of a broader public interest in fair outcomes. The Supreme Court, in one of the most famous expressions of this view, called the prosecutor "not [an] ordinary party to a controversy, but [a sovereign] whose obligation to govern impartially is as compelling as its obligation to govern at all."[1] Accordingly, the Court intoned, the prosecutor's interest "in a criminal prosecution is not that it shall win, but that justice shall be done."[2] In fact, however, prosecutors too often fall short of this aspiration, failing to discharge this overriding duty to see that justice is done and engaging instead in what is broadly termed "prosecutorial misconduct."

Frequently, when laypeople (or their self-appointed representatives in the media) talk about "prosecutorial misconduct," what they have in mind is *scheming*—such as when a prosecutor, perhaps assisted by other government agents (for example, the police), willfully manufactures evidence against an accused person she knows or believes is innocent, or suppresses evidence which indisputably would clear someone. While that does happen from time to time, we can be thankful that it's an anomaly.[3] Instead, what we encounter much more frequently in the contemporary American criminal justice system is better described as *overreaching*: oppressive tactics born of systemic institutional arrangements that reward (or fail to punish) prosecutors who "cut corners" in pursuit of a conviction. The government's resources and power so dramatically outweigh those of the accused that prosecutors, rather than scrutinizing their own behavior to guard against abuses of power, habitually focus only on their won-lost record and its political consequences. In the end, these institutional arrangements and their predictable consequences reflect the

---

This article was written in April 2002.

insight of Lord Acton's famous warning that "absolute power corrupts absolutely."

This essay describes two variations on the theme of prosecutorial overreaching.[4] It then reflects upon why the mass media, one social institution which has a real chance of checking prosecutorial excess, fails to challenge such practices. Despite priding itself in other contexts on its role as a "watchdog" alerting the public to government oppression, the media fail to see prosecutorial overreaching as a threat to the fundamental fairness of the criminal justice system. The regrettable result is a system in which prosecutors routinely act in ways that an impartial observer would characterize as oppressive and unfair, but which the corrective mechanisms of the legal system never address and which the media too often ignore.

1. Overreaching by Concealing Evidence which Might Help the Accused

The criminal justice system took a giant step toward basic fairness when the Warren Court formally recognized that the prosecutor has a duty to disclose evidence in its possession which might disprove a suspect's guilt. This doctrine—the *Brady* rule[5]—is a potentially powerful mechanism for correcting the structural imbalance of power between the state and the accused. It is beyond reasonable dispute that the prosecution's vast resources (armies of police officers, sophisticated crime labs, and so forth) and coercive power (including, but not limited to, the simple obligation witnesses feel to answer questions from the police) permit it to undertake a much farther-reaching investigation than the accused could ever mount. The *Brady* rule helps ensure that, to the extent that such a full-scale inquiry produces evidence favorable to the accused, he will have the benefit of it. Thus understood, this rule allows the accused (who is, of course, presumed innocent) to benefit from the extensive investigative resources and advantages enjoyed by the law enforcement apparatus.

Unfortunately, the courts' reading of *Brady* has created an incentive for prosecutors *not* to disclose evidence which might point to another suspect. Why? Because the legal standard for reviewing *Brady* claims *post*-trial, after a jury has already convicted the accused, places on him a very high burden to show that the undisclosed evidence would have left the jury with a reasonable doubt about his guilt. For several different reasons, this legal regime inexorably works to the prosecutor's advantage.

First, it is essential to appreciate that in most cases, the undisclosed evidence is not a "smoking gun" which indisputably clears the accused, but evidence which might have supported a defense if it had been further investigated, developed, and corroborated. As a result of its having been suppressed, of course, no such additional development and corroboration is likely to have occurred. Thus, in isolation, the undisclosed evidence may not appear particularly compelling or favorable.

Second, the retrospective harm analysis created by the courts is irreducibly and unfairly speculative. It's difficult to know exactly how defense counsel might have tried the case differently had she known about a particular piece of evidence in advance of trial. Trials unfold organically and it is often impossible reliably to recreate the path events might have taken if the prosecution had been forthcoming. In short, the pretrial disclosure of a single item of evidence, through a sort of "ripple effect," might have reshaped the entire trial. This effect makes backward-looking attempts to measure the effect of such non-disclosure singularly fruitless.

Finally, guilty verdicts have inertia. It is extremely hard for even a fair-minded court reviewing a *Brady* claim after trial to ignore the apparent strength of the state's case since it did, in fact, persuade twelve fair-minded jurors to convict. Simply put, a convicted person usually looks guilty, which tends to skew the reviewing court's judgment toward finding no harm from the prosecutor's pretrial suppression of potentially exculpatory evidence. Particularly where the favorable evidence has not been developed and corroborated by a full-scale defense investigation, it will shink in significance by contrast to the case actually presented by the prosecution at trial.

Thus, courts exaggerate when they suggest that the prosecution "assumes the risk" of an eventual reversal when it fails to disclose potentially exculpatory evidence before trial.[6] As a practical matter, the "risk" dissipates once the defendant has been convicted. The prosecutor need only succeed in suppressing the evidence until after trial, and then can preserve the guilty verdict by exploiting the tactical advantage it enjoys under the prevailing legal interpretation of *Brady*.[7]

2. Overreaching by Overcharging and by Coercing "Cooperation" with the Prosecutor

Another pernicious and commonplace variety of prosecutorial overreaching is *overcharging*, a tactic that can assume a number of different forms depending on the case and the jurisdiction. One type of overcharging occurs when prosecutors routinely frame charges at the highest degree of seriousness; for example, charging every homicide as the highest degree of murder. Such overcharging raises the stakes dramatically for an accused who contemplates going to trial. Even if he is represented by competent counsel who will vigorously challenge the prosecution's case, there is a substantial risk that the jury may convict him of the greater charge anyway. The risk is particularly great when the accused cannot hire her own counsel and so must rely on a court-appointed lawyer carrying an impossibly heavy caseload and armed with too few investigative resources to give every felony case the serious scrutiny it deserves.[8] Such bleak prospects tend to coerce the overcharged defendant into

giving up his right to trial (that is, pleading guilty) in return for the prosecutor's nominally reducing the charge against him. The "reduced"
charge may be the most serious charge that the prosecution could actually have proved at trial in any event—but unless the defendant is
willing to gamble that he can avoid conviction on the more serious
charge, he will not have a chance to test the prosecution's case on the
"reduced" charge itself.

A comparable type of overcharging is to enforce an inflexible policy of
seeking in every case the harshest sentence available for a given offense.
For example, since 1991 Texas prosecutors have had the discretion not to
seek the death penalty even if the defendant has been formally charged
with capital murder. If death is not sought, the mandatory sentence upon
conviction is life imprisonment with no chance for parole until the prisoner has served 40 calendar years. In some jurisdictions, such as Dallas
County, this development has led local authorities to seek fewer death
sentences because they view the non-death sentence as sufficiently punitive except in the most highly aggravated cases. In Harris County
(Houston), by contrast, the district attorney's office continues to seek the
death penalty in almost every capital murder case filed.[9] As above, this
tactic may coerce a guilty plea from the defendant in return for the prosecution's agreement not to pursue a death sentence, even if the defendant
has a potentially strong defense to the capital murder charge.[10] In addition to its coercive effect, such a policy (of seeking death in every case)
plainly amounts to an abdication of the responsibility of the prosecutor's
office to see that "justice is done" on a case-by-case basis.

In the federal criminal justice system, developments in the mid-to-late
1980s—the dramatic reduction in judicial sentencing discretion resulting
from the adoption of the federal Sentencing Guidelines, and the enactment by Congress of numerous mandatory minimum sentencing laws,
primarily in drug cases—gave birth to a new kind of prosecutorial overreaching. These draconian Reagan-era laws created harsh sentences
which a convicted defendant typically can evade only by "cooperating"
with the prosecutor. This constraint is imposed by the relevant statutes
and Guidelines, which give the prosecutor—not the judge—the power to
break the fetters on the judge's sentencing discretion. In practice, "cooperation" never means just telling everything the accused knows about his
own criminal conduct, or even the criminal conduct of other individuals
already in the prosecution's cross-hairs. Instead, in most federal jurisdictions the "cooperating" defendant cannot obtain the desperately sought
reduction in his own sentence unless he gives the prosecutor "bodies,"
that is, only if his information results in the prosecution and conviction
of additional suspects beyond those already identified by the authorities.

Just as the legal standard governing post-trial review has undermined
the effectiveness of the *Brady* doctrine in equalizing power between the
State and the accused, the courts' traditionally protective attitude toward

prosecutorial discretion has insulated systemic overcharging and "coop-eration"-driven plea and sentencing practices from meaningful judicial oversight. The Supreme Court has emphatically declared that "so long as the prosecutor has probable cause to believe that the accused committed an offense defined by statute, the decision whether or not to prosecute, and what charge to [bring], generally rests entirely in his discretion." [*Bordenkircher* v. *Hayes*, 434 U.S. 357, 364 (1978).][11] Unless a defen-dant can prove that these practices are the intentional product of a design to discriminate on a constitutionally impermissible basis (that is, against people of minority race, women, or people of a particular religious faith), the courts will not intervene.

3. The Failure of the Mass Media to Spotlight either Prosecutorial Overreaching or the Legal System's Continuing Refusal to Punish Prosecutors for Oppressive and Unfair Conduct

Prosecutorial misconduct of all types is abetted by the signal failure of legal institutions—courts and legal licensing authorities, for example—to identify and sanction prosecutors who break the rules. It has correctly been noted that courts frequently criticize prosecutors for improper con-duct, but that neither courts nor bar associations regularly pursue disci-plinary proceedings against prosecutors who likely acted wrongfully.[12]

Given that the forms of oppressive prosecutorial overreaching described above are not just the idiosyncratic actions of particular State agents but instead reflect structural features of the contemporary American criminal justice system—and therefore are present to some degree in almost every case—why have they not been exposed by the mass media? At least one possible reason is the dominance of entertainment-based values in news reporting about the criminal justice system.

As anyone who has had much contact with the mass media on any con-troversial topic will confirm, the narrative style which presently dominates feature news reporting, both in the press and on television, requires a sym-pathetic character at the center of every piece in order to personalize the otherwise abstract issue for the audience—to give the story a "human face." This sentimental narrative style does not lend itself to describing or addressing complex systemic institutional power relationships, which require time and careful attention to explicate. Publishing/airing deadlines and financial constraints press always in the direction of simplifying the story, which in the hands of too many correspondents becomes "oversimplifying."

Perhaps more important, the sentimental narrative style permits the reporter, whether unconsciously or by design, to avoid the political im-plications of the structural issue (for instance, large numbers of people are being oppressed because of their race or their poverty or their pow-erlessness, calling into question the legitimacy of the system oppressing them), which might alienate some significant proportion of the advertisers' target audience. Likewise, the history of particular prosecutorial practices, and their relationship to other institutionalized routines and power relationships, can be excised as too time consuming or distracting from the "personalized" story. Reducing the controversy to the micro scale, at which the problem is not a set of oppressive institutional arrangements that systematically deny fair treatment but instead the "bad" conduct of one actor who is oppressing a "good" victim, conveniently pretermits consideration of such questions. Instead, the dominant narrative mode is best suited to presenting black-and-white "hero and villain" scenarios in which the authorial sympathies of the reporter, while nominally under wraps for the sake of "objectivity," are evidently on the side of the designated "hero."[13]

Ultimately, the mass media are concerned with making money. Advertising fees fuel the engine of the media machine, and that means telling stories in an entertaining but sentimental fashion, taking care to offend as few viewers (that is, customers of the network/newspapers' primary advertising clients) as possible. This motivation is directly at odds with presenting the story of prosecutorial overreaching, which is at bottom not about the venality of particular prosecuting attorneys but about institutional structures which create a systemic imbalance of power that precludes a truly "adversarial" system of criminal justice. As regrettable as it may seem, the culprit in the mass media's failure to bring these issues into the public consciousness is the familiar one: capitalism.

Notes

1. *Berger v. United States*, 295 U.S. 78, 88 (1935).
2. Id.
3. That said, the fact that any prosecutor who has ever been found to have manufactured evidence against a suspect, or knowingly presented false evidence against an accused in court, could thereafter practice law (following interim punishment, however serious, by the bar) is an appalling comment on the nation's indifference to the lives and liberties of its people. A system appropriately protective of such fundamental values would treat a prosecutor who intentionally misused her office in this manner as having forfeited permanently the privilege of exercising discretionary judgments which may result, as their end product, in years of imprisonment or even death at the hands of the State.
4. These examples are illustrative, not exhaustive.
5. See *Brady v. Maryland*, 373 U.S. 83 (1963).
6. See, e.g., *Kyles v. Whitley*, 514 U.S. 419, 439 (1995) ("[N]aturally, [a] prosecutor anxious about tacking too close to the wind will disclose a favorable piece of evidence [rather than risk subsequent reversal]") (citation omitted).
7. This effect is more pronounced since Congress eviscerated the federal habeas remedy for state prisoners in 1996. Under the "Anti-Terrorism and Effective Death Penalty Act" ("AEDPA"), federal courts reviewing state convictions are forbidden from granting relief even where the defendant's rights were violated, unless the state court decision affirming the defendant's conviction was not only "erroneous" but "objectively unreasonable." In the half-decade or so of habeas cases governed by the AEDPA, a troublingly high proportion of state court judgments interpreting the scope of the federal constitution have been found to fall into this metaphysical cate-

gory of "wrong but reasonable." For the prosecutor who chooses to gamble on not disclosing potentially exculpatory evidence, the AEDPA adds an additional layer of protection from post-trial reversal.

8.   I have the greatest fondness, respect, and admiration for good public defenders. Their devotion and skill are a credit to the legal profession. Unfortunately, funding for many public defense agencies is so grossly inadequate that the quality of advocacy provided to their indigent clients suffers terribly. That is not the fault of the defenders themselves, but of the government officials responsible for providing the financial backing necessary to make real the promises of the Sixth Amendment.

9.   This particular type of overcharging is not unique to Houston. The Philadelphia district attorney's office likewise asserts that it will "seek the death penalty in all appropriate cases," which recently led to "contentious verbal sparring" with city council members over the cost and wisdom of such a policy. *See* Soteropoulos, "Budget hearing turns to bickering," *Philadelphia Inquirer* (March 14, 2002).

10. By seeking the death penalty, the prosecution guarantees that the jury will be "death-qualified," *i.e.*, that people with even moderate reservations about the wisdom or efficacy of capital punishment will not be allowed to serve. Both the experience of defense lawyers and some social science research tend to confirm that "death-qualified" juries are generally "pro-prosecution" and more prone to convict. See, e.g., *Lockhart v. McCree*, 476 U.S. 162, 167–168 (1983) (noting existence of social science studies supporting this inference). Thus, the prosecution can increase the likelihood of a conviction by insisting on seeking the death penalty if the defendant is convicted—effectively making up for any weakness or inadequacy in its evidence supporting a conviction. This insight was confirmed in the recent trial in Houston of Andrea Yates, a mentally ill woman accused of drowning her five small children. The prosecution insisted, as a formal matter, on seeking the death penalty. This permitted the State to cull the jury pool of any prospective jurors with doubts about the death penalty. Yet, once a "death-qualified" jury was seated and had convicted Ms. Yates of capital murder (rejecting her plea of insanity, despite the presence of extensive expert testimony supporting it and the absence of contrary expert opinion from the State), the State showed little enthusiasm for a death sentence. Prosecutors presented no additional evidence at Ms. Yates' penalty hearing, and at closing argument failed even to ask the jury directly to sentence her to death—settling instead for telling the jurors that whatever sentence they imposed would be satisfactory. See Dershowitz, "Yates' Prosecutors Guilty of Death Penalty Charade," *Houston Chronicle* (March 20, 2002). It is difficult to avoid the conclusion that the prosecutors in the Yates case asked for a death sentence only to increase their chances of obtaining a conviction in the first phase of the trial.

11. *Bordenkircher v. Hayes*, 434 U.S. 357, 364 (1978).

12. See Zacharias, "The Professional Discipline of Prosecutors," 79 *N.C. L. Rev.* 721, 723 (March 2001) (noting "the frequent references to prosecutorial misconduct in the case law" but the surprising "lack of ensuing [professional] discipline"); see also generally Davis, "The American Prosecutor: Independence, Power and the Threat of Tyranny," 86 *Iowa L. Rev.* 393 (January 2001).

13. This is not to suggest that accused and convicted persons are inevitably cast in the "villain" role. Despite the fact that television historically has relied on heroic depictions of cops and, to a lesser extent, prosecutors in entertainment programming—and thus has created a pervasive narrative convention in which those characters are the "good guys"—many of the "news magazine" programs (e.g., shows like *60 Minutes, Dateline,* and *20/20*) routinely present stories which paint law enforcement authorities as having accused or convicted the "wrong man," whether through malice or incompetence. The point is simply that the dominant simplified sentimental narrative form requires a "good guy" and a "bad guy," not which role the "cop" or the "robber" plays in a particular news drama.

Color Bind

Prisons and the New American Racism

PAUL STREET

Prison Dreams

Defined simply as overt public bigotry, racism in the United States has fallen to an all-time low. Understood in socioeconomic, political, and institutional terms, however, American racism is as alive as ever. More than 30 years after the heroic victories of the civil rights movement, Stanley Aronowitz notes, "The stigma of race remains the unmeltable condition of the black social and economic situation." That condition's seemingly insoluble persistence is seen in an inequitably funded educational system that "just happens" to provide poorer instruction for blacks than whites, an electoral system whose voting irregularities and domination by Big Money "just happens" to disproportionately disenfranchise blacks, and job, housing, health care, and financial labor markets that "just happen" to especially disadvantage and segregate African-Americans. It is evident in a political economy whose tendency toward sharp inequality "just happens" to especially impoverish and divide black communities. And it is evident in the glaring injustices of the U.S. prison system.

Consider a recent *Chicago Tribune* article that appeared well off the front page, under the title "Towns Put Dreams in Prisons." In downstate Hoopeston, Illinois, there is "talk of the mothballed canneries that once made this a boom town and whether any of that bustling spirit might return if the Illinois Department of Corrections comes to town." Seeking jobs and economic growth, Hoopeston's leaders are negotiating with state officials for the right to host a shiny new maximum security correctional facility. "You don't like to think about incarceration," Hoopeston's mayor is quoted as saying, "but this is an opportunity for Hoopeston. We've been plagued by plant closings." The mayor's judgment is seconded in the

This article was originally published in *Dissent*, Summer 2001.

Tribune's account of the considerable benefits, including dramatically increased tax revenues, that flowed to Ina, Illinois, after it signed up to become a prison town a few years ago.

Two things are missing from this story. The first absence is an appropriate sense of horror at the spectacle of a society in which local officials are reduced to lobbying for prisons as their best chance for economic growth. The second absence concerns the matter of race. Nowhere could the reporter or his informants (insofar as they are fully and accurately recorded) bring themselves to mention either the predominantly white composition of the keepers or the predominantly black composition of the kept in the prisons towns that increasingly look to the mass incarceration boom as the solution to their economic problems. As everyone knows but few like to discuss, the mostly white residents of those towns are building their economic "dreams" on the transport and lockdown of unfree African-Americans from impoverished inner-city neighborhoods in places like Chicago, Rockford, East St. Louis, and Rock Island.

The New Racism

This second absence is consistent with the politically correct rules of the new racism that plagues the United States at the millennium's turn. There is a widespread belief among whites—deeply and ironically reinforced by the demise of open public racial prejudice—that African-Americans now enjoy equal and color-blind opportunity. "As white America sees it," write Barbara Diggs-Brown and Leonard Steinhorn in their sobering *By the Color of Their Skin: The Illusion of Integration and the Reality of Race* (2000), "every effort has been made to welcome blacks into the American mainstream, and now they're on their own. 'We got the message, we made the corrections—get on with it.'"

"Going Downstate"

Nowhere, perhaps, is the persistence and even resurgence of racism more evident than in America's burgeoning "correctional" system. At the millennium's turn, blacks are 12.3 percent of the U.S. population, but they comprise fully half of the roughly 2 million Americans currently behind bars. On any given day, 30 percent of African-American males aged 20 to 29 are "under correctional supervision"—either in jail or prison or on probation or parole. And according to a chilling statistical model used by the Bureau of Justice Statistics, a young black man aged 16 in 1996 faces a 29 percent chance of spending time in prison during his life. The corresponding statistic for white men in the same age group is 4 percent. The United States' remarkable number and percentage of persons locked up by the state or otherwise under the watchful eye of criminal justice authorities—far beyond those of the rest of the industrialized world—is black to an extraordinary degree.

This harsh reality gives rise to extreme racial dichotomies. Take, for example, the different meanings of the phrase "going downstate" for youths of different skin colors in the Chicago metropolitan area. For many white teens, those words evoke the image of a trip with Mom and Dad to begin academic careers at the prestigious University of Illinois at Champaign-Urbana or at one of the state's many other public universities. But for younger Chicago-area blacks, especially males (just 6 percent of the state's prisoners are female), "going downstate" more likely connotes a trip under armed guard to begin prison careers at one of the state's numerous maximum or medium security prisons. Indeed, Illinois has 115,746 more persons enrolled in its 4-year public universities than in its prisons. When it comes to blacks, however, it has 10,000 more prisoners. For every African-American enrolled in those universities, two and a half blacks are in prison or on parole in Illinois. Similar differences of meaning can be found in other states with significant black populations. In New York, where the relevant phrase is "going upstate," the Justice Policy Institute reports that in the 1990s more blacks entered prison just for drug offenses than graduated from the state's massive university system with undergraduate, masters, and doctoral degrees combined.

In some inner-city neighborhoods, researchers and advocates report a preponderant majority of black males now possess criminal records. Criminologists Dina Rose and Todd Clear have found black neighborhoods in Tallahassee where every resident can identify at least one friend or relative who has been incarcerated. In many predominantly black urban communities across the country, it appears, incarceration is so widespread and commonplace that it has become what the United States' Bureau of Justice Statistics Director Jan Chaiken recently called "almost a normative life experience." Children there are growing up with the sense that it is standard for older brothers, uncles, fathers, cousins, and, perhaps, someday, themselves to be locked up by the state.

Labor Market Disenfranchisement

Researchers and advocates tracking the impact of mass incarceration find devastating consequences in high-poverty black communities. The most well known is the widespread political disenfranchisement of felons and ex-felons. The economic effects are equally significant. African-Americans are disproportionately and often deeply disenfranchised in competitive job markets by low skills, poor schools, weakened family structures, racial discrimination in hiring and promotion, and geographic isolation from the leading sectors of job growth. When prison and felony records are thrown into that mixture, the results are often disastrous. It is not uncommon to hear academic researchers and service providers cite unemployment rates as high as 50 percent for people with records. One study, based in California during the early 1990s, found that just 21 percent of that state's parolees were working full time. In a detailed study, Karen Needels found that less than 40 percent of 1,176 men released from Georgia's prison system in 1976 had any officially recorded earnings in each year from 1983 to 1991. For those with earnings, average annual wages were exceedingly low and differed significantly by race: white former prisoners averaged $7,880 per year and blacks made just $4,762.

In the most widely cited study in the growing literature on the labor market consequences of racially disparate criminal justice policies, distinguished Harvard economist Richard Freeman used data from the National Longitudinal Survey of Youth (NLSY). Limiting his sample to out-of-school men and controlling for numerous variables (drug usage, education, region, and age) that might bias upward the link between criminal records and weak labor market attachment, Freeman found that those who had been in jail or on probation in 1980 had a 19 percent higher chance of being unemployed in 1988 than those with no involvement in the criminal justice system. He also found that prison records reduced the amount of time employed after release by 25 to 30 percent.

More recently, Princeton sociologist Bruce Western has mined NLSY data to show that incarceration has "large and enduring effects on job-prospects of ex-convicts." He finds that the negative labor market effects of youth incarceration can last for more than a decade and that adult incarceration reduces paid employment by 5 to 10 weeks annually. Since incarceration rates are especially high among those with the least power in the labor market (young and unskilled minority men), the U.S. justice system exacerbates inequality.

This research is consistent with numerous experimental studies suggesting that the employment prospects of job applicants with criminal records are far worse than the chances of persons who have never been convicted or imprisoned. It is consistent also with evidence from labor market intermediaries dealing with ex-offenders. Project STRIVE, a renowned city job-placement program that mainly serves younger minority males in inner-city Chicago, reports that it placed 37 of 50 ex-offenders in jobs last year, leaving a 26 percent unemployment rate even for people who went through an especially successful program. The Center for Employment Opportunity in New York City is another "successful" program. Focused specifically on ex-offenders, it fails to place nearly a third of its clients. Another standard bearer in the field, "Project Rio" of the Texas Workforce Commission, claims to process 15,000 prisoners a year. After one year, just over two-thirds of parolees who go through Project Rio hold jobs. More telling, since most ex-offenders are thrown into the labor market without the benefit of a special transitional employment program, just 36 percent of a group of Texas parolees who did not enroll in Project Rio had a job one year after their release. And "even when paroled inmates are able to find jobs," the *New York Times* reported last fall, "they earn only half as much as people of the same social and economic background who have not been incarcerated."

The obstacles to ex-offender employment include the simple refusal of many employers even to consider hiring an "ex-con." Employers routinely check for criminal backgrounds in numerous sectors, including banking, security, financial services, law, education, and health care. But for many jobs, employer attitudes are irrelevant: state codes place steep barriers to the hiring of ex-offenders in numerous government and other occupations. At the same time, Western notes, "The increasingly violent and overcrowded state of prisons and jails is likely to produce certain attitudes, mannerisms, and behavioral practices that 'on the inside' function to enhance survival but are not compatible with success in the conventional job market." The alternately aggressive and sullen posture that prevails behind bars is deadly in a job market where entry level occupations increasingly demand "soft" skills related to selling and customer service. In this as in countless other ways, the prisoner may be removed, at least temporarily (see below), from prison, but prison lives on within the ex-offender, limiting his "freedom" on the "outside."

Savage Ironies

The situation arising from mass black incarceration is fraught with self-fulfilling policy ironies. At the very moment that American public discourse in racial matters has become officially inclusive, the United States is filling its expanding number of cellblocks with an ever-rising sea of black people monitored by predominantly white overseers. Echoes of slavery haunt the new incarceration state, reminding us of unresolved historical issues in the "United States of Amnesia."

Mass incarceration is just as ironically juxtaposed to welfare reform. At the same moment that the broader political and policy-making community is replacing taxpayer-financed "welfare dependency" with "workforce attachment" and "free market" discipline leading (supposedly) to "self-sufficiency" and two-parent family stability among the urban "underclass," criminal justice policies are pushing hundreds of thousands of already disadvantaged and impoverished "underclass" blacks further from minimally remunerative engagement with the labor market. It does this by warehousing them in expensive, publicly financed, sex-segregated holding pens where rehabilitation has been discredited and authoritarian incapacitation is the rule.

Droves of alienated men are removed from contact with children, parents, spouses, and lovers, contributing to the chronic shortage of suitable male marriage partners and resident fathers in the black community. Black humor on Chicago's South Side quips that "the only thing prison cures is heterosexuality." A connection probably exists between rampant sexual assault and sexual segregation behind prison bars and the disturbing fact that AIDS is now the leading cause of death among blacks between the ages of 25 and 44.

Incarceration deepens a job-skill deficit that is a leading factor explaining "criminal" behavior among disadvantaged people in the first place. "Crime rates are inversely related," Richard B. Freeman and Jeffrey Fagan have shown, "to expected legal wages, particularly among young males with limited job skills or prospects." The "war on drugs" that contributes so strongly to minority incarceration also inflates the price of underground substances, combining with ex-offenders' shortage of marketable skills in the legal economy to create irresistible incentives for the sort of income-generating conduct that leads back to prison. The lost potential earnings, savings, consumer demand, and human and social capital that result from mass incarceration cost black communities untold millions of dollars in potential economic development, worsening an inner-city political economy already crippled by decades of capital flight and de-industrialization. The dazed and embittered graduates of the prison-industrial complex are released back into a small number of predominantly black and high-poverty zip codes and census tracts, deepening the concentration of poverty, crime, and despair that is the hallmark of modern American "hyper-segregation" by race and class.

Meanwhile, prisoners' deletion from official U.S. unemployment statistics contributes to excessively rosy perceptions of American socioeconomic performance that worsen the political climate for minorities. Bruce Western has shown that factoring incarceration into unemployment rates challenges the conventional American notion that the United States' "unregulated" labor markets have been out-performing Europe's supposedly hyper-regulated employment system. Far from taking a laissez-faire approach, "the U.S. state has made a large and coercive intervention into the labor market through the expansion of the legal system." An American unemployment rate adjusted for imprisonment would rise by two points, bringing the the U.S. ratio much closer to that of European nations, where including prisoners raises the joblessness rate by only a few tenths of a percentage point. Counting prisoners would raise the official black male unemployment rate, which Western estimates at nearly 39 percent during the mid-1990s (including prisoners). Western and his colleague Becky Petit find that, when incarceration is factored in, there was "no enduring recovery in the employment of young black high-school drop-outs" during the eight-year Clinton employment boom.

By artificially reducing both aggregate and racially specific unemployment rates, mass incarceration makes it easier for the majority culture to continue to ignore the urban ghettos that live on beneath official rhetoric about "opportunity" being generated by "free markets." It encourages and enables the new, that is, subtler and more covert racism. Relying heavily on longstanding American opportunity myths and standard class ideology, this "new racism" blame inner-city minorities for their own "failure" to match white performance in a supposedly now free, meritorious, and color-blind society. Whites who believe that racial barriers have been lifted in the United States think that people of color who do not "succeed" fall short because of choices they made and/or because of inherent cultural or even biological limitations.

Correctional Keynesianism and the New Racism

The ultimate policy irony at the heart of America's passion for prisons can be summarized by what I call "correctional Keynesianism;" the prison construction boom fed by the rising "market" of black offenders is a job and tax-base creator for predominantly white communities that are generally far removed from urban minority concentrations. Those communities, often recently hollowed out by the de-industrializing and family farm-destroying gales of the "free market" system, have become part of a prison-industrial lobby that presses for harsher sentences and tougher laws, seeking to protect and expand their economic base even as crime rates continue to fall. With good reason: the prison building boom serves as what British sociologist David Ladipo calls "a latter-day Keynesian infrastuctural investment program for [often] blight-struck communities. Indeed, it has been phenomenally successful in terms of creating relatively secure, decent paid, and often unionized jobs."

According to Todd Clear, the negative labor market effects of mass incarceration on black communities are probably minor "compared to the economic relocation of resources" from black to white communities that mass incarceration entails. As Clear explains in cool and candid terms:

> Each prisoner *represents an economic asset that has been removed from that community and placed elsewhere* [emphasis added]. As an economic being, the person would spend money at or near his or her area of residence—typically, an inner city. Imprisonment displaces that economic activity: Instead of buying snacks in a local deli, the prisoner makes those purchases in a prison commissary. The removal may represent a loss of economic value to the home community, but it is a boon to the prison [host] community. Each prisoner represents as much as $25,000 in income for the community in which the prison is located, not to mention the value of constructing the prison facility in the first place. This can be *a massive transfer of value* [emphasis added]: A young male worth a few thousand dollars of support to children and local purchases is transformed into a $25,000 financial asset to a rural prison community. The economy of the rural community is artificially amplified, the local city economy artificially deflated.

It's a disturbing picture, even in this cynical age, full of unsettling parallels and living links to chattel slavery: young black men being involuntarily removed as "economic assets" from black communities to distant rural destinations where they are kept under lock and key by white-majority overseers. It is difficult to imagine a more pathetic denouement to America's long interwoven narratives of class and racial privilege. The rise of correctional Keynesianism is one of the negative and racially charged consequences of technically color blind political-economic processes.

An Analogy

Historical folklore romanticizes the large number of British and European convicts and ex-convicts who peopled and prospered in colonial North America and Australia. But, leaving aside the question of how many of those ex-offenders thrived, much less survived, the transplanted convicts of earlier eras landed anew in largely agricultural societies not yet based on waged and salaried labor and concentrated private monopoly in the means of production and distribution. It is entirely more difficult for an ex-offender to reenter the U.S. modern capitalist society in which the preponderant majority of working-age persons must find someone willing to "take the risk" (make the investment) of hiring them. A more telling and accurate historical analogy in their case—and the racial consistency rightly suggests considerable historical continuities of race and class—is found in the economic and labor market circumstances faced by America's suddenly "free" former slaves after the Civil War, all black and woefully short on capital, skills, and education, attempting to enter a society that still despised and coerced them.

To be sure, it is no simple matter to determine the precise extent to which mass incarceration is simply exacerbating the deep socio-economic and related cultural and political traumas that already plague inner-city communities and help explain disproportionate black "criminality," arrest, and incarceration in the first place. Still, it is undeniable that the race to incarcerate is having a profoundly negative effect on black communities. Equally undeniable is the fact that black incarceration rates reflect deep racial bias in the criminal justice system and the broader society. Do the cheerleaders of "get tough" crime and sentencing policy really believe that African-Americans deserve to suffer so disproportionately at the hands of the criminal justice system? There is a vast literature showing that structural, institutional, and cultural racism and severe segregation by race and class are leading causes of inner-city crime. Another considerable body of literature shows that blacks are victims of racial bias at every level of the criminal justice system—from stop, frisk, and arrest to prosecution, sentencing, release, and execution. These disparities give legitimacy to the movement of ex-offender groups for the expunging of criminal and prison records for many nonviolent offenses, especially in cases where ex-convicts have shown an earnest desire to "go straight."

Deeper remedies are required. These include a moratorium on new prison construction (to stop the insidious, self-replicating expansion of the prison-industrial complex), the repeal of laws that deny voting rights to felons and ex-felons, amnesty and release for most prisoners convicted of nonviolent crimes, decriminalization of narcotics, the repeal of the "war on drugs" at home and abroad, revision of state and federal sentencing and local "zero tolerance" practices and ordinances, abolition of racial, ethnic, and class profiling in police practice, and the outlawing of private, for-profit prisons and other economic activities that derive investment gain from mass incarceration. Activists and policy makers should call for a criminal-to social-justice "peace dividend": the large-scale transfer of funds spent on mass arrest, surveillance, and incarceration into such policy areas as drug treatment, job training, transitional services for ex-offenders, and public education regarding the employment potential of ex-offenders. They should call for the diversion of criminal justice resources from "crime in the streets" (i.e., the harassment and imprisonment of lower class and inner-city people) to serious engagement with under-sentenced "crime in the suites." More broadly, they should seek a general redistribution of resources from privileged and often fantastically wealthy persons to those most penalized from birth by America's long and intertwined history of inherited class and race privilege. America's expanding prison, probation, and parole populations are recruited especially from what leading slavery reparations advocate Randall Robinson calls "the millions of African-Americans bottom-mired in urban hells by the savage time-release social debilitations of American slavery."

The ultimate solutions lie, perhaps, beyond the parameters of the existing political economic order. "Capitalism," Eugene Debs argued in 1920, "needs and must have the prison to protect itself from the [lower class] criminals it has created." But the examples of Western Europe and Canada, where policymakers prefer prevention and rehabilitation through more social-democratic approaches, show that mass incarceration is hardly an inevitable product of capitalism. And nothing can excuse policymakers and activists from the responsibility to end racist criminal justice practices that significantly exacerbate the difficulties faced by the nation's most disadvantaged. More than merely a symptom of the tangled mess of problems that create, sustain, and deepen America's insidious patterns of class and race inequality, mass incarceration has become a central part of the mess. For these and other reasons, it will be an especially worthy target for creative, democratic protest and policy formation in the new millennium.

Sources

Anderson, Elijah. *Code of the Street: Decency, Violence, and Moral Life of the Inner City* (New York: Norton, 2000).
Aronowitz, Stanley. "Race: the Continental Divide," *The Nation* (March 12, 2001).
Blumstein, Alfred, and Allen J. Beck. "Population Growth in U.S. Prison, 1980–1996,"

pp. 17–62 in Tonry and Petersilia, eds., *Prisons*, vol. 26 of *Crime and Justice: a Review of Research* (Chicago: University of Chicago, 1999).

Buck, Maria. *Getting Back to Work: Employment Programs for Ex-Offenders* (Philadelphia: Public/Private Ventures, Fall 2000).

Butterfield, Fox. "Often, Parole Is One Stop On the Way Back to Prison," *The New York Times*, 29 November, 2000, A1.

Chaiken, Jan M. "Crunching Numbers: Crime and Incarceration at the End of the Millennium," *National Institute of Justice Journal* (January 2000): 10–17.

Clear, Todd. "Backfire: When Incarceration Increases Crime," in *The Unintended Consequences of Incarceration* (New York: Vera Institute of Justice, January, 1996).

Cose, Ellis. "The Prison Paradox," *Newsweek*, (November 13, 2000): 40–46.

Debs, Eugene V. *Walls & Bars: Prisons & Prison Life in the "Land of the Free"* (Chicago: Charles H. Kerr, 2000).

Fagan, Jefferey, and Richard B. Freeman. "Crime and Work" in *Crime & Justice: A Review of Research*, Volume 25, edited by Michael Toney (Chicago: University of Chicago Press, 2000): 225–90.

Foner, Eric. *Reconstruction: America's Unfinished Revolution 1863–1877* (New York: Harper and Row, 1988).

Freeman, Richard B. "Crime And The Employment Of Disadvantaged Youths," Working Paper no. 3875, National Bureau of Economic Research.

Gangi, Robert, Vincent Shiraldi, and Jason Ziedanberg. *New York State of Mind? Higher Education vs. Prison Funding in the Empire State, 1988–1998* (New York: Justice Policy Institute and Correctional Association of New York, December 1998).

Hagan, John, and Ronit Dinovitzer. "Collateral Consequences of Imprisonment for Children, Communities, and Prisoners," in Tonry and Petersilia, eds., *Prisons*, vol. 26 of *Crime and Justice: a Review of Research* (Chicago: University of Chicago, 1999).

Hagan, John. "The Next Generation: Children of Prisoners" in *The Unintended Consequences of Incarceration* (New York: Vera Institute of Justice, January, 1996).

Human Relations Foundation of Chicago. "Human Relations in Metropolitan Chicago, 2000" (Chicago, November 2000).

Illinois Board of Higher Education, IBHE Data Book at www.ibhe.state.il.us/

Illinois Department of Corrections, 1999 Departmental Data at www. idoc.state.il.us/news/1999_data. pdf

Interview with case manager, Safer Foundation, Chicago, December 23, 2000.

Interview with Chris Moore, Director, Male Improvement Program, Chicago Urban League, March 1, 2001.

Interview with Joan Archie, Director, Employment, Counseling, and Training Department, Chicago Urban League, March 1, 2001.

Ladipo, David. "The Rise Of America's Prison-Industrial Complex," *New Left Review* 7, (January/February 2001): 109–23.

Lowenstein, Thomas K. "Collateral Damage," *The American Prospect*, 12 (January 1–15, 2001): 33–36.

Massey, Douglas S., and Nancy Denton. *American Apartheid: Segregation and the Making of an American Underclass* (Cambridge, MA: Harvard University Press, 1993).

Mauer, Marc. *Race to Incarcerate* (New York: The New Press, 1999).

Moore, Joan. "Bearing the Burden: How Incarceration Policies Weaken Inner-City Communities," in *The Unintended Consequences of Incarceration* (New York: Vera Institute of Justice, January, 1996).

Moss, Philip, and Chris Tilly. *Stories Employers Tell: Race, Skill, and Hiring in America* (New York: Russell Sage Foundation, 2001).

Needels, Karen E. "Go Directly To Jail and Do Not Collect? A Long-Term Study of Recidivism, Employment, and Earnings Patterns among Prison Releases," *Journal of Research in Crime and Delinquency*, 33 (November, 1996): 471–96.

Nightingale, Demetra Smith, and Harold Watts. "Adding It Up: The Economic Impact of Incarceration on Individuals, Families, and Communities," in *The Unintended Consequences of Incarceration* (New York: Vera Institute of Justice, January, 1996).

Oliver, Melvin L., and Thomas M. Shapiro. *Black Wealth/White Wealth: A New Perspective on Racial Inequality* (New York and London: Routledge, 1997).

Parenti, Christian. *Lockdown America: Police and Prisons in the Age of Crisis* (London and New York: Verso, 1999).

Ritter, Jim. "AIDS Growth Alarming," *Chicago Sun Times* (March 11, 2001).

Robinson, Randall. *The Debt: What America Owes To Blacks* (New York: Penguin, 2000).

Steinhorn, Leonard, and Barbara Diggs-Brown. *By the Color of Our Skin: The Illusion of Integration and the Reality of Race* (New York: The Penguin Group, 2000).

Stier, Hayer, and Marta Tienda. *The Color of Opportunity: Pathways To Family, Welfare and Work* (Chicago and London: University of Chicago Press, 2001).

Taylor, Carl. "Growing Up Behind Bars: Confinement, Youth Development, And Crime," in *The Unintended Consequences of Incarceration* (New York: Vera Institute of Justice, January, 1996).

Testimony of Congressman Danny K. Davis, Expungement Legislation, Springfield, Illinois, February 23, 2001, in author's possession.

Tonry, Michael, and Joan Petersilia. "American Prisons at the Beginning of the Twenty-First Century," pp. 1–16 in Tonry and Petersilia, eds., *Prisons*, vol. 26 of *Crime and Justice: a Review of Research* (Chicago: University of Chicago, 1999), ed. by Michael Tonry and Joan Petersilia, *Prisons*, Volume 26 (Chicago and London: University of Chicago Press, 1999).

Tonry, Michael. *Malign Neglect: Race, Crime and Punishment in America* (New York: Oxford University Press, 1995).

United States Census Bureau. "Table 1: Population by Race and Hispanic Origin for the United States, 2000" [www.census.gov].

Western Bruce, and Becky Pettit. "Incarceration And Racial Inequality In Men's Employment," *Industrial and Labor Relations Review*, 54 (October 2000): 3–16.

Western Bruce, and Katerine Beckett. "How Unregulated Is the U.S. Labor Market? The Penal System as a Labor Market Institution," *American Journal of Sociology*, 104 (January 1999): 1030–60.

Wilson, William Julius. *When Work Disappears: The World of the New Urban Poor* (New York: Alfred A. Knopf, 1996).

Capital Crimes

The Corporate Economy of Violence

GEORGE WINSLOW

In 1980, after government regulators found two operators asleep at the controls of the Dresden nuclear power plant near Chicago, a spokesman for Commonwealth Edison tried to defend the company's somnambulant safety policy. Whether or not the operators were sleeping on the job "depends on your definition of asleep," he argued. "They [the workers] weren't stretched out. They had their eyes closed. They were seated at their desks with their heads in a nodding position."

In recent years, many politicians and officials at government regulatory agencies around the world have also been in the head nodding position—adopting sleepy regulatory policies while gleefully approving measures that have given major corporations more freedom to boost profits, expand their investments, pollute the environment, and exploit their workers.

Neo-liberal economists claim the current infatuation with sleepy regulators has liberated private enterprise from the shackles of red tape, thus dramatically increasing corporate profits, international trade, and foreign investment. But, the head nodding approach to deregulation has also allowed corporate crime to grow into a problem that costs the U.S. economy trillions of dollars each year and kills at least 150,000 Americans each year—far more than the 15,500-plus Americans murdered by street criminals in 2000.[1]

A graphic example of those costs occurred recently with the collapse of Enron, an energy trader that was the darling of Wall Street and Washington, D.C., in the 1990s. At the peak of its power in early 2001, Enron was the seventh largest company in the United States, with $100 billion in revenues and operations all over the world. President George W. Bush, who had received millions of dollars in campaign contributions from Enron, rewarded his largest political backer by hiring dozens of Enron

This article was written in May 2002.

employees to work in his administration or to sit on advisory boards. Academics touted Enron's ability to buy and sell supplies of electricity and other types of energy online as the greatest success story of the new economy and Wall Street analysts issued glowing research reports that pushed the company's stock into the stratosphere.

In the fall of 2001, however, revelations of insider trading, fraudulent accounting practices, and energy market manipulation forced the company into bankruptcy, the largest in U.S. history. Company employees, who were encouraged to invest their pensions funds in Enron stock while top management was selling $1.2 billion in stock, lost more than $1.3 billion in retirement funds, and institutional investors, many of which were pension funds, seem to have lost a mind boggling $25 to $50 billion worth of retirement funds. Overall, investors lost about $63 billion.

Those numbers only hint at the cost of the scandal. Beyond whipping out assets held by pension funds and investors, Enron and other energy trading companies have also been accused of using their power over the deregulated energy markets to bilk investors out of billions. Currently the state of California is attempting to recover $9 billion from utilities and energy traders, claiming they artificially created the electricity prices during the California energy crisis, and a number of federal, state, and local agencies are investigating Enron's trading unit. In an exhaustive research report the Foundation for Taxpayer and Consumer Rights argues that the deregulation of the California power industry, which produced exorbitant profits for Enron and other power industry companies, will eventually cost consumers in the state over $71 billion. But this number could go even higher. Internal Enron e-mails and documents released in early May 2002 by state investigators showed that the company had consciously attempted to manipulate electricity prices during the California energy crisis, producing massive profits for the firm.[2]

The lax regulation that allowed Enron to bilk investors, consumers, taxpayers, and employees out of well over $100 billion stands in a stark contrast to the current law-and-order approach to street crime. In 2001, federal regulators spent only $18 billion to fight corporate crimes that cost the economy $1 to $2.4 trillion a year and killed hundreds of thousands of people each year, while law enforcement agencies spent $147 billion in 1999—the most recent figure available in 2002—to fight street crimes. The Food and Drug Administration had an annual budget of only $1.4 billion in 2000 to regulate pharmaceutical drugs that produce 50,000 to 100,000 deaths each year from overdoses and improper use, while government agencies spend $30 to $40 billion a year to fight the illegal drug trade, which produces 8,000 to 10,000 deaths from drug overdoses.[3] A young man who tries to sell 10 pounds of pot worth maybe $16,000 can be sent to jail for life while a top executive at the Bank of New York who pleads guilty to laundering billions of dollars for Russian mobsters in 1999 is never sentenced and her employer never charged. Banks that laundered billions in heroin money during the civil war in Afghanistan in the 1980s and provided financial services for the Saudis and other U.S. allies who funded the Taliban remain happily in business. Yet, under California's "three-strikes-you're-out" law that sentences people convicted of three felonies to life in prison, a man who tried to run out of a store with a few golf clubs faces life behind bars.[4]

This chapter will explore these paradoxes and a number of other problems that have plagued our war on crime by focusing on the issue of corporate crime. To better understand the violence created by abusive corporate power, the essay will examine three main issues: the enormous costs of corporate crime, the political and economic trends that have shaped U.S. policies towards the problem, and the relationship between corporate crime and street crime.

The link between corporate crime and street crime—a connection long ignored by law and order conservatives—is particularly important. In the last 30 years, money laundering, tax fraud, environmental crimes, racism in the financial system, and a host of other corporate crimes have played a key role in the growth of street crime and the drug trade both by directly facilitating those crimes and by indirectly creating social problems that breed crime.

Understanding the links between street crime and corporate crime also reveals why violence has remained such a persistent fact of American life. The current law-and-order crusade, which has been embraced by both major political parties and every president since Ronald Reagan, is based on a larger conservative agenda that has reduced government spending for social programs to attack the causes of crime while spending huge sums to brutally incarcerate millions of poor people. A close look at the problem of corporate crime reveals that this policy has been a dismal failure, simply because it ignores the larger economic and political forces that create crime. Until there is a political movement to address these problems by creating a more just society, there is little hope of achieving justice in our prisons and courts.

The Trillion Dollar Gang

Examining the huge costs created by corporate crime provides the most obvious example of how the law-and-order crusade has allowed violence to proliferate. In one massive study of issue, Marshal Clinard and Peter Yeager found that 1,553 federal cases were brought in 1975 and 1976 against the 582 largest manufacturing and service corporations in the United States for violating criminal statutes, regulations, or civil laws. That rate of illegal activity means prosecutors accused the average major corporation of breaking the law 2.7 times over a two-year period. Similarly, Amitai Etzioni has found that 62 percent of the Fortune 500 companies were involved in one or more illegal acts between 1975 and 1985, and a survey by *Fortune* magazine in 1980 found that 11 percent of 1,043 large companies had been involved in a major crime during the preceding decade.[5]

In recent years, fines and penalties levied on major corporations and their executives have increased dramatically. Yet, these penalties remain small in terms of overall corporate profits. In 2001, Sara Lee was forced to pay only $200,000 and charged with a misdemeanor after Listeria-contaminated Ball Park Franks killed 21 people and seriously injured 100. No criminal charges have ever been brought against corporate executives who sold asbestos—a product that researchers in the 1980s estimated would kill 240,000 people over a 30-year period—or the tobacco companies who make billions peddling a legal drug that will kill one billion people in the twenty-first century unless smoking rates are reduced.[6]

In fact, many polluters and labor law violators are allowed to break the law repeatedly with little chance that they ever face serious sanctions. Consider, for example, the timber, paper, and wood products industries. Clinard and Yeager found that in 1975 and 1976 companies in the paper, fiber, and wood industries racked up 81 violations of federal regulations, including 28 serious and moderately serious violations. Most of these were for environmental infractions (50), labor law violations (15), and antitrust, price fixing, or restraint of trade laws (10).[7] Yet, over the next decade, two major paper companies, Louisiana Pacific and Weyerhauser, had made little effort to change their ways. In 1989, they were responsible for nearly one tenth (9.4 percent) of the 188 million pounds of toxic chemicals corporate America dumped into U.S. waterways. In 1992, the *Multinational Monitor* noted that pollution from Weyerhauser's operations has been linked to 13 Superfund sites, the company was a defendant in a $100 billion class action suit alleging widespread poisoning of U.S. streams with dioxin, and the Washington state Department of Ecology took 137 enforcement actions against the company between 1985 and 1991.[8]

Attempts to add up the costs that these crimes imposed on society have produced some mind-boggling numbers. This author's recent book, *Capital Crimes*, concluded that corporate crime costs the U.S. economy at least $1 trillion and Ralph Estes, who has published an extremely useful survey, estimates that corporate crime cost the U.S. economy over $2.4 trillion dollars in 1991. Estes' estimate included the cost of racial and gender discrimination ($165 billion), workplace injuries and accidents ($141.6 billion), deaths from workplace cancer ($274.7 billion), price fixing monopolies and deceptive advertising ($1,116.1 billion), cost of unsafe vehicles ($135.8 billion), cigarettes ($53.9 billion), other product injuries ($18.4 billion), environmental costs ($307.8 billion), defense contract overcharges ($25.8 billion), income tax fraud ($2.9 billion), violations of federal regulations ($39.1 billion), bribery, extortion and kickbacks ($14.6 billion), and a variety of other costs.[9]

Those two estimates exclude a number of major corporate crimes, such as money laundering, that would add trillions of dollars to the totals and they do not include the impact of a number of activities, such as the lack of affordable health care, that are quite legal but harm millions of people each year. Even so, this author's $1 trillion estimate dwarfs the largest available estimates of street crime. In 1996, researchers at the National Institute of Justice (NIJ) estimated that violent crime costs victims about $105 billion annually in medical expenses and lost property and productivity—about one tenth the cost of corporate crime. Even the NIJ's larger estimate of $450 billion, which includes controversial calculations of the cost of pain, long-term emotional trauma, and disability, is less than half the cost of corporate crime.[10]

Given these costs, one might suppose that law enforcement officials would mobilize huge budgets and staff to fight corporate crime. They haven't. Between 1980 and 1990, the United States saw some of the worst corporate crime scandals in its history, ranging from the S&L fiasco that cost taxpayers $135 billion to the insider trading scandals on Wall Street and the mounting cost of cleaning up toxic chemicals at Superfund sites, which will ultimately cost hundreds of billions of dollars. Yet, during that period, staffing at regulatory agencies dropped from 121,791 in 1980 to 114,684 in 1990, and funding in inflation adjusted dollars increased from $10.5 to $13.3 billion during this period, far slower than GDP.[11]

Even during the supposedly liberal Clinton-Gore years, funding dropped between 1992 ($14.98 billion) and 1996 ($14.95 billion) before creeping back up to $17.87 billion in 2000. In 2000, when Enron was secretly carrying out a wide variety of corporate crimes that would eventually cost consumers and taxpayers over $100 billion, there were only 129,815 people working at federal regulatory agencies, just a slight increase from the 125,818 in fiscal 1992. In contrast, in 1999, the most recent figure available, federal, state, and local governments spent $147 billion and employed 2.2 million people to fight street crime.[12] Commentators frequently justify this disparity in spending by saying corporate criminals do not terrorize their victims, and that these crimes harm very few people. In fact, corporate crime is a deadly business, as illustrated by the 55,919 American workers who died on the job between 1992 and 2000.[13] While corporations are rarely prosecuted for those deaths, some researchers estimated that about 30 percent of these fatalities could have been avoided if firms had followed workplace safety rules.[14] That would indicate that about 16,700 Americans died as a result of unsafe working conditions between 1992 and 2000.

That estimate only begins to hint at the carnage produced by unsafe workplace conditions. Many workers may die long after the initial injury and are not recorded in official statistics, or they may develop diseases from exposure to toxic chemicals. As many as 100,000 miners have been killed and 265,000 have been disabled by coal dust (black lung) disease. Another 85,000 textile workers suffer lung diseases from cotton dust (brown lung).[15]

Citing several studies on the long-term impact of toxic chemicals in the workplace, Estes believes that these chemicals cause $274.7 billion dollars worth of economic damage each year and that exposure to carcinogens on the job annually kills about 150,000 Americans. This annual death toll would produce more than 1.5 million deaths in the last ten years, far more than the entire battlefield deaths suffered in every American war since 1860 (a history of carnage that has killed 566,000 U.S. soldiers during the Civil War, World War I, World War II, the Korean War, and the Vietnam War).[16]

The Political Economy of Crime

These numbers raise an intriguing question: Why have government officials adopted such a schizophrenic policy towards crime, punishing the street crimes committed by poor people while paying only lip service to the problem of corporate crime?

These policies grew out of the rise of law and order politicians in the 1960s. By attacking rising crime, urban riots, and political turbulence in the 1960s, Richard Nixon and other conservatives were able to build political support for much larger conservative agendas. Over the last 30 years, this political swing to the right allowed conservatives to pursue a draconian law-and-order crackdown on street crime while simultaneously attacking government programs designed to address the social causes of crime and pursuing free market policies that deregulated the economy and boosted corporate profits.

The impact of the conservative law and order politicians on the politics of government regulation in the 1980s and 1990s is extremely complex, but in a general way, U.S. government officials began moving to the right in the 1970s. Then, during the Carter administration, the concept that the benefits of government regulation needed to be weighed against the economic costs was introduced. Carter, backed by both Republicans and Democrats, pushed forward deregulation of the airlines, trucking, banking, and financial markets. The growth in government regulatory spending and employment slowed for the first time in the last two years of the Carter administration and regulatory spending actually dropped during Reagan's first term in office.

Overall, regulatory spending increased by only 57.7 percent in the eight years of the Reagan administration, much slower than the 47.3 percent increase in the one-term Carter presidency. But the real turn to the right came during the Clinton years, when spending grew by only 37.7 percent over eight years. That was much slower than both the Reagan years and the one-term Bush administration, when spending jumped by 38.2 percent between 1988 and 1992. Meanwhile, both the executive branch and Congress encouraged this "head nodding" half-asleep regulatory policy by refusing to overhaul the regulatory system, much of which was based on laws passed in the 1930s, so it would be better adapted to a rapidly changing high-tech global economy.[17] Today each government regulator must oversee $76 million dollars worth of economic activity, a huge rise from the $14.8 million worth of GDP that each regulator oversaw in 1970. The lack of spending on government regulation becomes even more problematic when one considers changes in the global economy that have given corporations even more power over the global economy. The expansion of the European Union, the creation of NAFTA, reduced tariffs, the creation of free trade zones, the reduction of restrictions on foreign investment, privatization of state owned enterprises, the growing power of the World Trade Organization, the IMF, and the World Bank over developing economies are all part of a broader trend towards a vastly expanded global economy under the increasing control of major multinational corporations and their domestic political allies. Currently, $2 to $3 trillion flows across borders through the international financial system each day, up from $30 to $40 billion in the late 1960s.

This vast flow of cash dramatically changed the global economy, giving major corporations much greater power over political and economic processes, creating a climate in which political leaders reduced government programs designed to curb corporate crime while cutting social spending and waging a politically popular war on street crime. Here, once again, the Clinton years illustrate policies of neo-liberal politicians who were increasingly dependent on corporate contributions. Over an eight-year period, Clinton reduced welfare programs, dismantled federal programs for affordable housing, cut a quarter of a million federal jobs, paid little attention to antitrust enforcement, sold off billions of dollars worth of energy rights to major polluters, pursued policies that may destroy one-third of the ancient forests in the Pacific Northwest, did little to enforce campaign finance rules, and backed major legislation deregulating the telecommunications and financial services industries.[18]

But as the administration was offering regulatory relief and passing out huge subsidies to major corporations, it was engaging in a brutal war on street crime. The Clinton administration used cuts in federal agencies to provide funds for 100,000 local police officers. It supported mandatory sentences that put thousands of poor people behind bars for minor drug offenses, allowed massive human rights abuses to proliferate in U.S. prisons, ignored problems with police corruption and brutality, attacked critics who pointed out widespread racism in the criminal justice system, and ramped up federal spending for the war on drugs to record levels. Clinton's anticrime policies put more African-Americans and women behind bars than had any other president in U.S. history.

Many Enrons, Few Reforms

These disastrous policies were naturally popular with major corporate campaign contributors, who increasingly drive the political process. But, the orthodox law-and-order policy of coddling corporate donors and criminals while letting the poor eat prison has been a disastrous failure.

This failure is particularly obvious in the area of corporate crime. Tying the hands of regulators and delaying major regulatory initiatives, such as rules governing repetitive stress syndrome, during a period of rapid economic and technological change made it much easier for corporations to avoid real regulatory oversight. It is significant that all of the major corporate scandals of the last 20 years—the S&L scandal, the insider trading scandals of the 1980s, massive money laundering schemes at the rogue bank BCCI, investment fraud in the dot com bubble, and the collapse of Enron—are all directly related to the fact that government regulators have not adapted to the changing global economy.

In fact, the Enron scandal merely highlights regulatory problems revealed in these earlier cases. During the S&L scandal, executives used dubious accounting techniques—which were approved by government regulators—that allowed them to legally cook the books and make their institutions look like they were making money when in fact they were broke. That allowed insolvent S&Ls to pay executives huge bonuses and attract investment money by selling billions of dollars worth of stocks and bonds to unsuspecting investors. Unfortunately, the failure to address those well-documented problems allowed Enron executives in the 1990s to manipulate their financial reports, tricking investors and pension funds managers into thinking the company was more profitable than it actually was.[19]

In other cases that are strikingly similar to the Enron affair, S&L executives also recruited high-priced consultants—such as the current head of the Federal Reserve, Alan Greenspan—and Wall Street banks to tout their business strategies. Wall Street banks made billions from S&Ls by encouraging them to trade in junk bonds, mortgage-backed securities, and other relatively unregulated financial instruments. These investments were supposed to turn sleepy S&Ls into dynamic financial institutions, just as Enron's strategy of trading energy futures was supposed to transform this old natural gas producer into a powerful financial services company that traded everything from energy futures to bandwidth on fiber optic networks. Unfortunately, those unregulated investments failed to pay off, causing Enron and many S&Ls to collapse.

Like the S&L industry, Enron also used massive political contributions to protect it from government oversight. Between 1989 and 2001, Enron and its executives contributed over $6 million to political candidates, most of which, 74 percent, went to Republicans, and between 1995 and 2001, Enron spent another $7.5 billion lobbying federal officials. Meanwhile Arthur Andersen, the accounting firm that received huge fees from Enron to audit its books and for consulting services, spent $13.3 million lobbying federal officials between 1995 and 2001 and another $5.2 million in donation to candidates between 1989 and 2001. Equally large sums were probably spent lobbying local U.S. officials and foreign politicians.[20]

These massive contributions played a key role in the economic rise of Enron and the political clout of the Bush family. In 1992, the first George Bush's administration deregulated the energy business, and the chair of the Commodity Futures Trading Commission, Wendy Gramm, ruled that federal regulators had no power to regulate the trade in energy derivatives—a huge activity that eventually became Enron's largest business. (Subsequently, Enron put Gramm, who is the wife of Texas Republican Senator Phil Gramm, on the company's board of directors and paid her over $276,000.)

George W. Bush, who supported the deregulation of energy markets in Texas as governor, received more than $3 million from Enron during his career. Not surprisingly, Bush appointed dozens of people tied to Enron and Andersen to his administration in 2001, including the head of the Justice Department, John Ashcroft, who received $80,000 from Enron in contributions in 1999 and 2000, and the head of the Securities and Exchange administration, Harvey Pitt.

Prior to joining the SEC, which is playing a leading role in the investigation of Enron and its auditor Arthur Andersen, Pitt made his name defending Dennis Levine in the insider trading scandals of the 1980s. In the 1990s, he did legal work for Andersen and played a key role in defeating regulatory changes that would have prevented the fraudulent accounting techniques used in the Enron scandal.[21]

The Failed Crusade

While the Enron affair has produced a wave of headlines, much less attention has been paid to the failure of conservative policies towards street crime and the impact that corporate crime has had on street crime. Between 1968, when Nixon launched his law-and-order crusade, and 1992, spending for law enforcement grew from about $6 billion to $97.5 billion in 1993, and the number of people behind bars quadrupled. Over $1.5 trillion was spent to fight the war on crime between 1970 and 2000.[22]

Most conservatives and media commentators have considered this money well spent. But, despite spending $1.5 trillion, the production of many drugs skyrocketed during the height of the law and order crusade (global opium production quadrupled between 1970 and 1993), homicide rates exploded (jumping from 6.9 per 100,000 in 1968 to 9.5 in 1993, a 37.7 percent increase), the level of street crimes increased (victimization surveys show a 16.7 percent increase in the 1973 to 1993 period), global drug cartels dramatically expanded their power (in 1995 U.N. officials estimated that the cartels had over $1 trillion a year in revenue), and as just noted, the cost of corporate crime hit mind-boggling levels.[23]

In the last decade, improved economic conditions have dramatically cut crime rates. Yet it's worth remembering that the homicide rate in 1999 (5.7 murders per 100,000 Americans) is still much worse than it was in 1964 (4.7), when presidential candidate Barry Goldwater claimed the United States was the most lawless country in the world. Even with the recent declines U.S. homicide rates remain 3 to 10 times higher than any other developed country in Europe or Asia. Despite the popularity of this $1.5 trillion law-and-order crusade in Washington, America remains the most violent crime-ridden developed country in the world.[24] The failure of the current policies towards both street crime and corporate crime indicate that the entire issue needs to be systematically reexamined. While there are many causes of the high levels of violence in American society, abusive corporate power and crime have long played an unrecognized role in the problem.

One easy way to understand this connection is to take a look at the role corporate crime has played in the drug trade and organized crime: Virtually everyone in law enforcement worries about the growth of international organized crime groups who have capitalized on the growth of the drug trade. By the mid-1990s, the United Nations and other researchers "estimated" that organized crime groups had built up huge operations in Colombia (where drug cartels own 30 percent of the farmland and earn $5 billion a year from drugs), in Venezuela (where they control nearly one fifth of the nation's GDP), in Italy (where they earn $21 to $24 billion a year), in Mexico (where drug cartels earn $30 billion a year), in Panama (where banks launder $8 to $10 billion a year in drug money), in Asia (where the Chinese Triad gangs rake in $210 billion a year), in the former Soviet Union (where criminal gangs control 35 per cent of the commercial banks and over 2,000 corporations), and in the United States, where American crime syndicates employ 280,000 people and earn about $50 billion in profits.[25]

Much of this growth would not have been possible without dramatic changes in the global financial system, which made it much easier for crime groups to move their profits around the world and reinvest them in legitimate assets. Loosely regulated offshore banking havens in Switzerland and other places have a long history, but offshore banks proliferated rapidly in the Caribbean, Panama, and other places in the 1960s and 1970s. U.S. officials often supplied foreign aid to governments that set up offshore financial havens, and these banks played a key role in the expansion of multinational corporations, making it easier for them to move their profits around the world, invest in new markets, and avoid heavy taxes and regulations. Unfortunately, criminals also profited from this growing offshore system, using secret bank accounts, lax regulation, and low tax rates to launder money.

While the IRS attempted to investigate organized crime activities in offshore tax havens in the 1960s, most U.S. officials ignored the problem of money laundering. Nixon tried to fire one U.S. Attorney for proposing anti-money laundering legislation and he refused to enforce it when it was passed in 1970. The Carter administration began the first investigations under the law but little real attempt was made to crack down on the problem until the Reagan administration, which set up a multi-agency task force to deal with drug money. More resources were devoted to investigations of money laundering and organized crime groups, and U.S. law enforcement agencies began to work much closer with their international counterparts. A number of major organized crime figures, both in the United States and outside the country, were arrested in joint international investigations into money laundering cases.

Unfortunately, Reagan's larger conservative agendas completely sabotaged these long overdue initiatives. Without real evidence, the Reagan administration tried to blame the U.S. drug problem on liberals at home and left wing governments abroad while ignoring U.S.-backed dictators and military officials in Panama, Honduras, Argentina, Haiti, Pakistan, and Afghanistan who had close ties to major drug gangs. By the end of the 1980s, opium production in Afghanistan increased exponentially and U.S.-backed anti-Soviet guerillas, who received over $3 billion in aid during the decade, were the world's largest producers of opium.[26]

Closer to home, Reagan officials devoted a disproportionate amount of their antidrug program to catching low-level users and dealers. By 1994, a U.S. Justice Department survey found that more than one-third of all federal prisoners incarcerated under mandatory laws for drug offenses were considered "low-level" offenders and these "low-level" offenders constituted 21 percent of all federal prisoners.[27] In 1991, the federal government spent about $6.1 billion to house low-level drug offenders, way more than the $4.4 billion spent by federal authorities for treatment and prevention programs.[28]

But, as the administration was spending billions to put low-level offenders behind bars, it was also cutting government programs that could effectively fight money laundering. Between 1980 and 1984, the number of examiners at FDIC dropped from 1,698 to 1,389, the Controller of Currency axed 310 examiners, and thrift regulators reduced their ranks from 638 to 596, a move which sharply limited the government's ability to conduct sophisticated financial investigations and force companies to comply with anti-money laundering rules. As a result, during Reagan's first term, federal regulators failed to notice that sixty very large banks had been laundering huge sums of money throughout the 1970s and early 1980s. Treasury officials only became aware of the problem when the banks, not bank regulators, told the agency that they had violated the law. [29]

Close ties between Reagan and the gambling industry quashed efforts to curb money laundering in Las Vegas. As late as 1989, when U.S. and European officials were estimating that global crime groups were laundering $300 billion in drug money each year, the federal government spent only $120 million attacking money laundering—a tiny percentage of the $5.7 billion spent on the drug war that year. Not surprisingly, Reagan administration officials admitted in 1988 that they were seizing less than 1 percent of the drug money laundered through U.S. banks.

Today, the United States and many other countries have much tougher anti-money laundering laws and political pressure has forced many off-shore banking centers to provide banking records to outside investigators. Unfortunately, organized crime groups successfully capitalized on 30 years of lax regulation to dramatically expand the global drug trade. Poor regulation of the financial system allowed gangsters to invest in new sources of supply, create better distribution networks, and build up assets in the legitimate economy that they could use to buy political protection. The smugglers, crime groups, and heroin dealers who provided massive funding for the Taliban's rise to power in Afghanistan are, unfortunately, only one example of how these groups continue to create serious problems around the world.

The Corporate Causes of Violence

While some types of corporate crime directly encourage street crime, many have an indirect but equally devastating impact by creating social problems—such as poverty, unemployment, bad housing, and poor educational systems—that cause high rates of street crime. For example, in the 1970s and '80s, large job losses and declining wages helped boost crime rates in most urban centers. In 1992, *Business Week* pointed out that almost 3 million manufacturing jobs have been lost nationwide in U.S. cities between 1979 and 1990 and that certain light manufacturing industries, such as apparel, that employ many city residents have lost more than a quarter of their work force. During this same period, increased competition from low-wage offshore factories has reduced pay for many low-skilled jobs in the United States. Wages for low-skilled white men in their 20s fell by 14 percent between 1973 and 1989 while wages for white dropouts fell by 33 percent. Similarly wages for blacks who dropped out of high school fell by 50 percent and black men in their 20s, who must often turn to low-skill jobs to pay the bills, fell by 24 percent in this period.[30] Not surprisingly, researchers at the Urban Institute found "in 23 of the 30 largest cities, the poverty rate increased during the 1980s."[31]

These trends are particularly important because sociologists have long noted the relationship between job opportunities and street crime. In the early twentieth century, young men who joined street gangs in their teens often moved away from delinquent behavior in their early 20s when they found steady jobs in factories. But the disappearance of low skilled jobs in urban centers during the 1970s and 1980s forced many young men with limited educational backgrounds to turn to the drug trade to make a living.[32]

Over time, the lack of decent employment opportunities in high-crime communities was exacerbated by corporate policies—some illegal, some legal—that discriminate against minorities, cheat government agencies out of tax revenues, pollute the environment, and discourage investment in poorer communities. Racial discrimination made it much harder for minority groups who had migrated to large urban centers to find decent jobs in the 1950s and '60s, when U.S. crime rates began to rise, and the failure to aggressively enforce civil rights legislation during the 1980s, when Reagan gutted federal civil rights programs, imposed huge economic costs in high crime urban neighborhoods already suffering huge job loses. By 1991, when crime rates were reaching record levels, job discrimination against blacks, Latinos, and women cost the economy about $165 billion a year in lost employment opportunities.

Meanwhile, racism in the financial system made it much more difficult for poor urban communities to attract much-needed capital. Federal officials in the 1930s, '40s, and '50s, actually discouraged banks from making loans in urban areas with large black, Latino, working class, or Jewish communities. This practice, which is known as "red-lining," played a key role in the urban decay and rising crime rates of the 1960s and '70s. In the 1960s and '70s, racial discrimination in the lending and real estate business was outlawed but government officials made little attempt to enforce the laws and in the early '90s a detailed Federal Reserve study showed that racial discrimination was still widely prevalent in the home loan business.[33]

These problems, which make it much harder for poor communities to attract new investments, have been compounded by poor enforcement of environment laws. A number of studies from the 1980s and '90s have consistently shown that poor minority communities are much more likely to be exposed to severe environment problems, such as toxic waste dumps and air pollution. These dangerous environmental hazards not only impose huge heath problems and costs, they also make it much harder for poor communities to attract new investments or to retain more affluent minority residents.[34]

Other corporate crimes made it difficult for government officials to finance programs to address these problems. Lax regulation and political corruption probably adds $10 to $20 billion a year to the cost of issuing municipal bonds, and tax fraud by wealthy individuals and multinational corporations dramatically reduces the amount of money available for social programs. The IRS estimates that tax fraud costs the federal government about $100 billion a year and that about 70 percent of that fraud is committed by corporations and wealthy individuals. Increasingly large corporations also use low tax-offshore havens to reduce their taxes. Before its bankruptcy, Enron used hundreds of subsidiaries in the Cayman Islands to avoid paying taxes for most of the 1990s. Enron's use of offshore bank havens was of course quite legal. In fact, many of the worst social problems facing poorer communities can be traced to the structure of the legitimate economy, which gives major corporations the legal right to abuse and exploit people around the world. The major corporations who have moved their factories out of the United States into low-wage zones in Asia or Latin American did so because they knew these countries would legally allow them to employ child labor, fire union organizers, and expose workers to dangerous chemicals. These same corporations have also spent huge sums of money opposing national health systems even though the lack of decent health care kills, quite legally, thousands of Americans each year. Laws protecting American families from hunger, bad schools, homelessness, unemployment, or many other serious social problems are either nonexistent or poorly enforced. In fact, the legal legitimate economy encourages corporations that might attack the social causes of crime simply because those programs, which could save thousands of lives, cost money. And, as the Enron scandal illustrates, many politicians, who receive billions in corporate contributions each year, are happy to support corporate policies that kill, maim, and terrorize millions of Americans each year.

These examples suggest that both corporate crime and street crime are part of a larger problem of social justice. Corporate power currently allows companies to create serious social problems by legal and illegal means. Improved regulation of corporate behavior is important but until abusive corporate power over the economy and the political system is brought under tighter control, it is unlikely that any crusade against either street crime or corporate crime will be successful.

Sources

Much of the material in this article is based on the author's book *Capital Crimes* (New York: Monthly Review Press, 1999) and sources for most of the data can be found in that work. Other excellent sources of information on corporate crime include: *Multinational Monitor*; *Corporate Crime Reporter*; Ralph Estes, *The Tyranny of the Bottom Line: Why Corporations Make Good People Do Bad Things* (San Francisco: Berrett-Koehler, 1996); Russell Mokhiber and Robert Weissman, *Corporate Predators: The Hunt for Mega Profits and the Attack on Democracy* (Monroe, ME: Common Courage Press, 1999); Russell Mokhiber, *Corporate Crime and Violence: Big Business Power and the Abuse of Public Trust* (San Francisco: Sierra Club Books, 1988); Marshal Clinard, *The Abuse of Corporate Power* (New York: Praeger, 1990); Marshal Clinard and Peter Yeager, *Corporate Crime* (New York: Free Press, 1980); Frank Pearce, *Crimes of the Powerful: Marxism, Crime and Deviancy* (London: Pluto Press, 1976).

Notes

1. For sources on the costs of corporate crime see George Winslow, *Capital Crimes* (New York: Monthly Review, 1999), pp. 235–49 and Ralph Estes, *The Tyranny of the Bottom Line: Why Corporations Make Good People Do Bad Things* (San Francisco: Berrett-Koehler, 1996).
2. For a discussion of how this cost California consumers over $71 billion, see Foundation for Taxpayer and Consumer Rights, "Hoax: How Energy Deregulation Let the Power Industry Steal $71 billion from California Consumers." See also *Multinational Monitor*'s web site on Enron, *The Nation*'s web site on Enron; Common Cause, *Accounting for Disaster: Congress, Arthur Andersen, and the $60 Billion Enron Meltdown*, which is available on their web site, and Public Citizen: "Blind Faith: How Deregulation and Enron's Influence over Government Looted Billions from Americans." Estimates of losses from pension funds are from William Greider, "Crime in the Suites," *The Nation*, February 4, 2004.
3. Prescription drug estimate from Russel Mohkiber, "Top 100 Corporate Criminals of the Decade," in *Multinational Monitor*, July/August, 1999. See also National Institute on Drug Abuse, *Data from the Drug Abuse Warning Network (DAWN): Annual Medical Examiner Data*, [1981–1991]; Substance Abuse and Mental Health Services Administration, *Data from the Drug Abuse Warning Network (DAWN): Annual Medical Examiner Data*, [1992–1997].
4. See Winslow, *Capital Crimes*, the introduction and Part II.
5. Marshall Clinard and Peter Yeager, *Corporate Crime* (New York: The Free Press, 1980), p. 340; *Multinational Monitor*, June 1990, p. 6; *Time*, July 3, 1989, p. 4; *Fortune*, December 1, 1980, pp. 56–64; "Corporate Crime the Untold Story," *U.S. News & World Report*, September 6, 1982.
6. See Russell Mokhiber, and Robert Weissman, *Corporate Predators: The Hunt for Mega Profits and the Attack on Democracy* (Monroe, ME: Common Courage Press, 1999); Russell Mokhiber, *Corporate Crime and Violence: Big Business Power and the Abuse of Public Trust* (San Francisco: Sierra Club Books, 1988). Tobacco deaths are from the International Union Against Cancer.
7. Clinard and Yeager, *Corporate Crime*, p. 340.
8. *New York Times*, October 13, 1991, p. F10; *Multinational Monitor*, October 1992, p. 32.
9. Besides Winslow, *Capital Crimes*, see Chamber of Commerce, *Handbook on White Collar Crime* (Washington, D.C.: Chamber of Commerce, 1974); Jeffrey Reiman, *The Rich Get Richer and the Poor Get Prison* (Boston: Allen and Bacon, 1995), pp. 111–12; Clinard, *The Abuse of Corporate Power*, p. 15; Russell Mokhiber, "Soft on Crime," *Multinational Monitor*, June 1995, p. 25.
10. National Institute of Justice, *The Extent and Costs of Crime Victimization: A New Look*, (Washington, D.C.: GPO, January 1996).
11. See Winslow, *Capital Crimes*, Chapter 5 on corporate crime and Melinda Warren, *Federal Regulatory Spending Reaches a New Height: An Analysis of the Budget of the U.S. Government for the Year 2001* (St. Louis: Center for the Study of American Business, June 2000). This article is available online.
12. Id.
13. Bureau of Labor Statistics.
14. See Estes, *Tyranny of the Bottom Line*.
15. Russell Mokhiber, *Corporate Crime and Violence: Big Business Power and the Abuse of Public Trust* (San Francisco: Sierra Club Books, 1988, pp. 3–4.
16. See Estes, *Tyranny of the Bottom Line*, 181 and Winslow, *Capital Crimes*.
17. Computed from GDP and data on spending and staffing in Melinda Warren (see supra, note 11).
18. For a good discussion of the Clinton years see Michael Meeropol, *Surrender: How the Clinton Administration Completed the Reagan Revolution* (Ann Arbor: University of Michigan Press, 1998). Clinton's regulatory policies are covered in Winslow, *Capital Crimes*, Part III, particularly chapter 17, "Regulating for Profits."
19. One of the less well known but important aspects of the S&L scandal involved their losses from trading relatively unregulated financial instruments, such as mortgage backed securities and junk bonds. The Federal Deposit Insurance Corporation eventually alleged that 44 S&Ls that went broke purchased at least $28 billion worth of junk bonds, thus creating huge profits for the Wall Street firm of Drexel Burnham

Lambert and Michael Milken. Between 1983 and 1987, Milken alone earned more than $1.1 billion in salary and bonuses, and a group of more than 500 partnerships allied with the junk bond trading scheme paid out more than $2 billion in profits. Senator John Kerry alleged that S&L executives used offshore financial systems—the same system's widely used to launder drug profits—to steal at least $40 billion. See Winslow, *Capital Crimes*, Part III, particularly the chapter called "Financial Fraud."

20. Data on Enron and Arthur Andersen's political contributions from Center for Responsive Politics and Common Cause. See web pages for *Multinational Monitor* (www.essential.org/monitor/enron) for links to a number of articles and studies on political influence peddling by the companies. These contributions, of course, represent only a small portion of the money spent each year by major corporations to influence the regulatory system. Anywhere from $5 to $10 billion is spent each year by armies of lobbyists—most of whom represent the interests of the rich and powerful—at federal, state, and local levels. About 9,000 lobbyists are registered in Washington, D.C., and another 70,000 unregistered influence peddlers ply their trade in the nation's capital alone, with tens of thousands more working on a local level. In New York state alone lobbyists spent $39.1 million in 1994, more than double the 1988 figure, to influence state legislators. By 1996, another $2.65 billion was spent by candidates and political parties on federal elections, triple the amount spent in 1976. Much of this came from business interests that contributed $240 million in the 1996 election cycle thus outspending labor, which contributed $35 million, by a ratio of nine to one. Traditionally financial services companies, such as Enron and the S&L firms that went broke in the 1980s, are the largest contributors.

21. See Common Cause, *Accounting for Disaster: Congress, Arthur Andersen, and the $60 Billion Enron Meltdown*, which is available on their web site, and Public Citizen, "Blind Faith: How Deregulation and Enron's Influence over Government Looted Billions from Americans." Online at www.citizen.org. For a discussion of the California crisis, see Foundation for Taxpayer and Consumer Rights, "Hoax: How Energy Deregulation Let the Power Industry Steal $71 billion from California Consumers." Besides the contributions made by Enron, the accounting industry and its lobbying organization gave more than $27 million to federal candidates and political parties in the 1990s, money that also helped defeat plans to outlaw dodgy accounting practices.

22. *The Economist*, September 18, 1993, and Bureau of Justice Statistics.

23. See the introduction to Winslow, *Capital Crimes*.

24. Bureau of Criminal Statistics and the introduction to *Capital Crimes*.

25. See Agenzia ANSA, *Organized Crime*. Rome: ANSA Dossier, 1994; President's Commission on Organized Crime, *The Impact: Organized Crime Today* (GPO: Washington, D.C., April 1986); and International Scientific and Professional Advisory Council of the United National Crime Prevention and Criminal Justice Program, *Preventing and Controlling Money Laundering and the Use of the Proceeds of Crime: A Global Approach. Mont Blanc, Aosta Valley, June 18–20, 1994, General Reports* (Fondazione, Centro Internazionale su Diritto, Societa e Economia: 1994), p. 14.

26. See Alexander Cockburn and Jeffrey St. Clair, *Whiteout: The CIA, Drugs and the Press* (New York: Verso, 1999).

27. Edna McConnel Clark Foundation, *Seeking Justice* (New York: Edna McConnel Clark Foundation, 1995), p. 19.

28. *Seeking Justice*, p. 27.

29. See *Capital Crimes*, 269–96 for a discussion of U.S. money laundering regulation and Kathleen Day, *S&L Hell* (New York: W.W. Norton, 1993), p. 105.

30. *Business Week*, May 18, 1992.

31. Mark Alan Hughes with Julie E. Sternberg, *The New Metropolitan Reality*, The Urban Institute, December 1992), p. 22.

32. See *Capital Crimes*, pp. 127–89 for a discussion of the economic trends that have boosted crime rates in urban centers.

33. *Wall Street Journal*, March 31, 1992, p. 1.

34. See Robert D. Bullard, ed., *Wall Street Journal*, March 31, 1992, p. 1, *Confronting Environmental Racism: Voice from the Grassroots* (Boston: South End Press, 1993), pp. 17–20 and United Church of Christ Commission on Racial Justice, *Toxic Wastes and Race in the United States: A National Report on the Racial and Socio-Economic Characteristics of Communities with Hazardous Waste Sites* (New York: United Church of Christ, 1987).

Drug Policy as Social Control

NOAM CHOMSKY

In the typical Third World society, like Colombia, or India, or Mexico, or Egypt—they are all more or less the same—there is a sector of great wealth, enormous wealth, there are large numbers of people who live somewhere between suffering and misery, and then there is a sector who are just superfluous; they're of no use, that is, they don't contribute to profit. So you just have to get rid of them somehow.

Every Third World society has the same structure, and that structure is now being imposed on the United States. Inequality is growing, a large part of the population, probably a majority, is declining in earnings, wealth is enormous and very concentrated, profits are going through the ceiling. They have never had such profits before and a large part of the population is useless. Unskilled labor in urban slums, which happens to be mostly black and Hispanic, the superfluous people.

In these circumstances what do you do? Well, you have to do the same thing they do in the Third World. You have to get rid of the superfluous people, and you have to control the ones who are suffering. How do you control them? One of the best ways of controlling them is by increasing fear, and hatred, and making them hate each other and fear the super-fluous people. That's the way it's done everywhere, and it's happening in the United States. That's where the drug war fits in.

In the United States the drug war is basically a technique for control-ling dangerous populations internal to the country and doesn't have much to do with drugs. That's always been true. It goes back to England in the nineteenth century when they made gin illegal and kept whiskey legal. There was a simple class reason for it. Gin was the drink of the working class and whiskey was the drink of the upper class. This is a way of controlling the working class people.

This article was written in May 1997.

When alcohol prohibition was instituted in the United States, the purpose was to close the saloons in New York City where immigrants and working class people came, but nobody stopped anyone from drinking in the rich suburbs. In the case of marijuana, the marijuana legislation introduced right after prohibition ended started in the border states but it was aimed at Mexicans. Nobody even knew what marijuana was, it was just something the Mexican immigrants used and therefore it had to be criminalized so you could control the Mexican immigrant population.

The so-called drug war was started in the 1980s and it was aimed directly at the black population. None of this has anything to do with drugs. It has to do with controlling and criminalizing dangerous populations. It's kind of like a U.S. counterpart to "social cleansing."

Poor black males are criminalized the most by the drug war. The number of black men in the criminal justice system is enormous. That criminalizes a dangerous population. What about the population which is declining in earnings and jobs? They're frightened. The more you can increase the fear of drugs and crime and welfare mothers and immigrants and aliens and poverty and all sorts of things, the more you control people. Make them hate each other. Be frightened of each other and think that the other is stealing from them. If you do that you can control people. And that's just what the drug war does.

If we wanted to stop drug use in the United States there's an easy way to do it: educational programs. They work very efficiently, and they have made a big difference to the extent they have been used. Among the more privileged sectors, my children, probably yours, the use of drugs has been declining for a long time and so has the use of every other substance. My students don't smoke, don't use drugs, consumption of coffee is going down. In the United States, cigarettes are a class issue now. Students at universities almost never smoke cigarettes. But if you go to a poor section of town, you'll see a lot of teenage kids smoking cigarettes. It's a class issue, just like the use of drugs, just like the use of alcohol. This comes through changes in perception and understanding.

But today educational programs are on the decline; they're being cut back. The circumstances driving people to use drugs are intensifying. There's more poverty and fewer jobs, lower wages and fewer support systems. That's what's driving people to drugs and that's where the problem lies. But it's not being approached because the drug problem has been converted into a means of social control.

It's like when you turn on the television today, you hear all sorts of attacks on welfare mothers, even from some liberals. The idea is to get working people on the opposite side of the welfare mothers. The wages of working people are going down, their lives are getting worse, their children are not going to have even the opportunities they had. So what do you do? Do you tell them "We're trying to harm you"? Or do you tell them, "Welfare mothers are stealing from you"? Of course, you tell them welfare mothers are stealing from you.

Thus, if some teenage girl was raped and has a child, she's stealing from you, so you hate her. That's why they've made the welfare system so harsh and cruel, increasing cruelty and fear. These are all methods of social control. They're used everywhere.

In a country like the United States, where you can't really send out the paramilitary forces to murder people, as they do more and more in the Third World, you rely more heavily on techniques of social control. That's basically what the drug war is all about.

"Victims' Rights" as a Stalking-horse for State Repression

PAUL WRIGHT

How the ruling class defines and punishes "crime" goes a long way towards demonstrating whose class interests are being served by the criminal justice system. A key component of this strategy is to first define crime so that the poor are overly included, and the wealthy and powerful are largely excluded, weeded out of the arrest, prosecution, conviction, and imprisonment cycle. The flip side of this process lies in defining who is a victim and who isn't. Simply put, some victims are defined as "worthy" in the eyes of the law and the larger public discourse, while others are not. In recent years, there has been increased activity by victims' rights groups and legislatures who claim concern for the victims of crime. While there are more questions than answers regarding this complex issue, to date, "victims' rights" has been used primarily to expand state power and repression in a manner that police and prosecutors would otherwise have been unable to do directly.

The first step lies in defining who the "victim" is. An illustrative example is the move currently underway to add a victims' rights amendment to the U.S. constitution. This amendment would require that prosecutors notify victims of any court hearings involving the defendant, give victims an opportunity to speak at sentencings, and be consulted about plea agreements. A key change made after the bill was introduced was to define the term "victim" to include *only* the victims of violent crime. The victims of economic and property crime are excluded from coverage by this amendment. Since more people are victimized by economic and property crime than violent crime, apparently that victim majority is not worthy of protection.

The thousands of people bilked out of their life savings by the likes of fraudulent scamsters Charles Keating and Jim Bakker are among those not considered worthy of protection as victims. Just as criminal activity

---

This article was written in August 1999.

by corporations and the wealthy is effectively decriminalized through lax enforcement of the laws or diversion into the civil justice system, so too are the victims of predation by corporations and the wealthy "devictimized." Workers killed in accidents that result from a company's cost cutting measures to maximize profit are not victims. Consumers killed by dangerous products knowingly marketed by corporations to make more money are also not victims.

A miner killed because his employer cut costs on safety measures is not a victim. His widow who loses her life savings due to fraud by bank owners is not a victim, even having her car stolen by local thieves does not make her a victim. But if she is robbed at gunpoint of five dollars, she is now a victim worthy of constitutional protection.

Good Victims and Bad Victims

Beyond the definition of who is an official victim and who isn't, examine the victims of violent crimes against the person (murder, rape, robbery, and assault with bodily injury). Here the key issue defining a person as a victim is not merely a matter of economic loss but that of the identities of the victim and the victimizer. Or, not all victims are equal.

Some prosecutors who oppose the constitutional victims' rights amendment point out that a substantial number of violent crime victims are themselves criminals, their injuries the result of "dispute-settling" among members of the lower-class criminal element.

Sammy Gravano was given immunity for the murder of nineteen of his fellow Mafia compatriots, in exchange for his testimony against John Gotti. Obviously police, prosecutors, and a judge decided that Gravano's 19 murdered Mafia victims weren't worthy of the definition of "victim." Under a victims' rights amendment, would the families of Gravano's victims be allowed to speak out against his five-year sentence reached by plea bargain?

Every day across the United States police and prison guards kill, beat, and brutalize the citizenry. Prisoners are also assaulted, sexually and otherwise, and subjected to bodily injury by their fellow prisoners and prison staff. However, the political establishment is not calling for rights for these victims. Abner Louima, the Haitian immigrant in New York City who was sodomized with a police truncheon in a police station bathroom by New York's Finest, is not referred to as a "crime victim." We never heard the term "crime victim Rodney King," because even when police are convicted of criminal acts, to call the brutalized people "victims" necessarily implies the police perpetrators are criminals.

The political problem for the advocates of victims' rights becomes even greater when prisoners suffer injury. The political discourse that has been created around "victim rights" steadfastly implies what it cannot openly say: "worthy" victims are nice, middle- and upper-class people, usually white, who are raped, robbed, or killed by poor, violent strangers, especially black or Latino strangers. If the police, media, and politicians have made the universal face of crime that of a young black or Latino man, they have also strived mightily to make the face of the universal victim that of a middle- or upper-class white woman or child. Brutalized prisoners don't advance this political agenda. Hence, there is no concern whatsoever for the prisoner who is raped, robbed, beaten, or killed, whether by prisoners or prison staff. Not surprisingly, no one speaks of "victims' rights" for the prisoners subjected to violent crimes against their person.

Many states have specifically codified who makes a good victim and who doesn't. For example, in Washington, like many other states, no one who is victimized while confined in jail or prison can seek victim's compensation for their injuries. Other states, such as Ohio and Arkansas, deny victim's compensation to anyone who has ever been convicted of a crime.

The use of victims' rights laws readily shows how these political decisions defining who is and who is not a victim play out in the real world. Sylvia Cassidy was a 24-year-old North Carolina woman who was shot in the head and killed by her live-in boyfriend. When her family sought victim's compensation to assist with her funeral expenses, they were denied. The North Carolina Victims Compensation Fund Commission (VCFC) held that by living with her killer Cassidy was violating a 194-year-old law against cohabitation, thus she was a criminal. North Carolina, like many other states, excludes as victims anyone involved in criminal activity which leads to their death or injury. By "cohabitating" with her boyfriend, Cassidy was breaking the law, ergo she was a criminal and not a victim.("Quirk in Law Bans Claims of Victims in North Carolina," *Seattle Times*, April 1, 1999.)

VCFC director Gary Eichelberger noted that North Carolina law mandates denial of compensation if the victim was participating in any criminal activity. "We wrestle with this every time we get a claim like this, especially when the victim is otherwise innocent, " he said. Eichelberger went on to state that the Commission has denied compensation solely on the basis of cohabitation in 47 cases. Thirty-nine of these cases involved domestic violence victims.

Then we reach the forgotten victim: people wrongfully convicted and imprisoned or executed. Recent cases in Philadelphia, where hundreds of prisoners were released after successfully showing they had been set up and convicted on false drug charges by corrupt police, are but one example. Whatever the actual numbers, as a matter of statistical probability, of 1.8 million people imprisoned in U.S. prisons and jails, at least some are factually innocent. Few defenders of the criminal justice system claim it is infallible.

The U.S. Supreme Court has held that it does not violate the U.S. Constitution to execute the innocent, so long as the condemned received a "fair trial." Justice Blackmun commented in *Herrera v. Collins* that executing the innocent "bordered" on simple murder. If innocent people are convicted, imprisoned, or executed for crimes they did not commit, are they too not victims? Victims of a system no less, for unlike individual crimes committed by people acting alone, imprisoning and executing the innocent requires collusion by the police, prosecutors, judiciary, and sometimes juries and the media, to accomplish its end result. To call the imprisoned and executed innocents "victims" would raise the question of whether the entire criminal justice system is a victimizer.

The problem with defining who is and who isn't a "victim" is in the degree of impunity the victimizing perpetrators correspondingly receive. Not surprisingly, brutalized prisoners, citizens, and the wrongly convicted who suffer at the hands of police, guards, prosecutors, and judges are not considered worthy of the title "victim" because the victimizing institutions of social control—prisons, police, judiciary, and prosecutors—are rarely if ever held accountable for their misdeeds. People can't become a "victim" (not a worthy victim anyway) unless the social and political decision is first made by the ruling class to have a "criminal." The same reasoning applies to why people who suffer economic and physical harm due to the predation of the wealthy and corporations are also not considered worthy victims.

The Politics of Victims' Rights

The political use of the victims' rights movement is seen by the rise of this movement as part of the overall trend towards increased state repression that began in 1968 but which accelerated markedly with the Reagan presidency. Virtually all the well-funded victims' rights groups receive substantial portions of their funding directly from law enforcement agencies or groups linked to such agencies. The result, intended or not, is that these groups tend to parrot the party line of more police, more prisons, more punishment, more draconian laws. The Doris Tate Victims Bureau in California receives 85 percent of its funding from the California Correctional Peace Officers Association, the union that represents prison guards. The union also provides the Bureau with free office space in its Sacramento headquarters. Not surprisingly, the Bureau likes what the union likes, especially legislation like "three-strikes" laws which will help ensure full employment for prison guards.

The net result is that those with the biggest vested interest in maintaining and expanding the prison industrial complex—police, prosecutors, and politicians—eagerly use victims' rights groups as their stalking horses to expand repressive state police power in a manner that would seem crassly self-interested if they did so directly.

It is important to note, however, that not all victims' rights groups fall into this category. Murder Victims Families for Reconciliation (MVFR) and the restorative justice movement are the most notable examples of victims' rights groups that are not political pawns for those who seek to increase state repression. But much of MVFR's work goes unnoticed in public dialogue: they are neither well-funded nor well-publicized. Because their goal of actually helping the victims of property and violent crime deal with their loss do not advance a broader political agenda for the dominant class they are largely ignored.

The current criminal justice system ill serves the victims of crime and the criminal defendant. Most people who suffer the loss of property would prefer compensation to the thief's incarceration. Of course those robbed by the rich usually get neither compensation nor imprisonment as satisfaction.

For the victims of personal violent crime committed by poor individuals the current system offers only punishment. Punishment rarely gives the victim closure, nor does it provide the perpetrator with any type of real rehabilitation. But as long as the purpose of the criminal justice system remains that of the tool of social control over the poor, this is unlikely to change. Likewise, this is exactly what makes it unlikely that restorative justice will make inroads into the criminal justice system. Even less likely is that any organized voice will call for the inclusion of all victims of violence and theft, even if the perpetrators are agents of the state, the wealthy, and corporations; even if the victims of these crimes are poor, imprisoned, or socially disadvantaged.

For now, victims continue to be defined as the white, middle- and upper-class person who is killed, raped, robbed, or assaulted by a stranger. Unless critics of the criminal justice system begin to question and expose the current role of the victims' rights agenda and its veneer of legitimacy, its influence will go unchecked.

TWO MILLION SWEPT AWAY

With two million incarcerated, the experience of prison has now become normalized for many communities. From rural communities where prison has become the central industry to the effects of incarceration on the 1.5 million children who have a parent in prison—contact with prison is, for some, pervasive and immediate.

With more people in prison than in any industrialized country, and with the current boom in the female prison population, over 1.5 million children now have a parent in prison, meaning they suffer the secondary effects of prison along with their imprisoned parent. The disruptive effects of prison on a family are myriad and devastating. A child who loses a bond with an imprisoned parent never recovers from this loss: it will play out over the course of her entire lifetime.

And what of the small-town communities where the local auto parts factory—lost to the capital flight of the 1980s—is replaced with a prison? The community leaders of these economically devastated communities look to prison as economic panacea, only to find an incubator of social ills. In the rural communities where prisons are sited, rates of domestic violence and drug or alcohol abuse surge, with scant economic benefit to point to.

The following section explores the hidden impact of prison on communities, an impact usually neglected in the political discourse regarding crime.

—TH

Swept Away

NELL BERNSTEIN

Natasha Gaines came home recently to find an urgent message from one of her mother's lawyers: President Clinton had just commuted the sentences of four women and one man serving long prison terms for conspiracy under mandatory sentencing drug laws. It was good news, attorney Tracey Hubbard assured Gaines, whose mother, Dorothy, is serving a 19-year sentence in Tallahassee, Florida, for conspiracy to distribute crack cocaine. If Clinton had been moved by these women's stories, perhaps he would grant Dorothy's application for clemency. Maybe her mom would finally be allowed to come home.

But Natasha wasn't sure just how hopeful she should feel. Like the four women pardoned by Clinton, like tens of thousands of other women, her mother was sentenced to prison as a drug "conspirator," guilty of little more than having a man in her life who was involved with drugs. Clinton's decision to commute the five sentences received relatively little attention. There was no White House press conference and no press release.

Unlike his better-publicized grant of clemency to 12 Puerto Rican nationalists that year, which was perceived by some as an effort to win votes for Hillary Rodham Clinton in New York, Clinton's pardon of the drug "conspirators" appeared to have little or no political value as far as the White House was concerned. And political value is something that Dorothy Gaines and her daughter would understand. Political value has a lot to do with why Dorothy is in prison in the first place.

What the White House didn't say when Clinton ordered the release of Amy Pofahl, Serena Nunn, Louise House, and Shawndra Mills is just how unremarkable—and how political—these women's cases are. This was not a case of a president extending clemency to prisoners whose convictions were reached in error or were uniquely unfair. Their convictions

This essay was originally published in *Salon* magazine, July 20, 2000.

(and prison sentences) were completely routine under the federal conspiracy provisions passed as part of the mandatory sentencing movement of the late 1980s.

In fact, mandatory sentencing and conspiracy provisions have contributed to a boom in the female prison population that is unprecedented in its scope, and devastating in its impact on children and families. Female prisoners are now the fastest growing—and least violent— segment of the prison population nationwide.

According to a December 1999 report from the General Accounting Office, the number of women in prison has increased fivefold in the past two decades, from 13,400 in 1980 to 84,400 by the end of 1998. Between 1990 and 1997, the number of female prisoners serving time for drug offenses nearly doubled; in the federal prison system, a staggering 72 percent of female prisoners are serving time for drug offenses. The U.S. Sentencing Commission reports that 1,199 women were sentenced to federal prison on conspiracy charges in 1999, out of a total of 3,001 sentenced for drug trafficking in general. Given the length of the sentences mandated, that means that tens of thousands of women are in federal prison on charges similar to those of Pofahl, Nunn, House, and Mills.

In its report, the GAO attributes much of the increase in the female prison population to "tough on crime" measures such as mandatory sentencing. Mark Mauer of the Sentencing Project in Washington agrees; in his recent book, *The Race to Incarcerate*, he blames a shift in philosophy about the purpose of incarceration—from rehabilitation to punishment—for the move away from indeterminate sentencing (10 to 20 years, 15 to life, and so on) to mandatory minimums.

Rehabilitation, after all, is a mysterious and unpredictable process: Who can say how long it will take? For that reason, says Mauer, a sentence intended to rehabilitate was seen to require some built-in flexibility. Once offenders began to be defined exclusively in terms of their criminal acts, and the function of incarceration came to be seen solely as deterrent and punishment, such flexibility was no longer required. Enter mandatory minimums.

The 1986 Anti-Drug Abuse Act, passed at the height of the crack epidemic and signed by President Reagan just a week before Election Day, established most of the drug-related mandatory sentences currently in effect. The 1988 Omnibus Anti-Drug Act upped the ante, adding mandatory sentences for simple possession of crack cocaine and changing the drug conspiracy penalties so that a co-conspirator faces the same penalties as the person who actually commits the offense.

This is how mandatory sentencing works: If you are found to have possessed or distributed a specific amount of a particular substance, you will serve a legislatively mandated number of years, regardless of the circumstances of your crime, your character or any other mitigating factors.

The judge has zero discretion and must impose whatever sentence the legislature requires.

Conspiracy laws represent perhaps the nastiest twist in the mandatory sentencing statutes. Under mandatory sentencing, people who sell even small quantities of drugs can wind up with brutally long prison sentences. Under conspiracy laws, those who don't sell drugs—who merely have the bad fortune, or judgment, to be associated with people who do—can wind up with those same sentences.

The "conspiracies" that lead to these convictions rarely involve overt plotting and scheming to distribute large quantities of drugs. For a woman whose husband or boyfriend is involved in the drug trade, conspiracy may consist of having drugs in the house, taking phone messages from drug associates, or driving the husband or boyfriend to the bank where he makes an illicit deposit. In some cases, prosecutors have not been required to prove that a "conspirator" knew she was committing any of these acts; a finding that she should have known what her man was up to has been enough to secure a conviction.

Eric E. Sterling, now president of the Criminal Justice Policy Foundation in Washington, was counsel to the House Committee on the Judiciary from 1979 to 1989, advising the committee on its anti-drug efforts. As such, he had a front row seat as all this came to pass.

At the time mandatory minimums were enacted, Sterling says, he thought they were a bad idea, but he had no idea just how damaging they would prove to be in practice. Congress' intent in passing the laws, Sterling says, was "to give the Justice Department the tools and the impetus to prosecute the most important drug traffickers."

But the legislation was passed without hearings and Congress made some crucial errors that have allowed today's abuses, Sterling says. Mandatory minimums are based on a rigid schedule of "triggering quantities" of drugs that determine the length of a particular sentence. Many of the quantities are ludicrously low, leading to the prosecution of minor players as major kingpins.

This happened, says Sterling, in part because members of Congress knew very little about drugs, and without the benefit of expert testimony that hearings would have provided, they wound up with a fairly random set of numbers. Another problem, according to Sterling, is that those writing the legislation "didn't speak metric." Says the attorney, "Most members of Congress might have trouble telling you if a milligram is bigger than a kilogram."

When the conspiracy provisions were tacked onto the mandatory-minimum laws two years later, even less attention was paid to their potential impact. "To say that there was congressional intent would be to give too much significance to the way in which it was processed," Sterling says. The provisions attaching the same mandatory minimums to conspiracy as to drug trafficking itself were "characterized as a technical correction," Sterling says, and passed with very little notice. "They have resulted," he adds, "in the additional ensnarement of minor participants in drug offenses and in their being treated as though they were the central kingpins."

While this result may have initially been unintended, Sterling notes, Congress has very little motivation to undo its error. "First of all, the Congress in general is indifferent to claims of injustice and inequity in cases of accused persons," Sterling charges. "Secondly, [conspiracy laws are] a very powerful tool for eliciting testimony and coercing guilty pleas. The final reason is that any vote that would have the effect of lowering penalties for drug offenses runs the risk of being characterized as 'soft on drugs.'"

The fact that four out of the five prisoners whose sentences Clinton commuted were women is no coincidence. While women are actually slightly less likely than men to be sentenced on conspiracy charges, when they are, it is often because they are *not* involved in a major way (or at all) in the drug trade.

Under mandatory sentencing laws, the only way a person charged with a drug offense can get a sentence reduction is to help prosecutors build a case against someone else. Many women who wind up serving time on conspiracy charges are doing so because of the testimony of boyfriends or husbands who won sentence reductions for themselves on the basis of this testimony. The less involved a woman actually is, the less she has to offer prosecutors—and the more likely she is to do serious time.

The women whose sentences Clinton commuted have stories that are as appalling as they are typical. Amy Pofahl didn't know that her businessman husband, Sandy, was a major ecstasy importer until after he was arrested in Germany. When Sandy asked her to help him retrieve hidden drug profits so he could post bail, Amy complied. When Sandy offered testimony against his various associates, he threw in information about Amy's involvement with his finances. Sandy did four years in prison; Amy was sentenced to 24.

Serena Nunn's story is also typical. At 19, she got involved with the son of a drug dealer. Her role in his drug activities consisted of driving him to an occasional meeting, but because she refused to testify against him, she received a 16-year sentence.

Among the women currently serving decades-long sentences on conspiracy charges are many others with similar tales to tell. According to the advocacy group Families Against Mandatory Minimums, they include:

Sharvone McKinnon. McKinnon was a school bus driver; her boyfriend was a major crack dealer. McKinnon took messages for her boyfriend, occasionally let his employees drop off drugs at their house, and on one occasion delivered money for him. Eventually she left him, but not soon enough. He was arrested shortly thereafter, and she was convicted of conspiracy to distribute cocaine. McKinnon is serving a life sentence.

Kemba Smith. Smith was a college freshman when she fell in love with a drug dealer. After he was arrested, she collected money from one of his associates and secured a lawyer for him. When he was released on bail, she fled with him and they spent a year on the run. Eventually, Smith turned herself in and told the authorities what she knew about her boyfriend's whereabouts. By the time they found him, he was dead, and Smith's information was of no use. Smith was convicted of conspiracy to distribute cocaine, lying to federal authorities, and conspiracy to launder drug money. She is serving 24.5 years.

Sylvia Foster. Foster, a former prison guard who worked at a group home for handicapped adults, dated a crack dealer who used her home to cook and store crack. About six months into the relationship, Foster found cocaine in her house and broke up with her boyfriend. Foster claimed at her trial that she had not known about his activities and was innocent of any crime; as a result of this claim, she received a sentence enhancement for obstruction of justice. Foster is serving 24 years.

None of these women had any prior offenses.

Dorothy Gaines had one—writing a bad check for $155. Gaines, 42, was dating a drug user who was part of a crack ring in Mobile, Alabama. When the state came down on the ring, Gaines was caught in the net. At trial, she testified that she was unaware of any drug activity. Several of her alleged co-conspirators (including an aggrieved ex-husband with whom she had battled over child support) testified that she had kept crack at her house and delivered it when told.

Gaines was convicted in federal court solely on the word of witnesses who received sentence reductions in return for their testimony. Her sentence is longer than that of any other member of the conspiracy, including the so-called kingpin, who will be released eight years before she will.

Natasha Gaines, now 25, was a college student when her mother was convicted in 1995, and she followed the trial closely. She knew, she says, that her mother had never had anything to do with drugs—and also that her mother had always been "naive." Says Natasha, "You know how people say, 'Don't take my kindness for weakness'? Her kindness was her weakness.'"

Her mother's boyfriend, who refused to testify against her, told the judge that he had heard his codefendants, who were all kept in the same jail cell, "trying to get their stories straight" on Dorothy's supposed involvement. The fact that the trial proceeded anyway, and that her mother was convicted based solely on these men's testimony, taught Natasha some important lessons about the American judicial system in general and conspiracy laws in particular.

"My definition of conspiracy," Natasha says, "is that it's a way for the government to build a case when they have no evidence. They get people who are willing to work for them because they do have something on those people, and then it's like a Broadway play. 'We've rehearsed this over and over, and now we gotta convince these 12 people who've got tickets—the jurors—that we deserve a Tony award.' That's pretty much how I see it."

Natasha left college when her mother went to prison in order to take care of her younger sister and brother, now 17 and 15. Her brother Phillip, she says, has "taken it the hardest. He was only 2 when his daddy died, so he's always been the child that stays with my mom. Everywhere my mom went, he always tagged along. He's just mama's baby, and I've watched him suffer the worst."

In the early years of his mother's incarceration, Phillip made his own efforts to defend her reputation and secure her release. "Dear Judge," he wrote in a letter to the man who had sentenced his mother, "I need my mom. Would you help my mom? I have no dad and my grandmom have cancer. I don't have innyone to take care of me and my sisters and my neice and nephew and my birthday's coming up in October the 25 and I need my mom to be here on the 25 and for the rest of my life. I will cut your grass and wash your car everyday just don't send my mom off. Please Please Please don't!!!" Phillip included his phone number in case the judge had any questions.

When the judge didn't call, Phillip moved on. "Dear President Clinton," he wrote in March 1995, "I hope you can free my mom. I need her. Because I am just a little boy! I am just ten year old. I need my mom very much. Please get her out I need her."

Five years later, Phillip describes himself as "still holding on. I never did lose hope. I just thought they weren't interested.

"Words cannot explain how much I miss my mom," says Phillip, who belongs to a growing contingent of children orphaned by the drug war. The number of children whose mothers were in federal or state prison nearly doubled between 1991 and 1997, to 110,000. Most of these are the children of single parents; when mom is shipped off, they have no one left.

Because there are fewer state and federal facilities for women than for men, and because prisons are often built in remote rural areas, women are frequently sent hundreds of miles from their children. According to a 1997 survey of female state prisoners by the Bureau of Justice Statistics, more than half the women had never received a visit from their children, mainly because of the cost and difficulty of travel.

Phillip went a year between visits before going to see his mother in May 1999 in a borrowed car. Natasha had saved up to buy a car so she could take her siblings to see their mother, but the transmission went and she can't afford to fix it, so Phillip does not know when he will see his mother next.

The fact that his mother was convicted when he knows her to be innocent, Phillip says, has made it difficult for him to hold onto the values with which he was raised. "At the time, it made me feel like right was just wrong," he says. "I learned that no matter who you are and what you did, people don't really care. If somebody says you did this, they're gonna go by that. It's not right. I hope they just quit the conspiracy laws sooner or later."

Phillip is far from alone in that hope. New York, which launched the mandatory sentencing craze in 1973 with the passage of its draconian Rockefeller drug laws, is now reconsidering those laws. Rep. Maxine Waters, D-Calif., has introduced legislation in Congress that would repeal most federal mandatory sentencing provisions. The American Bar Association, the U.S. Sentencing Commission, and over three-quarters of the federal judges compelled to impose the sentences have all spoken out against mandatory sentencing laws. Even drug czar Barry McCaffrey has publicly criticized them.

Ultimately, however, the Clinton administration showed little inclination to take on the laws under which the four pardoned women were sentenced. According to Sterling, the federal prison population doubled during Clinton's tenure. The number of female prisoners rose even more quickly during that period than the number of male prisoners. If Clinton had done nothing but sign clemency orders for the remainder of his term, he wouldn't have come close to reversing this trend.

At the time, many hoped that the commutations would represent not a single feel-good gesture, but the beginning of a much needed reconsideration of mandatory sentencing policies.

Phillip Gaines has a more limited aspiration. "I was just thinking," he says, "that after he released four women, maybe he could release four more women. Maybe my mom."

An American Seduction

Portrait of a Prison Town

JOELLE FRASER

I've come home because the new High Desert State Prison needs teachers, and I need a job. At 8 a.m., I stop at the BP for the weekly paper: the first thing I notice is the place is full of prison guards. They're buying cigarettes and gas, stirring whitener into coffee. Each is decked out in full uniform, army green suit and parka with the California Department of Corrections gold patch, shiny black boots, belt hung with batons and pepper spray. Most are young and beefy; all have the soldier hairdo, trim mustache, crisp creases—these guys would pass any inspection.

Two more walk in. I should feel safe, but I don't. These uniforms are about keeping people in line. It feels more like a Central American border crossing than a gas station lobby in rural America. The young man with the ponytail apparently doesn't like the scene either; he walks in, then pivots coolly right back out.

Later, I learn this is shift change for Susanville's two prisons, when hundreds of guards switch places and traffic triples in this town, population 7,800. With 10,000 prisoners already, a federal prison on the way, and talk of a women's prison and a sex offender jail still to come, this is Prison County USA, where everyone and his brother works in some way for the prison, where there are more people behind bars than outside of them.

People told me the prison came to town just in time. The closing of two mines and an army depot, the shrinking logging industry, and a general feeling that the town was collapsing in on itself—all led Susanville to open its arms for High Desert State Prison, a 4,500-prisoner maximum security facility to be built just eight miles from Main Street, where it would sit beside the California Correctional Center, a smaller prison built in 1963.

This article was written in September 2000. A version was originally published in *The Verdict*, 2001.

In 1992, 57 percent of the voters said "yes" to the ballot proposal for another prison, mainly due to the public relations campaigns of the Chamber of Commerce and the Save Our Jobs Committee. A few months later, like a family preparing for the arrival of an important guest, the town readied itself for the prison.

And appropriately, this guest would bring gifts: a $57–70 million dollar payroll, 1,200 new jobs, and anywhere from 3,500 to 4,000 new residents, the families of prisoners and prison personnel who would buy their groceries, their gas, their meals, who would pay their rent and mortgages in this town. Annexing the prison into the city limits would mean more grant dollars for the city as the population total, now including prisoners, more than doubled to 16,000. The state Department of Corrections, eager to build another prison to stem the flow of a system already operating at 201 percent capacity, offered $2 million to compensate for impacts on schools, courts, and roads. It was the largest sum ever given to a community in which a prison was constructed, although it would be argued later that it was not nearly enough.

A banner stretched across Main Street: "WELCOME PRISON EMPLOYEES AND INMATES." Builders drew up plans for new condominiums and homes, motels advertised special rates for prison employees and prisoners' families. Sierra Video offered coupons for one free rental with a prison employee ID card. Uptown Uniforms displayed khaki jumpers and shiny black boots in its windows—a smart move considering $200,000 would be spent annually on uniforms. People lined up at the karate school for self-defense classes. The Susanville Supermarket hired four new people and structured work schedules around the state's first-of-the-month paydays. Carpet cleaners, hired out by real estate firms and landlords of rental property, were swamped.

News of the prison found its way to companies like Wal-Mart, Taco Bell, Country Kitchen, Blockbuster Video, all of whom came and set up shop in advance. During prison construction in 1995, every motel in town put up "no vacancy" signs as new prison employees and construction workers camped in trailers and filled parking lots for weeks.

Three years later, as the strip lengthened and the stoplights multiplied and many small businesses, unable to compete with Wal-Mart, quietly boarded their doors, Susanville is reminiscent of so many towns that have outgrown themselves and lost something in the process. But it is also unlike many small towns—there is the overwhelming presence of men with military haircuts and trim mustaches, the constant talk of prison scandals and violence (eleven prisoners have been killed or committed suicide since High Desert's opening), the clear division between locals and prison employees and prisoners' families. People complain about anonymity, about long lines at the bank, about traffic, about the rise in prices. The police department faces rising domestic violence, a 50 percent jump in juvenile delinquency and trade in hard-core drugs like heroin from gang members associated with the prison. The real estate community holds a glut of property because the new prison employees are a transient lot, eager for promotion and transfer, and they're not settling in like they were supposed to.

It would be easy to apply literary allusions to this collision of frustrated expectations—the prison was a Trojan horse, a Faustian bargain, a Pyrrhic victory, but that would deny the fact that some of the promises have come true, to a certain extent. The town does have more money, and graduating seniors, with job opportunities at the new prison, no longer have to flee to Portland and Sacramento and other faraway cities. People can make fewer shopping trips to Reno and choose from six movies instead of two. There's a health food store, and at Safeway, people can buy goat cheese and foccaccia bread. As one woman said, "Who knows, maybe we'll get a Mervyn's."

In a place where the economy is dying and the young people are leaving for places where it is not, the new prison was about money, about security and progress and hope for a better life. But as Susanville has discovered, a new prison requires that the community adapt to a rapid leap in a specific kind of population—those drawn to and associated with the work of corrections, an industry for whom the raw material is the systematic incapacitation of despairing human beings, in this case over 10,000 of them.

In the end, this was a town in which everyone was seduced in one way or another, and because a seduction is ultimately a mutual act, there was no one to blame the morning after. In this town everyone held out for a promise that, when kept, turned out to be less—or more—than bargained for.

For a century and a half, folks have been coming to this town looking for gold or some form of it in timber or ranching, full of hope and grit and then the scratch to survive when the dream is gone, a search so definitively American that I began to see that Susanville was not just a small town but The American Small Town, and that, like the Washo and Maidu Indians who lived here in the beginning, like the wolves who wandered this basin, it is an endangered species.

As the biggest town in Lassen County, Susanville sits in the middle of prime ranching country, about 100 miles from any good-sized city— Reno, Chico, Redding, and Red Bluff. Heading south towards Reno, drivers are treated to a comforting view of cattle scattered over ranchlands with high hills beyond like the warm backs of sleeping dogs. Here 4H is as important as church, and the Lassen County Cattlewomen hold an annual Mother's Day Beef Recipe Contest. Youth here are experts in barrel racing, goat-tying, and break-away roping, and they regularly prove it in local rodeos.

For these reasons it's often called cowboy country (or "redneck country," by the less generous). The weather is harsh—with its 4,500-

foot elevation, in the summer it tops 105 degrees, and in the winter snow can bury the town for weeks. It's a man's town, where fishing and hunting are part of every good boy's education, where the local community college offers more classes in auto mechanics and welding than English or history. It's a place where gunsmiths and well drillers receive the kind of recognition reserved for professors and doctors in other parts of the country; where gun racks are as ubiquitous as cowboy hats, and at the gas station convenience store on Highway 395, you can buy bullet key chains. The women, too, are tough, as adept at changing car parts or chopping wood or rolling a cigarette as the men; this is not a delicate place, and they grow old fast in the dry desert air, their faces lined and set.

But with the toughness of these people comes a respect for life and an enormous capacity to love. Ten years ago, lured by the gorgeous country and the promise of a small town life, my mother fled the Bay Area with my little brother and bought 22 acres of land covered with waist-high rye and the tracks of mule deer, coyotes, and jackrabbits. Over those years I've spent summers and holidays here; I've tutored at the vocational ed office and taught at the community college. I've made good friends and loved men and helped nurse my stepfather through a summer of . chemotherapy.

In this way I've come to know and admire the people of the town, but it is also as an observer and visitor that I have seen the changes. When I walk down Main Street, I am simply another stranger, now. I began to ask questions because in the space of two years I had seen Susanville change into another kind of place, and the change was one that was neither altogether good nor altogether inevitable. These changes seemed important, and though they were cropping up all over the country, no one was talking about prison towns.

On my mother's dining room table lies a polished cedar bowl, so smooth it seems lit from within, the kind of glow that requires an attention both precise and time-consuming. On the bottom of the bowl a typewritten note with a prison ID number is glued in place: For Victims of Crime. She bought it from the annual Prison Craft Fair, a charity event benefiting Lassen Family Services Domestic Abuse program, where you can buy everything from an oak coffee table to an embroidered leather belt.

"That place sells out in an hour," she tells me. "The craftsmanship is amazing."

The prisoners aren't there, of course, just their handiwork. For many of the townspeople, the fair is the closest they will get to the prison or its occupants. It is an example of the ways in which a town will ultimately co-exist with a prison, in partnerships that range from fundraisers to community work, where prisoners groom baseball diamonds, plant trees on county property, paint governmental buildings—even dry-clean school band uniforms. As the California Department of Corrections boasts in a brochure, "While the inmates are paid only cents per hour, the benefit to the community is far greater."

Those benefits are the icing on the economic cake that is offered to isolated communities like Susanville, far from any major port or city, who often try in vain to attract new industry. The town then relies on logging, mining, ranching, and government. Here, with more than half the town working for a government agency, acronyms spill out easily in daily conversations: BLM (Bureau of Land Management), CDF (California Department of Forestry), USFS (United States Forestry Service), DFG (Department of Fish and Game) and, of course, CDC (California Department of Corrections).

In 1963, the first prison, the 1,120-acre California Correction Center (CCC, "The Center"), was built to further conservation efforts. Prisoners lived at the boarding school-style center, spending their time helping reduce fire hazard, managing forests and watersheds, clearing streams, and improving fish and game habitat. In the cyclical nature of prison policy, this was the rehabilitation era, the time of liberal reform. One local man told me it wasn't unusual to get a work crew of prisoners to come out to help on someone's ranch. The Center, which began with only 1,200 prisoners, more than doubled in 1987 to accommodate the more than 2,000 rapists, kidnappers, and other violent offenders, who would be held behind razor wire in two-man cells with rifles trained on them 24 hours a day. It was a sign of the times—the "tough on crime" policies. Despite misgivings—there was no vote and hardly a public forum—the town adjusted to the expansion; after all, Susanville relied on The Center for 20 percent of its economy.

Over the past 10 years, as logging shrank and the mines and army depot downsized and then eventually closed, the idea of another prison seemed quite logical. After all, the state already owned the land, and it needed another prison to help with the dangerously overcrowded system. Even with High Desert, in mid-1998 the state's 33 facilities weren't enough to contain the state's criminals, whose number rises about 7 percent annually, the highest rate in the nation. (The state's punitive trends, the legacy of two tough-on-crime governors, included 1994's "three strikes" legislation, which sentenced three-time losers to 25 years to life, doubled terms for many second-time felons, and slashed time off for good behavior. The CDC's master plan predicted that prisoner population would exceed maximum operating prison capacity of 178,432 by the year 2000—sites are under discussion or planned for California City, Delano, Sacramento, San Diego County, and Taft.) But if The Center was a trickle that became a stream in Susanville, the $272-million High Desert State Prison was a river that became a flood.

Part of the problem was the state's bait-and-switch halfway through the process. Four months after voters approved a low- to medium-security facility, High Desert became a Level III and IV facility, housing the most violent offenders and those with 25-year-to-life terms. This required more staff, high security lights, and other requirements. The implications of this newer security level were far-reaching but hard to nail down. It meant, for example, that more prisoner families would move to Susanville to be near the incarcerated family member, stressing the social services more than anticipated.

County officials were furious, but there was little they could do. The state's mitigation money helped, and the city receives about $50 a year for each prisoner, but it doesn't help enough with the cost of building roads, increasing law enforcement, and expanding schools for an estimated 1,180 additional schoolchildren. The ranchers were against the prison from the start, claiming it exchanged open space and crop land for housing and infrastructure, and would siphon ground water now used for growing crops.

Perhaps the biggest problem with the prison is that, unlike private industry, which generates as much as $600 per job in property taxes, a government industry produces no direct county taxes, the money counties need to supply health care and police protection. And about half of Lassen County's existing industry is local, state, or federal government already.

When word of the new prison got out, former warden Bill Merkle saw 500 transfer requests for Susanville. "Lassen County is a good place to raise kids, has clean air and a nice environment," he said, a quote that began to take on a kind of mantra-like status, as every guard I talked to repeated it in turn. In all, nearly 1,800 guards, some veterans but most new on the job, made their way to Susanville from Southern California and the nearby larger cities of Sacramento, Reno, and Vacaville, a good number bringing families with them. For many of these men and their families, they might as well have crossed the border into another country.

Carol Jeldness, a licensed clinical social worker who contracted with the prison to provide counseling under the prison's Employee Assistance Plan, built her practice on guard relocation trauma. "A town like this, it doesn't welcome you much," she said.

The new guards needed to not only adjust to working in a brand new maximum security prison—with all of its start-up problems—but they had wives and children who'd come to a place with little to do, or at least it seemed so to many of them. There is no mall in Susanville, no factory outlet stores, no roller rink, no Boys & Girls Club—to find any of these requires a 160-mile round trip. The weather only exacerbates the isolation. It doesn't snow much in Orange or Sacramento counties, but in Susanville, for a good part of the winter, people need chains to get down Main Street. Cabin fever quickly became a popular topic.

Compounding the adjustment problem was the financial one. To be a guard, all you need is an AA degree (until recently it was only a high school diploma) and successful completion of a six-week training course.

As a result, many of the guards at High Desert are between 22–30 years old, and make about $40,000 a year with overtime. A stroll down "CO Row," the neighborhoods of Howard Court, South Mesa, and Fairfield Streets, offers a pretty good look at the lifestyle these new officers thought they could afford: fishing boats, ski jets, new American trucks and sport utility vehicles, all sitting in front of brand new ranch-style houses with two-car garages and manicured lawns.

The irony is that many of the younger guards are filing for bankruptcy, and those that aren't are struggling to make minimum payments on purchases that were bought too fast and in too many numbers. The Iron Horse Gym—a favorite of guards for its ample free weights—has many delinquent accounts; the monthly payment is about $30.

"It's a mess, and it spills over onto the family," Jeldness said. "They start pulling double shifts, working 60, 70 hours a week out there. Even those without financial problems have to pull the bad shifts in order to get seniority."

To make matters worse, California leads the nation in prisoner shooting deaths (12 since 1994, compared with six state prisoners shot across the entire nation during the same time period); High Desert accounts for three of those deaths over the past three years. Many of California's prisons, including High Desert, have recently been accused of scandalous activity on the part of the guards, everything from drug trafficking and torture (such as forcing prisoners to play "barefoot handball" on scorching asphalt) to pitting prisoners against one another like roosters in a cockfight, complete with spectators and wagering—and then shooting those who won't stop fighting. Two High Desert guards were charged early this year with filing a false crime report. Many of the guards I talked to were scornful of these activities, and some denied the existence of prisoner abuse, claiming that the shooting of prisoner is an easy thing to twist in the media.

Regardless, the current spotlight on guards has made work even more difficult: for most of their waking hours, these men (and a few women) are immersed in one of the most oppressive, stressful environments imaginable. As one shop owner commented about High Desert, "That place rock 'n' rolls."

"What kind of husband and father do you think they can be after what they've been around for 14 hours?" asked Jeldness. "The issues are complicated, but all seem to stem from men not talking.

"The CO [correctional officer] would say to me, 'My wife expects me to leave it at the door and be compassionate. It doesn't work like that.' It was awful," she said. "I had no authority to require time off. And the guards were always averse to that anyway. They're pressured to hide the counseling. It's all about being strong. And Lord, there's a lot of alcoholism. Many of my clients came home to a cleaned out house—the wife just couldn't take it."

Jerry Sandahl, a guard at High Desert with 14 years of experience, said it took him years to adjust.

"I spent 8 to 16 hours a day in solid bullshit," he said, looking out the window as a logging truck passed by. On the street, I would have guessed him for a salesman, an accountant maybe. "You hear cursing all day, and you come home and that's all you think about. It did tragedy on my family. When you come in there, they tell you family values are the most important thing, but it's not true. The state was. We're like a store, a warehouse. You bring in the merchandise—when someone wants to parole it, we send it back out."

Jeldness, who is also a mediator for Lassen County Family Court, saw her caseload—mainly child custody and divorce, jump from 167 to 320 in one year. During the two years after the prison opened, domestic violence as well skyrocketed in Susanville. Linda McAndrews, head of Lassen Family Services, said she got 3,000 crisis calls from women in 1996. She went to the warden and told him "he had to do something." He did—the number of crisis calls has decreased during the past year—but many believe that's due to the new law that states that if you've been convicted of domestic abuse, you're not allowed to carry a gun. If you can't carry a gun, you won't go far in the prison system. Consequently, women are much more reluctant to report abuse, fearing their husbands will lose their jobs, and then whatever problems they're facing will only spiral into something worse.

I thought about these interviews as I walked down Mesa Street, past the homes of the new guard families. I was struck by the emptiness—no children on bikes, no dads tinkering in the garage; it was if the sterility of the newness had not worn off, and wasn't about to any time soon.

Susanville, like most small towns, rests many of its hopes on its children, and so the jump in juvenile problems seems especially poignant. One afternoon, I met with Jason Jones, a juvenile probation officer, at Denny's, one of the most popular restaurants in town. While I waited for him, it struck me that many of the men in the restaurant, in particular the young ranchers and truckers, looked not unlike the prisoners I have seen: jean-clad, sporting tattoos, talking easily with their companions. The comparison made me uneasy, and I was glad when Jones arrived.

Over the past three years, he's observed the changes in Susanville's youth, and the bottom line: juvenile delinquency has steadily increased, in both the number and scope of incidents, including truancy, petty theft, vandalism, fighting, and problems associated with drugs and alcohol. There are gangs as well, especially the Latino North and South gangs; graffiti is scrawled on random walls, signifying affiliation with one group or the other.

Recently, the juvenile hall more than tripled its capacity to 50 beds. Jones has had to take two guns off kids in the past few months, one a loaded .357. He's seen the drugs get harder—from crank and the "blunt," a Philly cigar emptied and filled with pot, to heroin, which is smuggled in and out of the prison.

None of this surprised Jones or his colleagues much. What surprised them was the origin of most of the problems.

"We expected trouble with the inmate families," he said. "But what we got were problems with the CO families."

Very often, a facility with so many Level 3 and 4 prisoners, many of them 25-year-to-lifers, will draw families who relocate to be near their husband, father, brother, son. The repercussions of this—several hundred people, many on welfare, many of them Hispanic and black—could feasibly flood an insular small town with social service problems, from juvenile delinquency to racial strife. The high school administration had these kids "red-flagged" and were prepared for trouble, Jones said, but while he has handled only about five prisoner family cases, he's dealt with more than 50 guard family cases.

"We weren't prepared," Jones said.

The guards' kids, coming from urban centers, are more sophisticated, more impatient, and more noticeable in their urban-hip outfits, said Jones.

"These kids live in a para-military household," Jones said. "But really they don't have much supervision. They've got nothing to do."

The increase in domestic abuse and juvenile strife didn't surprise many people here. Susanville, like many country towns, is a place where violence is not just known but part of the natural order. One summer I leaned on our fence and watched our neighbor brand and castrate his herd. Several times, he had to stop and bring back his weeping, frightened grandson; the boy, perhaps 4 or 5, clapped his hands over his ears as his grandfather sliced the testicles off the bellowing, rolled-eyed calves and then seared their flanks with his brand, the smoke rising like campfires. The lessons are learned early around here; toughness is bred into you.

The acceptance of violence in a place like Lassen County, where living has always been hard and the soft rarely survive, makes its own kind of sense. A certain comfort with violence is necessary where the main sources of income come from the natural world—from felling timber, clearing land, digging for gold, breeding and slaughtering cattle. But when the second prison came in under the political wave of "get tough on crime," the colliding of the existing sense of violence—that it is one of necessity, of survival—with that associated with a maximum-security prison, mutated into a pervasive sense of antagonism.

"You can feel it in the air," Tony Esparza, who teaches landscaping skills at the prison, told me. "It's not just out at the prison, it's right here."

In a town where high school football takes on a kind of religious fervor ("If you don't play football you ain't nothin'," one young boy remarked), the pitting of "us against them" is an easy sell. There are the locals against the guard families, the guards against the prisoners' families, the bitter and random battles of the gangs. The most prevalent "them" are the prisoners, and the feeling is manifested in random and curious ways. Take this example: on a wall at the Iron Horse Gym hangs a large color poster. It depicts a group of about ten muscled, stone-faced prisoners, shirtless or wearing tank tops, all staring defiantly into the camera. The text reads: "THEY WORKED OUT TODAY: DID YOU?"

CCC has had many escapes over the years (in a two-year period, from August 1995 to August 1997, 33 to be exact). But High Desert hasn't had any, and doesn't expect to. Everyone in town knows about the state-of-the-art measures, the elaborate alarm system, the electronic display screens with schematic maps, the constant ID checking, the 6-times-a-day head count, the 13 gun towers with a 360-degree overlook of every foot of prison yard. These measures were, in fact, part of the sales package for the town. Escape, as the townspeople were reassured, is nearly impossible–a prisoner would have to be flown or smuggled out. No one can get by the 16-strand lethal voltage fence with enough electricity (85,000 kw) to kill a man eight times over. The "death fence" is, nevertheless, monitored 24 hours a day by a guard in a truck who circles it at a lazy 5 mph, gathering the charred ravens, rabbits, lizards and the occasional snake who get too close.

Like most prisons, High Desert spends more than half of its $81,533,000 annual budget on custody costs ($11,015 per prisoner, per year). The bulk of the $59,665,000 payroll goes to the guards. Lieutenant Paul Edwards escorts me through the series of gates and corridors that lead to one of the Level III yards. I show my driver's license and gate clearance form 10 times during the tour. Around us, guards are on their way to various areas, cell blocks, yards, the administrative offices. Most of the time they're quiet, but at other times there is the comradely feel of factory workers on their way to the line.

The staff oversee prisoners' movements every minute of the day, including when they sleep. During my tour, as I observed the "free hour" in the day room, in which the prisoners shower, play cards, watch TV, or stare at the walls, I was embarrassed to see a man, not 15 feet away, slip out of his clothes and begin showering with only a glass wall between us. Another prisoner shaved a friend's head with an electric razor. Others sat around in their underwear.

"This is their house," the guard remarked when he saw my surprise.

The lack of privacy is startling. Even the toilets are wide open to view via a picture window. Most unnerving are the halls with see-through ceilings, over which an armed guard strolls back and forth. The prisoners eye me and saunter around and hang out at the tables. They're segregated according to race and gang affiliation: blacks on the east end, Aryans and Southerns on the west. Day room feels very much like a recreation hall stripped of its foosball, pool tables, and vending machines. But it is much more sterile than any rec room—no posters, no rugs, no cushions, no color—just bolted down steel tables, chairs and benches on gray cement floors. And then there is the smell, the smell of an institution: that unpleasant mix of metal and disinfectant which almost covers the human scents of sweat, breath, and the faint trace of urine.

Three or four prisoners are out of their cells, and a guard addresses one, a slight Latino.

"Jorge, get me that push broom."

The prisoner says, "Okay," and heads for the broom. Such a simple exchange, holding within it the entire prison dynamic of authority, obedience, and order.

As I drive away, it occurs to me that it is only when I leave a prison that I most fully appreciate the meaning of the word "freedom," and I wonder what the prison employees think when they leave towards what is, for now, their home.

I flip through my notes and think about a conversation with my friend. We had talked of souls, of whether souls have a voice. If so, what happens when 10,000 miserable souls are confined in one small place? What kind of voice do you hear then? Of course there is no measuring, but it provokes the underlying question: can any economy based on human punishment be good in the end? And the employees who spend 8, sometimes 16 hours a day in that environment—how much can a small town bear?

When I go home it's different now, and of course that's the paradox, you can't go home again because you've changed. But in this case it's home that's changed. And I can no longer ignore a discomfiting idea: the profound truth of a prison town is that its future is sentenced as surely as the prisoners'. Most of the prisoners, can leave when their time is done, but the town will never leave the prison. Or more precisely: the prison will never leave this town.

It is ironic that the most concrete example of the change in Susanville—the prison itself—takes on its own abstract symbolism. During the day, no one could mistake the prison for anything but what it is, with its gray cement structures, high fencing with spiraling razor wire, guard towers with tinted glass, and silence.

But it is at night that the prison seems to take on a life of its own. At night, the proximity of the town to the prison is most evident because of the lights. Since more than half the prisoners are Level III and IV, the prison is surrounded by 30-foot-high poles topped with glaring amber lights. The resulting glow changes the night sky, affects the entire county—the yellow glow can be seen 50 miles away, and even planes flying over Sacramento, 200 miles to the south, can see the prison. On overcast nights, the clouds reflect the prison's light, casting the sky into an eerie, hellish spectacle, like embers from a tremendous firestorm, fallout from a war.

The town was furious: the lights illuminated not just the irrevocable change to their environment, but their powerlessness as well. If the state had stuck with the original plan of a low-security prison, which voters approved, fewer lights would have been needed. The Committee to Restore the Night Skies formed to lobby to shield the lights or to reduce their number. But after three years of outcry and meetings and petitions, for security reasons, the lights remain.

Despite the problems with the prison—the gangs and domestic violence, the increasing prices and strip-mall growth, the transience of the prison employees, the vacant housing, the would-be developers who scorn penal towns—what most people complain about are the lights. They have come to represent the ultimate, and intangible, cost of High Desert State Prison.

"When I first came to Susanville about 10 years ago," my mother told me, "it was at night and your brother and I drove over Highway 36 and saw the town below us like a little constellation of stars. It was so dark all around and the town seemed to just hang there in mid-air, like some fairy village. Now you see this tremendous area rimmed with horrible yellow lights—and it's all you can see."

My brother, returning after a year at college, said he will never forget the change.

"I came around the Bass Hill corner and I couldn't believe it. There was the prison, bright as day. It looked futuristic, unnatural, something out of a science fiction movie. Like some giant alien mother ship had landed."

Deadly Nostalgia

The Politics of Boot Camps

CHRISTIAN PARENTI

The short, stout eighth-grader Gina Score was never much of an athlete. But that didn't matter to the staff at South Dakota's Plankinton boot camp for girls, where military-style discipline and calisthenics were the modus operandi and, as staff put it, "Quitting is not an option." On her first day in boot camp, Gina—sentenced for stealing a beanie baby—was excoriated and ordered about in an official induction process that, according to one former staff member, "isn't successful unless someone pukes or pisses their pants."

The second day, July 21, 1999, began with a sweltering 2.7-mile morning run. Immediately Gina, at 5' 4" and 226 pounds, fell behind the rest of the pack and was showing signs of heat stroke. By the end, she was lying in a pool of her own urine, frothing at the mouth, gasping for breath, twitching, and begging for "mommy."

Staff denied the girl water, but did administer a full course of ridicule: calling her a faker, laughing at her, dragging her, dropping Gina's limp hand onto her own face and finally threatening to video tape the girl to prove "what a pathetic and uncooperative child she was."

When other girls attempted to shade Gina from the pounding sun, they were ordered to step away. After more than three hours of this, the staff finally called an ambulance, but Gina Score died en route the hospital.

This Lord-of-the-Flies scenario—outlined in a lawsuit filed by Gina Score's parents—is unfortunately an all too common feature of life in the social laboratory of "tough love." Since 1985, when Louisiana set up the country's first juvenile boot camp, these military "shock incarceration" or "shock probation" programs have been increasingly fashionable among politicians searching for policy mojos with which to charm fearful voters.

This article was written in March 2001.

Nationwide, there are now more than seventy-nine such camps in thirty states; most are county-run facilities catering to nonviolent and first time offenders. Many were started with federal grants from an $8 billion prison and boot camp building fund that was created by the massive, $30.2 billion, Crime Trust Fund established by the Violent Crime Control and Law Enforcement Act of 1994. The model's idea, as first conceived in Thatcherite Britain, was to give wayward youth a "short sharp shock" so as to nip deviance in the bud. The media usually loves boot camps: photo-ops of freshly shorn and uniformed thugs shouting "Yes Sir!" looks effective. But do the push-ups and yelling really work? Most researchers think not.

"They're made for TV and they're racist. These places are full of black kids!" says Jerome Miller, director of the National Center for Institutions and Alternatives. "They do nothing for the kids involved.

"And the dynamic between captor and captive can very quickly deteriorate into serious abuse," says Miller, who along with having served eleven years in the military and directed the juvenile justice systems in Massachusetts and Illinois, is the author of several influential books, most recently, *Search and Destroy: African American Males in the Criminal Justice System*. "One gets the impression that boot camps were set up by the sort of potbellied vets that hang around the local post," says Miller, adding that he knows of no credible research proving boot camps to be effective.

In fact, the overwhelming number of studies show the model to be a failure. The latest one—by the conservative Koch Crime Institute in Topeka, Kansas—found that boot camps have a 64 to 75 percent recidivism rate, making them less effective than any other sort of program.

But never mind the numbers: politicians like Governor Bill Janklow of South Dakota, who recently called youth prisoners "scum," just can't let go.

In defending his pet-project boot camps the Governor evades the evidence, instead preferring to tell the story of how he was a "wild youth" until joining the U.S. Marine Corp in the late '50s. And therein lies the power of boot camps: they pander to America's square nostalgia, by invoking an imaginary 1950s, when "dad was in charge." But nostalgia, because it is inaccurate, is also dangerous.

Death in the Desert

Nicholas Contreraz was another alleged "faker." At age 16, Nick was busted joy-riding in a stolen car around Sacramento, California. He was sent out of state to the privately run Arizona Boys Ranch, which had a boot camp component in its programming, and where staff were allowed to discipline youth by routinely striking and tackling them. According to extensive investigations by Arizona Child Protective Services and the

Pinal County Sheriff's Department, Nick's trouble started out typically enough: he was complaining of nausea and diarrhea. But Boys Ranch staff thought it was all a ploy to avoid physical exercise, and they called him "a baby" and told him the trouble was "in his head."

As Nick's condition spiraled downward, the staff escalated their yelling and abuse: at times waking Nick earlier than the rest, making him eat alone, and punishing him with push-ups and manhandling. Over the next two months Nick lost 14 pounds as he was racked by a 103 degree fever, muscle spasms, severe chest pains, and troubled breathing. All the while the staff forced him to continue with the discipline, calisthenics, running, and constant "Yes Sir! No Sir!" When he faltered during exercise the staff punched and shoved him onward.

Soon Nick was defecating in his bed and clothing and vomiting with clockwork frequency, complaining that his body was "hurting all over."

When staff could tell an eruption was imminent, they would mockingly count off "Three, two, one. . . ." On top of that, they forced Nick to tote a bucket filled with his own vomit, feces, and soiled sheets. For extra measure they made Nick do push-ups with his face just above this acrid slop.

Nick's struggle finally ended on March 2, 1998. Staff spent much of that evening throwing Nick to the ground, bouncing him off a wall and making him do push-ups. Before he lost consciousness, Nick lay in the dirt unable to move while above him bellowing staff commanded him to get up. According to witnesses interviewed by CPS, the boy's last words were a simple, "No."

The autopsy found that Nick's distended abdomen was flooded with more than two-and-a-half quarts of puss from a virulent hybrid infection of staph and strep. The boy's lungs held fluid that was, according to one official inquiry, probably inhaled when vomiting. And his body was covered with 71 cuts and bruises. The official cause of death was cardiac arrest and in the ensuing furor "neglect" became the operative word. "If you ask me, it was torture," says Joe Contreraz, Nick's uncle. "That was beyond abuse. I wonder if he was calling out Mom, Dad, Uncle Joe? It makes your heart hurt."

In the wake of Contreraz' death, California withdrew all its wards from the Arizona Boys Ranch, and it was revealed that the Boys Ranch had more than 100 complaints of child abuse lodged against it in the five years preceding Nick's murder. Shortly thereafter, four of the five ABR "campuses" were shuttered, five staff were indicted for murder, and the states of Arizona and California settled out of court with Contreraz' mother for more than a million dollars.

Since then all charges have been dismissed or dropped by the DA, except for one manslaughter and one child abuse charge against former Boys Ranch nurse Linda Babb, who cleared Nick for exercise and repeatedly penned reports to staff urging them to "hold Contreraz highly accountable" for his "negative behavior." Today, the ABR runs only one camp and the state of Arizona no longer allows them to use corporal punishment. A Boys Ranch spokeswoman would only say that the program is "now very different" before hanging up the phone and ignoring further inquiries.

The same month as the Contreraz death, a 24-year-old asthmatic named Eddie Bagby was pepper sprayed and killed by drill instructors during his first day at Arkansas' "young offenders" boot camp. Already in the midst of an asthma attack when he was sprayed, Bagby died a few hours later at a Little Rock hospital. He had been sentenced to 18 months for fleeing police and driving while intoxicated. Official investigations blamed Bagby's death on several pre-existing medical conditions.

Below the Radar

The gruesome deaths of Score, Contreraz, and Bagby are but the aberrant tip of a huge, largely unseen, iceberg of abuse. In South Dakota, for example, the publicity surrounding the Score case led to a class action lawsuit filed by the well-regarded Youth Law Center on behalf of fourteen other Plankinton boot camp veterans, many of whom had ended up in the juvenile prison as a result of resisting camp discipline. The boot camp has since been moved to the more remote town of Custer.

The suit alleges that the boot camp, which disproportionately targeted Native American youth, had inadequate medical and mental health care, poor educational programs, and that staff illegally censored the girls' mail and eavesdropped on their telephone calls and parental visits. It also details numerous examples of excessive force.

There is, for example, "four-pointing." This punishment involved up to six male staff physically restraining a girl, then shackling her into a spread eagle position on a raised concrete slab. From there the staff cut off the young woman's clothes with scissors and covered her naked body with blood- and urine-stained sheets, known as a "suicide gown." Girls at Plankinton have endured whole days and nights like this.

One of them was Patricia Demetrias, who was also forced to run with her ankles and hands shackled. The resulting cuts left permanent scarring. Running in shackles also offered staff an opportunity to force some girls to participate in the abuse of others, by making those not in chains drag those who were shackled. "If they'd fall, we'd have to pull them along by their chains," explains 17-year-old Vanessa Martin who spent three months in the boot camp and is now in foster care. "Doing that made me feel like crap—guilty," says Martin in a flat Midwestern accent.

Martin says that when there wasn't physical abuse, staff subjected girls to a steady stream of psychological cruelty, especially in the hour-long "group session" that capped every evening. "There were a lot of sexual abuse issues in there," she explains. "During group [the staff] would kind of use that. They'd always bring it up and keep asking questions even if a girl was, you know, really crying and didn't want to say any more." Neither the Governor's office nor the South Dakota Department of Corrections would comment on the suit or current conditions in the revamped boot camp in Custer.

Boot camps housing young adults, age 18 to 25, also have their share of abuses. Nineteen-year-old casino worker David Zamot learned this when he was busted for possession of marijuana and received a thirty-day sentence in Atlantic County, New Jersey's boot camp at May's Landing. Three days into his stay, "drill instructors" caught Zamot in the bathroom sharing a cigarette with two other prisoners. Instead of writing Zamot up, as is official policy, the "DIs" marched him out to "Bader's Coffin," a shallow, six-foot-long earthen pit laced with a cocktail of toxic wastes from the camp's laundry. The DIs forced Zamot into the pit to do several sets of sit-ups and push-ups.

"I was screaming, 'something's burning me!' But they were like, 'Shut up, we tell you when you can get out,'" explains Zamot from his mother's home in Egg Harbor City, New Jersey. When the DIs finally let Zamot out he was crying, begging for mercy, and his buttocks, back, scrotum, and penis were lacerated with third-degree burns.

Eventually Zamot required three major surgeries to repair damage to his skin and internal reproductive organs; he still suffers from numbness in his groin and right leg. But at the time he was given only cursory care and then locked in an isolation cell for the rest of his thirty-day sentence. "I was in a wheelchair, in this tiny cell and my scrotum was swollen and full of the chemicals," says Zamot. "They gave me Tylenol, that's all."

Camp and county officials eventually settled out of court for $900,000 but the county attorney's office still says the whole incident was just "an unfortunate mistake." Zamot's lawyer Paul D'Amato disagrees: "The muthafuckers knew the chemicals were in there! And we caught them lying about it." Zamot said he could have won higher damages if he had waited longer, but he just wanted to get the whole thing over with. "I still think about it a lot."

The Maryland Slugfest, an Official Rethink?

The mounting abuse and lawsuits may finally derail the boot camp fad. A number of states—among them California, Florida, and Maryland—are slowly backing out of the boot camp cul-de-sac. In Maryland, prison officials were so proud of their program they gave two *Baltimore Sun* journalists free access to the state boot camp, to follow a group of 14 inductees from start to finish. What the journalists saw shocked the entire state. Induction started with the so-called "TAC officers" punching and kicking the stunned and terrified boys. The rest of the program was full of the same: blatant physical abuse, coupled with little education. When the *Sun* caught up with the inductees a year later, back on the street, it was tragically apparent that the boot camp had done nothing for any of them: they were all back in jail, doing drugs, wanted on warrants, or MIA.

In response to newspaper photos of huge TAC officers reducing kids to tears and splitting open their lips, Maryland state officials swung into damage control mode: the head of corrections was fired, the national guard was brought in to take charge and then the camps were demilitarized altogether.

Georgia officials likewise have overhauled their boot camp program after a U.S. Justice Department investigation found that it was overcrowded and unconstitutionally dangerous. The California Department of Corrections closed its boot camp in 1997 after it was shown to be ineffective. Many California counties have also dropped the model after brief flirtations—many but not all.

Playing Army

"Lockup!" shouts the chubby drill instructor at the Kings County boot camp, in sun-baked Hanford, California. Before her are a squad of eight surly and very bored looking Latino teenagers in gray camouflage, heads shaved. "Drop!"

Boom! Down go the kids for another round of twenty push-ups. Their thirty-minute lunch of grilled cheese sandwiches and sodas has just ended. And because some of their number were slow, the whole squad is kissing the concrete. Their compound is a shabby patch of ground surrounded by a chain link fence topped by bright coils of concertina razor wire. The grounds hold six cinderblock buildings and a flagpole. Nearby, on the other side of the fence, sits a small obstacle course. The boot camp is wedged, as an architectural afterthought, into the back corner of the Kings County Government Center, a sprawling complex of flat buildings connected by open walkways.

"I never give them more push-ups than I can do," says the very fit Senior Officer Rick Yzaguirre. As we watch the chubby instructor yelling at her "cadets," I get Yzaguirre's point: some staff aren't so principled. In fact, camp Commander Robert Smiley says finding qualified staff is a problem, "because so many people have criminal convictions." Most of the day here is taken up by exercise, remedial classes, and "life skills" groups, all of which are punctuated by salutes, double-timing it, and following the camp's many rules about how to speak, walk, fold towels, and everything else. But the few prisoners I was allowed to speak with liked the regimen.

"It's difficult. They brainwash you. But it's good. You learn respect," says a skinny sixteen-year-old Latino kid named Nelson. He was busted for graffiti. His fellow cadet, Falando, agrees, and both say the staff treat them well and never hit them.

Up the road at the Fresno County Probation Department's Elkhorn Juvenile Boot Camp the story is pretty similar. This camp is bigger and sits amid 300 acres of flat orchards. Behind chain link fence I meet the camp director, Dick Simonian; he wears black fatigues and the military insignia of a general. His staff also dress in black or camouflage fatigues and wear military ranks from lieutenant up through major and colonel. But Simonian isn't what you'd expect: he never did time in the armed forces, his desk is a mess, and he hates Proposition 21, California's latest get-tough-on-youth crime ballot initiative. "I was a bartender going to grad school until a friend of mine talked me into becoming a probation officer," explains Simonian. He adds, "In the thirty years since then, we've gone from being social workers to cops."

Out on the compound his 130 fatigue-clad "cadets"—all nonviolent or first-time offenders, most of them Latino and Laotian—line up in formation: "Right face! Forward! March!" One of the cadet sergeants leads the cadence as "bravo platoon" marches off to class beneath their own homemade standard, a white flag bearing the image of an air brushed tank and, in graffiti-style letters, the slogan: "Bravo, No Limit Soldiers." "The guys make their own flags," explains Simonian, who almost seems a little embarrassed that the cadets aren't snapping to attention in his presence as would real soldiers before a real general. He goes on to show me the classrooms and barracks, and outlines an elaborate curriculum of anger management and life skills classes that cover everything from filling out job applications to doing mock interviews and public speaking. After the youth complete their five months in boot camp they go on to an aftercare program that involves intensive probation, drug testing, and a special community based school. Several cadets are picked out at random and away from the "TAC officers," comment freely on the program. "It's better than juvenile hall, we have more freedom here. If we don't mess up we can get weekend furloughs home. The structure is good," says a sixteen-year-old who was repeatedly busted for residential burglary. Others echo his sentiments: juvenile hall is boring, more confining, and dangerous; boot camp is less restrictive and at least offers some programming and classes.

As the day unfolds, the reality of Elkhorn emerges. Simonian, one of the top dogs in the Fresno County Probation Department, still believes in rehabilitation, and the only way he can get his old-fashioned forms of intervention funded is to dress them up in camouflage and apply for federal grants. In this regard the corny world of the Fresno boot camp embodies both the best and the worst of what correction can be. The extent to which the program is successful has more to do with its life skills classes and afterschool care than its marching and pseudo-military discipline.

All of which fits with Jerome Miller's analysis: "Even the military know that boot camp does very little for emotionally damaged youth.

That's why the military doesn't accept people with serious criminal records. Remember, many of these kids have been yelled at all their lives, they need more than that." So what does works? According to Miller anything is better than boot camps and the larger punitive policy trajectory they are part of. He recommends the old-fashioned stuff, programs "based in relationships" and run by good staff. "In Massachusetts we used to send kids mountain climbing in Norway," says Miller. "It was cheaper than incarceration, they got to rub shoulders with non-delinquent youth and it kept them out of town for a while." But, adds Miller, the Massachusetts legislature soon found out about the Norway trips and, for the sake of looking tough, shut them down.

Secrecy, Power, Indefinite Detention

MARK DOW

Kim Ho Ma is no angel. That's why we need to listen to him. At the age of two, Ma fled Cambodia with his family, and he entered the United States as a legal refugee at age seven. As a teenager, Ma endured taunts of "gook" and "chink" on the way to the corner store because his family ate rice and spoke differently. Fellow "foreigners" banded together, and eventually Ma was part of an Asian gang. At seventeen, Ma was convicted of manslaughter for his participation in a gang-related shooting, and after completing his two-year criminal sentence, he was taken into custody by the U.S. Immigration and Naturalization Service (INS) to be deported "back" to Cambodia—as if that were somehow where he belongs when his welcome in the United States wears out.

Kestutis Zadvydas was born to Lithuanian parents in a displaced persons camp in occupied Germany after World War II. His parents came to the United States legally as well, and he has been here for forty-four years. After a string of drug-related convictions, Zadvydas, too, was taken into INS custody after having served his time.

Repressive immigration legislation passed in 1996 and signed into law by Bill Clinton severely limited the judicial review available to legal residents such as Ma and Zadvydas. Before the 1996 laws, according to the INS's figures, half of such cases would have been granted relief from deportation based on ties, such as work and family, established in this country. Now such people are being deported, even when they do not speak the language of "their" home country.

But neither Zadvydas nor Ma can be deported. Zadvydas is stateless: there is nowhere to send him. The United States cannot return Ma to Cambodia because the two countries do not have a repatriation agreement. Ma was detained for about a year before a district court ordered

This article was written in July 2001, and a version appears in the Summer 2001 Index on Censorship, "American Gulag."

his release. The INS appealed that decision, and the case reached the U.S. Supreme Court, which heard oral arguments in February 2001 for the two cases together (*Reno v. Ma* and *Zadvydas v. Underdown*).

Of its total prisoner population of about 23,000, the INS is holding between four and five thousand such detainees who cannot be deported because their "home" countries will not accept them. The largest groups are from Cuba, Cambodia, Vietnam, and Laos, as well as Libya, Iraq, and former republics of the USSR. They are often called "lifers" or "unremoveables," but an INS spokesperson once told me that journalists are being melodramatic with this usage. The agency prefers the term "post-order detainees": they are confined beyond the statutory 90-day removal period since having been ordered deported.

Cases of "resident aliens" such as Ma and Zadvydas confront us with the fragile and ultimately arbitrary nature of our determination about who belongs here, about who "we" are. In Zadvydas' case, the agency has gone so far as to ask the Dominican Republic to accept him. Why? Because his wife, who lives in the United States, was born there. It's as if the government's position is: we don't care where he is "from"—the point is to ship him out of here. (Zadvydas, too, is out of detention pending a ruling by the Supreme Court.) Colorado attorney Carol Lehman has reflected on "the sub-constitutional nature" of this work and the realities it has shown her "outside everybody's understanding of how the government can treat people." She told me in 1999 that she likes to ask people what they think is most important about being a citizen here. Her answer is pragmatic, not patriotic: "They can't make you leave," she says. Then she repeats herself: "They can't make you leave."

These cases also highlight the unbridled authority which the INS claims as its prerogative in applying law-enforcement tactics to our geographical and psychological borders. To read the government briefs is to see that the INS is always arguing for more and more unchecked authority. Whatever the issue, the INS reminds the justices that courts traditionally grant wide discretion in matters of immigration and foreign policy, meanwhile itself attempting to construe these areas as broadly as possible. Clinton transitions to Bush, and the action's title, *Reno v. Ma*, becomes *Ashcroft v. Ma*. Whatever the attorney general's name, the executive's position remains the same: power demands more power.

The attorney general (who heads the Justice Department, of which the INS is an agency) must "remove" aliens within 90 days after their deportation is ordered. Criminal aliens, however, may be held beyond that period when found to pose a "risk to the community," or if determined to be a flight risk. That seems fair enough, assuming there are understandable delays in deporting someone. The INS is authorized to detain someone for the purpose of deporting him or her, not as a punishment. So how long can the agency hold someone in custody whom there is no reasonable chance of ever "removing"?

The court will decide "whether there is statutory authority for INS to indefinitely detain individuals it cannot deport, and whether such indefinite detention violates the individual's right to substantive due process," writes Jay Stansell, Ma's attorney. While much hinges on the interpretation of the word "reasonable," the U.S. government made its case to the Supreme Court that there is no limit on how long the INS can hold someone like Ma or Zadvydas. Deputy Solicitor General Edwin Kneedler told the court, "I do not believe there is any reasonable time limitation within the statute."

Attorney Laurie Joyce of the Catholic Legal Immigration Network notes that the quality of "custody reviews" for the release of indefinite detainees—the process by which their potential danger to the community and flight risk are supposedly assessed—has improved slightly since December 2000 as Washington INS officials have played a larger role. But she worried that an adverse ruling would give local INS officers "license to be even more abusive and arrogant" toward the prisoners whom she calls "eternally condemned."

At a reception hosted by the American Civil Liberties Union across the street from the Supreme Court building in Washington, D.C., Kim Ho Ma told me that he had recognized some of the local Seattle-area INS officials in the audience for the oral arguments. "It hurt them to see liberty and justice is served . . . 'cause, quote-unquote, they're the almighty government." Back in Seattle, detained with 120 other lifers, he says, "There wasn't even a single soul that heard the problem. . . . Nobody cares about these guys 'cause these guys didn't exist. . . . They were the scum of society."

Secrecy and intimidation are natural corollaries to excessive policing power, and the INS utilizes both. Dan Malone, a staff writer for the *Dallas Morning News*, says he was naive when he started looking into the circumstances of INS long-term prisoners back in 1997. One day he spoke with Russell Bergeron, the head of INS public affairs, who referred to a document summarizing the agency's detained population by categories such as nationality and length of detention. Bergeron told Malone that, according to the document, fifty-three detainees had been in custody for more than three years because their countries would not accept them. Intrigued, reporter Malone decided to "find out who they were."

Malone filed a Freedom of Information Act (FOIA) request to obtain the names and "alien numbers" of those fifty-three detainees. The response was a mind-boggling one-two punch of wholesale deception and petty lies. The Department of Justice/INS FOIA Unit responded that "no records" on this subject had been found "in a search of our Headquarters including our Public Affairs office." The FOIA specialist also said that public affairs chief Bergeron denied the existence of the document he had mentioned to Malone. When Malone tried to help out with the search by letting the INS's FOIA specialist know that Bergeron had identified one

Kristine Marcy as an INS field officer who was knowledgeable on the subject, the FOIA specialist responded that she was unable to locate any such INS employee; reporter Malone then called the INS switchboard, which gave him Marcy's number.

The INS continued its refusal to provide the requested information on the grounds that it was protecting the privacy of the detainees, and claimed that such a policy was consistent with Federal Bureau of Prisons guidelines. In one letter to the FOIA office, Malone pointed out that his own "request to the Bureau of Prisons for the names of all persons incarcerated under a federal death sentence was promptly answered by fax with the information requested." (That research culminated in the book *America's Condemned: Death Row Inmates in their Own Words*, co-authored by Malone.) After further denials, Malone and the *Morning News*, represented by attorney Paul Watler, sued the INS in Federal District Court to compel release of the requested information. In a settlement, the agency ultimately did provide a list of those detainees held over three years. They range from criminal aliens to asylum-seekers. And there were not fifty-three of them, as public affairs had first indicated, but 852. As terms of the settlement, the INS withheld the detainees' last names and identifying alien numbers, but did agree to deliver letters to all of them from the *Morning News*. The paper had the letter seeking further information about the individual cases translated into a dozen languages, and reporter Malone is finally getting to learn about them as hundreds of responses come in from around the country.

Malone told me his story originally characterized the INS's longest-held detainees as secret prisoners. So that his contacts at INS would not be caught off guard, he told the press office about this characterization in advance. As the story was being edited, an INS official complained to the newspaper about the characterization, and it was removed from the story. In the morning, however, the reporter woke to find his published story with the front-page banner "INS Faulted for Secret Detentions" (December 12, 1999): a headline writer at the *Morning News* had seen for himself what the story was about and titled it accordingly.

If the INS uses such tactics with reporters, imagine its license to suppress the outspokenness of detainees vulnerable to isolation cells and deportation. INS's media visitation standards even put in writing their intent to restrict media access to detainees who are the "center of attention." A New York-area attorney reports that detained clients have "felt alarmed and intimidated" by INS pressure on them regarding contacts with the press. Last year, when I arranged to talk to Olu Balogun, a Nigerian detained in Houston, the local INS told me that an interview was "not in [his] best interest." They told Balogun that signing the media interview authorization form might affect his pending case. "There is nothing else I have to be afraid of," Balogun said at the time. "They couldn't do more than what they have done already."

Mohammed Bachir has been a legal resident of the United States for twenty years. After he served two years for contempt charges related to a parental kidnapping conviction, the INS detained him for almost three years. Born in a Palestinian refugee camp in south Lebanon after his parents fled Haifa in 1948, Bachir is stateless, too, so he never got deported. In his years of detention, the INS held him in seventeen jails and detention centers in nine different states. The problem? He rallied other prisoners and the local media wherever he went, generating news stories from Southern California (where he was beaten badly for organizing a large-scale hunger strike) to upstate New York. "We had a problem keeping him in different facilities," Boston INS official Bruce Chadbourne told me. "He would kind of get some of the other detainees going. . . . [He was] sort of an instigator." Bachir was finally released from detention in April. Someone familiar with his case revealed that the main condition of his release was Bachir's agreement not to create "a media circus"—and he reportedly also agreed to keep that condition itself a secret.

Two years ago in Aurora, Colorado, a group of young Asian detainees who had already done more time in the Wackenhut-run INS detention center than they had served on their felony convictions told me that they had decided against a peaceful sit-down protest, knowing that it could prejudice the lone INS bureaucrat with the power to decide their fate. They were not being paranoid. Kim Ho Ma's participation in a hunger strike while detained in Seattle was still being used against him by the government in its Supreme Court brief.

"Indefinite detention," mused Ma as we discussed the terminology, "in other words, forever. They [used to] tell us every day, you're not getting out. I'm nobody to argue with them." As we stand up to say goodbye, Ma says, "I'm from a different country, but I'm as American as anybody." Immigration detention turned out to be a civics lesson for Ma, as it should be for all of us. "I didn't know I was from Cambodia," he says, "'til I went in there."

"Being detained" by the Immigration & Naturalization Service (INS) is not the equivalent of "doing time." INS detention is not a designated, punitive sentence. The INS has the authority to "detain" only for the purpose of deporting. This is the case even when the INS's authority to begin deportation proceedings against someone stems from the person's criminal record. But what happens when the INS becomes unable, apparently, to deport the person who is legally subject to deportation, because of the unwillingness of other countries to accept the deportee? Can the INS then hold the person indefinitely?

This was the main issue which the U.S. Supreme Court addressed in deciding the lawsuits described above. In an important victory for those trying to limit excesses of executive authority, particularly as wielded against immigrants, the Supreme Court ruled in favor of the detainees.

On June 28, 2001, writing for the 5–4 majority in *Zadvydas vs. Davis*, 533 U.S. 628 [99–7791 and 00–38; the two cases were consolidated], Justice Breyer wrote, "Based on our conclusion that indefinite detention of aliens . . . would raise serious constitutional concerns, we construe the [Immigration] statute to contain an implicit 'reasonable time' limitation, the application of which is subject to federal court review." Breyer went on to suggest, based on analogous statutes, that six months was "reasonable." (The decision did not cover a certain category of indefinite detainees known as "excludable aliens," who may be in U.S. jails but are nevertheless not legally considered to have "entered" the country.) In the weeks following the decision, while immigration lawyers reported varying compliance with the new law in different parts of the country, hundreds of INS "lifers" were released.

Then, after the events of September 11, the INS announced new emergency regulations. These extended from 24 to 48 hours the time the INS could hold someone without charge. But the new regulations allowed indefinite detention in circumstances deemed appropriate by the Attorney General. Congress then gave its approval to a new version of indefinite detention with the passage of the so-called antiterrorist USA Patriot Act, which did not rescind the emergency regulations, but added the necessity for the Attorney General to "certify" as terrorists those who might be indefinitely detained. The extremely broad meaning of "terrorist" under the Act, and the Attorney General's unreviewable power to make that certification amount to what Georgetown Law professor David Cole has called "detention by executive fiat." Judy Rabinovitz, senior staff counsel of the American Civil Liberties Union's Immigrant Rights Project, observed, "The legislation appears to have been drafted, at least in part, to get around the Supreme Court's recent decision in *Zadvydas*."

Meanwhile, in October 2001, an Ashcroft directive urged more restrictions on the release of government information through the Freedom of Information Act (FOIA), on which attorneys, historians, and journalists depend. In the immediate aftermath of September 11, the Justice Department had refused to release the identities or other information about persons being rounded up by the INS and the FBI, and Ashcroft at first justified this secrecy by shamelessly declaring that he was protecting the privacy of those detained. The American Civil Liberties Union and other groups, in a suit under FOIA, were eventually able to compel the release of certain, limited information about post-9/11 detainees. The government released a list giving the charging dates and country of origin for over 700 detainees. It blacked out the names, prisoner (or "alien") numbers, and detention/prison locations. Estimates of post-9/11 detentions reached some 1,200, but of course, there was no way to be sure: given all that we know about the Department of Justice and the simple fact that a lawsuit was required to get that minimal information, we can assume that there were many more "*desaparecidos*" in the system.

When the INS does release information, it is often *dis*information, as we see above in the case of reporter Dan Malone's efforts to find out how many "lifers" the agency held before *Ma* and *Zadvydas*. In the case of the 9/11 detentions, a *Washington Post* analysis of the information released to the ACLU found that "scores" of detainees "were jailed for weeks" without being charged at all (Dan Eggen, "Delays Cited in Charging Detainees," January 15, 2002). Journalist Jim Edwards reported that, while Ashcroft claimed "[t]he number of Muslim men jailed on minor immigration charges" went down to 450 in early/mid January, "numbers obtained from New Jersey jail officials and estimates from defense lawyers suggest that the total population of Muslim men detained may be closer to 600" (*New Jersey Law Journal*, January 17, 2002).

As this article on the indefinite detention cases of Ma and Zadvydas makes clear, INS secrecy and the agency's insistence on unchecked power began long before September 11. But the Justice Department has fully exploited the horrors of that day, and Americans' understandable fears which have followed, to extend the reach of its secrecy and power even further.

Trapped by the System

Parole in America

KELLY VIRELLA

On a rainy afternoon late last year, 47-year-old Joseph Bostic stepped off a Greyhound bus—homeless, jobless, and $37 shy of penniless—into New York's bustling Port Authority station. Bostic was returning to Brooklyn after finishing his second term in the New York state prison system. From 1983 to 1990, Bostic had served out his first prison term for a manslaughter conviction. After seven years he had been let out on parole, but knew that if he violated his parole conditions he'd go back to jail. So he did his best to stay clean.

He did a pretty good job, too, except for one small crime that society wouldn't normally take too seriously—in 1997, Bostic overdrew his checking account by $341. And for that, he spent three years in prison.

Statistics describing prison populations and crime in America reveal a paradox. Though crime rates are falling, the prison population is still growing. Why are more people going to prison than are committing crime?

In cases like that of Joseph Bostic, an explanation can be found in the dysfunctional institution of parole. An August 2000 Department of Justice (DOJ) study revealed that from 1990 to 1998, there was a 54 percent increase in the number of parole violators returning to prison. Of the 423,000 paroles that came to a conclusion in 1998, 42 percent ended up with the parolee going back to prison. In some states those percentages are much higher; in California, nearly 70 percent of the people entering prison last year were back because they violated their parole.

Some of these repeat offenders, to be sure, have committed serious crimes. But some of them, including many who are trying to go straight, are faced with parole conditions that are so strict that even things like

This article was originally published in *Alternet*, December 3, 2000.

chronic unemployment can be considered just cause for reincarceration. At the same time, services to help parolees reenter society are scarce, and laws protecting ex-offenders from housing and employment discrimination are virtually nonexistent. To make matters worse, when parolees are convicted of even the pettiest crimes—as Bostic was—due process is legally suspended and often violated in order to reincarcerate them.

"Parole sets people up for failure," American Probation and Parole Association president Carl Wicklund says. Wicklund calls the current approach to supervising ex-offenders "tail-'em, nail-'em, jail-'em." He scoffs at the idea that most parole supervision methods are "tests" to see if ex-offenders can make it in the outside world, saying the term is too mild.

"I would call them an obstacle course," he says.

Tail-'em

Parole is the period of law enforcement supervision that typically follows release from prison. For a prisoner who has served the minimum term of his sentence, it's an alternative to further incarceration.

Before a prisoner is granted parole, a parole board reviews his case to determine whether he is ready to be released. If the board judges that he is, it gives him a release plan, which prescribes the conditions of his parole. Release plans frequently include conditions like abstinence from drugs and contact with other ex-offenders, retention of gainful employment, and periodic reporting to a parole officer. If a parolee violates any of these conditions, or is charged with committing a new crime, he is subject to reincarceration.

After his first term in prison, Bostic's parole conditions required him to meet bi-weekly, then monthly with the parole officer assigned him by the parole division and to report all instances of police contact to him. During their meetings, the parole officer fills out a report detailing any problems Bostic reports any instances of police contact, and any change of address.

Bostic's parole officer was fairly easy-going, Bostic said. Others are much more stringent. Some make unannounced visits to parolees' homes, which are allowed by law, patrol the neighborhoods where parolees live, and try to catch them violating a parole condition or committing a new crime. Some parolees who have curfews report that they receive check-up calls and drop-by visits from their parole officers ten minutes after their curfews.

"Parole officers have plenty of incentives to reincarcerate parolees," University of Miami law professor Jonathon Simon explains. When states abandoned their efforts to rehabilitate prisoners in favor of retribution and public safety, the power to reimprison parolees shifted from parole boards to parole officers, Simon says. "Officers became first lines of defense against crime rather than case managers, or social services brokers," he says. "To keep their jobs, parole officers have to catch and confine the bad guys. They usually choose to do that at the first sign of relapse."

Nail-'em

With parole officers looking to nab them again, parolees are already facing poor odds. Add to that the difficulty of adjusting to life "on the outside," especially after long prison terms, and it becomes obvious that ex-prisoners need more help than they're getting.

The trend, unfortunately, has been to cut back such support services. Government funding for pre-release programs has always been inadequate, and both prison rehabilitation programs and social services for parolees were slashed during the '80s. Even the state of Washington, which has one of the best pre-release programs in the country, only treats 30–40 percent of all prisoners released.

Before Joseph Bostic was released, for example, the Department of Correctional Services did little to get him readjusted to society, besides help him put together a resume and prepare for job interviews. As he points out, "To someone who doesn't have food or a place to stay, a resume in a cruel job market doesn't seem like much of a ticket."

Furthermore, only a handful of states have laws that protect ex-offenders from housing and employment discrimination. That means that most landlords and employers are allowed to ask applicants if they've ever been convicted of a crime and discriminate against them if the answer is yes. Even the federal government restricts ex-prisoners' access to low income public housing.

These circumstances all contribute to our strikingly high reincarceration rates. To brings those rates down, instead of beefing up anti-discrimination laws or funding social services, during the '80s state governments tried hiring more parole officers and enforcing stricter terms. With more officers, the theory went, parole boards can give more individual attention and help to each parolee.

But, not surprisingly, the more individual attention is paid to a parolee, the more likely he is to be caught violating his terms of parole. A 1996 RAND study of 14 jurisdictions that had implemented more intensive supervision programs (ISP) found that 65 percent of ISP parolees were charged with violating some parole condition during the previous five years. In comparison, only 38 percent of routinely supervised participants were similarly charged.

The study also found that 37 percent of the ISP parolees had been rearrested and charged with committing a new crime, in comparison with only 33 percent of the routinely supervised ex-prisoners.

Jail-'em

Once accused of violating parole, ex-prisoners stand a very small chance of being exonerated: The federal constitution only requires states to grant parolees a subset of the full due process of law.

"Almost none of the procedural rules that must be observed during any other criminal proceeding apply to parole revocation hearings," New York attorney Steven Sanders says. Even in states whose standards are higher than federal standards, the handful of safeguards that do exist are frequently ignored, says Sanders, a 20-year veteran in this area of law who works for the Legal Aid Society's Parole Revocation Defense Unit.

Joseph Bostic's case provides a striking example of how limited due process can be in parole revocation cases. When Bostic pled guilty to overdrawing his checking account, he was living in Georgia, working for a successful construction business. Because he was on parole from New York, where he had committed his original crime, New York began the process of extraditing him to serve the rest of his original manslaughter term—eight years. Due to red tape and bureaucracy, Bostic sat in the Glynn County, Georgia, jail for four months, waiting to be transferred up north, without even having been charged with a parole violation.

"I lost my job and my ties to my family, defaulted on loans and ruined my credit while I sat in jail just waiting," he says.

Bostic was finally shipped to Rikers Island, New York, where he was held in waiting for six more months. Finally, the New York parole division held his parole revocation hearing and sentenced him, at first, to 15 months at Wallkill state prison. When the parole board conducted its review of his case, it modified his sentence to 8 years, reasoning that 15 months was too lenient.

Unlike in other criminal proceedings, the federal constitution does not require states to provide indigent parolees attorneys during their revocation hearings. Parolees don't even have the right to call witnesses or exclude hearsay testimony from their hearings. Court transcripts show that at Bostic's hearing, the parole specialist claimed that Bostic's former girlfriend had accused Bostic of making threatening phone calls to her. There was no proof that Bostic had made any such calls, but the parole specialist's testimony was still allowed into the hearing.

To make matters worse, parole departments are commonly exempted from judicial review, attorney Sanders says. "Parole revocation hearings are closed proceedings in which checks and balances are virtually non-existent," he says. New York courts, Sanders notes, have denied several recent high-profile requests from parolees who wanted their cases reviewed by someone less partial than the parole division. The New York courts told these parolees to appeal to the parole division itself.

Advocates Fear a New Clinton Initiative

Following the August 2000 DOJ study about parolee recidivism and prison growth, President Clinton released a statement calling for "a new public safety initiative aimed at providing greater supervision for offenders reentering the community." The statement announced that the fiscal year 2001 budget appropriates $145 million for the development and support of "innovative reentry programs that promote responsibility and help keep ex-offenders on track and crime- and drug-free."

The initiative, called Project Reentry, would allot $60 million to fund the development of "reentry partnerships" and "reentry courts" designed to prevent parolees from backsliding the way Bostic did. The money would also allow parole divisions to hire more officers and increase their officer-parolee ratio.

But Dr. James Austin, who has studied prisoner reentry extensively for the Institute on Crime, Justice, and Corrections at George Washington University, is skeptical that Clinton's budget initiative would produce results if adopted by Congress. "Compared to the $30–40 billion spent annually on adult corrections, $145 million is nothing," Austin says. Still others, like prison activist Dianne Williams, fear that Clinton's call for "a new public safety initiative" will result in even stricter parole supervision. "If the states who participate in the program use the money to pick up more parole violators, I think there will be issues," she says.

Williams, who is President of the Safer Foundation, a Chicago-based group that provides job-training for ex-offenders, does give Clinton credit for trying to address parolee issues. "Parole officers caseload is too high and I believe there needs to be a partnership between us and parole officers," Williams says. But, she adds, "I will always believe that social services are the best place to put the dollars."

Indeed, $75 million of Clinton's Project Reentry would fund Department of Labor job-training initiatives. And $10 million would fund Department of Health and Human Services substance abuse and mental health treatment for ex-offenders. This is the portion of the initiative that excites Williams, since private donations cover only 5 percent of Safer Foundation's budget.

"It is difficult to get funding for reentry projects," Williams says, "It is not a popular cause—not children, not battered women, not the arts. It's just not hot."

Other community organizations, like the Parolee Rights Project, recently started by the nonprofit where Joseph Bostic now works, are less enthusiastic about what Project Reentry will mean. The Parolee Rights Project is soliciting complaints about unfair parole supervisory practices to prove that there are systemic abuses that might be corrected through litigation. "We want to educate prisoners about how to navigate the system when they come up for parole," executive director Jennifer Flynn says.

"We have plenty of parole officers," Bostic says, regarding Clinton's initiative. "More job related programs, educational programs, and access to low income housing are what we need, but this initiative won't make a dent in those issues," he says. "$145 million is barely enough to pay the salaries of the bureaucrats who will run the programs."

[Editors' Note: "Project Reentry" was ultimately abandoned by the Clinton Administration. There are no current plans to revive the program.]

Relocation Blues

NELL BERNSTEIN

It is a sweltering summer morning in Washington, D.C., and in the silence of the basement of the Shiloh Baptist Church, 9-year-old Diamond is squirming in his seat. As an image forms on the color monitor before him, Diamond's eyes widen and the fidgeting ceases.

"Hi Dad!" Diamond shouts as if it were up to him to cover the distance that separates him from his father, DeWayne Mixon, who's incarcerated 360 miles away in the Corrections Corporation of America Northeast Ohio Correctional Center in Youngstown, Ohio. "Can you see me?" Diamond asks. Thanks to the efforts of activist Carol Fennelly and a pair of low-end computers connected through the Internet, Mixon—serving a three- to nine-year sentence for assault—can see and hear his son. After an extended visit earlier this summer, it is the second time in five years he's seen Diamond.

When the federal government initiated its takeover of Washington several years ago, one of its first moves was to close the decrepit Lorton Correctional Complex and start shipping the city's prisoners to distant private prisons. This practice reflects a national trend. The number of prison beds in for-profit facilities has grown from 15,000 in 1989 to more than 120,000 today, as state and federal authorities turn to the private sector to address overcrowding caused by the incarceration boom of the last two decades.

A side effect of this move toward private prisons has been the decimation of family bonds, as thousands of prisoners have been sent to serve sentences far from home.

Fennelly spent the '80s and most of the '90s advocating for the homeless in Washington, living in and running the city's 1,400-bed Federal City Shelter. Prolonged hunger strikes and other dramatic actions made

This article was originally published in *The Standard*, August 21, 2000.

Fennelly a household name in Washington. While the city's homeless population has decreased, the prison population has exploded, as it has across the country to two million nationwide. The transition to prisoners' rights was a natural one for an advocate accustomed to helping the most ignored segments of society.

"We have too many people in prison today whom most of the rest of the nation does not give a damn about," says Fennelly. "I don't know how to make people care about those two million prisoners, but I do believe they care about the children. And if I can make them care about the children, I can ultimately make them care about the dads." When Washington started moving prisoners to Youngstown, Fennelly went with them to look for ways to keep the city's emigré prisoners connected with home and family.

While watching television, Fennelly saw a mention of Internet software that allowed face-to-face teleconferencing. She immediately brought the idea to prison officials: Why not use the software to let Youngstown prisoners visit with their children at home in Washington?

It was not an easy sell. Security concerns made wardens wary of permitting online access behind prison walls. Fennelly responded by hiring Digital Access Corporation, which provides security programming to the Pentagon, among other clients, to strip down her PCs so they could be used for nothing but teleconferencing. Youngstown officials signed on and have supported her efforts ever since, Fennelly notes.

With an initial grant of $20,000 from Washington-based Cafritz Foundation, Fennelly acquired computers and software and launched the program. According to Mark Fellows, program manager at the Youngstown facility, the teleconferencing complements what prisoners are learning in parenting and drug-treatment classes, motivating them to change their lives both during and after their incarceration.

Fennelly commutes every other week between Youngstown, where she has two computers in the prison, and Washington, where two are installed at local churches. Using Microsoft NetMeeting software, prisoners' children are able to talk with their parents, introduce them to their friends, and show them school projects.

Fennelly doesn't intend her teleconferencing program to be a substitute for in-person contact; she also sets up offline visits and recently held a week-long summer camp for Washington children to spend a week in Ohio with their fathers. But for many Youngstown prisoners, online contact with their kids may be the only kind they get. And contact of any sort, Fennelly believes, is crucial to the future of the prisoners and their children. One study found that prisoners who did not participate in family visitation were three times more likely than those who did to violate parole after their release. And children of prisoners are more likely to become offenders if they don't get the support they need.

In a 40-minute teleconference with his son, DeWayne Mixon makes it clear that this concern is foremost on his mind.

"Be careful out there," he lectures Diamond, who lives with his grand-mother and three siblings in Washington's Edgewood Terrace housing project, which is known for drugs and crime.

"Now, you know right from wrong, don't you?"

"Yes."

"Don't be out there doing nonsense and acting crazy, you hear me?"

"Yes."

"'Cause you better than that, you hear me?"

"OK. . . . Daddy? Daddy?"

The connection has dropped, and not for the first time. The low-income neighborhoods in which the two churches are located aren't wired for cable modem or DSL, so Fennelly must use a standard tele-phone line. She does not have the bandwidth to run both sound and streaming video at once, and must alternate between the two, freezing the images in order for father and child to talk. Even so, the computer crashes regularly, requiring a pause of several minutes as it is restarted.

The disappointment on Diamond's face each time this happens high-lights not just the limits of the technology at hand, but the distance between father and son. The preciousness of the bits and pieces of their fathers these children experience though the computer underscores the magnitude of what has been taken from them—and from the 1.5 million other children who currently suffer the impact of parental incarceration.

"You be good out there," Mixon tells his son as the session draws to a close. "I love you, OK? Give Daddy a kiss on the cheek."

"How am I supposed to do that?" Diamond asks.

In a telephone interview from the Northeast Ohio Correctional Center, Mixon says he hopes the teleconference session will be the first of many and will give him the chance to be a good father. But it is also a painful reminder of the things he is not able to do for his son, and the risks Diamond faces as a result.

"It's killing me now," says Mixon. "I know that he definitely needs me. I just want to be careful what I say to him. Talk to him about doing good in school. Tell him to watch who he hangs around with, because a lot of them young boys out there can be bad little role models. And I just don't want him to follow in my footsteps."

Seeing Diamond at the summer camp and then on the computer mon-itor has given him a new resolve to make this his last time behind bars. "He listens to me," adds Mixon, "but being as I'm not out there, my hand is in the air. It's in the air. And I can't fault nobody but myself. He knows I'll do anything I can to make sure that he's all right. But basi-cally, the best thing for me to do now is just get out and act like I got some sense."

This kind of epiphany is exactly what Fennelly is looking to facilitate. Prison, she says, can offer a "redemptive moment in someone's life, when they have been taken out of the context where they were doing the things that got them there in the first place. A lot of times, because prisons are no longer focused on rehabilitation, that moment is lost. But if you can reach people when they want do to something in their lives—they want to be part of their family; they don't want to come back to this place—then that moment can become valuable, and it can lead to the redeeming of a life that might literally be lost."

There may be nothing so potentially redemptive as parenthood, explains Fennelly—an idea generally overlooked when it comes to men. When Washington's prisoners started heading out of town, Fennelly says, there was an outcry about mothers being separated from their children, but "nobody bothered to ask what would happen to the dads and their relationship with their kids. . . . Once a dad gets in prison, he's no longer considered a part of his family. Nothing in our society encourages this man to stay involved with his children."

Youngstown's Fellows agrees. "There are some things done for women prisoners," he says, referring to efforts to maintain family contact, "but very little for men." Fennelly's program has been well received by prisoners, says Fellows.

Since the program was launched, Fellows has gotten calls from administrators at private and state-run prisons interested in setting up their own teleconferencing programs. One ambitious effort already exists in two state prisons in Florida, where 100 women are able to talk with their children and read to them from storybooks using Microsoft NetMeeting. Florida Department of Corrections consultant Anne Holt hopes that "when the participants come home, it will be easier to reintegrate into the family and the community, and therefore they won't come back to prison."

The children's reaction to the teleconferencing program, adds Holt, has been powerful and immediate. Smaller children will climb up on the table and embrace the computer. One little boy asked, "Mommy, why can't you get out of the TV?"

Denise Johnston, a former pediatrician who heads the Center for Children of Incarcerated Parents in Pasadena, California, believes responses like this are cause for concern. While Internet visitation supplemented by periodic in-person visits are useful to older children, kids under six may find it confusing. Johnston says that because of television, "They're used to dealing with those kinds of images, and their understanding of them is that they're not authentic." A child whose primary contact with a parent is on a computer monitor, Johnston says, may wind up with the impression that "their parent is in the same place where TV shows take place. Wherever Drew Carey is, that's where Daddy is."

Another concern is that this technology may make it easier to justify shipping prisoners out of state. "If we come up with ways to address family needs when the correctional systems do something that is completely inhumane and untenable, we're going to facilitate more of these types of decisions," says Johnston. "'These people are in Ohio? Oh well, let's put them in Texas.'"

"The heart of locking somebody up," explains Johnston, "is the deprivation of love and touch." Teleconferencing's advocates on both sides of the prison walls would acknowledge the Internet can, at best, address only half of that equation. But as the prison population continues to grow, and more children are separated from their parents, a better-than-nothing solution looks pretty attractive.

"Do I think that teleconferencing will ever take the place of a hug?" asks Fennelly. "No. Neither do these kids, and neither do these men." But for children who are hungry for whatever parental affection they can scavenge from an impossible situation, a face on a screen can have a tremendous impact.

"I watch these little girls," says Fennelly, "and when Dad says, 'Hi, beautiful,' they sit up a little taller in their chairs."

MAKING A BUCK OFF THE PRISONER'S BACK

Today, tens of thousands of prisoners labor for little or no pay as the work force that runs prisons, either as janitors, cooks, laundry workers, and so forth. Several thousand more work in the "correctional industries" manufacturing items ranging from license plates, to office furniture and military equipment for the Pentagon. In some Southern states, like Texas and Louisiana, unpaid prisoners toil in the fields of former slave plantations just as chattel slaves did 150 years ago.

Some 3,000 prisoners nationally work for private corporations through subcontractors set up inside prisons. Among the companies using prison slave labor are Boeing, Nintendo, Starbucks, Trans World Airlines, and many others, as a strong conservative movement pushes to return prisons to their pre-Depression status as "factories with fences."

The economic role of prisons is not so much that of prison labor. In a $6 trillion economy, 3,000 prisoners working for private companies and another 20,000 performing manual farm labor on rural prison plantations is insignificant. What is nationally significant are the two million people, nearly all of working age, removed from the labor market, in addition to the 700,000 or more people employed by prisons and jails to guard, house, and administer the prisoners removed from national labor markets.

The real issue of prison labor is not so much the 3,000 prisoners working for private businesses, but the two million who aren't and the nonprisoners feeding at the public trough of the prison industry. If mass incarceration is the most thoroughly implemented social experiment in American history, then the labor incapacitation of two million Americans and the public employment of almost a million more who watch over this incapacitated work-force is the most thoroughly implemented government work program in American history since the New Deal.

—PW

Making Slave Labor Fly

Boeing Goes to Prison

PAUL WRIGHT

With the repeal of welfare, some political opportunists and right-wing pundits are turning their agendas to questions of law and order in general, and prison "reform" in particular. Right-wing politicos are pushing Congress to impose the same solution on prisoners as on welfare recipients: put them to work. During his bid for the '96 presidency, candidate Bob Dole promised that if elected president, he would issue an executive order requiring every able-bodied federal prisoner to work a 40-hour week to earn money to compensate victims. "Taking a portion of prisoners' earnings to pay their upkeep or reimburse their victims also seems appropriate to many Americans," quipped Dole to the *Atlanta Journal and Constitution*.[1]

Knut Rostad, head of the right-wing Enterprise Prison Institute (whose key players include Edwin Meese as chair of its national advisory board) is busy rallying support for the scheme. Citing Republican pollster Frank Luntz (who helped shape the "Contract with America"), Rostad told a Congressional committee that "the American public believes the greatest failure of government on a national level—other than welfare—involves crime and punishment." Rostad said Luntz's focus groups "reveal a negative emotional response to the prison system which is unlike anything he has seen in recent years." "The bottom line," says Rostad, is that the "state prison system should be changed from the ground up, and that inmate work programs should drive this change."[2]

Currently more than 90,000 state and federal convicts work in a variety of public and private enterprises while serving time.[3] The majority are employed in state owned enterprises, such as making license plates or furniture for government offices. Increasingly though, private businesses have contracted with at least 25 states to set up businesses inside prison walls to take advantage of state-supplied facilities and low

This article was written in March 1997.

wage nonunion workers, businesses which employ about 3,000 prisoners. The sales from these privately operated industries totaled $83 million, a relatively small but growing addition to the $821 million generated from sales of state agency industries products and services.[4]

Advocates for prison industry privatization argue that "legal restrictions, aided by bureaucratic inertia and labor union sensitivities, continue to hamper progress."[5] They propose repealing laws that protect prisoner laborers from the worst exploitation and protect free labor from unfair competition. In a May Day *Wall Street Journal* editorial, Meese proposed repealing Depression era laws that require paying prison workers making goods transported in interstate commerce at least the minimum wage.[6] Meese argues that if the labor market is opened up for them, prisoners can help pay the costs of their incarceration. The illogic of this position is that if the state really wanted to make money from prison industries, where its "profit" supposedly comes from a portion of the salary paid to the prisoner, it should push for higher wages. On the other hand, in a happy consequence not mentioned by Meese, the lower the wage, the higher the profits for corporations.

Testifying before Congress, Morgan Reynolds, director of the right-wing Criminal Justice Center, National Center for Policy Analysis, was not so circumspect. "State and federal prison systems," he said, "control a huge asset—convict labor—and largely waste its productive potential." He advocated changing the law to "allow private prison operators to profit from the gainful employment of convict labor. Encourage and publicize private sector proposals for enterprise prisons. Set up procedures for competitive bidding for prison labor. Diminish prisoner litigation against prison work by repealing the Civil Rights of Institutionalized Persons Act and the federal habeas corpus procedure. . . ."[7]

Prison Industries Making Out Like Bandits

Meese touts Washington state as a model for prison industries. In one Washington prison, the Boeing Corporation (then headquartered in Seattle) has discovered the benefits of a captive work force. In 1996, while the world's largest civil aviation manufacturer made more planes and more money than ever before, it cut the number of employees on its U.S. payroll. The only significant challenge to its drive to increase profits and executive salaries was a lengthy strike by the machinist union over eroding job security and disappearing pension and health benefits.[8] Like most corporations, Boeing has been cutting costs and countering organized labor's threat to its bottom line by moving factories abroad and out-sourcing to nonunion subcontractors in the United States. Its search for workers who are unable to unionize or demand a decent wage took it to two widely divergent, yet strangely similar places: China and the Washington State Reformatory in Monroe, Washington.

In China, where Boeing sold ten percent of its planes between 1993 and 1995,[9] the company operates at a fraction of its U.S. costs. According to the *Seattle Times*, "Employees live mostly on or next to the factory premises. Workers receive a salary of about $50 a month. They are forbidden to form independent trade unions. For those who step out of line on the shop floors in China, there is the notorious Lao Gai 'reeducation through labor' prison work camp. . . ."[10]

The newspaper could have written almost the same story by traveling 25 miles to the Washington State Reformatory where MicroJet employs prison labor to make aircraft components.[11] Among the company's customers is none other than Boeing. MicroJet, which lists its address as 16700 177 Avenue SE—the same address as the prison—currently employs a number of prisoners. The prisoners train for minimum wage and eventually progress to $7 an hour,[12] unlike those pesky machinists at Boeing's Everett plant who earn up to $30 an hour for the same work. Like all companies employing prison labor, MicroJet saves further by not paying benefits such as health insurance, unemployment, and workers' compensation. And if a prisoner worker is seriously injured, it is the state, through the prison system, that picks up the tab.

In addition to savings on salaries, prison industries also enjoy subsidized overhead. MicroJet's rent-free factory is in a 56,000-square-foot industrial building built and maintained by Washington state.[13] The arrangement offers a "just-in-time" inventory of labor: Prisoner workers can be simply left in their cells for weeks on end if there is no work, or they can be called in on short notice. Outside competitors, on the other hand, have to pay overhead and workers' wages even if no production is taking place. They must maintain a steady production line even when demand drops. Moreover, in prison, any attempt at labor organizing is met with immediate and harsh state repression which generates even less negative publicity than similar moves in China. Not a bad deal; not for MicroJet anyway. Nor for the other private employers at the Washington Reformatory, including Redwood Outdoors (a garment-making sweatshop that makes clothes for Eddie Bauer, Planet Hollywood, Union Bay, and other brands), Elliot Bay (a metals manufacturing company that makes crab pots and fishing industry equipment), and A&I Manufacturing (which makes blinds).

With these competitive advantages, prison industries can easily underbid any U.S. competitor. The real losers, then, are the free workers, whose jobs have gone to prisoner slave laborers or Chinese workers.

Wage Slave or Chattel?

If the *Seattle Times* had come to the Washington State Reformatory to describe the setup that these companies enjoy, it could have written, "Employees live right next to the factory premises. They are forbidden to form any type of trade union, much less an independent one. For those who step out of line on the shop floors of Washington prisons, there is the notorious Intensive Management Unit of 'reeducation through sensory deprivation' fame."[14]

In prison, the term wage slavery takes on a new meaning since prisoners are confined to their cells for much of the day. An industry job "consumes virtually all of your out-of-cell time," said Chris St. Pierre, who is serving a life sentence at WSR, "making you a virtual slave where all your time is spent at work or locked in your cell. This limits your ability to visit with your family and attorneys, do legal research, go to school, exercise, etc."

But while a $7 an hour wage clearly puts prison workers at a competitive advantage, it does not at first seem to exploit them. In fact, prisoners hired by MicroJet take home only a small fraction of their earnings. Right off the top, the state deducts 20 percent for "cost of corrections"; 10 percent goes into a mandatory savings fund controlled by the Department of Corrections (DOC); and 5 percent to a crime victim compensation fund.[15] In addition, the prisoner pays state and federal taxes, social security, and up to 20 percent more to pay off any victim restitution, child support, trial costs, and other court ordered financial obligations.[16] After prisoner Albert Delp works 40 hours a week making carabiners for Omega Pacific at $6 an hour, his weekly pay is $240. After three-quarters of that is eaten up by deductions, he takes home $60.[17]

"I don't support prison industries as they are run now," said prisoner St. Pierre. "Due to the deductions, the more you make, the more they take. You pay taxes and can't vote and have no say in how the money is used. You pay for room and board yet you're still subject to the same shit food and conditions. Even with the money you earn, there isn't much you can buy with it due to property limits. The employers treat prisoners poorly because they know the prisoners have limited employment options and aren't going anywhere."[18]

"It's not really slave labor because that implies it is compelled," argues a former Redwood Industries employee. "It's more like serfdom, [or like being] a domesticated animal."[19]

Few prisoners are willing to speak publicly against the program for fear of losing their industry jobs, being blacklisted by prison industry employers, or incurring retaliation from prison officials. In any case, most of Washington state's 12,800 prisoners would probably say that they support prison industries, regardless of any objective exploitation. Just like on the outside, people in prison work at jobs they dislike because they need the money, and there are long waiting lists for the 300 industry jobs available. While food, clothing, and shelter are provided, prisoners are required to pay for such basics as soap and toothbrushes and a $3 per visit charge for access to medical care.[20] Their situation is similar to that of sweatshop and maquilladora workers in South Asia and

Latin America who earn a few dollars a day. While such wages are exploitive and paltry by First World standards, in the Third World they make the difference between starvation and poverty and are thus highly sought after. Prison industries represent a Third World labor model in the heart of America. And while $1.50 an hour take-home pay for work that brings $30 an hour on the outside may not seem like much, it looks pretty good against the 38 to 42 cents an hour Washington convicts earn in prison kitchens, laundries, and janitorial services. And even those jobs have eager takers since overcrowding has created a prison "unemployment rate" of more than 50 percent. Like the maquilladora workers, the prisoners are objectively exploited but subjectively paid quite well. This disparity creates a relatively (by prison standards anyway) wealthy class of prisoners, a miniature labor aristocracy.

Working for Life

Prison industries prefer to hire people serving life terms to avoid the retraining and slow production associated with worker/prisoner turnover.[21] Reynolds tacitly admits that industry favors prisoners with longer terms, but explains it this way: "One of the difficulties of creating jobs for prisoners is that many of them are illiterate or semiliterate, or have low IQs. . . . The federal system may have the best prospects for high rates of payback because many of the prisoners are there for crimes typically committed by more intelligent criminals like counterfeiting, kidnapping and drug smuggling."[22] These are also crimes that tend to carry longer sentences.

This pattern of favoring lifers and long-termers calls into question the claim that such programs are intended to provide meaningful job skills. Also debatable is whether the skills are marketable on the outside. How many ex-prisoners will find work sewing garments in a sweatshop? Most of those jobs go overseas, and those that stay in the United States are often filled by undocumented immigrants and, increasingly, by prisoners. Skilled labor jobs such as those at MicroJet and Elliot Bay help ensure that such jobs become scarcer on the outside and the wages paid are forced downward.

And indeed, the interests of labor and most taxpayers may be ill-served by these programs. In touting the "revolutionary" impact of changing the system so that half of all prisoners could be employed by private industry, Meese cited the example of Lockhart Correctional Facility in Texas where the 180 prisoners who assemble circuit boards for Lockhart Technologies are paid minimum wage.[23] In fact, they actually take home about $.50 an hour. The example is indeed illustrative, but of how the system fails, not how it works. In 1993, Lockhart Technologies closed the Austin, Texas, plant where it paid about 130 workers

$10 an hour to assemble circuit boards and moved the whole manufacturing operation to the prison about 30 miles away.[24] Even if the prisoners were paid minimum wage, as Meese claims, Lockhart essentially cut its labor costs by more than half and it now pays $1 a year in rent. Meese says that this type of operation will reduce the "cost of incarceration," but says nothing about the social cost of driving down wages.

Another runaway shop that scampered behind bars rather than to Mexico or Indonesia is Omega Pacific, which manufactures carabiners (D-shaped metal rings used by climbers to secure ropes). In December 1995, the Redmond, Washington, company laid off 30 workers earning $7 an hour plus benefits and moved to the Airway Heights Corrections Center near Spokane. There, five free employees supervise some 40 prisoners who earn $6 an hour. Omega Pacific owner Bert Atwater told the *Spokane Spokesman Review* that he moved to prison because of the rent-free quarters where "the workers are delighted with the pay; [where there are] no workers who don't come in because of rush hour traffic or sick children at home; [and where] workers ... don't take vacations. Where would these guys go on vacation anyway?" Atwater was also pleased that he doesn't "have to deal with employee benefits or workers' compensation."[25]

One Washington prisoner who declined to be named for fear of retaliation dismissed the program as serving neither prisoners nor the public. The DOC industries program is "nothing more than a dog and pony show. The state spends millions on its prison industries bureaucracy alone just to say 300 prisoners are being employed by Class I industries. That's money that can't be used for educational programs, literacy, and vocational training, etc. The point is they're squandering taxpayer money, it just doesn't make sense."[26]

Others find prison industries sensible indeed and see the program as a sophisticated and palatable form of corporate welfare. EPI head Knut Rostad says his institute was formed after discussions "between me and Meese to fill a void in the market place that focuses on the management part of prisons. The market was extremely interested in prison industry."[27]

The program is attractive not only to industry on the make for a good deal, but to state governments and penal authorities overburdened by the highest per capita incarceration rate in the world. As the number of convicts explodes, so do the costs.

"Since 1980, the state and federal prison population has increased from 316,000 to 1.1 million," said Reynolds. "By the year 2002, the inmate population is expected to increase by another 43 percent. ... The expense has reached about $25 billion a year, or $250 a year for every household in America. One of the most obvious proposals to reduce the cost of criminal justice is to increase the amount of productive work by prisoners."[28] Senator Phil Gramm (R-TX) has proposed that federal prisoners pay 50 percent of their annual support through prison work.[29] Rostad predicts that: "Up to 60 to 80 percent [of wages paid prisoners in private industries programs] can end up going back to the state."[30]

The drive to make prisons pay–while racking up a hefty profit for the industry–fits well with the continuing transformation of America into a nation of small government, big corporations, and big prisons. And just like welfare reform, it gives the public a false impression that meaningful reform is taking place. Meanwhile, it takes pressure of a system that cannot provide enough decent jobs, and uses incarceration as the remedy for the ills of poverty, unemployment, inadequate education, and racism. If you've lost your job in manufacturing, garment or furniture fabrication, telemarketing or packaging, it could have simply been sentenced to prison.

Notes

1. Jeff Nesmith, "Prison Job Expansion Stirs Concern," *Atlanta Journal and Constitution,* September 18, 1996, p. A7.
2. Knut A. Rostad, president of the Enterprise Prison Institute, testimony before the House Judiciary Committee Subcommittee on Crime, September 18, 1996.
3. Nesmith, op. cit.
4. Rostad, op. cit. The figure of 25 states comes from Joyce Price, "License Plates Not All That Inmates Make," *Washington Times,* April 17, 1996, p. A6.
5. Dr. Morgan O. Reynolds, Ph.D. "The Economics of Prison Industries," testimony before the House Judiciary Committee Crime Committee on the Economics of Prison Industries, September 18, 1996.
6. Edwin Meese, "Let Prison Inmates Earn Their Keep," *Wall Street Journal,* May 1, 1996.
7. Ibid. In fact, neither the Civil Rights of Institutionalized Persons Act nor the *habeas corpus* provision has anything to do with the issue of prison labor litigation.
8. Boeing's 1995 profits rose 66 percent to $856 million with sales of almost $20 billion. At $1.66 million a year, Boeing's Frank Schrontz was the state's highest paid CEO. Meanwhile from 1989–95 the number of workers fell from 107,000 to 95,000. (Byron Acohido, "Top 5 Revenue Generators Hold onto Their Rankings," *Seattle Times,* June 11, 1996, p. G5.) This trend continues as Boeing announced its proposed merger with McDonnell Douglas in December 1996.
9. Ken Silverstein, "The New China Hands," *The Nation,* February 17, 1997, p.12.
10. Stanley Holmes, "Produce a Faulty Part, Be Punished," *Seattle Times,* May 26, 1996, p. A15.
11. They utilize a relatively modern technology that forces water through small nozzles at 55,000 pound per square inch to precision cut metals, plastics, ceramics and other materials. (MicroJet promotional materials.)
12. MicroJet hiring application.
13. Dan Pens, "Microsoft Out-Cells Competition," *Prison Legal News,* April 1996, p. 3.
14. Washington State Reformatory is a maximum security prison built in 1908 that houses about 730 prisoners.
15. *Revised Code of Washington,* 72.09.111(1)(a).
16. *Revised Code of Washington,* 72.111.
17. Tom Sowa, "Paycheck Deductions Make Inmates Hone Subtraction Skills," *Spokesman Review,* February 22, 1996, p. Al.
18. Interview with Chris St. Pierre, September 1996.
19. Interview with former industry worker, September 1996.
20. As part of a recent "get tough" legislation, Washington prisoners are charged fees for watching TV (whether they have access to one or not), schooling, family visits, some medical care, etc., as well as such small luxuries as coffee and tobacco. Those too poor to pay either have the fees deducted from monetary gifts or go without.

21. Although there are no national figures available, at WSR, of the 8 MicroJet workers 4 are lifers; as are 12 of the 15 who work for Redwood.
22. Reynolds, op. cit.
23. Edwin Meese, "Let Prison Inmates Earn Their Keep," *Wall Street Journal*, May 1, 1996.
24. "Forced Workforce," *Dollars and Sense*, July/August 1995, p. 4.
25. Tom Sowa, "Companies Find Home Inside State Prisons," and "Paycheck Deductions Make Inmates Home Subtraction Skills," *Spokesman Review*, February 22, 1996, p. A1.
26. Interview with former industry employee, September 1996.
27. Interview, October 4, 1996.
28. Interview, October 4, 1996.
29. David Frum, "Working for the Man," *The American Spectator*, August 1995, p. 48.
30. Reynolds, supra.

The Politics of Prison Labor

A Union Perspective

GORDON LAFER

What Does Labor Want? We want more schoolhouses and less jails, more books and less arsenals, more learning and less vice, more constant work and less crime, more leisure and less greed, more justice and less revenge.

—Samuel Gompers,
President, American Federation of Labor, 1893

In 2000, representatives of unionized workers across Oregon convened to identify the most important political issues facing working families. For the third year in a row, the state's labor federation named prison labor as one of its top priority issues. While unions around the country have routinely opposed the expansion of prison labor, the issue is particularly urgent for Oregon workers. During the past twenty years, over 30 states have enacted laws permitting the use of convict labor by private enterprise.[1] Oregon has taken things one step further, enacting the nation's most far-reaching statute, which not only permits but positively requires the establishment of prison industries. In 1994, voters approved Ballot Measure 17, which mandates that all prisoners must work 40 hours per week, and requires the state to pro-actively market prison labor to private employers. After only a few years, Measure 17 has already wrought dramatic effects. Thousands of public sector jobs have been taken over by prisoners; workers in the private sector have been laid off when their firms lost contracts to prison-based industries; and with the cost of supervising a full-time work force, the state for the first time in its history is spending more on corrections than on higher education.[2] This combination of concerns has galvanized union members around an issue no one used to think about, and has led state officials to reconsider the logic of mandatory prison labor. In one way, the Oregon law has

Another version of this article first ran in *American Prospect*, October 2001.

forced the debate to come to a head faster than in other states; and the outcome of this debate may offer a preview of the policy choices facing states across the nation as they confront what is fast becoming one of the primary threats to the job prospects of working class Americans.

When most of us think of prison labor, the image that springs to mind is of convicts making license plates, picking up trash, or performing other menial tasks that—whether serving as punishment or rehabilitation—have nothing to do with the jobs that people do on the outside. Indeed, this was the case for decades. Prisoner labor was largely outlawed until 1979, when Congress authorized states to once again use prisoners in for-profit ventures and sell the products of their labor in interstate commerce. Since that time, prisoners have come to be used by an increasingly wide range of industries. Travelers booking a flight on TWA are likely to be talking to prisoners, since the airline uses a California correctional facility for its reservations service. Microsoft used Washington state prisoners to pack and ship thousands of copies of Windows software; and Starbucks uses prisoners to distribute its gourmet coffees. AT&T uses prisoners to do telemarketing; a car parts plant used prisoners to manufacture parts for Honda; and Toys R' Us bussed prisoners in on the graveyard shift, to clean the stock shelves in preparation for the next day's customers.[3]

The Lure of Prison Labor

For all these employers, what's so attractive about using prison labor is precisely that it undoes everything that union members—and their parents and grandparents before them—have fought so hard to achieve. At times, prisoners have been used directly as a strike-breaking work force; TWA's reservations system was set up during a flight attendant strike, and according to the union involved, the prisoner program was a significant part of the company's strategy to undermine the strike.[4] In other cases, prisons have allowed employers to avoid unions even in well-organized industries; thus, the owners of an Arizona slaughterhouse shut down their unionized operation only to reopen in a joint venture with the state's Department of Corrections.[5] Even where it is not directly related to anti-union strategies, however, prison labor provides employers a means of avoiding or undoing virtually all of the gains won by working people over the past hundred years—creating islands of time in which, in terms of labor relations, it's still the late nineteenth century.

Prison labor is, of course, much cheaper than free labor for employers. In Ohio, for example, a Honda supplier paid auto workers $2/hour for the same work that the UAW had fought for decades to win $20–30/hour for. And in Oregon, private companies can "lease" prisoners for $3/day.[6] However, the attractions of prison labor extend far beyond wage rates. Prisoners don't merely make less than anyone else; they are also statutorily exempted from virtually every form of labor protection enacted during the past hundred years. Prison employers are excused from minimum wage and prevailing wage laws; they pay no health insurance, no unemployment insurance, no payroll or social security taxes, and no workers' compensation; they pay no vacation time, sick leave, or overtime. Prison workers can be "hired," fired, or reassigned at will. Not only do they have no right to organize or strike; they also have no means of filing a grievance or indeed of voicing any kind of complaint whatsoever: for example, they have no right to circulate an employee petition or newsletter, no right to call a meeting, and no access to the press. This is the ultimate flexible and disciplined work force. In all these ways, then, corporations have found a way to undo the achievements that working Americans fought so long and so hard to establish.

The prospect of windfall profits from prison labor has fueled a boom in the private prison industry. As with other public services, the companies operating private prisons aim to make money by operating corrections facilities for less than the state pays them. However, if they are also able to contract prisoners out to private enterprise—forcing prisoners to work for little or nothing and pocketing what would be their wages as corporate profit—they will have developed a second stream of revenue unavailable to other privatizers. In essence, a private prison functions simultaneously as a public service contractor and as the highest-margin temp agency in the nation. Partly for this reason, the past few years have seen such respected money managers as Allstate, Merrill Lynch, and Shearson Lehman investing in private prisons.[7]

The Oregon Law and the Expansion of Prison Labor into the Private Sector

In Oregon, the past few years have seen prisoners displace a growing number of unionized public sector jobs. The menial work of raking leaves or clearing trails has long proved insufficient to occupy the ever-expanding army that must be put to work. In order to meet its statutory mandate, the state has assigned prisoners to an increasingly sophisticated array of administrative tasks. Prisoners are now responsible for all data entry and record keeping in the Secretary of State's corporation division, along with answering the phones when members of the public call with questions about corporate records. Across the state, public agencies are now using prisoners for desktop publishing, digital mapping, and computer-aided design work.[8]

In recent years, the prison work program began taking jobs out of the private sector as well. In Eugene, church-owned Sacred Heart Hospital canceled its contract with a unionized linen service and redirected the work to a prison laundry. On the Columbia River Gorge, up to 100 construction workers lost out when the Umatilla prison used prisoners to expand its facility, taking away work that had previously been performed by unionized tradespeople.[9] And in the heart of the state's timber region, lumber executives set up two new prison mills in 2001, taking 60 jobs out of the local economy and leaving qualified County residents on the unemployment line.[10]

In both the public and private sectors, prison labor serves as a double-edged sword for working people. Most immediately, prisoner labor takes decently paid jobs out of the economy. At the same time, it also undermines the living standards and bargaining power of those who remain employed but whose firms are now forced to compete with prison industries. The imperative to compete with poverty level wages in the Third World has already wrought disastrous effects for American production workers. As manufacturing has declined, workers have increasingly relied on those sectors of the economy that cannot be exported, particularly the service sector. By chartering what is essentially a chain of maquilladora enterprise zones on American soil, the prison labor system makes it possible to force even service workers to compete at the level of the most heavily repressed laborers.

At this point, we are still just witnessing the infancy of this labor system. The Oregon program has not yet met its full-employment mandate, and the Department of Corrections is still working to develop streamlined procedures for providing local firms a safe, cheap, and reliable labor force. However, as administrators iron out the kinks in the system, the program is poised to grow exponentially. Like many other states, Oregon has adopted tough-on-crime mandatory sentencing laws. As a result, the prison population is projected to double in ten years. If this projection holds true and the state meets its requirement for full employment in the prisons, the number of prison workers will increase by 150 percent.[11] Nationwide, the Correctional Industries Association predicts that within a few years, 30 percent of prisoners will be working in for-profit ventures.[12]

The Fiscal Logic of Prison Industry

Oregon Governor John Kitzhaber has been an outspoken critic of the universal work requirement, and under his leadership the state legislature has opened up debate on the current policy. However, even with a well-intentioned governor—and even with the prospect of repealing the current law—the combination of mandatory sentencing and fiscal austerity makes the logic of prison labor hard to resist. In this sense, Measure 17 has simply forced Oregonians to confront early a set of pressures building up in states across the country. The equation is a simple one: sentencing laws have led to a steep increase in the prison population; it's expensive to maintain prisoners; but in a climate of fiscal restraint it is impossible to raise taxes in order to fund this expansion. Within these constraints, elected officials have only two options: either they allow the prison system to consume a huge share of the state budget—forcing deep cuts in public services—or they find a way to make incarceration cheaper.] As the size of the problem grows, the price of the first solution becomes less and less politically viable; thus, regardless of individual politicians' personal beliefs, states face mounting pressure to privatize corrections services, reduce other agencies' budgets by substituting prisoners for public employees, or hire prisoners out to local industries.

This potential explosion in prison work programs further threatens to create a vicious circle of poverty and imprisonment. When the economy goes into recession, the supply of decently paid jobs will shrink; more and more working class people will fall into poverty, and some number of these will engage in nonviolent crime (shoplifting, writing bad checks, drug possession) as a way of getting through. Those arrested will be incarcerated for long sentences and put to work for private companies, where their labor will serve to eliminate that many more decently paying jobs on the outside, thus reproducing the cycle. It is important to note that this cycle is not the result of a conscious conspiracy among public officials or private employers; it is, rather, the natural result of each party pursuing its own rational interests under current conditions. Indeed, the first signs of such a trend are already evident in the Oregon experience. In 2000, one of the union members who lost his job to prisoners was himself a former prisoner. Having worked in a prison laundry, he applied for a job in a private linen firm upon release. Less than two years later, however, his job was eliminated and the work sent back inside.[13] Thus, we are faced with the prospect of a self-reproducing cycle of full employment for prisoners and increasing hardship for free workers.

The legal requirement to put all prisoners to work holds whether the economy is booming or shrinking. In times of recession, the law creates a particularly dangerous dynamic. There is no guarantee of a job for American citizens, but the prison law essentially mandates a policy of full employment for prisoners. Even when thousands of free citizens are pounding the pavement or lining up at unemployment offices, the state is not allowed to pull back from its commitment to put all prisoners to work. As one union picket sign read, "Unemployed? Prison Inmates Aren't."[14] Thus, at exactly the point in the economic cycle that decently paying jobs become scarcer and more valuable, prison work programs will begin taking a larger share of jobs out of the economy. Moreover, since recession often leads employers to cut back production, the Department of Corrections may be forced to make special efforts—such as providing prisoners at even further discounted rates—in order to place all their wards in jobs. Since there is ultimately no limit on how low prison labor can be priced, prison officials may be forced to increase demand for prison labor by cutting wages even below their current level. This marketing strategy, however, will lead to prisons undercutting even more private sector employers and free workers. It is unclear whether this scenario will become reality; to date, the state has avoided such a destructive cycle by simply failing to carry out the full-employment requirement of the law. If the law is fully implemented however, it provides a formula for potentially devastating economic impacts in times of recession.[15]

Is It About Job Training?

Some proponents of prison labor insist that the industries serve an important rehabilitative function in providing prisoners with skills that will enable them to earn an honest living when they get out. While individual prisoners may benefit from their work, the prison industry is not designed to serve this function. If prison labor were part of a rehabilitative effort, we would see increased funding for education, training, and substance abuse treatment; but the reverse is true.

Nationally, the number of drug treatment slots in U.S. prisons was cut in half over the course of the 1990s, and is now available to just 10 percent of the prisoners in need of it.[16] In Oregon, drug and alcohol treatment programs have been cut even while the prison budget has expanded; and the prison labor law explicitly bans prisoners from substituting education or training in place of meeting their work requirement.[17]

Beyond this, prison work programs themselves are not operated along job-training lines. Prisoners are not selected for work based on their need for training, but just the opposite: employers look for prisoners who *already* have the skills needed for their jobs. Even those prisoners who do pick up skills often are being trained in jobs that do not exist, or do not pay living wages, in the free economy. For instance, both Oregon and California operate for-profit blue jeans industries, which sell denim-wear in the United States and abroad. But since the garment industry has moved almost all production out of the country in favor of lower-wage workers in the developing world, Oregonians leaving prison cannot expect to find family-wage jobs sewing blue jeans.

What are the critical skills that prisoners are imagined to be learning? One prison official concedes that prisoners may not learn a trade, but nevertheless insists: "Working is really good for offenders. Learning discipline, how to follow directions, how to work with others—these are really important habits."[18] But there's no secret to making disciplined workers out of people whose lives are subject to the total control of overseers; and this accomplishment in no way qualifies prisoners to earn a decent living upon release. It is telling that training is also the justification offered for the Chinese prison industries whose products are banned in the United States. "We want prisoners to learn a working skill," says the warden at China's maximum security Shanghai Jail.[19] At home and abroad, however, the prison industry system appears to be driven not by empowering prisoners to earn a living, but by exploiting their dependence and desperation to create windfall profits for politically connected entrepreneurs.

The Politics of Prison Labor: Whose Agenda Is This?

Oregon's prison labor law was approved by 70 percent of voters, including many union members. Five years later, many who supported the initiative now claim they were fooled. They wanted prisoners to work and to contribute to their own upkeep, but they never imagined they'd be taking jobs away from people on the outside. This is fair enough: for people who don't have time to analyze the small print of every proposal on the ballot, it's easy to be fooled. But if working people may have been deceived, those who wrote the initiative and funded the campaign promoting it knew exactly what they were getting.

Interestingly, the prime backers of the prison labor initiative were neither victims' rights associations nor conservative community groups. Instead, the campaign was almost entirely funded by a clique of conservative businessmen who have promoted a host of antiworker initiatives over the past decade. Led by the owner of the notoriously anti-union Shilo Inn chain, this group of wealthy businessmen joined together in the early 1990s to form the Oregon Roundtable, whose members each pledged to contribute $100,000 per year to promote a conservative political agenda. Of the $206,000 spent on the Measure 17 campaign, $193,000 came from this consortium, representing businesses in the sawmill, real estate, hospitality and medical supply industries.[20] This same group has backed virtually all of the most aggressively anti-labor proposals of the past decade, including regressive tax reform, cuts in unemployment benefits, an attack on public employee pensions, and a prohibition on using union dues for political action.

When we view Measure 17 as part of this broader agenda, the bill's draconian effects seem neither unintentional nor unwelcome. On the contrary, the proponents of this policy may have gotten exactly what they sought: a means of increasing profits by replacing living wage jobs with prison labor, and a point of leverage for disciplining the labor force as a whole by forcing a growing number of employers to compete with prison industry.

Security or Solidarity: Political Strategies for Curtailing Prison Labor

In the debate to date, opponents of prison labor have focused primarily on the security problems inherent in the system. Union representatives and progressive politicians alike have often focused on the danger of, for example, allowing people convicted of violent crimes to rake leaves in the parks where children are at play. Public safety *is*, in fact, a real concern. In seeking job placements for ever growing numbers of prisoners, the state has continually expanded the range of work and types of public interaction deemed appropriate for convicts. More alarmingly, the state has begun to compromise security standards in order to make prison work crews more affordable. Under the current system, employers may "lease" a ten-prisoner work crew for $30/day. However, the cost of providing a guard to oversee this crew is nearly $300 per day, and this cost has led many agencies to limit their use of work gangs. In order to put more prisoners to work, the Department of Corrections recently sought to cut operating costs by replacing guards with less trained but lower-cost civilian overseers.[21]

If the state has relaxed safety standards in order to expand the prison labor program, this is an important issue. Beyond this, politics is often a game of immediate pragmatics, and in this sense the right argument is whatever works. There is no question that, in the current atmosphere, attacking the safety of the prison labor system is a more effective political strategy than appealing for solidarity with prisoners. Nevertheless, there are two problems with this strategy. First, as the prison industry system works out the kinks in its operation, these security problems will be increasingly marginal. For instance, if Louisiana-Pacific (one of the financial backers of the prison labor initiative) decides to lay off union workers and construct a sawmill on prison grounds, there is no security argument that will effectively prevent the project from going forward. If we lay the groundwork for public opposition to prison work based exclusively on security concerns, we will be leaving ourselves vulnerable to better planned but equally devastating schemes in the future.

Beyond this, the most important dynamic propelling the expansion of prison industries is the fiscal logic of mandatory sentencing. Even if Oregon's work requirement is repealed, the simple equation of a booming prisoner population and limited state budgets will force both liberal and conservative administrations to take up any available means to make incarceration more affordable, and prison labor is likely to constitute an important part of this solution. Arguments about security may work in the short term. Ultimately, however, it will likely prove impossible to avoid a large-scale expansion of prison industries without undoing mandatory sentencing laws.

This is the task that faces the labor movement, together with allied organizations. This is a much more difficult project, involving much more challenging conversations among union members, than is the short-term argument about security. Both the strength and the limitations of the labor movement stem from the fact that—unlike any vanguard or issue-advocacy organization—unions do not selectively choose their membership from among those who are already ideologically sympathetic, but rather represent *all* workers in a given industry, and seek to mobilize a *mass* movement among average, nonpolitical citizens. Building a consensus around prison labor will be a slow and difficult process; but it is one we must take up if we hope to stop the prison train before it runs us all over.

Notes

1. U.S. Department of Justice, Bureau of Justice Assistance, *Prison Industry Program Fact Sheet*, Washington, D.C., 1995.
2. Maureen O'Hagan, "The Crime That Changed Punishment," *Willamette Week*, September 23, 1998.
3. Daniel Burton-Rose, Dan Pens, and Paul Wright, eds., *The Celling of America: An Inside Look at the U.S. Prison Industry*, Common Courage Press, Monroe, ME, 1998.
4. Report by Richard Holober, Assistant Research Director for the California Labor Federation, cited in Christian Parenti's, "Inside Jobs," *New Statesman and Society*, November 3, 1995, vol. 8 no. 337.
5. Arizona Hog Slaughterhouse Plant is Described in Steven Elbow, "Doing Time, 9 to 5," *Isthmus*, 1995.
6. Honda supplier Weastec Corporation paid prisoners $2.05/hour, of which the prisoners kept 35 cents, reported in Reese Ehrlich, "Prison Labor: Workin' for the Man," *Covert Action Quarterly*, Fall 1995. Oregon rates are reported in *Study of the Inmate Work Program*, Joint Legislative Audit Committee, Report no. 98–1, July 1998.
7. Eric Schlosser, "The Prison-Industrial Complex," *Atlantic Monthly*, December 1998.
8. Oregon Department of Corrections web page, www.or.state.us/doc.
9. Michelle Roberts, "Fight Brews Over State's Inmate Work Program," *The Oregonian*, December 22, 1998, p. D1.
10. Linn County Commissioner Cliff Wooten, personal communication with the author, July 12, 2001.
11. Based on figures reported in Office of Economic Analysis, *Oregon Corrections Population Forecast*, October 1998; and Michelle Roberts, "State approves plan to employ more inmates," *The Oregonian*, January 16, 1999, p. D1.
12. Matt Grayson, "Inmates, Inc.: In Favor of Prison Labor," *Spectrum: The Journal of State Government*, Spring 1997, vol. 70, no. 2.
13. Reported by Ron Teninty, union representative, International Brotherhood of Teamsters Local 206, conversation with the author, February 1999.
14. "Prison Labor Protest," *The Pacific Northwest Carpenter*, vol. 5, no. 8, p. 4.
15. Even without the worst case scenario envisioned here, Oregon Department of Corrections spokeswoman Nancy DeSouza warns that "If Oregon's economy takes a downturn, I foresee — and so do a lot of other people — more problems of competition with the private sector." Quoted in Michelle Roberts, "Fight Brews Over State's Inmate Work Program," *The Oregonian*, December 22, 1998, p. D1.
16. Eric Schlosser, "The Prison-Industrial Complex," *Atlantic Monthly*, December 1998.
17. Maureen O'Hagan, "The Crime That Changed Punishment," *Willamette Week*, September 23, 1998.
18. Walter Dickey, former Director of Corrections for the state of Wisconsin, now Corrections faculty at University of Wisconsin-Madison, quoted in Steven Elbow, "Doing Time, 9 to 5."
19. Quoted in Reese Ehrlich, "Prison Labor: Workin' For the Man," *Covert Action Quarterly*, Fall 1995.
20. Campaign contributions were provided to the author by the National Institute for Money in State Politics, www.followthemoney.org.
21. Michelle Roberts, "Truck Drivers Now Supervising Inmate Deliveries," *The Oregonian*, November 10, 1998, p. C1.

Work Strike Suppressed and Sabotaged in Ohio

DANIEL BURTON-ROSE

The October 16th, 1997, issue of the Cleveland black community newspaper *The Call and Post* printed a letter announcing a statewide work strike by Ohio prisoners on November 1. The letter was signed by Prisoners United For Equal Justice.

The purpose of the protest was to demand an end to the two-tiered system of sentencing created by Senate Bill 2, a "truth in sentencing" measure passed in July of 1996. Prisoners sentenced after the passage of SB 2 serve the time given to them by a judge. Prisoners sentenced before the bill took effect are under the thumb of Ohio's Parole Board—a dictatorial body of 12 who are appointed for life, whose decisions cannot be held to any objective criteria, and who are answerable to no superior.

Prisoners in Ohio regularly receive 10- and 20-year parole continuations—"flops"—and even "superflops" of 30 to 40 years. Prisoners United For Equal Justice contends this amounts to double and triple jeopardy at the hands of the parole board, and creates a dangerous "atmosphere of hopelessness" in Ohio's prison system. An estimated 39,000 prisoners out of Ohio's total 47,000 have their futures controlled by the Parole Board.

The letter to *The Call and Post* was itself the organizing tool for the strike, as many prisoners throughout the state subscribe to the weekly. At Trumbull Correctional Institution in Leavittsburg the impending strike caused a spate of dialogue between the prisoners and some prison employees, with several prominent employees reportedly acknowledging that prisoners "got to do what they got to do." But when the day of the strike came the general population was locked-down, and prisoners got to do nothing. A prisoner in segregation reported that guards circulated asking prisoners if they planned to strike, and demanding that they say it on video camera, with the video to be shown later at their parole hearing.

This article was written in May 1998.

A prisoner at the North Central Correctional Institution in Marion estimated 15 percent of prisoners participated there, and, according to Karen Thimmes of CURE-Ohio, 87 prisoners were transferred to other prisons to hurt the strike's chances of success. At Orient Correctional Institution in Columbus a prisoner activist reported that nearly 300 prisoners received conduct reports for refusing to work (200 of which were later dismissed), 30 to 50 prisoners were transferred, and several prisoner activists were put in the hole. Red Armstrong was one of those infracted: he was accused of writing the letter to *The Call and Post* and spent 15 days in disciplinary segregation for it. At Madison Correctional Institution in London, only a handful of prisoners reportedly participated in the strike. But at London Correctional Institution, also in London, where prisoners had only had two days notice of the strike, the level of prisoner cohesion was high, as only 150 prisoners went to lunch, and 400 to dinner, out of a population of more than 1,800.

A main obstacle to the strike was that it started on a Saturday, so food workers were disproportionately put on the line. The reason for this timing was unclear, but might have resulted from a desire by strike organizers to have their protest coincide with the 5th Ohio Prison Activists Conference at Oberlin College, which took place the same day.

But prisoners wanting nonviolent protest faced other problems, primarily a lack of support from prominent outsiders and prison reformists. At Grafton Correctional Institution a well-respected prisoner leader withdrew his support at the last minute because of his close ties to Cleveland senator and president of the Ohio Legislative Black Caucus Jeff Johnson, who urged against the strike.

Paula Eyre, Chair and President of CURE-Ohio, the state's largest reform group of prisoners and prisoners' families, authored a letter stating that CURE-Ohio was opposed to the strike, on the grounds that it "has too much potential to turn violent." She continued: "CURE-Ohio has worked hard over the last two years to bring a legislative solution to the unfair actions of the Ohio parole board," and such a violent turn in the strike "would quickly undo all that work. . . . We want to urge every prisoner not to participate in this work stoppage," she concluded. The letter was posted by the Ohio Department of Rehabilitation and Corrections (ODRC) in most cell blocks in every prison in the state.

At issue was the question of prisoners' right to act for themselves. CURE-Ohio seeks to work cooperatively with the Ohio Department of Rehabilitation and Correction, and does not support even nonviolent prisoner activism as a consequence. Senator Johnson epitomized the "sit tight, let us do it for you" attitude of Ohio's penal reformers by stating in his press release on the strike: "It is extremely important that Ohio's prisoners let the legislature and other advocacy groups do their job. Any type of drastic measure will offset any chances for positive reform in the future." (Johnson was later convicted of bribery and went to prison himself.)

ODRC head Reginald Wilkinson added threats to the urgings of reformists: "Inmates who attempt to lead, encourage, or coerce other inmates to participate in any form of boycott will be dealt with severely, including a potential loss of parole release," stated his letter that was posted in prisons throughout the state. "It is expected that all inmates respond to their assignments and not allow the desire of the few who would create chaos to make the lives of all Ohio's inmates much more difficult for a very long time."

CURE-Ohio's hopes for easing prisoner anger in Ohio rest on Senator Johnson's Senate Bill 182, which would equalize some of the more glaring injustices in Ohio's present parole system, such as making the parole board responsible to a set of guidelines, and getting rid of life terms for members (Ohio is the only state in the Union where parole officials have no term limits). Even optimistically, the bill will take a couple years to wind its way through a quite conservative legislature hostile to prisoners. Some prisoner activists contend the bill does not go far enough, as it ignores sex offenders, technical parole violators, lifers, or repeat offenders. Creating a just parole system would mean releasing thousands of prisoners who are doing more time than their judges originally intended; needless to say, a daunting prospect to any politician wishing to be reelected.

The mix of repressive measures and paternalistic sabotage that cut the strike short frustrated many prisoners, who see nonviolent protest as essential, so as not to give the mainstream media further chances to demonize prisoners or prison officials an excuse for further ratcheting up security levels.

Still, it would be wrong to call the strike a failure. Such events never fail to shake up prison officials, who have shown their fear of Ohio's prison movement by suspending with pay one ODRC employee who attended the activists' conference at Oberlin, and threatening to revoke the parole of an ex-offender who spoke there.

The Cleveland Plain Dealer acknowledged the validity of prisoners' concerns about an unjust parole system and recommended that the system be changed. They editorialize that the presence of the attempted work stoppage and at least five mini-riots or rebellions in Ohio in 1997 "suggests more tension than a prudent state should allow."

Several prisoners have continued to carry out protest individually. John Perotti, a long-time prisoner activist now at Trumbull, was in segregation at the time of the strike, so stopped eating in solidarity with the strikers. When the strike ended, he continued the fast, adding some grievances over his own case and brutal treatment to the generalized protest against the parole board. He fasted for over a month. Danny Cahill, another prisoner activist confined at Orient, began a fast without food or water January 1st, demanding the resignation of CURE-Ohio board members who signed the letter to Ohio prisoners urging them not to strike. Roughly 1,100 of CURE-Ohio's 1,800 dues paying members are prisoners, and Cahill contends they need committed activists, not advocates, supporting them. Cahill's hunger strike lasted seven days and no members of CURE-Ohio resigned.

Cahill stated in regards to prisoner activism: "We have endured far too many abuses and degradations. We have a right to stand up and resist." He summed up the situation in Ohio's prisons, not as a threat but as a lament: "If we can't have peaceful protest, what's left?"

Staughton Lynd, a long-time labor activist currently doing prisoners' rights work in Youngstown, addressed the dilemma faced by prisoner activists in Ohio seeking substantive changes: "People on the inside want to feel like there are people on the outside with whom they can take joint action. And I think they're in a state of confusion as to who that is."

Prison Jobs and Free Market Unemployment

ADRIAN LOMAX

In May 1996, the Fabry Glove & Mitten Company opened a production facility in Wisconsin's Green Bay Correctional Institution. The company hired 70 prisoners as laborers, later adding 30 more. The prisoners, who operate cutting and sewing machines, earn $5.25 per hour. The Department of Corrections keeps 65 percent of the prisoners' wages to offset the expense of imprisoning them.

A year earlier, Wisconsin's legislature had approved Republican governor Tommy Thompson's plan to amend the state's labor laws in order to allow private firms to set up shop inside the state's prisons. Thompson won passage of his proposal only after assuring legislators that the convict-labor program would not be permitted to steal the jobs of any workers outside prison walls. Michael Sullivan, secretary of the Wisconsin DOC, affirmed that prisoner labor would be used solely to make products not currently being produced in this country.

At the beginning of 1996, the Fabry company employed 205 workers at its three Green Bay-area plants. By April 1997, less than a year after the company began hiring prisoners, Fabry's outside-the-walls work force had fallen by 40 percent, to 120 employees.

Fabry laid off the fabric cutters at its city plants in August 1996. The following month, the firm issued orders for prisoners to cut fabric for 50,000 gloves, hats, scarves, and other products. Many other workers were laid off or fired in the ensuing weeks. In the first nine months of the prison shop's operation, prisoners cut or sewed 461,000 items.

Before the prison venture began, Fabry's outside workers earned up to $11 an hour. Employing free workers also entails nonwage expenses like health-care benefits, vacation benefits, unemployment compensation, and workers' compensation insurance premiums. Fabry pays none of those expenses for its prisoner employees.

This article was written in May 1998.

Democratic state senator Charles Chvala, the senate majority leader, called the Fabry layoffs outrageous. "I challenge the governor to go to Green Bay, stand eye to eye with those laid-off workers who have played by the rules all their lives, and explain why he believes inmates should have their jobs," Chvala said. "Law-abiding citizens—working Wisconsin citizens—are being forced into competition with prison inmates for jobs, and this is indefensible."

Company president John Fabry said the layoffs were unrelated to his firm's employment of prisoners. He explained that the company had been planning layoffs since 1995. If the opportunity to hire prisoners had not materialized, Fabry claimed, the company would likely have moved production facilities to Asia.

The DOC supports Fabry's assertion that the layoffs occurred independently of the convict-labor deal. "With the information we have at this point in time, displacement [of Fabry workers with prisoners] did not occur," DOC secretary Sullivan said. "To stay viable, Fabry did reduce some operations, but I am unaware of any displacements resulting from the agreement with us."

John Matthews, Governor Thompson's chief of staff, agrees. "The marketplace was forcing him to find a different place to produce these products," Matthews told a reporter. "It came down to a choice between the Pacific Rim and the prison."

Senator Chvala took issue with these denials. "There can be no mistaking the connection between Fabry's downsizing and their use of prison labor," Chvala wrote in a letter to Sullivan. Chvala called on the DOC chief to cancel the Fabry contract "before more honest, law-abiding working people lose their jobs."

Federal law mandates that private companies hiring prisoners must not displace outside workers. The U.S. Department of Justice is investigating the Fabry ordeal, but the law is unclear. The term "displacement" is not defined and the statute has not yet been tested in court.

Job loss was not the only change that awaited Fabry workers after the company shifted production to the prison shop. Four months after it began hiring prisoners, Fabry slashed the wages of its remaining free employees up to $5.50 an hour. "If you want to work for what the prisoners make," said Penny Vande Voort, a former sewing-machine operator who quit following the pay reduction, "go ahead and work for John Fabry."

The phenomenon of people outside prison walls being thrown out of their jobs by companies employing convicts is not confined to Wisconsin. A replay of the Fabry affair occurred in Texas, where U.S. Technologies sold its electronics plant in Austin and laid off 150 workers; 45 days later, the company's owners opened a facility using convict labor in a Texas prison.

Nationwide, more than 100 private firms have reached convict-for-hire agreements with 29 states. Microsoft, IBM, Victoria's Secret, and TWA are among the companies that have exploited prisoner labor.

Source

Wisconsin State Journal, Milwaukee Journal Sentinel, Green Bay Press Gazette, U.S. News & World Report.

THE PRIVATE PRISON INDUSTRY

In 1984, private prisons made their reappearance in the United States after a fifty-year hiatus. The private prison industry had been abandoned in the early 1930s when state and local governments removed private administration of prisons and jails because of rampant brutality and corruption. Despite this history of failure, in recent years companies have scrambled to return prisons to the realm of private enterprise.

Promising to run prisons more cheaply and efficiently than the government, by 2001 the private prison industry had won the contracts to imprison nearly 5 percent of the U.S. prison and jail population. Using campaign contributions and lobbying, private prisons have grown—despite evidence that they are more expensive and dangerous (both for prisoners and the public), and overall, much shoddier enterprises than their public counterparts. After the private prison industry almost imploded in 2001 due to poor management, scandal, and financial chicanery, the federal government rescued the industry from collapse through sweetheart contracts and subsidies.

Whether private versus public prisons are "better" is largely immaterial and irrelevant. It is like comparing rotten oranges to rotten apples from the prisoner's perspective. But, at least in public prisons, when prisoners are raped due to inadequate staffing, transport vans burst into flames killing the occupants due to no maintenance, or prisoners are held past their release dates, no one can say prison officials did so to line their own pockets and personally profit from the misery of others. With private prisons, most shortcomings can be traced to a conscious decision to enhance the company's bottom line. After all, the purpose of private prison companies is to make money for their owners, and not to promote public safety, rehabilitate prisoners, protect the public, or ensure a safe working environment for their staff and the safekeeping of their charges. If that happens it is a mere by-product of the goal of making money.

—PW

Bailing Out Private Jails

JUDITH GREENE

The private prison industry is in trouble. For close to a decade its business boomed and stock prices soared. Across the country state legislators recognized the opportunity, and a frenzy began to contract with private companies as prison populations soared under the new, more severe sentencing laws. At first, prison privatization seemed a great boon, for it allowed legislators to appear both tough on crime and fiscally conservative. But then reality set in as media reports about the gross deficiencies and abuses at private prisons accumulated, along with the resulting lawsuits and million-dollar fines. By 2000, not a single state solicited new private prison contracts. Many existing contracts were rolled back or even rescinded. The companies' stock prices went through the floor.

Here was one experiment in the privatization of public services that might have limped to a well-deserved close. But instead, the federal government seems to be rushing to the industry's rescue. Consider a one-year sample of news reports, from August 2000 to July 2001, that chronicle problems in prisons run by the Corrections Corporation of America (CCA), the country's largest private prison company.

- August 2000: Two prisoners escaped from a CCA prison in Bartlett, Texas. State investigators found that doors had been left unlocked at the facility. No one was watching the closed-circuit TV surveillance monitors. When the prisoners cut their way through the prison's perimeter fence, a security alarm sounded, but staff in the prison's control center turned it off and did nothing.[1]
- October: Two guards at a CCA prison in Walsenburg, Colorado, who had repeatedly beat a prisoner while he was handcuffed, shackled, and unable to resist, pleaded guilty in federal court.[2]

This article was first published in *American Prospect*, September 2001.

- November: The Bartlett facility erupted in a disturbance that left five prisoners injured. Two days later, five guards were stabbed and three others were injured when prisoners at a CCA prison in Estancia, New Mexico, took them hostage.[3]
- December: Jurors in Columbia, South Carolina, found that guards at a CCA juvenile prison had abused a youth confined there and that their use of force was so malicious it was "repugnant to the conscience of mankind." The jury awarded $3 million in punitive damages.[4]
- April 2001: Prison guards at CCA's Cibola County Correctional Center in New Mexico tear-gassed nearly 700 prisoners who had staged a day-long nonviolent protest of conditions at the facility.[5] The same day, in Oklahoma, the addiction treatment manager at CCA's Tulsa Jail resigned. The warden, she said, had directed her to make a "sales pitch" to local judges, urging them to sentence offenders to a treatment program in the jail even though the program had been eviscerated in order to cut operating expenses.[6]
- May: Three prisoners were mistakenly released from the same Oklahoma jail,[7] and nine guards at CCA's District of Columbia Correctional Treatment Facility were indicted. Federal prosecutors alleged that they had accepted money from an undercover FBI agent in exchange for smuggling two-way pagers and cash into the prison.[8]
- June: Back at the Tulsa Jail, a CCA guard resigned his post after 10 Valium tablets were reportedly found hidden in his sock during an employee shakedown.[9]
- July: 400 prisoners exported from Indiana to a CCA prison in Wheelwright, Kentucky, started a riot in the prison recreation area that spread to four housing units before it was over, with prisoners setting mattresses on fire and tossing TVs and toilets through the windows. Two weeks later, CCA fired the warden and his top assistant, citing "policy violations."[10]

CCA is not the only private prison company with a record of continuing abuses. Prisons run by the Wackenhut Corporation in New Mexico have repeatedly erupted in violence and disturbances. (Together, CCA and Wackenhut control 75 percent of the U.S. private prison market.) Between December 1998 and August 1999, four prisoner-on-prisoner homicides were committed in Wackenhut's New Mexico facilities; and then, in August, a guard was murdered as well. Most people think that kind of violence is the norm in America's prisons. But the best available data on prison homicides—compiled by the Criminal Justice Institute, publishers of *The Corrections Yearbook*—show otherwise: In 1998, when American prisons held 1.3 million prisoners, there were only 59 prisoner-on-prisoner homicides. That's a rate of one murder for every 22,000 prisoners. The homicide rate in Wackenhut's New Mexico facilities in those nine months was about one for every 400 prisoners—and that's not counting the death of Ralph Garcia, a Wackenhut guard.

But if the company changed its ways after that explosion of violence, it's hard to tell. The following year, its Jena Juvenile Justice Facility in Jena, Louisiana, was shut down. A Juvenile Court judge in New Orleans found that the youngsters held there had been treated no better than animals.[11]

The Great Escape

Industry executives will tell you that these prison management disasters were isolated events, confined to a handful of "underperforming" facilities. But the available evidence suggests that the problems are structural and widespread.

A research project I directed in 1999 compared the quality of correctional services in a medium security private prison run by CCA in Minnesota with the three medium security prisons run by the state.[12] We found many more operational problems in the CCA prison, from program deficiencies and unreliable methods of classifying prisoners for security purposes, to high rates of staff turnover that resulted in inadequate numbers of experienced, well-trained personnel. And this was in a private prison that was not notoriously troubled—a facility that the company, in fact, considered to be exemplary.

There have been few other studies of the quality (as opposed to the cost) of private prison services, but evidence is mounting that serious operational problems are not confined to just a few institutions.

- An industry-wide survey conducted in 1997 by James Austin, a professor at George Washington University, found 49 percent more prisoner-on-staff assaults and 65 percent more prisoner-on-prisoner assaults in medium and minimum security private facilities than in medium and minimum security prisons run by government.[13]
- National data reported in *The Corrections Yearbook* indicate that guard turnover was 41 percent for the private prison industry in 1998, compared with 15 percent in publicly run prisons.
- A tally of news reports in 1999 showed at least 37 escapes of adult prisoners from secure private prisons that year. (This did not count escapes from juvenile facilities, from transportation vans, or during escorted hospital visits.) For comparison, one can look at New York's state prisons, which hold roughly the same number of prisoners as the entire system of private prisons in the United States. Between 1995 and 1999, there were only eight escapes from secure institutions in New York—a rate of less than two per year.[14]

The problems seem to be endemic to the enterprise—a result, in great part, of the private companies' mission to hold down costs. Most important, wages and benefits substantially lower than those in government run prisons have resulted in significantly higher employee turnover, with dramatic ill effects. But other kinds of corner-cutting have also taken a toll. Spending on prisoner health care and on staff training also tends to be inadequate at the private prisons, which is another reason why the industry has fallen behind the public prison system both in maintaining prisoners' basic human right to a safe and humane environment and in protecting the safety of the prison staff and the public.

Yet for all that, it's unlikely that the states will save much, if any, money by contracting with the private companies. Private prison cost cutting primarily serves to boost company profits. As early as 1996, a report of the U.S. General Accounting Office thoroughly reviewed a series of academic and state studies and concluded that there was no clear evidence of cost savings. The most optimistic academic advocate of privatizing prisons, Charles Thomas (a criminologist who directed the Private Corrections Project at the University of Florida), had claimed that savings of 10 percent to 20 percent could be expected. But then it came to light that he'd been paid $3 million in consulting fees by private prison corporations. He was penalized by the Florida Ethics Commission, which enforces the state's conflict of interest laws, and had to shut down his research institute at the university.

Moreover, the financial advantage that may have been most attractive to state legislators—the private companies' ability to construct prisons unhindered by public debt limits or by the need to get voter approval for bonds—has turned out to be the industry's downfall. From 1991 to 1998, according to Charles Thomas's data (unfortunately, the only data available), the growth in private adult prison beds averaged 36 percent per year.[15] But with the states pulling back from the trouble-plagued facilities and Wall Street reacting even more strongly to the deaths and scandals, the companies have found themselves overleveraged and under-capitalized. CCA, for example, built new prisons "on spec," assuming that contracts to fill them would follow, and by my estimate the company had more than 8,500 prison beds standing empty in 2001. The firm came close to a financial meltdown: its stock lost 93 percent of its value in 2000, and its accountants reported a fourth quarter loss of more than a third of a billion dollars.[16]

Human rights advocates, public employee unions, prisoners' rights activists, and student groups have not let these developments pass unnoticed. Many activists have rallied together in protests targeting annual stockholder meetings of the major private prison companies. A national wave of student protests on college campuses last year forced Sodexho Alliance, CCA's largest corporate stockholder, to divest its shares. These diverse opponents have helped put these problems under the media spotlight, including a now well-reported discussion of the industry's many scandals and operational disasters. Thus, it should be no surprise that so many states are now backing away from for-profit companies.

But while most state correctional managers are taking a hard look at the private prison industry, the federal government stepped up to fill the breach. Says Steven Logan, the CEO of Cornell Corrections, "On the federal side, there's an unprecedented [new market]—to the tune of approximately 20,000 beds that are expected to be set out for people to bid on over the next 24 months."[17] If Logan is right, the feds have been poised to take up a lot of the slack—and, in fact, to spur new construction—by showering the industry with contracts that will be worth $4.6 billion over the next 10 years.[18]

Until recently, the Federal Bureau of Prisons (FBOP) had moved relatively slowly down the road to privatization. It awarded its first private prison contract only in 1997 to Wackenhut for operation of a 2,048-bed prison complex for low and minimum security federal prisoners in Taft, California. A second contract was awarded to CCA in 1998 for a 1,500-bed facility in Eloy, Arizona. But as the industry's troubles escalated, Congress required the FBOP to contract for more private beds, insisting on private prisons for at least half the prisoners at the District of Columbia's prison complex at Lorton, Virginia, which was scheduled to shut down. And then the FBOP launched a massive privatization initiative of its own throughout the country.[19]

In part, this was a response to the rapid growth of the federal prisoner population. Between 1995 and 1999, while the incarceration rate nationwide grew by 16 percent, in the federal prison system it rose by 31 percent. By June of this year, the FBOP was responsible for some 127,000 sentenced criminals and perhaps 25,000 other detainees; its prisons were operating at 33 percent over their capacity. And like the state legislators before them, members of Congress were madly building new prisons (26 were under construction or in the development pipeline in 2001), searching for cheap new private prison beds, and refusing to consider changes in the draconian sentencing laws that were causing most of the increase in prisoners.

In fact, the Illegal Immigration Reform and Immigrant Responsibility Act and the Antiterrorism and Effective Death Penalty Act, new laws passed by Congress in 1996, have conveniently created a special population of prisoners—immigrant prisoners—whom the feds seem comfortable segregating from the rest of the prison population and turning over to the private companies.

Find and Deport

It's common knowledge that the harsh drug sentencing laws Congress enacted in 1986 have greatly increased the federal prison population. (In 1984 just 30 percent of federal prisoners were drug offenders; today 57 percent are.[20]) Less known is the impact of federal immigration policies. Since at least 1994, Congress has put enormous pressure on federal officials to find and deport troublesome immigrants (both legal residents and undocumented immigrants). This trend has accelerated in the wake of September 11 attacks in New York City and Washington, D.C. In the 1996 Immigration Reform Act, Congress widely expanded the list of crimes for which a noncitizen must be deported after serving his or her sentence. These crimes, called "aggravated felonies," are now defined to include many offenses that are neither aggravated nor even, in many jurisdictions, felonies. Fueled by this statute and political pressure, an all-out law enforcement campaign has erupted to find crime-committing immigrants (even relatively petty offenders, and those whose only "crime" is attempting to re-enter the country). With this campaign has come an explosion in the number of non-U.S. citizens in federal prison, the so called "criminal alien" population.

There were more than 36,000 noncitizens serving criminal sentences in federal prisons at the end of February 2002, up from 18,929 only eight years before. About half of them were Mexican citizens, 10 percent Colombians, 7 percent Cubans, and the rest an assortment of other nationalities. In addition, several thousand other noncitizens are being held in federal prisons, not as convicts serving criminal sentences, but as pretrial or pre-deportation detainees. These include many "lifers," or people awaiting deportation who have completed their criminal sentences in state or federal prison, but who remain incarcerated because no country will take them. A U.S. Supreme Court ruling[21] in June 2001 prohibited the indefinite detention of certain lifers, but according to Judy Rabinovitz, senior staff counsel at the American Civil Liberties Union's Immigrants' Rights Project, the decision is unlikely to affect most of those in FBOP facilities.

Telling evidence that the federal law enforcement campaign specifically targets immigrants comes from Peter H. Schuck, a professor at Yale Law School. In 1998 Schuck found that while immigrants (legal as well as undocumented) made up 9.3 percent of the American population and a roughly comparable 7.6 percent of the prison population of the states, they made up a vastly disproportionate 29 percent of those in federal prisons.[22]

The "criminal aliens" in federal prison are apparently a relatively unthreatening group of prisoners. According to the federal Bureau of Justice Statistics (BJS), about a third of them were sentenced for immigration violations, and just 1.5 percent of them were sentenced for violent offenses (compared with 15 percent of the U.S. citizens in federal prison). A BJS research project found that even those convicted of drug sales are likely to have played a lesser role in the transaction than did U.S. citizens convicted on drug sale charges. This may also help to explain why these prisoners have been singled out for incarceration in privately run prisons. Criminal aliens typically require only low security prisons, since most of them have been classified as low security prisoners. And as

Mike Janus, privatization administrator at the FBOP, points out, they face deportation at the end of their sentences and therefore do not require the kinds of education and counseling programs available in regular federal prisons.[23]

Off the record, the FBOP officials say that they're confident they can oversee the private companies better than the states have. On the record, they say they are simply seeking "management flexibility" to deal with this burgeoning segment of the prison population in a less program-rich environment than other prisoners require. But that's not far from acknowledging that they think they can get away with providing second-class prisons for these second-class prisoners.

If We Build It, They Will Come

The FBOP's first request for proposals to provide up to 7,500 low security beds for this population was issued in September 1999. As phase one of the plan, private contractors were to meet the prison system's "criminal alien requirements"—this phase was called CAR-I for short. The beds were to serve California, Arizona, New Mexico, Texas, and Oklahoma.

A CAR-I proposal by Cornell Corrections to house almost 2,000 prisoners at a facility near Santa Fe that the company hoped to lease from the state of New Mexico was eliminated from the competition as a result of vigorous opposition from a local coalition of immigrant rights advocates, civil rights and church leaders, and prison reformers.[24] But in June of 2000, two other CAR-I contracts were signed with CCA: one for 2,304 beds at the company's long-empty "spec" prison at California City, California, and the other for 1,012 beds at its Cibola facility in Milan, New Mexico. (This is the facility where, some months later, guards tear-gassed hundreds of prisoners who were protesting conditions.) These contracts are for an initial three-year term, followed by seven one-year renewal options. They will be worth about $760 million over 10 years.[25]

For CCA, which carried more than $1 billion in outstanding indebtedness in 2000 and was in violation of its credit agreements, the two contracts provided a virtual bailout.[26] The company's many creditors were willing to extend it waivers. But without the federal contracts, John D. Ferguson, the company's new CEO, frankly admitted that CCA would likely have been forced into bankruptcy.[27]

A second request for proposals, CAR-II, was issued in July of 2000 for private prison beds to be located in Alabama, Florida, Mississippi, and Georgia. Five private companies and one Mississippi county proposed 14 possible CAR-II sites. In the fall of 2001, the field was narrowed to two recommended sites. The apparent winners of this sweepstakes were CCA and Cornell, but by April 2002 the contract awards were still pending final review by the FBOP. CCA's proposed site was a "spec" prison already built by the company in McRae, Georgia, that had been standing empty for almost two years. Cornell Corrections proposed an undeveloped site in McComb, Mississippi, that would require new prison construction from the ground up.[28]

A CAR-III solicitation was issued in November 2000 for three 1,500-bed facilities in California and Arizona. By the January 2001 deadline, six companies, one town, and a sheriff's department had submitted 20 prospective sites.[29] Less than a week later, the FBOP filed public notice that it anticipated a CAR-IV as well, for Delaware, Kentucky, Ohio, Virginia, and West Virginia.[30]

The momentum of the contracting process appears to have been slowed by the post-9/11 anthrax incidents, when public comments on the CAR-II environmental impact statements that were mailed to the FBOP were held up for examination for possible contamination. As months passed with no news of the impending contracts for either CAR-II or CAR-III, company executives remained bullish on the future, predicting that the "War on Terrorism" will increase the level of federal contracts. In February George Zoley told the stock analysts who follow his company that Wackenhut stands to gain new business from stepped-up efforts to detain undocumented immigrants:

> It's almost an oddity that . . . given the size of our country and the number of illegal immigrants entering our country that we have such a small number of beds for detention purposes, and I think this has become an issue under the "homeland security" theme, and I think it's likely we're going to see an increase in that area.

Then, in mid-March 2002, a sudden development stunned anti-privatization activists in Arizona and California, the target states for CAR-III contracts. On March 15 the FBOP notified public officials that the Bureau had cancelled the CAR-III solicitation, citing new prison population projections that indicated a reduced rate of growth.[31]

The End of the Bail-Out?

At the time of the CAR-III cancellation, the future of the FBOP CAR contracting initiatives was impossible to predict. No word was forthcoming about the status of the promised CAR-II contracts. No information was available about the new FBOP forecast for future prison bed needs. The private prison industry had worked hard for many years to develop powerful political allies at the highest levels of the federal government. Michael J. Quinlan, the FBOP director under the first President George Bush, had recently announced that he would be stepping down from his post as the chief operating officer of CCA as soon as a replacement could be found. But Norman Carlson, a director of the FBOP under President Ronald Reagan, remained a member of Wackenhut's board of directors, as did Benjamin R. Civiletti, who served as Attorney General during the Carter Administration.

Meanwhile, generous federal campaign contributions ($528,000 between 1995 and 2000) and the best lobbyists that money can buy have spread the influence of private prison companies beyond the personal networks of their executives and board members to the halls of Congress. There are grassroots pressures for expanding private prison contracts as well, coming from desperate pockets of rural America where prisons are seen as a source of new jobs. And there is every reason to expect that the current administration will not easily back off from efforts to expand privatization in the future. With 42 private prisons located within its borders, President Bush's home state of Texas is the world capital of the private prison industry.

To be sure, political opposition to privatization of prisons is growing. The private prison industry's record of human rights violations, violence, and prisoner escapes has fueled an unusual alliance between prison reform advocates and guards (union members in government run institutions), who ally with student groups and community organizations. Though the interests among these groups are often widely varied, the end goal is the same: to fight further expansion of prisons for profit. In most states where prison population growth is finally slowing or halting, enthusiasm for privatization seems to have waned, and contracting opportunities have almost disappeared. But prison privatization is unlikely to be permanently abandoned by the federal system unless the growth of the federal prison population is brought under firm control. And that means that the effort to reform federal sentencing guidelines and change the immigration laws must continue.

It's a good cause. The anti-immigrant laws adopted by Congress in 1996, especially as they interact with federal drug laws, create particularly unfair punishments for noncitizens, most of whom are subject to harsh and rigid sentences for drug offenses, with no consideration of mitigating circumstances or the offender's actual role in the crime. And then they are further punished with deportation. The federal plan to create and expand a huge second tier of segregated immigrant prisons— whether public or private—is an irrational and expensive way to avoid coming to terms with those fundamental injustices.

Notes

1. Monico Polanco, "Bartlett Jail Faulted in Escape Study, Criminal Justice report cites 16 Problems, Human Error," *The Austin American-Statesman*, October 18, 2000.
2. Associated Press Newswires, "Ex-prison Supervisors Told They will be Jailed for Beating Prisoner," *Associated Press*, October 27, 2000.
3. Associated Press, "Five Prisoners Injured in Jail Melee," *The Houston Chronicle*, November 9, 2000.
4. *William P. v. Corrections Corporation of America* C/A No.: 3:98–290–17 "Verdict, Phase I" document, filed on December 14, 2000.

5. Associated Press, "Torrance County Prison Gets New Warden in Wake of Riot," *The Albuquerque Tribune,* December 1, 2000.
6. Susan Hylton, "Jail Warden Ignores Rehab, Ex-staffer Says," *The Tulsa World,* May 4, 2001.
7. Staff Reports. "Jail Error Lets Out Another Prisoner," *The Tulsa World,* May 30, 2001; Associated Press. "Another Prisoner is Mistakenly Released from Tulsa Jail," *AP State & Local,* June 5, 2001.
8. Bill Miller, "10 D.C. Guards Charged in Smuggling Sting," *The Washington Post,* June 1, 2001.
9. Susan Hylton, "Jail Staff Member Resigns Amid Drug Allegations," *The Tulsa World,* June 13, 2001.
10. Ty Tagami, "Riot Rocks Private Prison in Floyd, *The Lexington Herald-Leader,* July 7, 2001; Associated Press, "Top Two Prison Officials Fired in Wake of Uprising," *The AP,* July 18, 2001.
11. Fox Butterfield, "Privately Run Juvenile Prison in Louisiana Is Attacked for Abuse of 6 Prisoners," *The New York Times,* March 16, 2000.
12. Judith Greene, "Comparing Private and Public Prison Services and Programs in Minnesota: Findings from Prisoner Interviews," *Current Issues in Criminal Justice,* Vol. II, No. 2.
13. James Austin and Garry Coventry, "Are We Better Off? Comparing Private and Public Prisons in the United States," *Current Issues in Criminal Justice,* Vol. II, No. 2.
14. Personal communication with Paul Korotkin, director, Program Planning, Research and Evaluation, New York State Division of Correctional Services.
15. Charles Thomas, "Ten Year Growth in Rated Capacity of Private Secure Adult Correctional Facilities," December 31, 1998. *Private Adult Correctional Facility Census* online at http://web.crim.ufl.edu/pcp/
16. Getahn Ward, "CCA Reports Big Quarterly Loss," *The Nashville Tennessean,* March 14, 2001.
17. Steven Logan comments during a teleconference with investment analysts, transcript on file with author.
18. This figure is calculated from the announced value of the first two "CAR" contracts received by CCA in June 2000.
19. See Requests for Proposals for "Criminal Alien Requirement" phase II and III, posted at http://www.bop.gov/ under the "Acquisitions" link.
20. Allen J. Beck, and Paige Harrison. *Prisoners in 2000.* Washington, D.C.: Bureau of Justice Statistics. August 2001.
21. *Zadvydas v. Davis,* 533 v.s. 628 (2001).
22. Peter H. Schuck, "Removing Criminal Aliens: The Pitfalls and Promises of Federalism," *The Harvard Journal of Law and Public Policy,* Vol. 22, Issue 2, Spring 1999.
23. Comments by Michael Janus during a presentation at a World Research Group conference, "Privatizing Correctional Facilities," held in San Antonio on September 25–26, 2000.
24. Dale Lezon, "Cornell Passed Over for Contract," *The Albuquerque Journal,* April 14, 2000.
25. CCA Press Release. "Corrections Corporation of America Contracts With BOP for 3,316 Beds," *PR Newswire,* June 12, 2000.
26. Getahn Ward, "Default Waiver, New Pact Give Prison Realty Some Breathing Room," *The Nashville Tennessean,* June 14, 2000.
27. Comments by John Furguson during a teleconference with investment analysts, transcript on file with author.
28. *Federal Register.* Vol. 65, No. 145, July 27, 2000.
29. *Federal Register.* Vol. 65, No. 182, September 19, 2000.
30. Federal Bureau of Prisons Property and Procurements Branch, "Correctional Facility, Privately Owned and Operated," *Commerce Business Daily,* January 17, 2001.
31. Letter from Connie Tatko, FBOP Contracting Officer, to California State Senator Wm. J. "Pete" Knight, dated March 15, 2002.

Juvenile Crime Pays—But at What Cost?

ALEX FRIEDMAN

According to a study by the Office of Juvenile Justice and Delinquency Prevention (OJJDP), from 1991 to 1995 the population of youthful offenders held in privately operated facilities grew 10 percent to an estimated 35,600. The juvenile justice system has become enormously profitable as youths are channeled from the schoolhouse to the jailhouse in ever-increasing numbers. In 1997 Equitable Securities Research released a report entitled "At-Risk Youth: A Growth Industry," which indicates there are 10,000 to 15,000 private juvenile justice service providers; publicly traded juvenile corrections companies made $75 million in net profit in 1996 alone. An estimated $3 billion is spent each year on services for juvenile offenders at the federal, state and local levels, and up to $50 billion is spent annually on programs for at-risk youth.

Private-sector companies that primarily provide adult corrections services are jumping on the "jails for juveniles" bandwagon: The Corrections Corporation of America (CCA) and Wackenhut operate seven juvenile facilities each, and the Corrections Services Corporation operates six. In May 1997, Cornell Corrections, another adult prison contractor, announced its interest in acquiring the privately held Abraxas Group, a leader in juvenile supervision services that provides residential, educational, and treatment programs to over 1,300 youths. Cornell already manages a Youth Development Center in Georgia and is in the process of converting a county jail in New Mexico into a juvenile detention facility.

Most privatized services for youthful offenders, however, are provided by companies that specialize in that field. One of the industry leaders is Youth Services International (YSI). As of January 1997, YSI was managing 20 juvenile facilities with over 4,000 beds in twelve states; the com-

---

This article was written in February 1998.

pany has annual revenues of approximately $100 million. Youthtrack, another service provider, operates juvenile justice programs in Colorado; the company recently entered into a contract to manage a detention facility for youthful offenders in Bayamon, Puerto Rico. Other established companies in the for-profit juvenile corrections industry include Rebound, Inc. and Children's Comprehensive Services.

The privatization of corrections-related services for youthful offenders, including incarceration, has received mixed reviews. Cash-strapped state and local governments faced with burgeoning juvenile offender populations have embraced the concept. "The private sector is financially better able to fill the immediacy of the need to offer the kinds of programs that [are] necessary," says John Joyce of the Florida Department of Juvenile Justice. Judy Brisco with the Texas Youth Commission agrees: "They fill a vital role because we can't meet the needs of every kid."

The public's reaction to private juvenile justice services has been less conciliatory. In early 1997, for example, YSI's plans to build and operate detention centers in Pennsylvania and New York were canceled after the company met with stiff resistance from local community members. Such opposition is partly a "not in my backyard" attitude, while other criticisms mirror those leveled against private companies that operate adult prisons: An industry that profits from crime has a conflict of interest in rehabilitating offenders, it is immoral for companies to profit from people who are incarcerated, and it is ethically questionable for the government to contract its custody and control of prisoners to the private sector. (In reference to juveniles this could be termed "in loco parentis for profit.")

Some communities have also voiced concerns about safety and security issues, and these concerns are entirely justified in light of past incidents that have occurred at private juvenile centers. In 1994 Rebound lost a three-year, $150 million contract with Baltimore County, Maryland, to manage the Charles R. Hickey School, a facility for hardcore youthful offenders, after the company allowed too many escapes. One year later a Rebound facility in Brush, Colorado, was harshly criticized in an independent evaluation that found "a consistent and disturbing pattern of violence, sexual abuse, clinical malpractice, and administrative incompetence at every level of the program." Colorado's juvenile corrections division admitted that it had to lower its contract performance standards for the facility because the state was dependent on Rebound to provide bed space. Further, in March 1997, Florida canceled a detention center contract with Rebound due to inadequate performance.

Other juvenile justice service providers have had similar problems. In July 1994, the same week that YSI assumed Rebound's canceled contract to operate the Charles R. Hickey School, a juvenile escaped from the facility. Four months later a female employee was raped by a youth at the school's sex offender unit; she had been left alone with the juvenile, which was a violation of the terms in YSI's contract. The senior staff member at the school was fired. And on June 5, 1995, seven juveniles overpowered a bus driver and three counselors and escaped as they were being driven across campus; several other youths were injured when the bus crashed.

Sometimes the problem is not with the juvenile offenders but instead with the company contracted to incarcerate them. The worst-case scenario in this regard resulted in South Carolina's June 1997 decision to decline to renew a $14 million contract with CCA to operate the 400-bed Columbia Training Center. Seven youths escaped in August 1996, and the facility's administrator was replaced. A review of operations at the training center three months later found that staff members had used excessive force; this was confirmed in an independent evaluation commissioned by the governor's office in January 1997. CCA employees were accused of hog-tying the juveniles, and several of the youths claimed they had been subjected to physical abuse and were denied food, medicine, and toilet facilities. After eight more juveniles escaped from the training center in February 1997, CCA agreed to withdraw from the contract, stating it was "inordinately distracting to both parties."

Despite these setbacks, the private juvenile corrections industry continues to grow as state and local governments attempt to cope with decreasing budgets and increasing numbers of youthful offenders. And despite a 9.28 percent drop in violent juvenile crime in 1997, enthusiasm for building even more private juvenile facilities has not dampened. Diane McClure, CEO of Securicor New Century, speaking at the Second Annual Privatizing Corrections Conference said, "Our market analysis shows that despite recent reports of decline, juvenile crime will continue to rise and demand for beds will remain solid."

But whether society will benefit from privatizing the juvenile corrections system remains in doubt—especially considering that for-profit juvenile justice companies are accountable to their stockholders and not to the tax-paying public that foots the bill for the services they provide. The true measure of the effectiveness of the private juvenile corrections industry will not be realized until the youthful offenders incarcerated in privately-managed facilities today grow up to become the law-abiding, or law-breaking, adults of tomorrow.

The National Juvenile Detention Association estimates that 5 percent of the nation's juvenile detention facilities are privately operated, and the construction of for-profit prisons, jails, and boot camps for youthful offenders is a rapidly expanding industry. By slashing operating costs and providing subsistence level services, companies can reap handsome profits from the millions of dollars they receive through largely unregulated government contracts.

As a result of this profit-margin mentality, an increasing number of privately operated juvenile detention facilities are being cited for alarming conditions, with reports ranging from all-out torture and abuse of children housed in the facilities, to rampant administrative and staff misconduct and mismanagement.

Fear and Loathing in Louisiana

The Justice Department filed suit November 5, 1998, against the state of Louisiana for failing to protect juvenile prisoners from brutality and for providing inadequate education, medical, and mental health care.

"It's incredibly unusual," said David Utter, director of the Juvenile Justice Project of Louisiana, which has also filed suit against Louisiana over conditions at one of its four juvenile prisons, the privately owned Tallulah Correctional Center for Youth. "I don't even know when the Justice Department ever filed suit in a case like this."

"Over the past two years," the Justice Department told the *New York Times*, "the Justice Department has repeatedly advised state officials of the specific deficiencies and the corrective action needed. The state has failed or refused to address the Justice Department's findings in many critical ways."

A 1997 investigation by the Department of Justice (DOJ) found that guards at the Tallulah prison routinely beat juveniles at the facility, and a 1998 DOJ report cited Tallulah's lack of treatment for mentally ill adolescents who, investigators say, are dumped into the general prison population where they are frequently victimized.

In a one-week period in May of 1998, 70 of the 620 boys at Tallulah were sent to the infirmary after being involved in fights. Many had cuts and bruises; one had been raped. Another youth begged not to be returned to a dormitory where he said a fellow prisoner had been sexually abusing him for weeks. And a former juvenile offender, a 16-year-old who served 18 months at Tallulah for stealing a bike, said youths often fought each other over food and clothes.

State prison officials disputed many of the DOJ findings, but conceded that mentally ill juveniles were improperly placed in the general prison population. Investigators said many of the deficiencies were due to high employee turnover (up to 100 percent in one year). Tallulah guards are paid just $5.77 an hour.

Tallulah is operated by TransAmerican Development Associates Inc., which receives $16 million a year—$71 a day per juvenile. The company's principal owners/directors include George Fischer, a campaign manager for former Governor Edwin Edwards, who was later convicted of racketeering; Verdi Adams, a former state highway engineer who has other business dealings with Fischer; and James R. Brown, the son of late state senator Charles Brown.

On July 22, 1998, Louisiana officials took temporary control of the Tallulah facility following a disturbance by 15 youths and the resignation of the prison's warden. A team of 35 guards was sent in from the state's adult prison system and state officials announced plans to create a special facility for Louisiana's mentally ill juvenile offenders. One likely candidate to operate the proposed facility, they say, is TransAmerican Development.

Louisiana has repeatedly insisted that it has tried to make changes at Tallulah and its three state-run juvenile prisons and that Federal investigators have exaggerated the problems.

The owners of Tallulah have also complained that the improvements demanded by the Justice Department would be so expensive that it would put them out of business.

Misconduct in Colorado

The High Plains Youth Center in Brush, Colorado, a 180-bed facility operated by Denver-based Rebound, Inc., was closed by state officials in April 1998, following an investigation that revealed abuse and mismanagement.

High Plains was originally built for adult prisoners, but after the initial investors went bankrupt Rebound acquired the facility to incarcerate children. The company charged between $140 and $180 a day to house juveniles—many of them violent offenders—from jurisdictions as far away as Washington, D.C.

Juveniles at High Plains told investigators they had been choked and kneed in the back by company guards; records indicate that some youths were physically restrained up to five times a day. Several female staff members were suspected of having sex with children at the facility and two employees were fired for sexual misconduct. From January to April 1998, state officials documented seven cases of physical abuse, four of sexual abuse and ten of neglect.

Colorado authorities finally took action and began an intensive investigation after 13-year-old Matthew Maloney, a mentally ill youth from Utah, hung himself in February 1998. When his body was found he had been dead almost four hours.

According to state investigators many of the problems at High Plains were related to low pay and excessive staff turnover—25 of 164 employees had left the facility within a three-month period. The work force was stretched so thin that juveniles said they had to help staff members restrain other prisoners. Only half the required number of employees were on duty the night that Matthew died.

Other problems were attributed to mentally ill juveniles housed at the facility. Rebound had advertised High Plains as providing services for youths with mental illnesses, although the center did not have adequate mental health care and was not licensed to provide such services. State investigators found 22 youths on psychotropic medication when they audited the facility.

Privately-managed facilities routinely accept mentally ill youths because they can charge higher fees to house them, even though they frequently are unable to provide sufficient mental health care. Mental health authorities estimate that up to 20 percent of incarcerated juveniles have serious psychiatric problems. Consequently, youths with mental illnesses pose a danger to staff members, other adolescent offenders, and themselves.

The Colorado Department of Human Services revoked Rebound's operating license for High Plains on April 20, 1998, citing unsafe conditions and inadequate care. Company officials called the closing of the center "inappropriate." Rebound spokesperson Tom Schilling insisted, "High Plains remains a safe facility for youths and always has been safe."

Other Rebound facilities have been closed by state authorities in Florida and Maryland; Florida officials described one of the company's programs as being "largely out of control."

Not Isolated Incidents

The above examples of misconduct and mismanagement at privately-run juvenile facilities are not isolated incidents. Arkansas recently canceled a youth detention center contract with Associated Marine Institutes, a Florida-based company, following allegations of abuse and questions about financial accountability.

In 1997, in Florida, Dade County Circuit Judge Thomas Petersen criticized a Pahokee detention center managed by Correctional Services Corporation. Youths at the facility said they had been stripped to their underwear or left naked locked in solitary confinement and prohibited from sitting down or falling asleep.

This is not to imply that privately operated juvenile facilities have a monopoly on abuse and malfeasance as opposed to their public counterparts. Systemic deficiencies exist in many state juvenile justice departments, largely the result of a politically driven trend to incarcerate more and more youthful offenders. When lawmakers authorize spending for the construction and expansion of juvenile prisons they often neglect to appropriate adequate finds for educational, vocational, and treatment services. According to Georgia Department of Juvenile Justice Chairman Sherman Day, it is "much easier to get new facilities from the legislature than to get more programs."

University Professor Shills for Private Prison Industry

ALEX FRIEDMAN

Much of the statistical and academic information regarding prison privatization that is reported in the media (and consequently relied upon by lawmakers deciding whether to contract with private prison companies) comes from Charles W. Thomas, director of the Private Corrections Project at the University of Florida, Gainesville.

The Private Corrections Project is funded by grants from the private prison industry—including CCA, Wackenhut, Cornell, U.S. Corrections Corporation, and Correctional Services Corporation—that amount to $50,000 to $60,000 annually. The money is channeled as unrestricted donations through the University of Florida Research Foundation. Documents supplied by the university indicate that the project received over $250,000 between 1990 and 1996; according to Dr. Thomas, the amount is more than $400,000. Although Thomas's salary is paid by the university, his expenses and summer salary ($26,845 in 1997) are funded by the Research Foundation.

In an interview with *The National Times*, Thomas admitted he had money invested in "substantially all" of the private prison companies, but refused to say how much. On April 25, 1997, the *Wall Street Journal* reported that Thomas was being named a board member of the CCA Prison Realty Trust; he receives an annual salary of $12,000 with options to buy 5,000 shares of stock. The chairman of Prison Realty was Doctor R. Crants, who was also chairman and CEO of CCA. CCA merged with Prison Realty Trust on January 1, 1999.

According to a Prison Realty document filed with the Securities and Exchange Commission, "Charles W. Thomas, a member of the Prison Realty Board and a director of New Prison Realty, has performed and will continue to perform, certain consulting services in connection with the merger for a fee of $3 million."

This article was written in February 1999.

An ethics complaint was filed against Professor Thomas for his financial involvement with the private corrections industry while conducting research in that field. The ethics complaint against Thomas was filed by the Florida union that represents prison guards. Kathy Chinoy, chairperson of the Florida Commission on Ethics, stated on June 2, 1998 that "[t]here is probable cause to believe that Dr. Thomas violated [ethics standards] by having a contractual relationship with private corrections companies or companies related to the private corrections industry, which conflict with his duty to objectively evaluate the corrections industry through his research with the University." Professor Thomas and the Florida Attorney General's office have failed to negotiate a settlement of the case, which is being referred to the Division of Administrative Hearings.

Professor Thomas has denied there is a conflict of interest.

Sources

The National Times, The Wall Street Journal, Prison Privatization Report International, Corrections USA, press release.

[Editor's note: Thomas was eventually found to have a conflict of interest and subsequently resigned from his position with the university.]

Campus Activism Defeats Multinational's Prison Profiteering

KEVIN PRANIS

Times are hard. So hard that in many states, politicians are talking more about closing prisons than building new ones. The 1990s was the golden age of prison expansion in America. During that decade, the number of men and women behind bars nearly doubled, from 1.1 million in 1990 to almost 2 million in 2000, and spending on incarceration approached $40 billion. Recognizing an opportunity to make fortunes off the backs of prisoners and their families, Corporate America—including architects, bankers, building contractors, and telephone companies—lined up at the prison trough.

And it wasn't just American companies. The sweet smell of profit attracted foreign multinationals as well—among them Sodexho Alliance, a Paris-based catering company. Unlike the company's rivals in the food service industry, Sodexho was not content to make money by feeding prisoners. Instead, in 1994, Sodexho entered into a strategic alliance with the world's largest private prison company, Corrections Corporation of America.

Over the next few years, Sodexho became not only CCA's largest shareholder, but also the private prison company's partner in a joint venture to spread the gospel of private prisons across the globe. By the end of the decade, the ties that bound the two companies together included joint ownership of private prison subsidiaries in the U.K. and Australia, with interlocking boards of directors. (Sodexho was given the only contractually guaranteed seat on CCA's board of directors, while top CCA executives served not only on Sodexho Alliance's board of directors, but also on the board of Sodexho's U.S. subsidiary, Sodexho Marriott Services.) The companies also had mutual membership in, and financial sponsorship of, the American Legislative Exchange Council—a right-

---

This article was written in January 2002.

wing state lobby group that pushes prison privatization and "tough-on-crime" legislation along, with a host of other conservative causes.

By 1998, it looked as if everything was coming up roses for the two companies. CCA's stock shot to an all-time high of $46, and the jointly owned Australian and U.K. subsidiaries were pulling down new private prison contracts. Then things started to go horribly wrong. As prison expansion slowed and opposition to privatization grew, CCA suddenly found itself stuck paying for empty prisons that the company had built "on speculation." Once shareholders and analysts realized that the company was cooking its books all hell broke loose, and the price of CCA stock went into a free fall, reaching an all-time low of 18 cents before bouncing back to just over a dollar.

During the next year, Sodexho worked with CCA management and other key investors to put the prison company back on its feet. But by this time Sodexho had its own problems. A national network of student activists working under the banner "Not With Our Money!" had launched a series of protests on campuses served by Sodexho Marriott Services. Within a year, the Dump Sodexho campaign had spread to more than 60 colleges and universities across the United States and Canada, and the company had lost contracts at seven active schools. On May 19, 2001, the business headline in *The Tennessean* read, "CCA majority shareholder to sell stocks: French food catering giant pressured by college students."

The "Dump Sodexho" campaign was waged by college students who not only took the industrial part of the "prison-industrial complex" head-on, but who also successfully linked prison issues to critical issues of campus democracy, workers' rights, and corporate power through a medium that virtually every student (or former student) in America can understand—the dreaded dining hall!

> Everywhere we go,
> people wanna know
> why we're here.
> So we tell them,
> "We hate private prisons
> and Sodexho's food!"

December 5, 2000. The cadence floats on winter winds across the campus of Buffalo State College, an urban, working-class school where more than a hundred students and community members have gathered to protest the school's catering contract with Sodexho Marriott Services. The marchers arrive at their destination and shiver in the cold as they listen to an unusual group of speakers—including a member of the City Council, a prison guard and a former prisoner—condemn both private prisons and those who seek to profit from them.

The administrators who need to hear the message are hiding in the brick fortress of Cleveland Hall, insulated behind locked doors and campus police officers, but the students are resourceful. At the appointed moment, the students slip into the building and up the stairs until they reach the locked door outside the President's office.

After a boisterous hour of chanting and door-pounding, thirty-five students get what they're looking for—an opportunity to grill Vice-President Hal D. Payne. How, an African American student asks Payne, can an African-American administrator of a public college, which is itself being drained of resources by prison expansion, defend doing business with a company connected to punishment for profit?

Payne tries to tell the students that they've got it all wrong—it's the state's Rockefeller Drug Laws that are responsible for the shameful number of young men and women of color behind bars, not Sodexho. In theory, Payne is absolutely right. To paraphrase the NRA, "Prisons don't sentence people; people are sentenced to prison." Anyway, New York's prisons are *public*, so isn't Sodexho's involvement in the *private* prison industry beside the point?

But the student protesters are unmoved by Payne's words, which are too little and too late. Where were the State University administrators when a broad coalition began calling two years ago for the repeal of the Rockefeller laws? For that matter, where were they when governors Mario Cuomo and George Pataki shifted $600 million a year from higher education to prisons? And why the newfound interest in sentencing reform just as students have discovered an outpost of the prison-industrial complex lurking on their doorstep?

Buffalo State will keep its Sodexho contract since, for reasons nobody can explain, Sodexho's is the only bid that met the school's qualifications, but the work that Buffalo students have begun will continue.

Sodexho executives are still struggling to understand how the largest food service provider in North America became better known for its relationship to the private prison industry than for its mystery loaf. Here's the inside story:

1995. The best kept secret in America is that there are roughly two million men and women living behind bars—mostly young, poor, and of color. Few Americans are aware of the social costs, from the criminalization of a generation to the draining of funds from education and social services, and fewer still are aware of the social forces driving prison expansion, particularly the use of prisons as a form of "economic development" for poor rural communities. Twenty years of research and advocacy on alternatives seems like so much spit in the wind, and many have either given up or started to spit in the other direction.

But there are stirrings among a few progressive activists who are talking about the need to oppose a "prison-industrial complex" which functions much like the military-industrial complex. All of us believe that the fate of American democracy depends on stopping the gears from turning. We just don't know how.

Over the next several years, prison organizing made slow progress while media coverage skyrocketed. In 1995, major papers ran a story about prison issues every few weeks. Soon it was once a week, then once a day, and then we stopped trying to keep track. The coverage was driven in part by the work of Washington, D.C.-based groups like Justice Policy Institute and The Sentencing Project but equally important were the sheer volume of fascinating and scandalous stories generated by the nation's vast gulag.

Racial profiling, racial disparities, mothers in prisons, rape in prison, costly prison expansion, corporate prisons—all of the stories that were reported by the media and reinforced by the consciousness-raising efforts of prison activists—began to generate rage among young activists and unease in the public at large.

At the same time, there was an activist renaissance on campuses and in the streets that had much (although not everything) to do with the new leadership of the labor movement. In the Fall of 1996, graduates of the AFL-CIO's Union Summer internship, who had learned to knock on doors and talk to strangers about social issues, took their newly acquired skills into dormitories and dining halls. A series of labor teach-ins took place around the country, adding momentum to campus and community movements for workers' rights. The sweatshop movement exploded by providing students with an easy way to connect economic justice abroad to purchasing decisions made by their college administrators.

In November of 1999, the WTO ministerial in Seattle and subsequent (now famous) mass protests focused the nation's attention on growing opposition to corporate power and top-down globalization. But another battle took place in Seattle outside the media spotlight. A mile from the downtown "security zone," a peaceful march of a hundred or so people marching for political prisoner and death row prisoner Mumia Abu Jamal was attacked by police who fired dozens of rounds of tear gas into a residential community. While not as well publicized, this incident was part of growing resistance to police brutality, racial profiling, and other forms of criminal injustice in communities of color.

The "Dump Sodexho" campaign was launched in the wake of Seattle, on the day when, according to a report issued by Justice Policy Institute, the number of people behind bars in the United States was projected to reach two million (February 15, 2000). "Dump Sodexho" spread like wildfire across college campuses where the coalitions and campaign demands reflected a sophisticated understanding of the links between multiple forms of oppression and injustice.

For example, at Oberlin College, where every student is required to take a full meal plan, the Sodexho-prison connection was the catalyst for bringing together prison, labor, socialist, environmental, and student co-op activists around a set of demands that included dumping Sodexho, including temporary workers in the bargaining contract and purchasing more organic food. At the State University of New York at Albany, the Sodexho-prison connection added fuel to a struggle for union recognition on the part of workers organized by the Hotel Employees and Restaurant Employees International Union. At the University of California at Santa Cruz, students of color and members of student government waged a referendum campaign in which students voted overwhelmingly to kick Sodexho off campus.

At the same time, students have adopted tactics that directly challenge "business as usual" on campus while projecting a vision of how things could be different. As students discovered in the course of the campaign, campus food service is basically a scam in which one company is given a monopoly contract to serve in exchange for keeping the administration worry-free. The company often accomplishes this by providing the school with no-interest "loans" for capital improvements that are then repaid through the "contract"—that is, the money students pay for their (often mandatory) meal plans. In fact, students discovered an eerie parallel between the outsourcing of food service and the privatization of prisons—in both cases, companies have little incentive to provide good service, because those most affected by the services have little or no voice in contracting.

Under such circumstances, sustained boycotts are counterproductive (the company just makes less food and more money), and students have taken to organizing one-day symbolic boycotts at which a food alternative is provided. On April 4, 2000, the State University of New York (SUNY)-Binghamton and Earlham College used student organization funds to feed almost 1,000 people, while Hampshire College students organized a potluck that virtually shut down the dining hall. In May, 800 Oberlin students sat on the lawn and ate food cooked by activists, courtesy of the school's vibrant co-op system, while listening to music and speeches about private prisons. In every case, students find that free, good food reminds students why they hate bad expensive food—especially when the company that makes it feeds prison expansion.

It's one thing to fight and quite another to win. Ninety-nine out of one hundred campus administrators agree: the fact that a company is 48 percent owned by prison profiteers, or by the KKK for that matter, should have no bearing on contracting decisions. How else are we going to ensure high-quality food for a low, low price?

Activists in this fight soon discovered what sweatshop and anti-apartheid activists learned before them. Administrators from across the political spectrum will fight tooth and nail to prevent students from having real power on campus. On December 6, the day after the Buffalo State occupation, seven Ithaca College students took over the school's financial aid office. After 34 hours, during which time they were denied food, water, and even the use of a bathroom, the students got what months of letters, meetings, and protests had failed to deliver: a serious meeting with President Peggy Williams. The students won major concessions, including a public forum with national Sodexho representatives. As friends in the sweatshop movement say, "Direct action gets the goods!"

On February 12, 2001, Sodexho Marriott Services' Senior Vice-President and General Counsel, Robert Stern, came to Ithaca College to face the music, in the form of a bunch of angry students and me, representing the campaign entitled "Not With Our Money!" Stern quickly discovered that he had underestimated the activists, who grilled him with pointed questions, not only about Sodexho's ties to the private prison industry, but also about the company's poor record on workers' rights. Stern's most serious misstep came when he was asked what he, personally, thought of prison privatization. Stern replied that, as with any other business, he thought the private sector could "add value" to the operation. To students, Stern might as well have said that South Africa was "like any other country" or sweatshops were "like any other factory."

Ithaca College was the beginning of the end for Sodexho's partnership with CCA. In order to preserve his company's contract at Ithaca, Sodexho CEO Pierre Bellon personally wrote Peggy Williams in early March to inform her that he had received authorization from his board to sell the CCA stock. On campuses, however, the campaign continued to escalate. The Ithaca sit-in was followed by a similar action at Arizona State University, a pair of lost contracts at Oberlin and American University, a week long sleep-out at Xavier University, a sit-in at the University of Texas, and a lost contract at DePaul University, along with dozens of smaller skirmishes at more than 60 campuses where the campaign had taken root.

On May 19, "Dump Sodexho," which had by now received coverage in major national and international publications including *The New York Times*, *The Washington Post*, and *The Evening Standard*, received coverage in CCA's hometown paper. Just eight months earlier, CCA spokeswoman Susan Hart had described the student campaign as "ineffective," but in the *Tennessean* article, which bore the headline "CCA majority shareholder to sell stocks: French food catering giant pressured by college students," the CEO John Ferguson made no attempt to hide the truth—the students had won.

The official announcement came on May 22, during CCA's shareholder meeting, when Ferguson announced that Sodexho had reached an agreement to sell its shares, and Sodexho executive Jean Pierre Cuny had resigned from the CCA board of directors. The news was greeted with great enthusiasm by the odd assortment of students, prison guards, and community activists who had come out to protest the meeting.

Next Steps

The Sodexho victory was a major step forward, but hardly a solution to the problem of prison privatization, much less that of the larger prison-industrial complex. While losing the company's largest shareholder was undoubtedly embarrassing and somewhat painful for CCA, the Sodexho loss couldn't make up for the helping hand provided by the Federal Bureau of Prisons, in the form of lucrative contracts, and Wall Street, in the form of forbearance on CCA's loans. Meanwhile Sodexho, which was forced to abandon its position with CCA, had not yet renounced its global private prison ambitions, which the company continued to pursue through wholly owned subsidiaries in the U.K. and Australia.

After a series of discussions, including a national student strategy conference attended by more than 50 activists, the "Not With Our Money!" campaign made two decisions. First, we decided to work with allies in Australia, France, and the United Kingdom to get Sodexho out of the private prison industry for good. Although Sodexho executives assumed that American students would lose interest once the company divested from CCA, activists have continued to keep the heat on the company here, while in Europe the campaign has just begun to heat up.

In October, a group of more than one hundred immigrants' rights and prison activists occupied a Sodexho owned tour-boat launch in Paris to protest the company's involvement in a number of highly controversial privatization schemes—including the operation of private prisons and detention centers as well as a voucher scheme that advocates say exploits refugees. A week later, *Maximal* (the French version of the men's magazine *Maxim*) published a major feature story on the Sodexho-prison connection. Sodexho's troubles are far from over, as European activists begin to connect the dots and build alliances with U.S. comrades.

Meanwhile, "Not With Our Money!" is taking the campaign against the private prison industry in the United States to the next level by going after Lehman Brothers—a global investment bank that has become the number one dealmaker for the private prison industry. While the rest of Wall Street kept its distance from the troubled industry, Lehman Brothers helped Cornell Corrections, the number three private prison company, set up stock offers and an Enron-esque "special-purpose entity" that netted the prison company $217 million in additional capital.

This year, Lehman Brothers is trying to pull off the biggest-ever private prison financing bailout by helping Corrections Corporation of America refinance a $1 billion credit agreement. The catch is that Lehman Brothers, like Sodexho, does millions of dollars worth of business with public and nonprofit institutions where ordinary people have leverage.

Students at a half-dozen schools—from North Carolina State University to the University of Wisconsin at Madison to the University of California at Riverside—kicked off the Lehman campaign with Valentine's

Day actions (featuring candy hearts printed with messages like "Prison = $$ 4 Lehman"). Meanwhile, in New York, where Lehman makes millions underwriting public bonds, Jews for Racial and Economic Justice has targeted Lehman for a Passover picket (complete with giant inflated frogs representing the plagues that may be visited upon Lehman if they don't get their house in order).

So far, Lehman has chosen to ignore protests against the company's involvement in the prison industry, but that may be a bad move on the part of the investment bank if history is any judge. As Sodexho is still discovering, emotions regarding prison issues run high. The food service company just lost a contract at Cabrillo Community College, where activists found the company's current global prison operations as repugnant as Sodexho's former investments in CCA. Two Jesuit campuses, Wheeling Jesuit University and Xavier University, are also reconsidering their relationship to the company.

Clearly, the best strategy for companies invested in prisons for profit is to get out before it's too late.

Juveniles Held Hostage for Profit by CSC in Florida

ALEX FRIEDMAN

According to a consultant hired by the Florida Department of Juvenile Justice, the Pahokee Youth Development Center operated by the Correctional Services Corporation (CSC) kept ten juvenile detainees beyond their release dates for no reason other than to beef up corporate profits.

Consultant David Bachman wrote in a November 1998 report to the state that the youths were detained beyond their release dates so they would be included in a quarterly head count used to determine the amount of funding that CSC receives.

The Sarasota, Florida-based CSC has a three-year, $30 million contract to manage juvenile detention centers in the city of Pahokee and Polk County. The company operates 15 other juvenile facilities nationwide and in Puerto Rico.

The state of Florida pays CSC an average of $68.40 per detainee/day at the 350-bed Pahokee lockup; the local school district pays the company an additional $2.5 million annually to provide educational services.

The juveniles who were kept beyond their release dates were scheduled to go home a week before the quarterly school board head count. Delaying the release of the ten youths to include them in the count "increased the educational funds and the per diem costs to the state," said Bachman.

Correctional Services vice president Jim Irving denied juveniles were improperly detained to increase the company's income; however, he failed to offer any other explanation why the youths weren't released as scheduled.

The delayed releases cited in Bachman's report are the latest in a series of problems that have plagued the privately operated Pahokee lockup since it opened in January 1997. State officials have confirmed 15 cases of staff abuse; ten employees have been fired; one has resigned and seven

This article was written in June 1999.

have been reprimanded for excessive or improper use of force. The state has repeatedly warned CSC about its failure to train staff in the proper use of force.

In July 1998, juveniles complained to Dade County Circuit Judge Thomas Petersen about conditions at the center, saying they had been stripped to their underwear (and sometimes naked), placed in solitary confinement, and prohibited from sitting down or falling asleep. They also claimed they were kept in their cells for up to 16 hours a day.

After an on-site visit, Judge Petersen harshly criticized the facility and concluded it was at best unsuitable for many of the juveniles incarcerated there, many of whom are nonviolent property offenders. CSC officials denied the youths' accusations and disputed the judge's findings.

Miami-Dade County juvenile court judges have since been ordered by prosecutors to stop committing sentenced offenders to the Pahokee Youth Development Center. The state is appealing the order to the Third District Court of Appeal.

Bachman noted in his report that problems similar to the ones cited at the Pahokee lockup are likely to occur at other state juvenile facilities, most of which are operated by the private sector. He recommended the legislature take steps to ensure that private companies operating juvenile detention centers are not given authority over when youths are to be released.

Sources

Palm Beach Post, Prison Privatization Report International

MALIGN NEGLECT: PRISON MEDICINE

From the most ordinary of maladies to the most lethal, prisoners are only constitutionally entitled to adequate, or minimal, medical care. This standard translates as such: prisoners must pile up in a body count before anyone on the outside takes notice, which usually occurs in the form of a lawsuit, and only after so many prisoners have suffered or died.

The problem is due to dismal care from shady doctors and health care staff often barred from practice in the free world. It is not uncommon for prison doctors to come to their positions after their medical licenses have been revoked in other states, or even after being convicted of violent crimes. While such outrageous professional backgrounds would never be acceptable in the free world, apparently they are acceptable for prisoners. And though there are some successful medical neglect suits, they occur only after many prisoners languish.

The vast majority of prisoners are at the whim of health care staff who too often are simply not qualified to treat them, and a prison culture suspicious of prisoner requests for care as "attention" or "drug-seeking" manipulations.

The following chapter demonstrates an overall standard of malign neglect in prison medicine.

—TH

The New Bedlam

WILLIE WISELY

Gary Hahn walks his dog, tugging at the leash, back and forth on the hard-pan track at Lancaster prison's maximum security D Facility in California. Right arm folded, fist crammed into the small of his back, Gary walks bent over, his curved spine and emaciated frame belying the muscular build of just a decade before. Eyes bloodshot, pupils pinned, his gaze darts wildly back and forth beneath an angry tangle of graying hair. Gary raises a small commotion among other prisoners as he shuffles by, talking nonstop to his little dog. They snicker, point, and make faces behind his back. That's because there's really no dog, no leash. Gary is psychotic.

Every morning, Gary gets out of bed and frenziedly beats his abdomen trying to kill the evil pig living beneath. He carries all of his important paperwork stuffed into the waistband of his jeans. Sometimes Gary forgets to shower. For weeks. When he leaves the dining table, he might suddenly spin about, walk back and rap his knuckles on the table three times before making an exit. Gary carries on a rapid conversation as he walks, cursing loudly, sometimes spitting. He's talking to people only he can see. Gary is just one of an estimated 20,000 mentally ill people in California prisons. And they're driving the other 162,000 prisoners crazy.

The Pacific Research Institute, a San Francisco think tank, reported in 1996 that arresting, prosecuting, defending, jailing, imprisoning, and treating the mentally ill costs taxpayers between $1.2 and $1.8 billion a year. "Mentally ill inmates are not like typical prisoners. They are very labor-intensive," said Christine Ferry, director of mental health services at the Santa Clara County Department of Corrections, in the *San Jose Mercury News*. In prison, the mentally ill are heavily sedated. Psychiatric medications are used not to cure or treat mental illness, but instead to make disturbed, often volatile prisoners easier to manage.

In a classic example of political ideology trumping good sense, then-

---

This article was written in June 2000.

president Reagan cut the budget for state mental hospitals in half, forcing thousands of mentally ill people onto the streets. Cast from hospitals, thousands of mentally ill became victims of violent crime, drug addicts, alcoholics, their illness often leading them straight to jail and prison. The number of mentally ill people in jail, prison, or on some form of supervised release from custody dramatically increased as a result of Reagan's budget cuts. Rather than costing the public some $17,000 to $20,000 annually to treat in a psychiatric hospital, the mentally ill prisoner may cost $50,000 a year to keep in the prison environment where their problems are largely ignored and often exacerbated, and where their impact on the health of other prisoners is decidedly negative.

In prison and jail, the mentally ill are often victimized both by other prisoners and staff, either maliciously or for entertainment. Some mentally ill prisoners are extremely violent, assaulting or stabbing prisoners and staff alike. Just being locked up in the same dorm, or same cell, with someone suffering from mental illness heaps added stress on the already full plates of prisoners without emotional problems. For those not afflicted with psychiatric problems, life in prison is enough in itself to wear away one's mental health.

Tank fills his days begging for coffee, cigarette papers, tobacco, and the use of a lighter. He gets out of bed in the morning, rolls a cigarette out of toilet paper, eats breakfast, and crawls back on his bunk to sleep. But sometimes he just sleeps for 18-hour stretches at a time. After three years in prison, he has no toothpaste, soap, or shampoo. Tank can fit all his wordly possessions in a state lunch sack. Though family members live nearby, he doesn't get visits.

Diagnosed with psychosis, paranoia, epilepsy, and impulse control problems, James "Tank" Clem has been in and out of psychiatric hospitals since age 15. Living under bridges, in cardboard boxes, and abandoned cars, he used cocaine, heroin, and drank heavily. When he began to binge on crank, his mental illness became more pronounced. In a paranoid state, he shot and killed a fellow crankster after a night of slamming speed. Leaving a young wife and infant son to fend for themselves on the streets, Tank is serving 45-years-to-life for first degree murder at Corcoran prison.

Tank has lived in every building on the yard. He spends an average of three to five weeks in one cell before his new cellie throws him out. An epileptic who suffers from frequent grand mal seizures, he regularly fails to wake up to get his medication. He's indifferent about washing his hands, cleaning up after himself, or washing his clothes. Tank tries to get moved in with prisoners who have their own televisions or radios. He'll lie on his bunk watching television until three in the morning, it doesn't matter what's on. He never reads, has no goals, plans, hopes, or hustle.

Although he's attempted suicide twice and is clinically depressed (in addition to the other mental health problems), Tank receives no treatment or psychiatric medication.

I spent five weeks with Tank as my cellie. Every day, I felt myself slipping a bit deeper into depression just being around him. I couldn't turn the light on because he slept most of the day. He kept me awake watching my television because he didn't own an earphone. I'd come back after visiting all day to find him still lying on his bunk, dirt and food scraps on the floor, staring blankly at the ceiling. A sergeant asked me to let Tank stay in my cell "just for a few days until we find another place." His last cellie threw him out on the tier and refused to let him back into the cell. The few days turned into weeks. The housing unit guards wouldn't move Tank unless I found him a place to go. Since no one wanted him, that was impossible. I couldn't concentrate to write. I began to think of nothing other than getting rid of him.

Psychiatrist Dr. Terry Kupers, who has studied the impact of segregation upon mentally ill prisoners nationwide, stated: "The psychotic inmates are unequivocally the most disturbed people I've ever seen. They scream and throw feces all over their cells. In a mental hospital you'd never see anything like that! Patients would be sedated or stabilized on drugs. Their psychosis would be interrupted." With little or no meaningful health care, the mentally ill free-fall in an ever increasing maelstrom of madness. For those prisoners forced to live with and around the mentally ill, subsequent damage to their own mental health is inevitable.

The majority of people in prison have histories of drug and alcohol use. Many are victims of sexual, emotional, and physical abuse. They don't enter the system with highly developed coping mechanisms, and they have little opportunity to develop any inside. Prisoners don't have the luxury of getting away from stress, of simply being alone to reflect and to think. Philosophical or spiritual ways of being that give great consolation and hope to people outside, such as Yoga or Buddhism, depend in large part on the ability to be alone for uninterrupted meditation and reflection. But, in the New Bedlam, prisoners are never alone. Not when they shower, sleep, or defecate. Someone is always watching. The constant bombardment of unrelenting stress takes its toll like a flurry of well-placed punches on a tired boxer's head. As the Three Strikers and other lifers grow old in the current "tough on crime" political climate, the line of prisoners at the clinic window keeps getting longer.

"After about 15 years, prisoners suffer irreversible mental health damage from being in prison," said Dr. Anderson, a psychologist at Lancaster prison, which is near Los Angeles. Dr. Anderson points out, in the post-rehabilitation age, most California prisons are bleak, harsh, dangerously boring human warehouses. As the prisons slowly crumble, so do the prisoners they house. At Lancaster, several hundred prisoners cue up at the clinic window every evening for their meds.

Bob (not his real name) looked like an ordinary guy when he walked into the eight-man cell in the Orange County, California, jail. Well-groomed, clean, wearing new eyeglasses and arrested for unpaid traffic tickets, he should've spent a few short hours in lockup. He talked to the other men in the cell, moved to the front of the cell and watched the sunset through the narrow Plexiglas slits in the concrete outer wall. After several minutes, Bob gripped the cell bars tightly, his knuckles popped and sweat rolled down his face.

Bob shook the bars so hard it sounded like rumbling thunder. Then he threw his head back and let out a wail that chilled the spines of hardened convicts nearby. It took six men to pry his hands from the bars. Guards strapped him onto a gurney and carted him to the rubber room, a padded cell in the jail's clinic area with a small hole on the floor for a toilet. There, he was stripped naked, strapped into a straight jacket, injected with Thorazine, and left drooling on the floor. At some point between being arrested, booked into the county jail, and deposited in the jail—Bob absolutely lost it.

How long can a person maintain their own mental health when they live in an insane environment, surrounded by unbalanced people on both sides of the fence? "It disturbs me when I see someone I've known years ago, and now he's crazy," says James Christie, a 30-year-old prisoner at Corcoran prison, in California. "I could choose to let go, to let prison, the guards, and life push me over the brink. But I hang on, find ways to cope." Though prison guards and other staff are supposed to watch for, and report, warning signs of mental breakdown in prisoners, "they usually don't. More often, they provoke mentally ill prisoners for fun," says Christie.

"There was this one black guy in Corcoran SHU [security housing unit]. He was on serious hot meds [psychiatric medication]. He tried to cut his dick off once. He shouted the menu out through his cell door every day," recalls Christie. "The guards would rack his cell door open and shut—bam, bam, bam—to set him off. At night, they'd shine flashlights from the control tower into the his cell until he started to bang his head against the wall and howl like a wounded animal." Segregated housing units, administrative segregation, and security housing units are filled with mentally ill prisoners. Tortured, alone, suicidal, and violent.

Mentally ill prisoners are used as tools and torture devices to either drive otherwise normal prisoners over the edge or spark a struggle. Guards will often mix the dangerously mentally ill prisoners in with prisoner activists, jailhouse lawyers, or others they don't like. It's a win-win situation for the guards. Either the mentally ill prisoner drives his cellie crazy or provokes him to fight, giving the guards an excuse to use force to break up the carefully coordinated melee. Sometimes the sane prisoner beats his demented cellmate, throws him out on the tier, and then gets a serious rule infraction. The mentally ill prisoners used in this game are seldom punished. In doesn't take long for them to realize they're free to act with impunity.

"My name is Sin. I was put on earth to take on the sin for Mankind. I hold the key between this world and the other. Do you want me to unlock the door for you?" said the six foot, seven inch, gangly wraith standing in the center of my new cell in New Folsom's administrative segregation unit. Another jailhouse lawyer sent to the hole on drug charges, I knew what time it was. Sin was moved from cell to cell, section to section, and building to building in segregation. He was in the hole for a fight. When a guard saw the disturbance, hit his alarm, and ordered him to get down at gunpoint, Sin yelled, "Fuck you coward! You can't kill me! Shoot punk!"

The guard fired two shots from the military assault rifle. With every other prisoner lying face down on the yard, Sin stood, unscathed. Sin fought with every cellie he had. Officially, violent, disturbed prisoners are supposed to be on single-cell status. Unofficially, New Folsom guards knew exactly what they were doing. They wanted to provoke a fight, giving them an excuse to either shoot me or write me up for fighting. They refused to move either of us unless there was an incident, making the end inevitable.

Sin had nightmares. The ghosts of his father and uncle sexually assaulted him in his sleep. He would spring from his bunk in the middle of the night, swing his arms wildly, scream, and spit at thin air. The staff—including guards, Sin's counselor, and medical assistants—all knew Sin was gravely mentally ill, a danger to himself and others. Sin told me he belonged to the FFA, Fist Fuckers of America. He described how members competed to see how many inches up their rectum they could take a greased arm.

After three days without violence, a guard told Sin I killed his mother before we were released to the small, concrete segregation yard. The fight was brief. A rookie gunner yelled a warning before firing. Sin was moved. Off to another cell, another prisoner chosen for special treatment, perhaps execution. "To get through the door to the other side," Sin confided, "you've got to die in this world."

The average person in prison, like the average person outside, never notices that many of their neighbors are mentally ill. In prison, crazy people often look like just another convict. They have prison tattoos, smoke hand-rolled cigarettes, and drink instant coffee. They might make pruno (home-made wine) or chase drugs on the yard. The insane learn to mask their symptoms from the casual attention of others. But, in the relative safety of their own cells, the mask slips. It's in the unforgiving confines of those concrete coffins that exposure to the mentally ill is most likely to adversely impact their cellmates.

Prisoners housed in maximum security facilities in California are in a constant state of movement from cell to cell, section to section, yard to yard, and prison to prison. Part of this movement is the department strategy to "keep the cons from getting comfortable," according to a

Captain at Corcoran prison who declined to be identified. But a large percentage of the moves occur when prisoners simply can't put up with their mentally ill cellies any longer.

California is far from unique in its treatment of mentally ill prisoners. "Criminal" acts that are actually the byproducts of mental illness acts are rarely, if ever, evaluated as such: instead, such behavior is shunted into the criminal justice system, the "perpetrator" abandoned to his madness, left to deteriorate in prison.

Wreaking Medical Mayhem on Women Prisoners in Washington State

TARA HERIVEL

In 1993, prisoner Gertrude Barrow crawled to the clinic at the Washington Corrections Center for Women with a ruptured peptic ulcer. Barrow's previous requests for treatment had been dismissed by health care staff who diagnosed her ulcer as a bad case of gas. When Barrow vomited on the clinic floor, a nurse tossed a towel at her, and told her to clean it up. Barrow died just a few hours later.

Barrow's death served as the catalyst for a six-year legal struggle to upgrade the Washington Corrections Center for Women's (WCCW) failing health care system from shameful to adequate.

Seattle's Columbia Legal Services' Institutions Project, the Washington ACLU and the Northwest Women's Law Center have waged a protracted battle with WCCW, with the current legal challenge aiming to extend judicial oversight over the institution's faltering health care system. The current litigation seeks to enforce a settlement agreement reached as a result of a class-action filed against WCCW in 1993 by prisoners. The '93 suit, *Hallett v. Payne*, was born out of a litany of health care horror stories, including Barrow's death from a common, treatable illness, which occured during discovery. Institutions Project attorneys David Fathi and Patricia Arthur speculate that Barrow's death led to the quick capitulation of WCCW, who settled the case immediately.

Among the suit's chief complaints, the foremost was that WCCW's health care staff are overwhelmingly incompetent. Besides the usual fare for prisoners (that often amounts to institutional neglect), WCCW staff performed bizarre "procedures," like removing a prisoner's mole with a Bic lighter and a paperclip, and the prison had no coherent system of medical records.

Against a backdrop of appalling medical care, a court-ordered Stipulation and Judgment was approved in '95, setting forth requirements includ-

---

The article was written in November 1999.

ing oversight by outside medical investigators, improved health care services, and employment of qualified health care staff. This past March, attorneys from Columbia Legal Services went back to court, claiming that WCCW has virtually ignored the mandates of the Stipulation.

Currently, prisoners' dental care is performed by a dentist whose vanity plate reads "Dr. Yank": as can be imagined, there are many unnecessary extractions under "Dr. Yank's" brand of "care." And women at WCCW suffer regular degradation, their requests for health and mental health care typically dismissed by staff as manipulative, "attention-seeking" behaviors. Several women who had requested, and regularly been denied mental health care attempted suicide, and one prisoner was even able to set herself on fire with lighter fluid.

The central claims leveled at WCCW included haphazard mental and dental care and second-rate supervision and training of staff. In the original complaint, attorneys for the plaintiffs also argued that WCCW provides substandard medical care. Because of procedural problems, Magistrate Judge David Wilson barred the medical complaints from the current suit.

"Care" at WCCW

Currently, only eight mental health care professionals serve a population of about 730 women. Since the intial suit, there are now fewer nurses at WCCW, though the population there has tripled. Former Nursing Supervisor Pat Wiggins wrote in a memo in 1998, "With the increased hours and workload [for health care staff], I have seen increased numbers of errors and incidents reported. There is a need for concern." Wiggins also stated that medication errors quadrupled between April and October of 1998.

An investigation by the Department of Health (DOH) conducted in October of 1998 seconded Wiggins' concerns, finding that WCCW's failure to ensure that policies and procedures were established and implemented resulted in "errant infection control standards." For example, the DOH discovered that a temporary hire, nurse Jeanette Johnston, used the same needle on two successive patients, an incident which went unreported until one of the patients filed a grievance. The investigation also found that nurses routinely recap needles (presenting a risk that the needle will be mistaken for a new one, and therefore be reused), carry needles in their pockets, and improperly dispose of needles.

The lack of staffing at WCCW has resulted in tragedies, near misses, and overall atrocious patient care. For example, one patient was left unattended on a gurney in a hallway overnight. During the night, she had a seizure, fell off the gurney, and was rushed to a hospital in Tacoma.

Rain or shine, the women at WCCW form long lines outdoors waiting for their medication. Some prisoners refuse to take their meds because of the hassle of the med lines, which sometimes take two hours to work through. While waiting in the med line, one frustrated prisoner sliced a 4-inch cut into her arm with a razor blade, exposing the bone.

Self-harm and Suicide

Over the past year alone, there have been over 100 acts of self-harm by WCCW prisoners. Prisoner requests for mental health consultations go unanswered; or worse, prisoners' requests are rebuffed, and then they are punished for resulting acts of self-harm. Prisoner Allissa McCune testified at the hearing that when she sought help from mental health counselor Mike Walls, he told her he was too "overwhelmed with work" to talk with her. McCune attempted suicide soon after.

Justine O'Neill requested emergency help from her mental health counselor, Levette Dearmon. When O'Neill told Dearmon that she was hearing voices and struggling with suicidal thoughts, the counselor kicked O'Neill out of the office. Ms. O'Neill sat outside Dearmon's door for 45 minutes, crying. A prisoner passing by saw O'Neill crying and wanted to help, but was told by a counselor to "just walk by." That night O'Neill cut herself with a razor in five different places. O'Neill testified that she received no counseling following her suicide attempt, but instead was infracted with a loss of ten days "good time."

Women at WCCW are typically infracted, or punished, for their acts of self-harm. Under Washington Administrative Code Rule 712, prisoners may be infracted for self-harm. Though prisoners across the state are subject to Rule 712, women at WCCW are off the charts in numbers of infractions and correlative acts of self-harm performed. In a recent deposition, Associate Superintendent Gary Fleming stated that he's seen more acts of self-harm at WCCW than in any other prison he's worked at.

Infractions may result in loss of good time, segregation, extra work, cell confinement, or loss of employment. Because of the threat of infraction, prisoners are discouraged from seeking out help from mental health staff. As one prisoner stated, "If I'm going asking for help and I'm punished for it, then I guess I won't ask for help anymore."

Dr. Cassandra Newkirk, an independent monitor who evaluated WCCW's mental health program, noted in trial testimony that women in prison are particularly inclined toward self-harm. Newkirk explained that women in prison typically have experienced some form of sexual, physical, or emotional abuse prior to incarceration, and that restraining, punishing, or secluding women who have been abused retraumatizes them. WCCW psychiatrist Dr. Jan Loeken estimates that 95 percent of the women she sees have histories of abuse.

Further, in response to punishment or isolation, women who have been abused "will engage in self-harm behavior as a way of trying to get a sense that they are actually alive," stated Newkirk. Self-harming may either be a response to a lack of meaningful attention, or because women prisoners intend to commit suicide. "If we [women] need attention, want attention, [we] engage in many different kinds of ways to get that attention," said Newkirk.

Some women at the prison have even suffered sexual abuse while at WCCW. A mentally ill prisoner was forced by former mental health counselor Robert Perry to perform oral sex on Perry. Perry (who has since been fired) threatened to kill her if she told anyone.

And even the most obvious prisoners-at-risk are handled without care. In February of 1999, Dorine Crawford tried to set herself on fire using a match and nail polish remover. Though Crawford is severely mentally ill, her treatment plan had not been updated to include her well-documented self-destructive tendencies, and she was allowed to keep the flammable materials she later used to attempt self-immolation in her cell. (Though, in a morose twist, her treatment plan did provide for the use of pepper spray against Crawford.) Crawford was burned over 30 percent of her body. The prison responded by issuing Crawford a written reprimand under Rule 712.

Prisoners who threaten self-harm are placed in "one-on-one," or isolation cells. Prisoners confined to one-on-one may receive no mental health counseling at all. Neshelle Wood, a prisoner at WCCW, described one-on-one: "You get no counseling. They don't want to make it a reward process, is what Counselor Walls told me. You are locked back there 24 hours a day." Wood also said that one-on-one provokes flashbacks of childhood abuse, when she was often locked in the closet by her abuser.

Prisoners with self-harming impulses may also be placed in segregation, a unit with numerous design features that could be, and has been, used in suicide attempts. With "modesty walls" to hide behind, and sprinklers to hang themselves on, prisoners with self-destructive tendencies are routinely placed in this particularly dangerous environment. When Cassandra Taylor tried to hang herself in segregation, unit sergeant Hope Counts made no attempt to intervene, but instead left the unit, returning an hour later to videotape Taylor cutting herself for prison records.

Nineteen-year-old Naomi Riojas also tried to hang herself in segregation. Though WCCW psychologist Michael Robbins admitted that "extended stays in seg appear to be difficult for Riojas," she nevertheless was placed in segregation, despite repeated objections by her counselor.

Most acts of self-harm at WCCW involve razors which are distributed at the prison. WCCW saw a 111 percent increase in self-harm incidents involving razors between 1997–1998. In response, Superintendent Alice Payne convened a "Razor Consideration Group" to evaluate whether double-edged razors should be eliminated from the prison. Payne overruled the Group's recommendation that razors be eliminated from the institution, and has allowed razors to remain at WCCW. Payne's reasoning was that banning razors would only increase their use as contraband. In contrast, the distribution of double-edged razors was banned from men's prisons in Washington in 1995.

During the recent hearing to extend judical oversight, Superintendent Payne and psychologist Michael Robbins characterized prisoners' self-harming as "manipulative," "attention-seeking" behavior. Dr. Robbins pointed to Naomi Riojas as an example of a prisoner he believes attempted suicide as a manipulative means to gain transfer out of segregation. When asked whether he realized that Ms. Riojas' suicide attempt was related to sexual harassment she suffered from a guard, Dr. Robbins responded only that he was unaware of the circumstances leading to Riojas' suicide attempt.

Prison as the New Overflow for State Hospitals

With the dismantling of public mental hospitals in the 1960s, and the race to incarcerate of the past two decades (and concurrent legislation affecting such incarceration numbers), prisons have become home for alarming numbers of the mentally ill. Within the population at WCCW, over 60 percent of the prisoners suffer from serious mental illness. Forty percent of the women at WCCW are on some form of psychotropic drug, and that number appears to be on the rise. Washington State Department of Corrections' Chuck Cummings stated that, in comparison, 9 percent of the men in Washington prisons are on psychotropic drugs.

WCCW's Dr. Judith DeFelice, Dr. Jan Schaeffer, and Dr. Michael Robbins, and all of the mental health experts who testified at the recent hearing, concluded that staffing is inadequate to meet the needs of the population.

Despite the admission by WCCW's own staff that the prison is dangerously understaffed, and staff poorly trained or supervised, Superintendent Payne insists that WCCW offers quality health care, while alternately complaining of a lack of funds to increase psychiatric and nursing coverage.

Dental Care Courtesy of Dr. Yank

Attorneys for the women at WCCW also highlighted the prison's shoddy dental care as an example of prison's deliberate indifference to inmates' pain and suffering. Cheri Fletcher first visited WCCW's dentist Dr. Carl Weaver in October of 1998. With a vanity plate that reads "Dr. Yank," Weaver is infamous for his fetishistic preference for extractions. When Fletcher requested a cleaning and repair of a bad enamel chip on one tooth, Weaver told her, "All I do is pull them and fill them. I don't clean them; that's not my thing." Another visit to Weaver over a toothache resulted in an extraction, but of the wrong tooth. When Fletcher returned with the same toothache, Weaver made a bite guard for her. When Fletcher chewed through her bite guard because of the constant and continuous pain, Weaver finally pulled the tooth that Fletcher had originally indicated as the source of pain.

Mary Eastwood had 16 teeth removed in eight visits to Dr. Weaver. In trial transcripts, Eastwood stated that Weaver would ram the needle in so fast "you end up with a big sore spot worse than the tooth afterwards." And during the extractions, Dr. Weaver was "just yanking . . . pulling them so quickly, they are just snapping off."

After several such extractions, Eastwood experienced fevers and chills. She asked if she should be taking antibiotics, but Weaver told her he didn't think it was necessary. A note written by Weaver on her chart stated, "This patient's history makes me extremely skeptical of the solidity of her complaint." When Eastwood's neck began to swell, she went to Weaver for help. Weaver told her she'd "put on a little weight." He also told her that he thought she was only visiting him because of her "drug-seeking behavior."

Months later, a visiting doctor diagnosed Eastwood's swollen neck (now with a lump as big as an orange) as the result of an infected gland due to lack of antibiotics. Eastwood now suffers from a variety of health problems related to the infection, including occasional flareups, weight loss, and the inability to eat hot and cold foods. Eastwood recently tried to commit suicide, in part because of the pain and humiliation of her experience.

A Sinking Ship

With this outrageous track record of medical mishaps and deliberate neglect, it's no surprise WCCW has seen a rapid rate of turnover in its health care staff. Between 1996 and 1999 there have been six different mental health supervisors, and a slew of other key mental health staff have quit—many in frustrated desperation. Dr. Linda Thomas, a former psychologist at WCCW, testified that she resigned her position because she felt "hopeless." Dr. Jan Schaeffer left WCCW after two-and-a-half years because of the rootlessness of mental health programming. Feeling that the program lacked a mission, Dr. Schaeffer said: "I felt I was beginning to work in a very unsafe setting."

The Long Wait

Attorneys at Columbia and the women at WCCW now wait in limbo while Magistrate Judge David Wilson ponders whether to recommend extension of judicial oversight at the prison. The plaintiffs' requests seem basic: decent health care provided with integrity. With a prison system that often runs amok if unchecked, it seems obvious that prisoners should not be dying of ulcers, their health complaints dismissed as manipulative fantasy. But behind the locked doors of American prisons, scant or nonexistent oversight of prison staffs' wayward tendencies continues to provide a grim harvest of horror stories.

[Editor's Note: The motion to extend judicial oversight was denied in a sixty-page opinion by Magistrate Judge David Wilson that cited absolutely no case law. The opinion was rubber-stamped by Judge Burgess. The 9th Circuit rejected the appeal in April 2002, see Hallett v. Morgan, 287 F.3d 1193 (9th cir. 2002).]

Hepatitis C

A "Silent Epidemic" Strikes U.S. Prisons

SILJA J. A. TALVI

It's been called the nation's most insidious virus. A "silent epidemic" that has swept the nation, hepatitis C is now the most common chronic blood-borne infection in the United States. Because the virus often causes no noticeable symptoms for up to 20 or 30 years after infection, most of those who are infected have no idea they are living with hepatitis C.

Conservative estimates show that some 4 million Americans are now infected with hepatitis C (HCV). In comparison, less than 1 million Americans are infected with HIV, the virus that causes AIDS. And the nation's 2 million prisoners aren't even included in that estimate. While the number of new HCV infections in the nation has declined over the last decade, the incremental progress made in educating and testing the general public is now severely threatened by what amounts to staggering infection rates behind bars.

The nation's prison populations are now harboring the highest concentrations of hepatitis C in the country. From state to state, from 20 to 60 percent of the current national prison population is believed to harbor the virus, which can lead to chronic liver disease, cirrhosis, and liver cancer. There is no vaccine or foolproof cure for HCV. In response, state prison administrators have been implementing varied and divergent approaches to address the rates of infection.

Some state prison systems, including Oklahoma's, have gone so far as to adopt a "don't ask, don't tell" policy as a way of avoiding costs affiliated with treatment of HCV. Faced with 28 percent and 37 percent infection rates among male and female prisoners, respectively, the Texas state prison system chose a different approach. In 2000, the Texas Department of Corrections (DOC) drafted a plan providing for HCV testing, monitoring, and treatment for those with chronic infections.

Other state prison systems, including those in New York, Washington,

This article was written in January 2001.

Colorado, and California, say they provide testing and treatment upon request—*if* a prisoner can pass certain criteria. But prisoners and their advocates insist that too little is being done, too late. The bottom line, they say, comes down to money, and not the welfare of prisoners, or the community at large.

"Prisoners are going in expecting to do 10–15 years, and they're ending up with a death sentence," says Jackie Walker, AIDS Information Coordinator for the National Prison Project of the American Civil Liberties Union, in Washington, D.C. "They're not getting the [medical] treatment that they deserve to receive."

Often, says Walker, prison officials cite the high cost of treatment for prisoners as the reason for the denial of HCV treatment. And treatment is expensive. Only two antiviral drugs are currently approved for use in treating HCV: Interferon and Ribavirin. Standard treatment per person, per year, can run between $8,000–$20,000.

Unlike HIV, HCV medications are usually given over the course of one year. And the drug therapy is not guaranteed to work. According to the Centers for Disease Control and Prevention (CDC), Interferon has a 10 to 20 percent success rate when used alone. Combination therapy, using both drugs, is effective 30 to 40 percent of the time. Both Interferon and Ribavirin are also known to have potentially severe side effects, including flu-like symptoms, a worsening of psychiatric conditions, and a decrease in white blood cells.

Yet not every prisoner infected with HCV requires or wants treatment, say those involved in advocating for the medical rights of prisoners. Many simply want to be informed of their status, to receive information about the virus, and to be monitored to make sure that the virus is not progressing to life-threatening levels.

"This is an area where, ultimately, the patient should be able to choose whether to go on the treatment. But in [the prison system], that's not the way it works," says Jack Beck, a Supervising Attorney of the Prisoner's Rights Project of the Legal Aid Society in New York. "If someone knows what the risks and benefits are, they should be able to receive treatment as long as it's within medical guidelines. And that is not currently the case."

Beck, who has been involved in a decade-long case against the New York DOC related to the care of HIV-positive prisoners, says that while study of the prevalence of HCV in New York state prisoners is still pending, he and others believe that upwards of 30 to 40 percent of all prisoners are infected, amounting to roughly 25,000 prisoners. Co-infection of HIV and HCV, according to Beck, is also very high among the prisoners.

But only slightly over 100 prisoners are currently receiving treatment, says Beck, out of more than 70,000 prisoners statewide. That number is as low as it is, he says, because the diagnostic process in prison can drag on for months, and the criteria for treatment is very difficult to meet. "I believe part of the strategy [of prison officials] is to 'filter' as much as possible, and to restrict the number of people on therapy, because if they really started treating all the people who are infected, the cost would be phenomenal." The NY DOC would not respond to this allegation, or to questions about treatment policies.

Beck and other prisoners' advocates say that not treating prisoners in need of care is both a violation of the Eighth amendment (prohibiting "cruel and unusual punishment"), as well as a violation of a landmark 1976 Supreme Court ruling in *Estelle v. Gamble*, which determined that prisoners have a right to adequate medical care for serious medical needs.

Of those infected with HCV, about 85 percent develop chronic, life-long infections, according to the CDC. Fully 70 percent of those infected will develop chronic liver disease, and 15 percent will develop cirrhosis of the liver. People at particular risk for infection include past or present injection drug users, medical care workers exposed to contaminated blood, and those who received blood transfusions before 1992, before tests screening for HCV were widely implemented. According to the CDC, roughly 20 percent of recent cases of HCV infection are due to sexual activity. Unsterilized tattoo or piercing equipment, as well as intranasal drug use, also puts people at higher risk for HCV.

Some 10,000 deaths per year are currently attributed to chronic HCV infection—the CDC has predicted that this number will triple in the next 20 years. HCV infection is also the most common reason for liver trans-plantation in the United States One transplant can easily cost over a quarter-million dollars, and takes both luck and years to procure for people on the outside.

From an economic standpoint, Beck insists, it doesn't make sense to ignore treatment while prisoners are incarcerated. "Treatment is not effective at the end stages [of this disease]," he says. "If you don't take this opportunity, these people are going to be out on the street, and we're going to have these terrible expenses with liver failure and the costs associated."

Research presented at the 1999 National HIV Prevention Conference in Atlanta confirms the basis for these concerns. According to a study commissioned by the National Commission on Correctional Health Care, and presented by Dr. Theodore Hammett of AN Associates, one-third of all people with HCV infection in 1996—some 1.4 million people—passed through a correctional facility in that year. Anthony Nicholas Ware, a 42-year-old prisoner serving a 22-year-sentence at the medium security Luther Luckett Correctional Complex in La Grange, Kentucky, had been begging for treatment for his HCV since 1997.

Only after he joined a lawsuit against the Kentucky DOC was he finally granted the right to start treatment, early in 2001. He notes that only one other prisoner currently being given treatment for HCV infection. The rest, he says, "have been kicked out [of treatment] for unfounded reasons."

Raymond James Hannum, a prisoner at F.C.I. Coleman in Florida, also has HCV. Hannum, who has been moved three times since entering the federal prison system, says that he has been pleading to be treated for his HCV infection for six years, with no success. Hannum concedes that his blood is tested regularly, but says that requests for a liver biopsy—which would indicate the extent to which the infection has progressed—have thus far been denied. Hannum's medical records clearly indicate that he has been classified with "chronic persistent hepatitis C."

"Generally, in terms of health care, it's better to be in the federal system than the state system. There's a greater level of oversight," says Walker of the ACLU's National Prison Project. But Walker says that the regular number of letters she receives from federal prisoners indicate an obvious problem surrounding the treatment of HCV infection. "I'm just not seeing that prisoners in federal prisons are receiving [adequate] treatment for hepatitis C."

"Not knowing you have HCV is one thing, but the F.B.O.P. [Federal Bureau of Prisons] is well aware of my problem, so there is no excuse for nontreatment in my case," says Hannum. "I can tell you exactly why I'm not getting treatment: Money." The Federal Bureau of Prisons did not respond to general questions about testing and treatment procedures. In the past, the Bureau has commented that prisoners are tested for HCV infection if they shows signs of infection, and that treatment is available to those who qualify.

Alan S. Rubin, a Louisville-based attorney representing Ware and roughly 50 other prisoners in their complaint against the Luther Luckett Correctional Complex (LLCC), says the prison has always maintained that treatment is available, but that no one was able to meet strict treatment criteria. The prison's criteria allow treatment only for those who are also HIV-positive and for those who have a history of illicit drug use in the preceding 12 months.

Already, says Rubin, at least two people at LLCC have died behind bars because of complications from HCV. And he continues to receive letters on a weekly basis from prisoners who, upon learning that they're HCV-infected, want to be monitored and treated.

"It's not right," says Rubin, who points to testimony from Kentucky's DOC that one-third of prisoners are likely infected with HCV. "In the next 5–10 years, if something doesn't change, we're going to see the death rates from liver disease skyrocketing among prisoners and among those who have been recently paroled."

Rubin won a single, significant legal victory on the issue of HCV treatment in the case of Michael Paulley, an Army veteran serving a 20-year sentence at LLCC. Paulley tested positive for HCV and had already developed cirrhosis of the liver when he was seen by a hepatitis specialist, Dr. Cecil Bennett, at the Louisville Veterans Affairs Medical Center.

Although the VA was willing to pay for Paulley's treatment, the DOC refused to treat him, saying that he did not meet the prison's medical guidelines for drug therapy. Rubin, in turn, argued that the DOC was using those guidelines as a pretext for denying all prisoners treatment for HCV for fear of the costs involved.

In March 2000, Federal Judge John Heyburn II agreed with Rubin, and issued an injunction ordering the prison to treat Paulley.

"Money, not medicine, was the driving force behind the department's decision," wrote Magistrate Judge C. Cleveland Gambill in his findings to Judge Heyburn.

"Prisoners have a moral and legal right to medical care," says Dr. Bennett, who specializes in treating hepatitis in Louisville, and who advocates that all prisoners be tested for HCV and told of their status upon entry to the prison system.

In the Luther Luckett Correctional Facility—as in most other state prisons in the country, according to prisoners' rights advocates—no formal prevention or peer education program currently exists which is specifically geared toward HCV. This is so despite the fact that many prisoners nationwide are apparently getting infected for the first time behind bars, whether from unprotected sex with other prisoners, or from unclean drug or tattoo needles. Ware explains that he only discovered his HCV status after going through the state's Open Records Act and paying for copies of all of his lab work. "There it was: hepatitis C," says Ware. "I thought, 'Oh my God, where did I get that?'"

Judy Greenspan, of the prisoner's advocacy group California Prison Focus, says she sees this same neglect in California prisons. "Mostly, we've found that when prisoners have tested [positive for HCV], they haven't been told," says Greenspan. "People find out, for instance, when they're told they're not eligible for a job in the kitchen because they have hepatitis. That's the first they hear that they even took the test. Obviously, they're doing some sort of routine screening, somewhere. But most people are not being informed of their status."

Terry Thornton, Spokesperson for the California DOC, explains that prisoners are medically evaluated upon entry to the California Department of Corrections, and may request medical attention when they have health questions or concerns. "Hepatitis testing is done when medically appropriate as indicated by history, physical examination, laboratory testing showing abnormalities, or by prisoner request," she explains.

The California state prison system is, in fact, one of the few that has taken the initiative of completing a comprehensive seroprevalence study of HCV, indicating how common HCV is in the blood of incarcerated men and women.

A March 1996 research study, completed in cooperation with the California Department of Health Services, demonstrated that the rates of infection among incoming prisoners were 54.5 percent for women and 39.4 percent for men. Among HIV-positive men, 61.3 percent were found to be co-infected with HCV, while HIV-positive women were found to have an astounding 85 percent co-infection rate with HCV.

Greenspan says that those who are infected with HCV are finding it difficult to get treatment, or to receive adequate medication for their infections. Last year two HIV-positive women in California prisons suffered painful, protracted deaths from complications related to HCV.

But treatment for HCV is available in California state prisons, answers Thornton, and includes treatment for those who are co-infected with HIV.

"Prisoners are treated on a case-by-case basis," says Thornton. "We treat patients for hepatitis C, if they have otherwise healthy medical parameters and continue to do well while on the hepatitis medications. Many have successfully completed such therapy."

But budgetary restrictions are likely to prevent the implementation of more widespread treatment. In fiscal year 99/00, the California DOC was granted $325,000 in funding specifically earmarked for Interferon treatment. By the Department's own estimates, it costs $12,000–$20,000 per year, per patient to treat HCV. Even on the low end of that scale, only 27 prisoners would be eligible for a full course of Interferon treatment, out of a current state prison population of over 161,000 men and women.

Thornton says that the DOC is currently seeking approval to supplement the existing health care budget to cover additional costs for diagnosis, treatment, and prevention.

Greenspan worries that more prisoners will die behind bars in the interim. "The tragedy about the hepatitis C epidemic is that we're finding out about it in the sundown years of the AIDS activist movement," says Greenspan. "The mass activism [around HIV] has faded, and trying to get people motivated about this issue is difficult because most people infected [with HCV] have a history of injection drug use, are mostly poor people of color, and people who are in prison.

"For many people who are in and out of the prison system, the only time they access medical care is on the inside. That's their reality," adds Greenspan. "If the system doesn't want to provide medical care, then they shouldn't lock up so many people."

Walker, of the ACLU's National Prison Project, insists that Americans have to begin thinking of prisons "as part the community," on both humanitarian and public health grounds. "The majority of people are not in there for extreme, violent crimes," she says. "The majority are in there for nonviolent crimes, doing time for 5, 10, 15 years. These are people who are going to be returning to our communities. Do we want people coming back out sicker than they were when they went in?"

Dying for Profits

RONALD YOUNG

Marvin Johnson, a 28-year-old diabetic, required 100 units of insulin per day to stay alive. On the morning of July 27, 1995, he was arrested and jailed in Little Rock, Arkansas, for driving an acquaintance's car without permission. Less than three days later, Johnson lapsed into a coma in his jail cell and died for lack of insulin.

Johnson was charged with misdemeanor unlawful use of a vehicle but ended up being sentenced to death. Johnson died on July 29, 1995, early in the morning of his third day in the Pulaski County Jail. In his 30-hour wait for insulin, Johnson told three nurses and six sheriff's deputies that he was an insulin-dependent diabetic and needed medicine, according to an investigative report reviewed by the *St. Louis Post-Dispatch*.

Despite his pleas for help, the jail's medical provider, Correctional Medical Services (CMS), denied Johnson his life-sustaining shots, claiming that they could not confirm his prescription because Johnson was vague about his medical history. Jail staff refused to treat Johnson even though Johnson's girlfriend, LaJeanna Hawkins, called the jail's satellite holding area to tell them Johnson was diabetic. Hawkins even offered to bring insulin to the jail, but the deputies told her Johnson would be well cared for.

The nursing supervisor reportedly accused Johnson of "faking" his condition. "He was not forthcoming about his medical history, and he exhibited behavior that he was faking," David Fuqua, a lawyer for Pulaski County, told the *Post-Dispatch*. "They get a lot of that from inmates," he said. Susan B. Adams, CMS's director of marketing and communications, claimed in a 1996 written rebuttal to a New Jersey newspaper's investigation of the incident, "We were not informed of a call to the jail by Johnson's girlfriend."

"This gentleman had his diabetes ignored, to let it go 30 hours, even

---

This article was written in December 2000.

after he got sick, he wasn't evaluated for hours after that," said Dr. Neil White, an associate professor at Washington University School of medicine and vice president of the St. Louis region's American Diabetes Association. "It's clearly negligence," he said. "This is not even the appropriate minimum level of care. If they had started monitoring when he first came in . . . he'd probably be alive today."

Annie Johnson, who helped her late sister raise Johnson and his three siblings, sued the sheriff and CMS, alleging medical malpractice, negligence, and wrongful death. By November 1997, Pulaski County and CMS paid Johnson's family a settlement. Pulaski County's portion was about $20,000, said Pulaski County's attorney, David Fuqua. CMS, which demanded a confidentiality agreement, won't say how much it paid Johnson's family.

This is just one chapter in a litany of abuses and deaths suffered by prisoners nationwide at the hands of CMS, the largest private health care provider to jails and prisons in the country. *The Detroit News* reported in June 2000 that CMS contracts with physicians and health care workers who serve more than 260,000 prisoners in 315 prisons and jails in 27 states. CMS runs statewide prison health care systems in Alabama, Arkansas, Idaho, Massachusetts, Michigan, Minnesota, Missouri, New Jersey, New Mexico, and Wyoming. CMS controls approximately 45 percent of the over $1 billion market.

In November 1994, CMS hired Gail R. Williams, MD, to direct mental health services in Alabama prisons, even though Oklahoma had revoked his license to practice the year before for sexually battering and harassing a nurse and other female staff members. CMS helped persuade Alabama's Medical Licensure Commission to give Williams a license restricted to practice in prisons. CMS was fully aware of Williams' history and discussed it with the board of examiners, CMS's Adams told the *Journal of the American Medical Association* (JAMA). "We are confident that we have measures in place to prevent him from repeating his past mistakes," she said.

Apparently these measures weren't enough to prevent Williams from making new mistakes concerning prisoner mental health services. A wrongful death suit was filed against Williams, CMS, and other CMS health care providers after the February 21,1996, death of Alabama state prisoner Calvin Moore. Moore, 18, died in an isolation cell after serving only seven weeks of a two-year sentence in the Kilby Correctional Facility, a few miles east of Montgomery. According to JAMA, prison records show that, shortly after being admitted to Kilby on January 3, 1996, Moore began to display severe psychiatric symptoms. He stopped eating, and although he lost 56 pounds (over one-third of his body weight), he received no medical treatment other than one injection of the antipsychotic agent Haloperidol.

When Williams took charge of the mental health services in Alabama's prisons for CMS, he ordered the medical staff to greatly reduce the number of prisoners who receive psychotropic medications. He also discontinued the policy of sending the most severely mentally ill prisoners to Taylor Hardin, the state's secure medical facility. Instead, such prisoners had to be treated within their respective prisons, despite a shortage or all-out absence of psychiatric beds or competent staff to serve the acutely mentally ill in the state's twelve prisons. Moore's isolation cell in the P-1 unit of Kilby was an austere administrative segregation cell not intended to house severely mentally ill prisoners. Critics of the Alabama prison system say the P-1 unit, and others like it around the state, also serve as warehouses for an overflow of mentally ill prisoners.

Moore spent the last several days of his life in the P-1 isolation cell sitting or lying in his own urine in a catatonic state. For more than a week, until a few hours before his death, no one even bothered to take his vital signs. An official state report said Moore died of natural causes "possibly related to an unidentifiable heart lesion." However, Robert H. Kirschner, MD, senior forensic consultant to Physicians for Human Rights, who served as an expert witness in the case, called the report a "whitewash," saying Moore's death was a homicide caused by dehydration and starvation resulting from criminal negligence.

CMS settled the Moore lawsuit without an admission of wrongdoing for an undisclosed amount on August 31, 1998. According to spokeswoman Adams, the CMS staff at Kilby provided Moore with "appropriate and compassionate care." Adams insists "[t]he settlement was for the compromise of a doubtful and disputed claim." Adding that "a consideration in CMS's decision to settle this case was the anticipated high cost of trial and the health care provider's time and attention would be diverted from their duties."

Williams isn't the only CMS-employed physician working in Alabama's prisons with dubious credentials. Walter F. Mauney, MD, who was medical director at Kilby when Moore died, was also named in the Moore wrongful death lawsuit. According to CMS records reviewed by JAMA, Mauney was hired in 1995 shortly after being released from a drug addiction treatment center. It was also discovered that in 1979, a Monroe County, Tennessee, grand jury charged Mauney with three counts of having oral sex with and sexually penetrating a 16-year-old mentally retarded boy. Mauney, who was 40 at the time, pleaded guilty to one count of "crime against nature" and was sentenced to ten years in the state penitentiary. The sentence was suspended.

Louis Tripoli, MD, CMS's chief medical officer, defended the company's hiring of Mauney. "Given Dr. Mauney's remorse, his desire to make amends, and based upon a review of his professional credentials and record available to us at the time, CMS believed that Dr. Mauney was a satisfactory candidate to provide inmate health care services," he told JAMA.

The hiring practices of CMS are part of an overall policy on the part of some states to allow physicians who have had their licenses revoked to practice in state prisons—apparently prison becomes the last resort for such doctors. Sidney M. Wolfe, MD, director of Public Citizen's Health Research Group in Washington, D.C., believes the public should be very concerned about such policies. "It is unethical and inhumane to say that a physician isn't trustworthy or good enough to treat people in the community, but that he or she is good enough to care for inmates of correctional facilities or mental hospitals," he told JAMA.

The Norfolk City Jail in New Jersey severed its contract with CMS in 1994, after the deaths of seven prisoners between 1993 and 1994, many because of medical reasons, jail officials reported. Norfolk Sheriff Robert McCabe said publicly in 1996 that his jail's health care was in a state of crisis. The U.S. Justice Department investigated CMS's Norfolk operation and concluded that the company's medical services there were "grossly deficient and violated inmates' constitutional rights."

In a written rebuttal on behalf of CMS, spokeswoman Adams stated to the *Gloucester County Times* (in New Jersey), "At Norfolk, CMS was unfairly blamed for the problems of the jail, which were actually symptoms of much larger and more chronic issues such as inadequate funding for jail services, an antiquated facility, and extreme overcrowding." In the meantime, a suit filed by one of the deceased prisoners' families was settled out of court by CMS. In that case, Jerome J. Walton, Jr., 28, arrested on probation violations and a marijuana charge, died when a CMS medical assistant at Norfolk simply forgot to schedule him for a much needed dialysis treatment.

Despite the death at Norfolk, the State of New Jersey awarded CMS a three-year, $187.2 million contract in 1996, to provide health care services to the state's approximately 26,000 prisoners in state prisons. The body count began almost immediately. The first death occurred only three days after CMS took over in April 1996, when John Orriello, serving ten years for burglary, stopped breathing and died after a succession of oxygen tank failures. CMS blamed a defective regulator it had inherited from the state. Still, within less than a month after taking charge, four prisoners died due to problems with the health care delivery system provided by CMS.

CMS currently has a three-year contract with New Jersey for $90 million a year, employing some 1,200 doctors, nurses, technicians, and health aides in the state's prison system. The contract expires in 2002.

On June 14, 1999, Hatari Wahaki, 41, a prisoner at the New Jersey State Prison in Trenton, wrote a letter to the American Friends Service Committee complaining of searing temperatures in the ad-seg wing of the 100+-year-old prison, and lack of medical care for prisoners under CMS's jurisdiction. "I have been trying to get medical attention for months regarding a chronic respiratory condition whereas my lungs are rapidly deteriorating," Wahaki wrote. "I constantly have severe headaches where it feels like the flow of oxygen is being cut off from my brain causing sudden surges of pressure that be so intense it knocks me off balance. I have been experiencing these symptoms for over a year, yet the medical department steadfastly refused to treat me."

Wahaki, along with prisoner Vidal Prince, 48, was found dead on July 4, 1999, in a cellblock described as a "brick oven." Authorities claimed that both men died of "natural causes" and not from the extreme heat or lack of medical care.

CMS makes much of its capacity to win accreditation for contracted facilities from the National Commission on Correctional Healthcare (NCCHC). But B. Jaye Anno, a doctorate-level expert in prison health care and a co-founder of the NCCHC, explained to the *Garden State News Service* that the accrediting organization focuses more on whether a facility has the "infrastructure" to deliver proper health care, not whether the facility does in practice deliver that care. "It's fair to say they look at minimum standards," Anno said.

CMS's Adams pointed out that CMS was able to obtain accreditation through the NCCHC for both the Norfolk and Pulaski County jails. Yet, at least in the case of the Norfolk lockup, Adams put partial blame for prisoners' deaths on an "antiquated facility." In light of Anno's statement that NCCHC accreditation focuses mainly on a facility's infrastructure, it would appear that Adams' attempt to shift the blame from CMS to inferior facilities must be looked upon with a suspicious eye. NCCHC certification shows that the necessary minimum medical infrastructure was in place at Norfolk. If it can be shown otherwise, as Adams originally maintained, then this would prove that NCCHC certification is basically meaningless. Whichever may be the case, this bit of contradiction shows that CMS is being purposely evasive and even misleading as to what or who actually caused the deaths at Norfolk.

Lawyers for the State of New Jersey and CMS appeared in federal court on July 17, 2000, to fight efforts by New York-based Human Rights Watch (HRW) to obtain access to progress reports regarding psychiatric treatment provided to mentally ill state prisoners. Bruce Cohen, a Chatham, New Jersey, lawyer handling the case for HRW, told the Associated Press that the broad secrecy imposed by the state and by CMS was disturbing. "The public of New Jersey doesn't realize that the situation in New Jersey prisons for the mentally ill was horrendous," Cohen said.

The Center for Social Justice, a public-interest group based at Seton Hall University law school, filed a class-action lawsuit on behalf of mentally ill prisoners in New Jersey that was settled in a confidential agreement in July 1999. Follow-up reports on conditions in New Jersey prisons are also confidential under the settlement.

Jamie Fellner, a staff attorney for HRW, said she was disturbed by the secrecy maintained by attorneys representing the private firms. "It would be a disaster for democracy, and certainly for the criminal justice system, if the fact that you privatize suddenly means the public cannot know how its responsibilities and the state's responsibilities are being met, and yet that would seem to be the argument that the subcontractors would like to make," she told the Associated Press.

CMS spokesman Ken Fields said Fellner was incorrect. "We welcome any independent examination of the health care services we provide," he told AP. "The fact that CMS is a private company has nothing to do with the fact that those monitoring reports were confidential."

In Michigan, United Auto Workers (UAW) Local 6000 filed a suit on May 25, 2000, in federal court seeking a temporary restraining order to keep the state from replacing approximately 70 prison health care workers with CMS employees. Since February 1998, Michigan has had a $37 million-a-year contract with CMS to cover off-site hospitalization and specialty care for the state's approximately 45,000 prisoners. The UAW suit concerns the latest expansion of the contract, which grants CMS sole jurisdiction over all on-site primary care; under the contract, CMS essentially is the gatekeeper to all medical care and access, and may make all determinations regarding which prisoners will receive off-site services. CMS's cost-based interest in keeping off-site visits to a bare minimum raises concerns with many prisoners and prisoners' rights advocates.

Without the remedy, the UAW lawsuit says, CMS—as the nation's largest supplier of medical care to prisons—would expose state prisoners to "the so-called care of a company whose track record shows a profound and continuing defiance of constitutional standards of care."

The UAW suit points to a North Carolina case where CMS is facing an involuntary manslaughter charge for the 1996 death of prisoner Clarence Junior Cousins. Cousins, a 37-year-old textile worker, was put into a special medical-watch cell at the Forsyth County Jail, where CMS provides prisoner health care services. An autopsy showed that Cousins died from alcohol withdrawal.

Prosecutors allege that Cousins' alcohol withdrawal went untreated after a CMS nurse, Arthelia Moser, who was untrained in alcohol withdrawal, misdiagnosed Cousins as having a mental disorder. Moser was indicted in October 1998 for involuntary manslaughter. Cousins had told a nurse when he was admitted into the jail that he had been drinking heavily. The indictment against Moser stated that a person exercising ordinary care or reasonable caution would have seen that Cousins needed treatment, and that Moser's inaction contributed to Cousins' death.

Sheila Cousins, Cousins' wife, and his children filed a wrongful death suit in March 1997 against Moser and CMS. Both settled the lawsuit out of court in March 1998 for $175,000.

In response to the involuntary manslaughter charge against CMS, spokesman Fields told *The Detroit News*, "The allegations are false." He said the allegations against CMS primarily concern staffing levels, and insists that staffing levels at the time of Cousins' death exceeded required levels. He also said CMS still operates at the Forsyth County Jail. Prosecutors dismissed the manslaughter charge before trial.

The UAW suit also cites an opinion from an Idaho judge, who, in May 2000, citing scandalously poor treatment in the state's prison health care system operated by CMS, subsequently ordered the probationary release of an ailing, elderly man sentenced to up to six years in prison for vehicular manslaughter.

In ordering the release of the prisoner, Kenneth L. Pool, Fifth District State Judge Monte Carlson commented on the level of health care being provided by CMS, stating, "Mr. Pool deserves to be punished and he deserves to be in prison. His sentence is well within the punishment authority given to district court judges, and in my opinion is appropriate. But his treatment in the first five months of custody in the Idaho State Prison more closely resembles physical torture than incarceration. His treatment violates the standards of decency in today's society."

Judge Carlson also said that a private physician who examined Pool concluded that a doctor providing such medical care to a patient outside prison would be guilty of malpractice. Idaho DOC spokesman Mark Carnopis defended CMS. "We've contracted with Correctional Medical Services . . . to provide our medical care since October 1996," he told the AP. "They've done a very good job in providing that care and we're happy with them providing that care."

In South Carolina, state officials there weren't singing the praises of CMS either, after having contracted with the company for nearly three years to provide health care services in 10 of the state's 32 prisons. That contract was terminated in January 2000. A report released in May 2000 by the South Carolina Legislative Audit Council found $632,698 in overpayments to CMS for providing HIV treatment to prisoners. The report also said that there was a severe lack of oversight by the state of CMS operations. In particular, the report found that prison officials were lax in monitoring CMS prisons and fining CMS for violations; additionally, CMS failed to meet standards for distributing medications to mentally ill prisoners at the Lee Correctional Institution. Counseling staff at both CMS and South Carolina Department of Corrections (SCDC) prison sites also did not meet the minimum qualifications required for their positions.

In prisons where the SCDC provided health care services, the report found only one of 40 required medical audits was conducted during the two years ending in June 1999. Likewise, none of the 21 required dental audits were conducted during the same two-year period. The report said that absent the necessary audits, it's impossible to determine what level of service is being provided.

The South Carolina report underscores the fact that the health care services provided to prisoners by the state, even in the absence of privatization, is often far from adequate. Often the bad health care services of the state are made even worse when private contractors take control. Adding a profit incentive to the mix presents a clear conflict of interest, exacerbating the already abysmal medical care given to prisoners.

A 1999 survey by the University of Massachusetts and Local 285 of the Service Employees International Union (SEIU) accused CMS of "buffing up" in anticipation of state audits, and failure to adequately address staff shortages. CMS also runs the statewide prison health care system in Massachusetts. The survey indicated that some employees work without adequate medical supplies and are asked to sign-off as having received training that they do not actually receive. 98 percent of the survey respondents said they work routinely short-staffed, and 88 percent said they work without essential supplies. Only 19 percent reported that their facility had enough staff on hand to handle emergencies. The anonymous survey was distributed to 215 health care workers at five prisons in central Massachusetts.

Corrections Digest reported that complaints about Minnesota's $9.4 million-a-year contract with CMS soared from 118 in 1998, the year CMS took over the state's prison health care system, to nearly 200 in 1999. The Minnesota Nurses Association, which represents nurses who work within the Minnesota prison system, has complained that there are pharmaceutical errors and delays in obtaining medications. "I get calls where [nurses] are just frantic," association official Mary Kay Haas told the AP.

"I still haven't received any medical attention whatsoever," New Jersey prisoner Hatari Wahaki said in a letter he wrote three days before he died. The health care provider that ignored him to death was none other than CMS. "I consider what they are doing as literally playing with my life," Wahaki wrote.

The increasing privatization of prisoner health care is, indeed, playing with the lives of prisoners. And in an increasing number of instances, this setup is resulting in prisoners literally dying for profits. Following the death of Diane Nelson, 46, a mother of three and a prisoner at the Pinellas County Jail in Florida, nurse Diane Jackson quipped, "We save money because we skip the ambulance and bring them right to the morgue." Though Prison Health Services, Inc. (CMS's primary corporate competitor) provided health care services at Pinellas, Jackson summed up an attitude that is a deadly reality now in control in many of the nations' prisons and jails.

"The Judge Gave Me Ten Years. He Didn't Sentence Me to Death."

Prisoners with HIV deprived of proper care

ANNE-MARIE CUSAC

In prisons and jails across the country, prisoners with HIV or AIDS are being denied proper treatment. In many cases, guards and medical staff block prisoners from getting their vital drug regimens, sometimes for months at a time, or prescribe regimens that are dangerous. Such negligence can lead to drug resistance. It can also lead to death.

"We routinely get letters from people who are not getting their medications," says Christine Doyle, research coordinator for Amnesty International, U.S.A.

The mistreatment appears to be widespread and may affect thousands of prisoners. It may also be illegal.

The Supreme Court has ruled that prisoners must receive adequate medical care. The 1976 decision in *Estelle v. Gamble* states:

> Deliberate indifference to serious medical needs of prisoners constitutes the unnecessary and wanton infliction of pain ... proscribed by the Eighth Amendment. This is true whether the indifference is manifested by prison doctors in their response to the prisoner's needs or by prison guards in intentionally denying or delaying access to medical care or intentionally interfering with the treatment once prescribed.

Since 1996, combinations of three antiretroviral agents, including one protease inhibitor, have dramatically improved the health of many people with HIV and AIDS. The basic government recommendations for HIV and AIDS medications, as outlined by the National Institutes of Health and Human Services, urge three-drug combination therapy for "all patients with symptoms ascribed to HIV infection." Using a combination of two drugs, or one drug alone, is strongly discouraged.

But some state systems deny prisoners treatment, including the three-

This article was first published in *The Progressive*, July 2000.

drug regimen, as a matter of policy. For years, the Mississippi State Prison at Parchman required prisoners with HIV or AIDS to prove they could handle a two-drug regimen for six months before they were allowed access to expensive protease inhibitors. This prison-wide policy applied even to those prisoners who successfully followed a three-drug regimen outside prison.

On March 5, 1999, ten HIV positive patients at Parchman filed a motion for a preliminary injunction as part of an ongoing class-action lawsuit at the prison. They alleged that the medical care they were receiving was endangering their lives.

U.S. Magistrate Jerry Davis responded by filing a preliminary injunction ordering the state of Mississippi to provide its HIV positive prisoners with triple-combination therapy in accordance with the standard of care established by the federal government.

"The court finds that the HIV positive prisoners are entitled, at a minimum, to the degree of care outlined in the guidelines of the National Institutes of Health," reads the court's Memorandum Opinion of July 19, 1999. "Simply because they are incarcerated should not subject these prisoners to a level of care that will significantly lower their chances of surviving with the virus, especially since the treatment that will give maximum suppression is known."

"In case after case I reviewed, prisoners were deliberately denied the standard medical treatment for HIV infection," Robert Cohen testified for the plaintiffs. "It is my professional opinion that the grossly inappropriate care currently being provided is resulting in unnecessary pain and suffering and will be responsible for unnecessary deaths for patients who would respond to appropriate treatment."

Cohen, a medical doctor in New York, has worked in the field of prison health care for twenty-five years. He served as the director of the Montefiore Rikers Island Health Service, where he oversaw health care for 13,000 prisoners, and he has reviewed medical care for the Department of Justice. "What they were doing [at Parchman] was barbaric," he says.

Cohen filed a "Report on the Medical Care of Prisoners with HIV Infection at the Mississippi State Prison Parchman Farm," dated February 25, 1999. "There is a policy at Parchman, clearly stated within the medical records, that patients cannot receive [the protease inhibitor] Crixivan until they have received two medications alone for six months," he wrote. "Adding one new drug to a failing two-drug regimen assures the early development of resistance. This is almost always the wrong approach, and it is the only approach taken at MSP/Parchman."

One prisoner whose medical records he examined was mistreated for more than a year. "Contrary to standard practice, the patient was started on two medications, AZT and 3TC" on September 16, 1997, Cohen wrote. Beyond that, the prisoner had trouble getting any care at all, even when he developed potentially serious symptoms.

"The abysmal care this patient received, and continues to receive, is shocking," Cohen wrote. "He is left to waste away in his cell, constantly having seizures and uncontrolled diarrhea, while the medical staff ignore him, refuse to examine him, make no effort to find out what is wrong with him. When they discover a serious abnormality in the brain, they ignore it. He receives inadequate doses of medication to control his seizure. He complains of loss of vision, and no evaluation takes place. He was intolerant of his medications, yet no effort was made to give him medications which he could tolerate."

Cohen documented another patient who "had been treated on Crixivan, AZT, and 3TC for two years prior to his incarceration." Once this prisoner got to Parchman, he was not allowed Crixivan. Three months later, his viral load "was found to be 38,113," wrote Cohen. (Viral load refers to the amount of virus in the blood.) Even with the patient's elevated count, which indicated resistance, the prison continued to give him the medications that had been proven ineffective.

The prisoner's written notes to the medical staff reveal his anxiety over not receiving his medications. "I was taking Crixivan, before I got to prison, in the free world for two years, but since I got to Parchman I have not been able to get my Crixivan," he wrote on September 8, 1998, according to Cohen's report. "I request once again for my Crixivan. I have been out now for almost three weeks. Please refill my medication." The prisoner received this reply: "You will be started on Crixivan after you have been proven compliant on Combivir [AZT and 3TC combined in one pill] for six months."

Cohen's conclusion: "This is almost unbelievable. A patient doing well on standard combination therapy is taken off his effective treatment. Why? The reason is the MSP [Mississippi State Prison]/Parchman standing policy that you must take six months of therapy with two drugs before you are eligible to get a protease inhibitor. In this case, stopping the Crixivan resulted in the predictable development of resistance. Even with the results of the viral load available, he was restricted on medications which weren't helping him, and he was still denied access to medications that would help him. This is reprehensible."

The Mississippi Department of Corrections disputed Cohen's conclusions. "It is our position that he was incorrect, that he just didn't have enough to go on," says Leonard Vincent, a lawyer for the Mississippi Department of Corrections. He says that Cohen "came in and looked at sixty to eighty records in one day."

However, the Department of Corrections did agree with the judge who ordered the preliminary injunction. "It was our position all along" that health care for prisoners with AIDS and HIV needed to change, says Vincent.

The situation at Parchman is not unique. According to a March 2000 South Carolina Legislative Audit Council report entitled "A Review of

Medical Services at the South Carolina Department of Corrections," the state's approach "begins with a two-drug regimen with the addition of a third drug as needed." That policy, warns the Legislative Audit Council, "is not generally recommended."

Since that audit, the department has asked the South Carolina Department of Health and Environmental Control to review HIV and AIDS care in the prison system, says John Barkley, spokesman for the South Carolina Department of Corrections.

In California, two women's prisons, Central California Women's Facility in Chowchilla and the California Institution for Women in Frontera, were sued in the mid-1990s over allegations of medical negligence and other abuses. Among the plaintiffs were HIV-positive women who claimed they were denied necessary care and medications. In an August 1997 settlement, the prisons agreed to drastic changes in medical care and to award the plaintiffs' attorneys $1.2 million in fees.

Keith Carter, an HIV-positive prisoner doing time for armed robbery in the Florida prison system, says he got his medications. The problem was, he got them at mealtime. In late 1999, he was housed at the Tomoka Correctional Institution in Daytona Beach, Florida. One of his drugs was Crixivan. "I can't eat till an hour after I take it," says Carter. "If I eat, I have to wait two hours. For the longest time, they would wake us up at 8:30 in the morning, give us our medication, then take us directly to breakfast."

Crixivan is made by the Merck pharmaceutical company. According to company literature, eating a heavy meal with the drug can lessen its absorption by 77 percent. One of the drug company's guidelines for administration of Crixivan reads: "Do not take Crixivan at the same time as any meals that are high in calories, fat, and protein (for example, a bacon and egg breakfast). When taken at the same time as Crixivan, these foods can interfere with Crixivan being absorbed into your bloodstream and may lessen its effect."

"So he had a choice of not taking the medication or he could skip breakfast," says John Doellman, who holds power of attorney for Carter.

Carter had carefully researched his medications before he started to take them. Fearing he would become resistant if he did not follow the manufacturer's guidelines, he decided to start skipping breakfast. He says he began to buy extra food from the canteen.

At night, the medication came at the wrong time again. "So I would keep it in my cheek and not swallow it, then get out of there and put it in my pocket," he tells me over the phone. "I did this for months. It was very risky. I could have been locked up in disciplinary confinement for trying to save my own life."

In this way, Carter says he managed to take his medications according to the manufactures' directions. But he says some of his fellow prisoners weren't so wily. "Those guys, a lot of them, don't have people on the outside. They're ignorant—they don't know they're risking their lives taking those meds at the wrong time. Some of them don't realize they're killing themselves. Others think they're dying anyway; it's not worth it. Others don't want to put themselves forward. They're frightened."

Doellman finally contacted Jackie Walker, AIDS coordinator of the ACLU's National Prison Project. "I am writing to you on behalf of Keith E. Carter, #417290, a prisoner living with HIV incarcerated at your facility," wrote Walker to the superintendent of Tomoka Correctional Institution. "I am deeply concerned about reports regarding access to medication for Mr. Carter. . . . He is faced with the difficult choice of abstaining from meals or eating but knowing insufficient levels of Crixivan are reaching his bloodstream. Because of this problem, he skips breakfast and seldom eats lunch. In June, he was diagnosed with anemia, and vitamins were prescribed."

"It took only one letter from Jackie on the ACLU National Prison Project letterhead to straighten that situation out," says Doellman.

The Florida Department of Corrections said that it could not comment on Carter's case.

Carter, who now lives at a halfway house, remains concerned about his health. He says that, despite his efforts, he missed several doses during his time at Tomoka. "It's a terrible, terrible feeling to be powerless over your own life," he says. "The judge gave me ten years. He didn't sentence me to death."

According to the Bureau of Justice Statistics, 25,483 state and federal prisoners were HIV positive in 1998 (the latest numbers available). Not all of these showed symptoms that would require the three-drug regimen. But many who did present such symptoms were refused the care they needed.

In September 1999, the University of Pittsburgh and Stadtlanders Pharmacy (the largest pharmaceuticals supplier to prison systems in the United States) released a study that examined "pharmacy records for all inmates on active antiretroviral therapy receiving medications through Stadtlander Corrections Division between 2–1–99 and 2–28–99." The study, which looked at prisons and jails, found that 36 percent of inmates receiving medications during that month were "on not generally recommended or not recommended antiretroviral regimens," as established by the U.S. Department of Health and Human Services. The study suggests that more than 1,200 prisoners who received medications from Stadtlanders were not being treated in the preferred manner. According to Grant Bryson, vice president of operations for Stadtlander Corrections Division, the pharmaceutical company provides drugs to 330,000 prisoners, or approximately 17 percent of the total "market" of 1.9 million.

If Stadtlander's sample holds true for the rest of the jail and prison population, then approximately 7,400 HIV positive prisoners were not receiving recommended treatment at the time of the study.

But the number may have been much higher. The Stadtlanders study considered only those prisoners who were prescribed inadequate regimens. The study did not consider cases where prisons or jails failed to deliver medications to prisoners, or cases where prisoners received their medications, but did not get them at the appropriate time.

Cary Chrisman, clinical director of Stadtlander Corrections Division, says that treatment rates are improving. Currently, he says, 10 to 13 percent of prisoners are not receiving the preferred drug regimens.

Advocates and health experts say the problem with delivery of AIDS medications appears to be worse in jails than in prisons. People who end up in jail often do not have their medications in their possession at the time of arrest. Sometimes, their friends and family members are prevented from bringing those medications to them. Advocates also say that jails have more trouble than prisons establishing regular medical regimens for people with AIDS or HIV because prisoners stay in jail for short stints or are transferred to other institutions.

There is an "attempt being made" to practice adequate health care for patients with HIV in the prisons, says Ronald Shansky, a physician who monitors health care in correctional facilities all over the country. "I think you're finding a much bigger problem when they get into a small jail." Shansky cites common jail policies of "confiscating personal property, including medicine" as a problem.

On October 12, 1998, sixteen prisoners submitted a grievance letter to the Fulton County Jail in Georgia. "This is an urgent matter related to blatant neglect of AIDS/HIV inmates housed in 3 South 500. We are not receiving adequate medical treatment," they wrote. "We are not receiving antiviral drug therapy medications as prescribed by infectious disease clinics protocol, nor are we being taken seriously about our AIDS related complication[s]. . . . Our lives are being placed in high risk environment as well as grave danger." The letter was signed, "The entire 3500 (3S500) Zone."

"Basically, people are entering the jail at their own risk," says Tamara Serwer, a lawyer with the Atlanta-based Southern Center for Human Rights. Serwer represented prisoners in a 1999 lawsuit against Fulton County. Many of these prisoners were denied their HIV medication for weeks.

"During the intake process on May 25, 1999, I slept on the floor in an overcrowded, filthy holding cell for two days containing no mattress. I did not receive any medication until July 7, 1999," reads the affidavit of Willie Bass, a prisoner at the Fulton County Jail. The suit led to a settlement agreement to improve jail health care, including adequate treatment for prisoners while in the jail and several days' worth of medicine upon release.

Robert Greifinger, a former head medical officer at the New York State Department of Corrections and the New York City Jails, now serves as the monitor for the court. On March 2, he filed a quarterly document entitled, "Report on Medical Care for HIV-Infected Inmates at Fulton County Jail, Initial Assessment."

"I reviewed the mortality report on prisoner W, who died during 1999 with HIV infection," he wrote. "Even after months in custody, he never got to an HIV specialist, and never got medication. His death may be attributable to this delay in access to care. In the case of H, who also died during 1999, there were serious lapses in care. For example, physician orders for medications were never picked up by the nursing staff, and the prisoner did not get medication."

Greifinger also looked at the medical care received by women at the jail. "I reviewed the medical care of two HIV+ women who had been sent to the emergency room during the few months preceding my visit," he wrote. "Patient C.S. had known HIV infection for fourteen years. It took eleven days for her to get her physical examination and more than 3.5 months to get to the HIV specialist. There is no documentation as to the reason she was not given medication. She was not immunized against pneumonia, as recommended for HIV+ persons. One consequence of this delay was a hospitalization for pneumonia for a week."

Greifinger concluded, "The medical care for HIV-infected prisoners at the Fulton County Jail does not meet the expectations set out in the Final Settlement Agreement." On March 13, Greifinger's report led to a consent order to correct "gross inadequacies of medical care."

Shortly after this report, Greifinger filed another, observing that the Fulton County sheriff had replaced Correctional Healthcare Solutions, Inc., formerly in charge of health care at the jail, with another company, Correctional Medical Associates, Inc., and that the place appeared cleaner and better run. The jail was again ordered to improve care. The monitoring process is ongoing.

The new medical provider "is doing what the judge has ordered" so that prisoners who are sick when they come to the jail don't "leave us sicker and still untreated," says Captain David Chadd, public information officer of the Fulton County Sheriff's Department.

Meanwhile, a similar suit in nearby DeKalb County, Georgia, is just getting started. "HIV-positive prisoners receive a virtual death sentence immediately upon incarceration at the DeKalb County Jail, especially those who are being treated with antiviral drug regimens prior to their incarceration," says the complaint filed by fourteen prisoners. "Such prisoners are routinely deprived of such regimens for days, weeks, and even months despite repeated requests for medical attention and despite having made proper jail personnel aware of their HIV-positive status." The DeKalb County Sheriff's Office denies the charges. "No prisoner is deprived of any medical care once incarcerated in the DeKalb County Jail," says Cherlea Dorsey, the public information officer.

Robert Sullivan, of Tacoma, Washington, says a few days in the Pierce

County Jail destroyed his health. Sullivan is in the final stages of AIDS. Both he and the jail told the court in a recent lawsuit that he did not receive his medications for at least two days. His wife was finally permitted to bring them in on Sullivan's last day in jail.

"The virus had time to mutate," Sullivan tells me by phone from his home in Tacoma. "I've tried eight different drug combinations since then. Consecutively, the drugs have failed." Sullivan sued Pierce County.

Sullivan, who is 6'2", now weighs 115 pounds and is bedridden. According to his lawyer and his caseworker, he came so close to dying he was taken off life support.

"I don't know how you can tie [the drug failure] to two days in jail without your medications," says Frank Krall, Pierce County deputy prosecuting attorney. "I have a specialist from Swedish Medical Center in Seattle, Washington, who testified that two days didn't do anything to Mr. Sullivan."

Krall agrees that Sullivan did not get his protease inhibitor and antiretroviral medications for two days, but he says that did not result from deliberate indifference. "People need to know that we tried to get Mr. Sullivan his drugs," says Krall. "He got to see a nurse within minutes of getting there. He got to see a doctor within four hours. We contacted his physician."

On April 21, 2000, the United States Court of Appeals for the Ninth Circuit overturned a previous decision, which had dismissed Sullivan's lawsuit against Pierce County. The jail had claimed that since it did not stock Sullivan's medications, it was under no obligation to provide them to prisoners. The appeals court soundly rejected that argument.

"It is undisputed, that, for at least forty-eight to seventy-two hours, Sullivan was deprived of his medication, although PCDCC [Pierce County Detention and Corrections Center] medical officials knew that Sullivan was in the final stage of AIDS and that he was in dire need of that medication—in particular, his protease inhibitor, Invirase," wrote judges Stephen Reinhardt, David Thompson, and Thomas Nelson. "Both Doctors Flemming and Bay [Dr. Flemming is Sullivan's physician; Dr. Bay is the head physician at the Pierce County Jail], as well as Joyce Newlun, booking nurse at the PCDCC, testified that it was common medical knowledge that an AIDS patient taking protease inhibitors as part of an AIDS cocktail had to remain in strict compliance with that regimen at all times and without exception, lest the cocktail become ineffective."

"It would have been simple for them to do the right thing," says Sullivan's lawyer, B. Michael Clarke. "All they had to do was have his wife bring in the medicines. And if they had a problem with that, they could have gone down to the drug store. He'd been literally given his life back, and the jail took it away."

Why do some jails and prisons persist in providing substandard care? "Interviews with staff and prison advocates in several major correctional systems indicate that a combination of factors—including high medication costs; prisoner reluctance to seek testing and treatment based on denial, fear, and/or mistrust; and uneven clinical competence and lack of uniform treatment standards—may limit the availability of appropriate HIV treatment regimens to prisoners," says a July 1999 report sponsored by the National Institute of Justice, the Centers for Disease Control and Prevention, and the Bureau of Justice Statistics.

The U.S. government estimates that costs for antiretroviral therapy run approximately $12,000 per prisoner per year. Says Cohen, "These medications are so expensive that in many cases there is a tremendous incentive to miss them. There should be no financial incentive to miss them. There should be no financial incentive to limit access to medications or to medical care."

Anne De Groot, co-chair of the HIV Education Prison Project at Brown University, is a staff physician at a number of women's correctional institutions. "The system just constantly fails," she says. "It fails because the medicines are not delivered to the prison—so prisoners will get one or two of the three drugs. Or the medications will be rationed by inconvenience" when staff have trouble following complicated protocols for obtaining the drugs. "Meanwhile, the treatment is in suspension," and the prisoner does not receive medicines.

"I'm giving you examples from some of the places where I work," she says. "I happen to work in some of the best places on the East Coast for care. I don't even want to think about what goes on elsewhere."

De Groot mentions one doctor, whom she describes as "excellent." However, that single doctor, she says, is responsible for all the prisons in a single state system on the East Coast. "If you're taking care of 300 people [with HIV or AIDS] in one prison, then 300 in another, there's no way you can do anything but put out brush fires."

Mistreating HIV-positive prisoners can be devastating to the afflicted. But the effects are not confined behind prison walls.

"Failure to adhere consistently to the regimens may have serious public health consequences if drug-resistant strains are transmitted to others," says the July 1999 report from the National Institute of Justice, the Centers for Disease Control and Prevention, and the Bureau of Justice Statistics.

"This is going to create an enormous public health crisis on the outside—as well as inside the prisons," says Cynthia Chandler, director of the Women's Positive Legal Action Network in Oakland. "It would not surprise me if we start finding large amounts of drug-resistant HIV as a result of people coming back into their communities after having been denied their medications while in prison."

FDOC Hazardous to Prisoners' Health

MARK SHERWOOD AND BOB POSEY

Imagine discovering that your doctor has lost multiple malpractice suits, and has also been sued by former patients for fraud and sexual abuse. Imagine that you next discover your doctor has subsequently had his license revoked, and is barred from practice. Most likely, you would be horrified to discover such claims, and assume that your doctor must be a complete incompetent. Such doctors—those found incompetent to practice in any other jurisdiction—are sought after and employed by prison systems across the country, prison systems that get cut-rate deals on third-rate physicians.

A recent investigation in Florida unearthed exactly the above scenario within the Florida Department of Corrections (FDOC). In a series by the *St. Petersburg Times,* reporters discovered that 30 percent of the 129 doctors employed in Florida prisons have serious black marks on their records for acts ranging from malpractice to sexual abuse of patients to fraud (September 26–28, 1999). And because of inadequate care by such "professionals," Florida prisoners are dying at alarming rates.

Additionally, prisoners' families who subsequently pursue wrongful death claims against the DOC are often barred from doing so by state and federal legislation (like the Prison Litigation Reform Act) making it extremely difficult to successfully sue the DOC for medical malpractice— even when malpractice results in disfigurement or death. Further, even without such bars to legal recourse, prison doctors would be shielded from personal liability anyway, with taxpayers inevitably footing the bill for judgments against prison doctors.

The special report by the *Times* showed that the DOC has been a dumping ground for years for incompetent (if not all-out dangerous) physicians. Doctors who have repeatedly lost malpractice claims, have

This article was written in May 2000.

been found guilty of sexually abusing their patients, found guilty of fraud, and who only have temporary or restricted licenses, or who have been disciplined by the State Board of Medicine, are a bargain for the DOC. And that appears to be the real incentive for the DOC, which is constitutionally required to provide at least some health care for the 68,000 prisoners in its custody.

Life and Death Cost-Cutting

The average doctor straight out of medical school earns $120,000 a year. The DOC pays far less, with salaries ranging from $72,000 to $86,000 a year. Because prison doctors are indemnified by the state, the prison system offers a safe haven for doctors with troubled professional pasts by allowing them to avoid paying the exorbitant malpractice insurance they would otherwise be required to purchase on the outside.

David Thomas, the Florida DOC's chief doctor, admits that economic considerations figure predominantly in the department's hiring practices. "Clearly, you would prefer people that don't have any problems," Thomas said. "But I do think there is a place for well-trained people who have made a mistake, and we may be well placed to do that because we have a degree of control over our doctors that the outside world does not."

Some question why the DOC hires doctors with questionable histories and puts them in charge of a $225-million health care system, and the lives of prisoners.

"Those numbers are pretty atrocious," said Randall Berg, a lawyer with the Florida Justice Institute in Miami. "It shows they really don't care what level of care is provided—they're operating on the cheap."

Shady Physicians

The *Times* investigation discovered that of the 129 doctors employed by the DOC, 16 have lost medical malpractice claims against them in Florida, some more than once.

Fourteen prison doctors have disciplinary records with the state medical boards, a relatively rare distinction: in comparison, last year less than half of one percent of the nation's doctors were disciplined by the state medical board.

Seven of the FDOC doctors have been disciplined more than once by medical boards and nine are listed in a book entitled *Questionable Doctors* that is put out by a national consumer group. In addition, three of the doctors have a history of sexual misconduct with patients, and 15 doctors are practicing on temporary or restricted licenses. Under an exception in Florida law, doctors with restricted licenses, or those who have not passed either the Florida or national medical exam but are licensed in another state, may work in Florida's prisons.

Overall, only one-third of all the DOC's doctors are certified in a specialty, a requirement generally necessary to work at a hospital or for an HMO.

Between 1996 and 1998, the Florida DOC admits it only reported three doctors to the state medical board. Two of those doctors, Abigail Rosario-Rivera and Frederick Vontz, are still employed by the DOC—even after being complained against before the state's medical board for negligence resulting in the death of several Florida prisoners.

The department is even willing to hire doctors with criminal records. Dr. Robert Briggs, the chief medical executive at Charlotte Correctional Institution, pleaded guilty in federal court in 1981 to filing fraudulent Medicare payment invoices.

Another doctor, Dr. Effong Andem, was disciplined in 1994 by the army, with charges including "lack of attention to detail, failure to assume responsibility for patients, failure to admit or recognize errors, and failure to learn from mistakes." The next year, he was hired by the DOC.

Dr. Mireya Francis was disciplined by the Florida Board of Medicine in 1993 for dispensing drugs to mentally ill patients without first performing psychiatric evaluations. In 1995 she was again disciplined for lying on an application about being barred from practicing medicine in Ohio. Nevertheless, the DOC hired her.

Dr. Arnold Azcuy is a medical executive at the North Florida Reception Center. He is in charge of reviewing prisoners' medical cases statewide and makes the ultimate decision as to whether a prisoner receives care. Dr. Azcuy paid out on three medical malpractice suits before coming to work for the DOC. Two of the claims against him involved the deaths of his patients.

Another DOC doctor, Stanley Dratler, lost his medical license for three years in 1986 for fondling female patients. Before coming to the DOC, Dr. Jose Gonzalez was disciplined by the medical board after giving the wrong medicine to a pregnant woman, causing her uterus to rupture and the fetus to die.

Dying by the Dozens

The DOC maintains that the medical care provided to prisoners is as good as one can get on the outside. But then they never thought anyone would care enough to take a closer look, or that DOC Secretary Michael Moore would unintentionally open the Pandora's box of Florida prison health care.

In 1999, Moore proposed to Governor Jeb Bush that money could be saved if three oversight committees—the Florida Corrections Commission (FCC), the Correctional Medical Authority (CMA), and the Correctional Privatization Commission (CPC)—were done away with. Despite the fact that the three entities provide an important measure of oversight of DOC operations, Moore told Bush that they were unnecessary, that the department could more efficiently supervise itself.

The proposal backfired, and wound up instead focusing public scrutiny upon the responsibilities and mandates of the commissions. The CMA, a group established by the Florida legislature to audit prison medical care in 1993, balked at Moore's proposal to do away with the oversight committees, and instead released a flood of information about Florida prison doctors' shady pasts and horrendous professional records to the media, blowing the lid off the otherwise neglected topic.

According to the CMA, since January 1994 at least 56 Florida prisoners have died from inadequate medical treatment. That's almost one in eight of the 463 death records that the CMA reviewed for that period.

"These deaths could have been prevented," said Linda Keen, executive director of the CMA. CMA records indicate that Florida prisoners have been dying by the dozens as a direct result of substandard and negligent medical care while incarcerated.

To obtain unbiased peer review of their findings and to confirm their suspicions, the CMA hired private doctors with no ties to the DOC to review a sampling of deaths at the state's prison hospitals.

Every few weeks the CMA sent the findings of the consultants to various lawmaking bodies, including the governor, the legislature, and the DOC. But CMA's authority to mandate any real change was severely limited under Florida law, which allows the entity only the power to make recommendations, recommendations the DOC may choose to implement or not.

Kay Harris, who prepared the CMA reports, said that despite the obvious problems illustrated in the reports, no fundamental changes occurred and public concern was little to nil. "The average John Q. Citizen doesn't care about inmate health care," Harris said.

John Burke, chief administrator of the DOC's health care system, disputes the accusation that the department is at fault. Despite the CMA's assertions, the department's record is a good one, he insists. "A percentage of people are going to die no matter what you do, and I don't think our percentage [of deaths] is inordinately high considering the population we take care of," said Thomas. "We're not perfect. People make mistakes, and other people suffer for it."

Mentally Ill Prisoners Fare No Better

The *St. Petersburg Times* series also explored care received by mentally ill prisoners—a population consistently overrepresented in prisons across the country. The *Times* reported that within the state prison population at least one of every nine prisoners suffers from serious mental illness, and that mental health staff are often overwhelmed by enormous caseloads. Some mental health staff members also complained of a lack of institutional support for their work, citing the pervasive belief among administrators and guards that mental health workers are "coddlers" who are easily manipulated by prisoners.

"Often it's security who [make] the call that inmates [fake mental health problems], so that it's okay not to provide treatment for them. There's an attitude that all inmates are [faking]," said Helen Cunningham, who quit the DOC in August 1999, as Baker Correctional Institution's senior psychologist. Cunningham said she often had to wait days before guards would bring prisoners requesting mental health care to her. She said she was treated worse by prison guards if she wrote up reports on allegations that prisoners had been abused, as she was often required to do.

The Florida DOC spends over $46 million a year on mental health but still is falling behind, with need far outpacing care provided, and existing care being reduced even further. In the last two years at least 65 mental health staff positions have been cut. The numbers of mentally ill entering the system and the cost of psychotropic drugs are rising faster than the DOC budget.

"It's being tightened down as tight as we can get it," said Florida DOC's deputy director, John Burke. "[But] we think we're still providing care that meets the constitutional standard." Yet Burke concedes that the prison setting may be wholly inappropriate for the mentally ill. "Once these guys are put in prison they've got to function in a structured environment, a very structured environment, and some of them can't. But that's not a correctional officer's fault."

Others see mistreatment of the mentally ill in Florida prisons as an entirely foreseeable consequence of lack of funding and inattention on behalf of the Florida DOC and the state's various lawmaking bodies.

"As they cut mental health services, which is what they're doing, you are going to have more and more inmates who are unmanageable because of mental illness," said Connie Schenk, a former Florida DOC psychologist who quit in frustration in 1999. "The way [the DOC] deals with mentally ill inmates who can be problematic is just to put them into close management [sensory depriving confinement], where they don't get near the access to help that they used to," said Schenk.

Social science and clinical literature consistently reports that when any person (whether mentally ill, or not) is subjected to social isolation and reduced environmental stimulation, that person is likely to psychically deteriorate, and in some cases may actually develop psychiatric disorders. The effects of such isolated confinement almost certainly create more problems for those already suffering from mental illness. "A prison is absolutely the worst place for somebody with severe mental illness, and absolutely certain to exacerbate their symptoms," said Ron Honberg, legal director for the National Alliance for the Mentally Ill.

Kay Redfield Jamison, a professor of psychiatry at the John Hopkins School of Medicine, notes that, "The incarceration of the mentally ill is a disastrous, horrible social issue." Subjecting the mentally ill to isolated confinement situations "can exacerbate their hallucinations or delusions," Jamison said.

Despite a wealth of well-researched and documented studies showing that isolated confinement of the mentally ill has destructive and damaging effects, the Florida DOC has actually increased the use of isolation techniques, and plans to increase its use even further without consideration of the long-term effects or the eventual cost to society or taxpayers. Such prisoners will eventually be released into the community with real, preventable damage to their psyches and spirits.

Decades of Neglect

The present allegations and mounting heaps of evidence against the Florida DOC and its shamefully below par health care staff are not new to the state's prison system. For 20 years, between 1973 and 1993, Florida's prison system was under the control of federal courts as a result of a consent decree won in *Costello v. Wainwright,* a 1973 case challenging the poor quality of medical care provided to state prisoners.

In *Costello,* court-appointed medical teams found that prison officials provided substandard medical care as a routine norm. After costly improvements and under pressure from the federal court for a showing of real progress, *Costello* was finally settled in 1993, when the state promised to provide medical and mental health treatment equivalent to the outside community's standard of care.

Bill Sheppard, the lawyer representing prisoners in *Costello* said that the problem today is the same as it was two decades ago: Lack of money.

"Every damn death I've seen is a sad story," Sheppard said. "And the legislature is the. . . . damn cause of it."

Randall Berg, an attorney with the Florida Justice Institute, said medical care did improve in the prisons up until the lawsuit's dismissal in 1993. "Things got measurably better. But it didn't take long for it to get back where it was. . . . And it's getting progressively worse," Berg commented.

It has become so bad and problems are so rampant that even Florida's normally prison-myopic legislators have begun to take notice. According to Senator Skip Campbell, vice chairman of the Senate Criminal Justice Committee, "I can assure you I get a letter a month from inmates saying, 'I'm not getting proper care.' I'm starting to believe now that maybe they aren't getting the treatment [they need]."

Bill Clinton's Blood Trails

JEFFREY ST. CLAIR

The year Bill Clinton became governor of Arkansas, the Arkansas state prison board awarded a hefty contract to a Little Rock company called Health Management Associates (HMA). The company got $3 million a year to run medical services for the state's awful prison system, which had been excoriated in a ruling by the U.S. Supreme Court as an "evil place run by some evil men."

HMA not only made money from providing medical care to prisoners, but it also started a profitable side venture: blood mining. The company paid prisoners $7 a pint to have their blood drawn (about half what urban skid row bloodsuckers pay for winos' blood). HMA then sold the blood on the international plasma market for $50 a pint, with half of that going to the Arkansas Department of Corrections.

Since Arkansas is one of the states that does not pay prisoners for their labor, prisoners were frequent donors at the so-called "blood clinic." Hundreds of prisoners sold as much as two pints a week to HMA. The blood was then sold to pharmaceutical companies, such as Bayer and Baxter International; to blood banks, such as the Red Cross; and to so-called blood fractionizers, which transform the blood into medicines for hemophiliacs.

HMA's contract with the Arkansas DOC and its entry into the blood market came at the same time as the rise of AIDS in the United States. Regardless, HMA did not screen the torrents of prison blood, even after the Food and Drug Administration issued special alerts about the higher incidence of AIDS and hepatitis in prison populations.

When American drug companies and blood fractionizers stopped buying blood taken from prisoners in the early 1980s, HMA turned to the international blood market, selling to companies in Italy, France,

This article originally appeared in the February 1–15, 1999 issue of *Counterpunch*.

Spain, and Japan. But the prime buyer of HMA's tainted blood, drawn largely from prisoners at the Cummings Unit in Grady, Arkansas, was a notorious Canadian firm, Continental Pharma Cryosan Ltd.

Cryosan had a shady reputation in the medical industry. It had been nabbed importing blood taken from Russian cadavers and relabeled as from Swedish volunteers. The company also marketed blood taken from Haitian slums.

Cryosan passed the tainted Arkansas prison blood on to the Canadian Red Cross and European and Asian companies. The blood was recalled in 1983 after the FDA discovered the contamination. But less than one-sixth of the blood was recovered. In Canada alone more than 7,000 people have died from receiving contaminated blood, many of them hemophiliacs. More than 4,000 of these died of AIDS. Another 40,000 people in Canada have contracted various forms of hepatitis.

A $300-million class action suit has been filed on behalf of the Canadian victims of Cryosan's tainted blood. According to one of the attorneys for the plaintiffs, David Harvey, the suit names Bill Clinton and officials at the Arkansas DOC as co-defendants.

Cryosan's former president, Ted Hecht, doesn't believe his company did anything wrong. "Don't look upon me as a villain in the piece. We supplied U.S.-government licensed product and never denied its origins," he told the *Ottawa News*, which first broke the story in September 1998. "I never forced anyone to buy my product. If they didn't want it, they didn't have to buy it. I didn't shove it down their throats."

Hecht may have a point. His plasma packages were labeled, "ADC, Grady Arkansas." But the Arkansas DOC and its contractor, HMA, have few excuses. They oversaw a shoddily run prison blood-drawing operation that cross-contaminated prisoners and let loose on the global blood market thousands of pints of plasma they had good reason to believe were contaminated with lethal disease.

Dr. Francis "Bud" Henderson founded HMA in the 1970s. As the company began to expand, he brought in a Little Rock banker named Leonard Dunn to run the firm, while he served as its medical director. Dunn was a political ally and friend of the Clintons. He was appointed by Clinton to sit on the Arkansas Industrial Development Commission and served as finance chair of Clinton's 1990 gubernatorial campaign. Later that same year, Dunn bought the famous Madison Guaranty Savings and Loan from Clinton's business partner James McDougal. Dunn now serves as chief of staff to Arkansas Lieutenant Governor Winthrop Rockerfeller.

In 1983, the Food and Drug Administration stripped HMA of its license to sell blood after it found that the company failed to exclude donors who had tested positive for hepatitis B, often a precursor of HIV. A state police report compiled as part of an investigation into the company's operations at the Cummings Unit noted that the FDA pulled the

HMA's license to sell blood "for falsifying records and shipping hot blood." The report goes on to say that "the suspension was for collecting and shipping plasma which had been collected from donors with a history of positive tests for [hepatitis B] ... the violations were directly related to using inmate labor in the record and donor reject list."

Dunn's ties to Clinton served HMA well. He and Arkansas DOC officials convinced the FDA that the fault lay with a prison guard who was taking kickbacks from rejected prisoners in order to let them get back into the blood trade. The license was quickly restored and the tainted blood once more began to flow.

That didn't end the investigations, however. HMA's contract was up for renewal by the prison board and its slipshod record posed a big problem for the firm. When investigators began probing the company's practices, including allegations of prisoner abuse, Dunn repeatedly boasted of his ties to Bill Clinton.

"Mr. Dunn spoke openly and freely and explained to these investigators that he was the financial portion of the corporation as well as its political arm," investigator Sam Probasco noted in his report. "Dunn advised that he was close to Gov. Clinton as well as the majority of state politicians presently in office."

The allegations against the company involved numerous health and safety violations, failure to test for diseases such as hepatitis and syphilis, bad bookkeeping and outright falsification of records. HMA officials maintained the problems were minor and that the blood program was actually driven by a need to give prisoners "pocket money" to buy cigarettes and other personal items.

"The inmates had no way to earn hard dollars except by selling plasma," said HMA's Dr. Henderson. "The prison population was fairly restless anyway." Of course, many of the prisoners paid a heavy price for the miserly $7 they got for each pint. It seems that even with the onset of AIDS, the Cummings blood center often skimped, drawing blood from multiple patients with the same needle.

According to Michael Galster, who worked as a medical specialist at the Cummings Unit at the time, HMA hired Vince Foster, then with the Rose Law Firm, to help squash the state's investigation. Foster seems to have accomplished the task; the state's internal investigation of HMA cleared the company of any wrongdoing.

But an independent review by the Institute for Law and Policy Planning, a California firm, concluded that HMA's work in the prisons was extremely deficient. Their report cited more than 40 contract violations and was replete with instances of negligent care of prisoner patients and in its handling of the blood center. Much of the blame was placed on another Clinton pal, Art Lockhart, head of the Arkansas DOC.

When the independent review came out, pressure mounted for Clinton to fire Lockhart. Clinton swiftly nixed the idea, telling reporters that he didn't believe the allegations were serious enough for him to "ask Mr. Lockhart to resign."

The Arkansas State Police launched a half-hearted investigation into allegations that HMA was awarded a renewal of its contract after bribing members of the state prison board. The investigation soon focused on an attorney named Richard Mays, a close friend of Bill and Hillary Clinton. Mays was given at least $25,000 by HMA to act as an "ombudsman" for the company, a position that apparently carried no job description and no responsibilities.

Mays, who served as a vice-president for finance at the Democratic National Committee, is at the center of several Clinton scandals. In 1996, he was credited with securing Little Rock restaurateur Charlie Trie's $100,000 contribution to the Democratic Party's coffers. He also pops up in the Whitewater probe, where he tried to stave off the federal prosecution of David Hale. Mays and his wife have been frequent visitors to the White House, including an overnight stay in the Lincoln bedroom. Dunn claims that Mays was recommended to him by Clinton and prison board chairman and Clinton intimate Woodson Walker.

In 1986, HMA's contract was revoked. But that didn't stop the Arkansas DOC's prison blood program. A new company, Pine Bluff Biologicals, took over the blood center and expanded it to include two other Arkansas prisons. The new company's safety record turned out to be about as dismal as HMA's. Screening for AIDS was particularly lax. Pine Bluff's president Jimmy Lord dismissed such concerns and suggested that AIDS was not a problem in Arkansas.

"If anyone [prisoners] got caught in a homosexual act," Lord recently told Arkansas reporter Suzi Parker, "we took them off the [blood donation] roster."

By the late 1980s, Arkansas was the only prison system in the United States still running a blood program. In 1991, a reporter for the *Arkansas Times* asked John Byus, medical director of the Arkansas Corrections Department, how much longer they planned to continue the operation. "We plan to stick with it till the last day, to the last drop we're able to sell."

The program stayed in operation until Bill Clinton moved to Washington. It was finally shut down in 1993 by his successor, Jim "Guy" Tucker.

RAPE, RACISM, AND REPRESSION

When most people think of prisoners, they think of monstrous men who rape and terrorize other prisoners. And a few prisoners fit the stereotype. Then there is the growing public awareness of guard brutality, as the more sensational stories eventually wind their way to the public: guards who routinely rape and harass female prisoners; staff who stage fights between prisoners with histories of antagonism for "entertainment"—just to name a few of the stories of prison violence now familiar even to free world people.

But the picture, when filled out, shows a culture that not only allows prisoner rapes and other acts of brutality, but in fact encourages or propagates them. Violence necessarily permeates the institution of prison, and it serves an important purpose. Routine prison brutality keeps prisoners from challenging the conditions of their confinement and organizing en masse against their captors. The raped, raping, brutalized, or brutalizing prisoner has little left to contribute to an organized resistance.

In this chapter, the portrait of human cruelty that emerges shows, in the larger framework, what an institution of violence will necessarily produce: the byproducts of rape, racism, and repression for all of its participants.

—TH

The Restraint Chair

Safe and Humane?

ANNE-MARIE CUSAC

Jail and prison employees call it the "strap-o-lounger," the "barca-lounger," the "we care chair," and the "be sweet chair." Prisoners and their lawyers have other names for the device: "torture chair," "slave chair," and "devil's chair." They are not referring to the electric chair, but to a restraining device that has led to many serious abuses, including torture and death. Belts and cuffs prevent the prisoner's legs, arms, and torso from moving. The restraint chair is designed for violent prisoners who pose an immediate threat to themselves or others. But according to interviews with prisoners, lawyers, and restraint chair manufacturers, as well as a review of court cases, jail videotapes, coroners' reports, and scattered news stories, it is clear that the restraint chair is being used in an improper and sometimes sadistic manner.

The chair has been used against children in custody for nonviolent behaviors. Prisoners and detainees have been left in restraint chairs for as long as eight days. In some cases, the jail staff failed to manipulate the prisoner's limbs to protect against blood clots. While in restraint chairs, prisoners have been interrogated, forced to testify, tortured while hooded and pepper-sprayed, beaten or threatened with electrocution. Some prisoners have been strapped in the chair completely nude. At least eleven people have died under questionable circumstances after being strapped into a restraint chair.

The restraint chair has become extremely popular and is in widespread use: jails, state and federal prisons, the Immigration and Naturalization Service, the U.S. Marshals Service, state mental hospitals, and juvenile detention centers are all equipped with the chair.

Amnesty International has called for a federal inquiry into use of the restraint chair. The device "is an issue of great concern to us," says Angela Wright, an Amnesty researcher on the United States. "It appears

This article was originally published in *The Progressive*, 2000.

to be used in some jurisdictions as a frontline, or even routine form of control, including as a punishment for disruptive or annoying behavior."

Michael Valent, a mentally ill prisoner, died after spending sixteen hours nude in a restraint chair in a Utah prison in March 1997. The deputy chief medical examiner, Edward Leis, confirmed that Valent's prolonged restraint "is the main precipitating factor leading blood clots and his death." A lawsuit brought by Valent's mother ended in a $200,000 settlement with the state of Utah. Although it was not a stipulation of the lawsuit, the state stopped using the restraint chair.

Scott Norberg died in June 1996, of what the Maricopa County Medical Examiners Office called "accidental positional asphyxia" after he was gagged and pushed into a restraint chair, his head forced to his chest and shocked with a stun gun. Maricopa County and its insurance carrier settled a wrongful death lawsuit with Norberg's family for $8.25 million in 1998.

Katalin Zentai, a former journalist, died in late 1996 at the Connecticut Valley Hospital after being held in a restraint chair at a local jail for thirty-three hours. She died, after being released from the chair, as the result of blood clots that had formed in her legs and traveled to her lungs.

On April 17, 1995, Carmelo Marrero died in the Sacramento County Jail while strapped in a restraint chair. The County Coroner's Office said his death was an accident. Officially, his death was listed as the result of "probable acute cardiac arrhythmia, due to probable hypoxemia, due to combined restraint asphyxia and severe physical exertion, due to apparent manic psychotic episode." As Supervising Deputy Coroner Phil Ehlert explained to the *Sacramento Bee*, hypoxemia is "a lack of oxygen caused by a highly agitated state exacerbated by imposed restraint." A class action lawsuit against the jail, which was eventually settled for $750,000, claimed that the device had repeatedly been used for torture at the jail and that Marrero's death was a direct result of his time in the restraint chair.

Demetrius Brown, a twenty-year-old, mentally ill man, died in Jacksonville, Florida, on October 31,1999, after a guard held him in a choke hold while others attempted to strap him into a restraining chair. "The manner of the death," concluded the medical examiner's report, "is homicidal."

In early December 1996, twenty-two-year-old Anderson Tate was arrested after a routine traffic stop and taken to the St. Lucie County Jail in Florida. He informed the jail personnel that he had swallowed a large amount of cocaine. He was denied medical care and "died while strapped in a restraint chair," reported Amnesty International in 1998. As Tate died, "he was in the chair for three hours, moaning and chanting prayers, while jailers taunted him and ignored his pleas for help. Two deputies were dismissed after an administrative investigation by the Sheriff's Department, but no criminal charges were filed." The incident was recorded by a video camera.

On March 5, 1997, Daniel Sagers died in an Osceola County, Florida, jail after guards placed him in a restraint chair and beat him, using a towel to force his head back so violently that they damaged his brain stem. Sagers was being held at the jail for firing a shotgun while on a golf range. His family eventually won a $2.2 million civil lawsuit. In February 1999, a former guard was convicted of manslaughter in Sagers' death and sentenced to one year in jail. He has filed an appeal. Two other guards pleaded no contest to charges of battery and were placed on probation.

On December 20, 1994, Shedrick Brown died after struggling with guards while being forced into a restraint chair in the Hillsborough County Jail in Tampa, Florida. After four hours in the chair, he was found unresponsive, having suffered a stroke. He died an hour later. In March 1995, the Hillsborough County Medical Examiner's Office ruled his death a homicide.

On August 30, 1997, Anthony R. Goins died in a Kansas City, Missouri, jail of cardiac arrest after struggling with guards who squirted him with pepper spray and strapped him in a restraint chair. When the officers returned a few minutes later from washing the spray off themselves and planning to clean up Goins, they found him dead. The coroner said that the drug PCP and Goins' struggle with the police were contributing factors in his death.

In December 1998, Kenneth Vincent Bishop died at the Pueblo County Jail in Colorado shortly after being placed in a restraint chair. Although the Pueblo County coroner ruled that his death resulted from an excessive level of amphetamines, the sheriff has denied the ACLU's open-records request of the video of Bishop's treatment. According to Mark Silverstein, legal director of the American Civil Liberties Union of Colorado, the sheriff has also refused to hand over the jail's restraint policy.

On the night of July 6, 1999, James Earl Livingston had a psychotic episode. Suffering from delusions, he believed his brother in-law was chasing and trying to kill him. Livingston, a thirty-one-year-old man with schizophrenia from Tarrant County, Texas, ran to the police for protection. In about eight hours, half of that time spent in a restraint chair, Livingston was dead.

The Tarrant County Medical Examiner's Office ruled in August 1999, that Livingston's was a natural death caused by bronchial pneumonia. But that's not the whole truth, says Richard Haskell, a lawyer who is representing Livingston's mother, Maxine Jackson, in a suit against the Tarrant County Sheriff's Department. He says Livingston's last stint in the chair killed him. "So far as we know, he was pepper-sprayed in the face and then placed in a restraint chair," says Haskell. Livingston was not allowed to wash the pepper spray out of his eyes or off his face in apparent violation of Tarrant County Sheriff's Department procedures, says Haskell. "He was not decontaminated, and he was left alone in a room. Within twenty minutes he was dead."

Pepper spray "inflames the mucous membranes, causing closing of the eyes, coughing, gagging, shortness of breath, and an acute burning sensation on the skin and inside the nose and mouth," said Amnesty International in a 1998 report on human rights abuses in the United States. "There is considerable concern about its health risks."

Deputy Mark Lane Smith was the first person to perform artificial respiration on Livingston in an unsuccessful attempt to revive him. When another deputy took over, wrote Smith in a Detention Bureau Report, "I then removed myself from the area and walked into the sallyport, where I threw up from inhaling pepper gas residue from inmate Livingston."

It's hard to imagine the terror someone feels who is buckled into a restraint chair after being pepper-sprayed, says Haskell. "'You wouldn't do that to a dog."

The chair that held James Earl Livingston for more than four hours, on and off, on the night of July 6, 1999, is manufactured by KLK, Inc., of Phoenix Arizona. The KLK chair sells for $2,290, plus a $190 crating charge. This "Violent Person Restraint Chair" (the company's name for the device) "has been in use by the sixth largest sheriff's office jail system in the nation for four years, with a ninety percent reduction in injuries compared to the previous four years," brags the company advertising. "Special sizes and colors available upon request."

I telephone KLK for their take. Teresa Dominguez, production coordinator with the company, tells me the chair is sold mainly to prisons and mental hospitals but says she can give me no other information. On her advice, I submit a fax of questions for the company's officers. After more than a week without a response, I call back. "They basically said they can't answer the questions," says Dominguez. "The owner saw the fax and said, 'No, we won't answer these.'"

The company also declined to answer questions about the death of James Earl Livingston. But Dominguez says the chair isn't to blame. "How they use the chair, I imagine, would be the question," she says.

Another manufacturer is more forthcoming. Dan Corcoran is president of AEDEC International Inc., of Beaverton, Oregon, which manufactures the popular Prostraint Violent Prisoner Chair. Corcoran says his chair is "humane" and was designed to be so. "You know, when you take a little bird and it's lost and confused, and at first its heart is beating?" he asks. But if you fully cup that bird in your hands and immobilize it, the bird, he says, "calms down." So, too, says Corcoran, with human beings. The chair "makes a real nice sit for them."

What about allegations that the restraint chair has been linked to several deaths and that it is easily misused? "The people who want to do good start gainsaying it, calling it a medieval instrument of torture," says Corcoran, who "has no patience" with this stance. "It's a way of getting attention."

When I ask Corcoran for a press packet, he tells me he doesn't have one "because every lawyer who doesn't have a job" will want to get hold of the press packet and take his words out of context. He will, however, tell me the chair's cost—$900. If you get the accessories, $1,300. He will also tell me who his customers are—"mostly county jails," but also state prison systems, the U.S. Bureau of Prisons, the U.S. Immigration and Naturalization Service, the U.S. Marshals Service, and the Forest Service. "Park Service, too," he says. "Every state, every province has it."

Corcoran also exports his restraint chairs, but "only to the countries that really believe in human rights," he says. "A lot of countries are looking into this right now. We're kind of ticklish about selling these to Third World countries that don't have human rights because there really is a possibility that they might be abused."

Among those countries that have gotten Corcoran's OK and now have AEDEC restraint chairs is the United Arab Emirates. According to Amnesty International reports on the United Arab Emirates, "Cruel, inhuman, and degrading punishments, including flogging and amputation, were repeatedly imposed" in 1999. In 1998, "Torture and ill-treatment were reported and the use of cruel judicial punishments increased significantly." In 1997, said the human rights group, "Torture and ill-treatment of detainees in police custody continued."

Corcoran says he has sold "thousands" of the chairs. But as to the exact number, "We don't tell anybody that, in court or otherwise."

A flier for the chair recommends its use for "interrogating prisoners and for detaining people in Holding Tanks in Mass Entertainment Facilities (Concert Halls, Collisiems [sic], etc.)." It appears to be used primarily in the intake and booking sections of local jails. Many of those who end up in the chair have not been convicted of a crime and have landed in jail for minor offenses, such as public drunkenness.

"The mere presence of the restraint chair is asking for abuse," says Charles T. Magarahan, an Atlanta attorney. On June 5, 1997, Magarahan's client, Christopher Stone, was beaten, strapped into a restraint chair, and then beaten again after he was arrested for drunk driving and brought to the Cherokee County Jail. "He had not been uncooperative," says Magarahan. "He kept saying, 'I'm with you guys.' They put him in the chair, but they didn't push it like you'd push a chair. They dragged him by his head, with him screaming in pain."

"When Plaintiff was in the holding cell, totally restrained, Defendant [Deputy Sheriff Donald] Ware returned to the outside of the cell and sprayed pepper spray underneath the door," says the legal complaint that Stone filed against Ware, Cherokee County, and two other jail employees (the suit is currently in court). No one bothered to decontaminate Stone. Then, once the cloud of gas subsided, says the complaint, Deputy Ware returned and sprayed under the door again.

In a separate suit, Ware was also prosecuted for using excessive force against Stone. On November 4, 1999, he pleaded guilty. He was sentenced to one year probation and fined $1,000. He has also been dismissed from his position.

In February 1999, the Sacramento Sheriff's Department settled a class-action lawsuit alleging that deputies were torturing people, many of them women and minorities, with a restraint chair. The cost of the settlement was $755,000, the largest for alleged officer misconduct in the department's history. The lawyers who brought that suit are demanding that the restraint chair be banned.

The Sacramento case alleged numerous and repeated forms of torture, including mock executions, where guards strapped prisoners into a Prostraint chair and told them they were about to be electrocuted. Katherine Martin, a 106-pound woman with a heart condition, claimed she spent eight and a half hours in the chair after she was wrongly accused of touching a guard. She alleged that the straps had been pulled so tight that they had sliced skin from her back and shoulders and cut off circulation to her extremities, causing permanent nerve damage. She also claimed that she was given no liquids and that she was taunted and mocked. She was denied her requests to use the bathroom and ended up urinating on herself. Martin had originally been brought into the jail on suspicion of public drunkenness. This charge was later dismissed.

Videotapes of the Sacramento Jail's restraining methods played an important role in the case. In one tape, Ronald Motz calls through the window of his cell, asking for his lawyer. "Motz, this is the last time we're going to tell you, sit down," says a police officer, "Your attorney's not here, and the phone doesn't work." Motz continues to call out. After a break in the tape, guards wrap a spit mask around his face and pull him into a chair. "I just want to call my attorney," says Motz. "You don't get to call an attorney," says the officer. "Why?" asks Motz. The officer tells him that he can't make the call because he was "drunk in public." A few seconds later, the guard says, "You were going to be released in about five hours, now you're not."

"What did I do wrong—ask for my attorney?" asks Motz.

"You weren't following directions," says the guard.

The videotapes also show a woman named Gena Domogio being put into the chair naked. She yells at the guards who are kneeling on her back and spits blood on the floor, apparently because her mouth has been injured. The guards respond by wrapping her face in a towel. They keep the towel on her face and at one point appear to hold it against her mouth as they force her into the chair, although she repeatedly says that she has a thyroid problem and that she can't breathe.

Kimberly Byrd was reportedly taken to the hospital after she passed out in the chair where she had been hooded and tightly bound, according to a letter Amnesty International wrote to the Sacramento County Sheriff's Department in March 1999. In the videotape of her restraint, she is obviously terrified. "I'm going to die. Please don't let me die," she says over and over again.

The Sacramento case, *Geovanny D. Lobdell vs. County of Sacramento et al.*, listed AEDEC International, Inc., as a defendant. AEDEC's Corcoran gave a deposition on June 8, 1998, to attorney Stewart Katz. Many of Katz's questions referred to a "Manufacturer's Warning" sheet Corcoran distributes to his clients: "The purpose of the Prostraint Chair is to provide law enforcement and correctional officers with the safest, most humane, and least psychologically traumatizing system for restraining violent, out-of-control prisoners," reads the statement of purpose included on the warning. "The chair is not meant to be an instrument of punishment and should not be used as such."

The following are selections from Corcoran's deposition:

Q: What testing did you do?
A: I put various friends in there. I yanked on that as hard as I could, and I'm physically apt. I could cause no pain to them whatsoever.
Q: Now, does your manufacturer's warning make any reference to minimum age constraints for persons to be restrained in the restraint chair?
A: It does not.
Q: And does it refer to any maximum age constraints for people to be placed in the restraint chair?
A: No, it does not.
Q: Does it convey any warning as to whether individuals with specific health problems should not be placed in the restraint chair?
A: No.
Q: Well, are there any physical conditions that you believe should lead to a person not being restrained in the chair?
A: No arms, no legs.
Q: All right. So you don't believe the chair should properly be used on amputees or people born without fully developed limbs.
A: The chair wouldn't be functional unless they had appendages.
Q: Is it a fair statement that it's your opinion that the chair is less psychologically traumatizing than the alternatives you mentioned [these included, in Corcoran's words, "four-pointing, chained to a bench, strapped to a bed"]?
A: Yes.
Q: Is that opinion based upon any medical or psychological expert work in the field?
A: No.
Q: Now [your statement of purpose reads]: "It is an especially useful tool for restraining drug or alcohol affected prisoners." Period. My question, sir, what is your evidence for believing that it is especially useful for people who are on drugs?

A: Because medical restraints at that point are very dangerous.

Q: And what is the basis for saying the medical restraint at that point is dangerous?

A: Because they have not diagnosed what is in their bloodstream already, and whatever is put in there is compounded.

Q: Was there any scientific literature you relied on to come to this conclusion?

A: That's common sense.

Q: Did you do any testing on people who were under the influence of drugs or narcotics?

A: No.

Q: Did you do any testing for people who are under the influence or feeling the effects of alcohol?

A: No.

Q: All right. Now, the last statement under your Statement of Purpose: "The chair is not meant to be an instrument of punishment and should not be used as such." Why did you include that sentence?

A: Because Mexico asked to purchase 200 of them, and I wouldn't sell them to Mexico.

Q: And why wouldn't you sell them to Mexico?

A: As any instrument, car, toilet plunger, they can all be abused. There was too high a potential because we have a high, much higher standard in this country than other countries do. That's why the chair does work here and people will buy it.

Q: People go to the bathroom while they are seated in the chair. Are there provisions in the design of the chair to evacuate those excretions?

A: Yes.

Q: What are those?

A: The thing is cupped. Blood-borne pathogens and bodily fluids are contained in the person's clothes. I felt that was a better choice than let the pathogens go into the cell and infect other people.

Q: Have you looked at any of the literature regarding how long a person can safely be restrained in a Prostraint Chair?

A: There is no literature that I know of.

Q: Have you done any studies, research, as to the maximum amount of time an individual can be restrained in your restraining chair without causing a physical injury?

A: No.

Q: Now, if you thought the chair wasn't punishing, why wouldn't you sell those chairs to Mexico?

A: Because I have seen enough movies, and I may be stereotyping, but there could be interrogations. I didn't want that to happen.

Q: Is it a correct statement that you marketed the Prostraint restraining chair for use which includes interrogating prisoners?

A: Yes.

Efforts are now under way to restrict or ban use of the chair. In August 1999, a Knox County, Tennessee, judge ruled that the confession of robbery suspect E.B. "Boyd" Collier was involuntary and illegal because it came while he was confined in a restraining chair during his five-hour interrogation. "While such a chair may be useful, it easily crosses the line as a coercive force," wrote Criminal Court Judge Mary Beth Leibowitz.

A March 1996 Department of Justice investigation of the Maricopa County Jails in Arizona found that the sheriff's department used stun guns on prisoners while they were confined in restraint chairs, including one case where jail staff used a stun gun against a prisoner's testicles. According to Amnesty International, one prisoner, Richard Post, was forced into a restraint chair in a manner that is "reported to have caused compression of his spine and nerve damage to his spinal cord and neck, resulting in significant loss of upper body mobility." On August 19, 1999, Maricopa County agreed to pay Post $800,000 to settle his claims that jail guards had used excessive force against him. In 1997, jail officials told Amnesty International that the jail system owned sixteen chairs and that it had used them about 600 times in the past six months. The Maricopa County Jails have since altered their restraint policy and say that they no longer use the chairs for punishment. A Department of Justice lawsuit against the jail system was dropped in June 1998.

Alleged misuse of the restraint chair led the U.S. Department of Justice to file a 1996 lawsuit against the Iberia Parish Jail in Louisiana, claiming that the jail deputies, as a matter of course, subjected prisoners to "cruel and unusual punishment and physical and mental torture" by confining them to restraint chairs for hours and forcing them to sit in their own excrement. One prisoner was allegedly held in the chair for eight days, another for forty-three hours. In a pretrial settlement, the jail authorities agreed to stop using the restraint chair.

In early January of 2000, a group of Erie County, Pennsylvania, prisoners asked a federal judge to ban use of the chair. The suit against the prison alleged that prisoners had been held for two to eight hours in the chair for such behaviors as "making insolent remarks," cursing, and throwing towels at one another.

In Ventura County, California, a class action lawsuit led a federal judge to issue a preliminary injunction banning the chair on November 15, 1999. That order is being appealed. The lawsuit alleged that during one eighteen-month period, 377 people had been strapped into the chair at the Ventura County Jail and that one prisoner had been left in the chair for thirty-two hours. "Data shows that the Sheriff's Department's misuse of that chair flows from a practice of restraining nonviolent arrestees for extended periods of time in violation of the arrestees' Fourteenth Amendment rights," wrote U. S. District Judge Lourdes Baird in her fifty-page decision. "The policy allows deputies to require restrained arrestees to either urinate or defecate on themselves and be forced to sit in their own feces or 'hold it.'"

On December 13, 1999, Amnesty International issued a statement calling for an inquiry into police actions at the WTO protests in Seattle. Among the allegations that troubled Amnesty were several incidents involving restraint chairs at the King County Jail. "People were allegedly strapped into four point chairs as punishment for nonviolent resistance or asking for their lawyers," says the group's press release. "In one case a man was stripped naked before being strapped into the chair." Martin Mijal, a building contractor in Portland, Oregon, participated in the WTO protests. He was arrested with other Direct Action Network protesters and charged with "failure to disperse." After ten hours of waiting in several jails, and hearing that a lawyer was on her way, the group decided to resist the deputies' attempts to transfer them to individual cells. According to Mijal, they linked arms. Mijal says the deputies responded by bringing in several restraint chairs. They then began to separate the protesters. "I was holding myself in a ball with my arms locked under my legs," writes Mijal in his complaint to the ACLU of Washington. "As they carried me, I cried out 'Lawyer!' three times because I was very scared and I thought they might be close by."

Mijal says he did not resist as the guards placed him in the restraint chair. "Then, as I remained entirely incapacitated in the wheelchair, and totally by surprise a male guard put pepper foam directly into my eyes. It was very, very painful. Instinctually, to get the foam out of my eyes, I wiped my forehead against the nearest thing, which was a guard's leg, who was standing to the side of me and I heard him yelp when the chemical burned through his pants."

Mijal's action angered the guard. "Then he took a cloth and put it over my face," he writes in his ACLU complaint. "He put his hand on the cloth and with his finger found my left eye socket and rubbed the poison in my eye, forcing my eyelid up. Then he lifted the cloth and put another pad of thick cloth over my mouth and gagged me. I couldn't breathe at all, because of the pain and the fear. I was in immense agony."

"We would dispute that account," says Jim Harms, Public Information Officer for the King County Department of Adult and Juvenile Detention. He claims that the deputies were simply following procedures and that the activists shouldn't have expected to see their lawyer so quickly upon arriving at the jail. He also says that the officers used a standard use-of-force progression on Mijal, that he struggled with the guards and refused to be restrained, and that he was pepper-sprayed just so the deputies could get him into the chair. As for being pepper-sprayed while restrained, hooded, poked in the eye, and gagged, "There is nothing in the report or the follow-up review to show that actually happened," says Harms.

"If you've ever seen the film *Brazil*, it's like a scene from the torture chamber," says Robert Smith of San Francisco. Smith, an activist with Art and Revolution in San Francisco, was arrested along with Mijal and backs up his claims. "He's being held down, he's got a bag over his face, there's people in riot gear all around him. This is after being pepper-sprayed. I'd never seen human beings doing something like that to other human beings."

Cowboys and Prisoners

WILLIE WISELY

It was trumpeted as the pinnacle of high-tech prison architecture when it opened in 1993. The Federal Correctional Complex in Florence, Colorado, contains two lower security facilities, one maximum security prison, and, since 1994, the *Clockwork Orange*-inspired U.S. Penitentiary Administrative Maximum. The steel and concrete citadels of the prison are rimmed by verdant hills covered in dense grass. But, inside the model modern maximum security prison, an old-fashioned rodeo of brutality plays out, where guards who call themselves The Cowboys are pitted against prisoners bridled by chains.

On August 8, 1996, four guards punched, kicked, and body slammed William Turner, according to an indictment filed November 2, 2000, in the U.S. District Court of Colorado. The guards contended that Turner, a slightly built 45-year-old robber, stabbed two of them with a sharpened toothbrush. Turner was charged with assault, bound with restraints, and thrown into a small holding cell. Unable to wash and covered in his own excrement due to injuries suffered in the beating, he pleaded unsuccessfully with medical staff over the next four days to be taken to the infirmary for X-rays and treatment. Turner also told anyone within earshot he didn't stab the guards, but was fearful they would be back to finish him off.

"They're going to jump on me and kill me," he declared in one videotaped exchange with a medical technical assistant. "Look at me, man. I didn't stab nobody. I'll take a polygraph on it, man, I have never stabbed anybody in my entire time in this system." Turner's attack formed the foundation of the government's case. But Turner was by no means the first prisoner at Florence to suffer. Prisoners there were often falsely accused of assault, with fabricated incident reports created to cover up the brutality.

This article was written in 2001.

In a series of hard-hitting articles in *Denver Westword,* writer Alan Prendergast revealed a pattern of misconduct, violence, and official acquiescence at Florence (see "Marked for Death," 5/25/00). As a result of media exposure, multiple lawsuits filed by prisoners, and complaints by other prison staff, the U.S. Justice Department conducted a two-and-a-half-year criminal investigation. That probe quickly zeroed in on the guards called The Cowboys.

The star witness for the Justice Department was David Armstrong, a former Florence lieutenant and confessed member of The Cowboys. Armstrong pled guilty in July, 1999, in Denver's federal court, admitting that he and other Cowboys participated in "retaliatory beatings against disruptive or 'problem' [prisoners and] routinely joked, bragged, and related tales of their abuse of inmates to each other." Armstrong also recounted how David Pruyne, 36, came up with the group's nickname during a confrontation with a prisoner who belonged to the Crips. "We have a new gang here," whispered Pruyne. "It's called The Cowboys."

Armstrong, who faced ten years in prison and a $250,000 fine, revealed in his plea agreement that The Cowboys formed in 1995 as a secret gang for dissatisfied guards. The Cowboys were angry because they felt prisoners assigned to the Special Housing Unit (SHU) for assaulting staff were getting off too lightly. Their solution? Punch, kick, and torture chained and cuffed prisoners, then file false reports claiming the victims provoked the violence. Other staff were warned to keep quiet about the abuse. "Officers who expressed disapproval of The Cowboys' actions ... were often threatened with physical harm," recounted Armstrong. "Officers who did not support them could be at risk of harm from an attack by an inmate because Cowboys would delay or avoid providing help."

By the time The Cowboys attacked Turner in 1996, the scope of their plan had broadened. Turner was a jailhouse lawyer, someone who prepares and files lawsuits and legal briefs for himself and other prisoners.

Seven members of The Cowboys were indicted by a federal grand jury November 2, 2000. The guards were charged with 52 specific acts of misconduct against some 20 named prisoners from 1995 to 1997. It's unlikely that the number of The Cowboys, or casualties in their war against prisoners, will ever be known. The indictment provided a rare glimpse at how guards regularly abuse prisoners. Guards there kicked prisoners, smashed their heads into floors or walls, and mixed feces and urine in their food. Guards Mike Lavallee, 33, and Rod Schultz, 36, contaminated food served to prisoners with human waste several times. Lavallee and Pruyne tossed burning paper into a locked cell to justify spraying two prisoners with fire retardant. The guards were also charged with stomping prisoners' testicles.

According to federal prosecutors, Lavallee told Armstrong and other conspirators they had the "green light" from prison authorities to "take care of business." Lavallee and Schultz advised The Cowboys to "lie until you die" if questioned about their actions, and threatened payback for guards who didn't back them up.

A news release from the U.S. Department of Justice explained the "object of the conspiracy was to unjustifiably injure and physically punish restrained or compliant [prisoners] at the prison." In furtherance of that conspiracy, the charges revealed how guards "falsified incident reports, and fabricated injuries and allegations of prisoner misconduct in order to falsely justify the use of force." The criminal action was hailed by officials as a positive step in the direction of ending abuse of prisoners by guards.

"Today's indictment demonstrates that no one is above the law," United States Attorney Thomas Strickland boasted in the press release. "Those who deprive others of their constitutional rights while acting under color of law will be held accountable." Bill Lee, Assistant Attorney General for Civil Rights added that the federal investigation and indictment proved the resolve of the Justice Department to insure that prisoners aren't mistreated while in custody. "This is the biggest indictment of Bureau of Prisons employees in recent history, if not ever," said Jess Dorschner, spokesman for the U.S. Attorney's Office in Denver. The charges came as no surprise to the guards union.

In April of 1996, Dale Lewsader, then president of the American Federation of Government Employees local union wrote to prison officials, "We have employees that are engaged in acts of physical abuse against [prisoners]. Management knows this is happening and is condoning these actions. We understand that in some cases, supervisors are ordering the assaults."

Chris Kester, a former Florence guard who worked at the prison from 1993 to 1997, said he and others tried to end the abuse. "We brought this [abuse] up to management more times than I can count," Kester explained in a telephone interview with *The Gazette*, April 29, 2001. "The rumors were everywhere. These [Cowboys] could not have done what is alleged without someone higher up protecting them." So far, no charges have been filed against prison administrators or Bureau officials.

Turner eventually received a $17,000 settlement in one of his civil rights suits against the federal government for the abuse he endured at Florence. That award, while not large by comparison to civil judgments generally, is significant because federal judges often dismiss claims of misconduct brought by people in prison.

Ronnie Beverly, another former Florence prisoner, was repeatedly beaten by Lavallee, Schultz, and other Cowboys while in the SHU in 1996. Beverly said brutality at the hands of guards was common in Florence. "It was a situation where your human rights were being violated and it was covered up from the top to the bottom," he told *The Gazette*. Not everyone believes these eyewitness accounts, however.

"These people are in prison because they are cheats and liars," said Robert Liechty, an attorney representing guards named in one of Turner's lawsuits. "I think these charges are trumped up," he claimed. Liechty said prisoners frequently falsely accuse guards of abuse. And it seems the indicted guards have other supporters.

"These are good officers," said Steve Browning, president of the local union at Florence and an employee there since 1995. He said the guards were falsely accused. "They are treated as if they are guilty," Browning lamented. "The prosecutors claim there is a big conspiracy, but I don't think these things happened that way."

The former union leaders who complained to the Bureau of Prisons about The Cowboys were tossed out in an election dominated by candidates who denied that anything wrong had happened. Under Browning, the union was turned into a support group for the indicted guards. They set up a legal defense fund and a separate account to provide assistance to the families of those charged while the case was pending. At Christmas, the wives of union officials dropped off gaily decorated gift baskets and succulent holiday dinners at the homes of the accused Cowboys. Despite this support, evidence of their guilt was clear.

In addition to Armstrong, two other guards offered to cooperate with federal prosecutors in exchange for leniency in their own pending cases. Jake Geiger and Charlotte Gutierrez are expected to be sentenced after the criminal trial of the other seven Cowboys concludes. Armstrong, first to break the code of silence, awaits sentencing for his part in the conspiracy at his New Jersey home. In 1998, Steve Mills, another former Florence guard, was sentenced to 33 months in prison for beating a prisoner.

Gutierrez, the only woman involved in the conspiracy, pled guilty to kicking Harold Lane in the ribs. Lane, handcuffed and wearing leg irons, was picked up by another guard and thrown to the tile floor face first. After Gutierrez kicked the helpless Lane, a lieutenant told her to "fix this," according to statements made in the plea agreement. She cleaned blood from the floor and walls, then hit her shins several times to make them look red and swollen. Her report claimed Lane provoked the violence by kicking her in the legs.

Was the indictment and public exposure the last round-up for The Cowboys? Probably not. Unlike the romanticized version of the shoot-out at the O.K. Corral where the Earps and Doc Holiday reputedly killed or disabled the leaders of a group of Tombstone toughs who called themselves The Cowboys, the story of guards brutalizing prisoners won't be made into a feature film starring the latest crop of dewy-eyed actors. Neither the public nor law enforcement cares much about the safety of people in prison. If not for the self-serving "cooperation" of former guards who participated in the beatings and cover-ups, and the relentless reporting of a local writer, The Cowboys might still be riding 'em hard and putting 'em away wet at Florence, the rodeo in the Rockies.

Deliberate Indifference

State Authorities' Response to Prisoner-on-Prisoner Sexual Abuse

JOANNE MARINER

[Editors' Note: The following is excerpted from "No Escape: Male Rape in U.S. Prisons," a comprehensive report by Human Rights Watch on male prisoner-on-prisoner rape in the United States. The report is based on three years of research, during which time information was collected from over 200 prisoners spread among thirty-seven states.]

I've been sentenced for a D.U.I. offense. My 3rd one. When I first came to prison, I had no idea what to expect. I'm a tall white male, who unfortunately has a small amount of feminine characteristics. These characteristics have got me raped so many times I have no more feelings physically. I have been raped by up to [7] men at a time. I've had knifes at my head and throat. I had fought and been beat so hard that I didn't ever think I'd see straight again. One time when I refused to enter a cell, I was brutally attacked by staff and taken to segragation [sic] though I had only wanted to prevent the same and worse by not locking up with my cell mate. There is no supervision after lockdown. I was given a conduct report. I explained to the hearing officer what the issue was. He told me that off the record, He suggests I find a man I would/could willingly have sex with to prevent these things from happening. I've requested protective custody only to be denied. It is not available here. He also said there was no where to run to, and it would be best for me to accept things.... I probably have AIDS now. I have great difficulty raising food to my mouth from shaking after nightmares or thinking to hard on all this.... I've laid down without physical fight to be sodomized. To prevent so much damage in struggles, ripping and tearing. Though in not fighting, it caused my heart and spirit to be raped as well. Something I don't know if I'll ever forgive myself for.

—A.H., Indiana prisoner, August 30, 1996[1]

For Human Rights Watch, 2000.

The letter excerpted above was one of the first to reach Human Rights Watch in response to a small announcement posted in *Prison Legal News* and the now defunct *Prison Life Magazine*. Having been alerted to the problem of prisoner-on-prisoner rape in the United States by the work of activists like Stephen Donaldson of the organization Stop Prisoner Rape, we decided to conduct exploratory research into the topic. When we put out a call to prisoners for information, we were deluged with letters. Rape, by prisoners' accounts, is no aberrational occurrence; instead it is a deeply-rooted, systemic problem. It is also a problem that prison authorities do little to address.

Rape plagues U.S. prisons because of a lack of attention or concern by prison authorities or politicians. In too many institutions, prevention measures are meager and effective punishment of abuses is rare. Nor does the criminal justice system protect sexually abused prisoners. Few prosecutors are concerned with prosecuting crimes committed against prisoners, preferring to leave internal prison problems to the discretion of the prison authorities; similarly, prison officials themselves rarely push for the prosecution of prisoner-on-prisoner abuses. As a result, perpetrators of prison rape almost never face criminal charges.

Internal disciplinary mechanisms, the putative substitute for criminal prosecution, function poorly in those cases in which the victim reports the crime. In nearly every instance evaluated for this study, prison authorities imposed light disciplinary sanctions against the perpetrator—perhaps thirty days in disciplinary segregation (if that). Often rapists are simply transferred to another facility, or are not moved at all. Their victims, in contrast, may end up spending the rest of their prison terms in protective custody units whose conditions often approach those in disciplinary segregation: twenty-three hours per day in a cell, restricted privileges, and no educational or vocational opportunities.

The federal courts have played an insignificant role in curtailing prisoner-on-prisoner rape. Because few lawyers are willing to litigate on behalf on prisoners, only a fraction of sexually abused prisoners bring their cases to courts; and because such cases are often filed by prisoners acting as their own counsel, they rarely survive the early stages of litigation. The cases that do survive hardly ever end in a favorable judgment. While there have been a few generous damage awards in cases involving prisoner-on-prisoner rape, they are the exceptions to the rule.

In sum, the failure to prevent and punish rape results implicates more than one government body. The primary responsibility in this area, however, is borne by prison authorities. Rape prevention requires careful classification methods, prisoner and staff orientation and training, staff vigilance, serious investigation of all rape allegations, and prosecution of substantiated allegations. At the least, it requires a willingness to take the issue seriously, to be attentive to the possibility of victimization, and to consider the victim's interests. Without these basic steps, the problem will not go away. Rape is not an inevitable consequence of prison life, but it certainly is a predictable one if little is done to prevent and punish it.

Failure to Recognize and Address the Problem—and the Perverse Incentives Created by Legal Standards

> Regrettably [rape] is a problem of which we are happier not knowing the true dimensions. Overcrowding and the "anything goes" morality sure haven't helped.
>
> —High-level state corrections official
> who spoke on condition of anonymity[2]

No empirical study has yet analyzed the prevalence of rape in prisons nationwide. But a number of smaller-scale, state- or institution-specific studies have been conducted, many of which have found a high incidence of prisoner-on-prisoner rape. For example, a 1996 survey conducted by Professor Cindy Struckman-Johnson in the Nebraska prison system showed that 22 percent of male prisoners had been pressured or forced to have sexual contact against their will while incarcerated.[3] Of these, over 50 percent had submitted to forced anal sex at least once.[4] Extrapolating these findings to the national level would give a total of over 140,000 prisoners who have been anally raped.[5]

Official data (to the extent such information even exists) tell a very different story. Only half of all state jurisdictions tabulate separate statistics regarding the incidence of rape (a telling indicator of their lack of seriousness in addressing the issue); and those that do collect such data report that rape is an infinitely rare event. But since the causes of underreporting are well known to prisoners and prison administrators alike, a low frequency of reported cases is no reason for correctional authorities to turn a blind eye to the problem.

Human Rights Watch surveyed the prevention practices of state and federal correctional departments and found that few departments take specific affirmative steps to address the problem of prisoner-on-prisoner rape.[6] Almost none of the departments who responded to our request for information had instituted any type of sexual abuse prevention program; and only a very few—such as Arkansas, Illinois, Massachusetts, North Carolina, New Hampshire, and Virginia—stated that correctional officers receive specialized training in recognizing, preventing, and responding to prisoner-on-prisoner sexual assault.[7] Similarly, not many departments had drafted specific protocols to guide staff response to incidents of assault.[8]

High profile class action lawsuits helped spur correctional authorities to take the problem of custodial sexual abuse seriously. Normally, the threat of litigation creates an important incentive for state authorities to come to grips with certain problems. Notably, the state of Arkansas—one of the only states that was able to provide Human Rights Watch with a concrete description of the training and orientation measures that it takes with regard to the problem—included a discussion of litigation and staff liability for prisoner-on-prisoner sexual abuse at the very beginning of its training curriculum on the subject.[9]

Yet the legal rules that the courts have developed relating to prisoner-on-prisoner sexual abuse create perverse incentives for authorities to ignore the problem. Under the "deliberate indifference" standard (applied in legal challenges to prison officials' failure to protect prisoners from inter-prisoner abuses such as rape), the prisoner must prove to the court that the defendant-prison staff had *actual knowledge* of a substantial risk to him, and that they disregarded that risk. As the courts have emphasized, it is not enough for the prison to prove that "the risk was obvious and a reasonable prison official would have noticed it."[10] Instead, if a prison official lacked knowledge of the risk—no matter how obvious it was to anyone else—he cannot be held liable.

The incentive this legal rule creates for correctional officials to remain unaware of problems is regrettable. Indeed, in many lawsuits involving prisoner-on-prisoner rape, the main thrust of prison officials' defense is that they were unaware that the defendant was in danger. More generally, officials in such cases often argue that rape in their facilities is a "rarity"—"not a serious risk."[11] They certainly have no reason, under the existing legal standards, to try to ascertain the true dimensions of the problem.

The North Carolina Pilot Program

An encouraging exception to the overall absence of particularized attention to prisoner-on-prisoner sexual abuse can be found in North Carolina. In 1997, the legislature passed a law establishing a pilot program on sexual assault prevention in the prisons.[12] Covering only three units of the state prison system, the program is otherwise a laudable attempt at addressing the problem of prisoner-on-prisoner sexual abuse. It provides that the orientation given prisoners will include information on reducing the risk of sexual assault and that counseling on the topic will be provided to any prisoner requesting it. It also requires that the correctional authorities collect data on incidents of sexual aggression and develop and implement employee training on the topic.

The program's rules on classification and housing are particularly valuable. They provide that all prisoners must be evaluated and classified as to their risk of being either the victim or perpetrator of sexually assaultive behavior. These classifications are to be taken into account when making housing assignments. In particular, prisoners deemed vulnerable to assault are barred from being housed in the same cell or in small dormitories with prisoners rated as potential perpetrators.

Improper Classification and Negligent Double-Celling

Among the goals of prisoner classification policies is to separate dangerous prisoners from those whom they are likely to victimize. At one extreme are "supermax," or administrative segregation units, where prisoners with a history of violence or indiscipline are held; at the other are protective custody units where the most vulnerable prisoners are held.[13] Yet even between these extremes, the existence of various security levels (e.g., minimum, medium, maximum, or close custody), and the range of categorization alternatives within these levels, are supposed to allow prison authorities flexibility in arranging prisoners' housing and work assignments so as to minimize inter-prisoner violence and victimization.

In the overcrowded prisons of today, however, the practical demands of simply finding available space for prisoners have overwhelmed classification ideals. Prisoners frequently find themselves placed among others whose background, criminal history, and other characteristics make them an obvious threat.

In the worst cases, prisoners are actually placed in the same cell with prisoners who are likely to victimize them—sometimes even with prisoners who have a demonstrated proclivity for sexually abusing others.

A Connecticut prisoner described how he was raped by his cellmate, a prisoner with a history of raping other prisoners:

> [I] was sent to the orientation block to be cellmate with another prisoner already occupying a double cell. I did not know at the time that I was to share a double cell with him, that he was a known rapist in the prison. . . . I must point out that only a month and a half prior, he was accused of raping another man. On my fourth day of sharing the cell, I was ambushed and viciously raped by him. After being raped, I remained in shock and paralyzed in thought for two days until I was able to muster the courage to report it, this, the most dreadful and horrifying experience of my life.[14]

The pressures of overcrowding facing so many prisons today mean that double-celling is much more common than in the past—often with two men being placed in a cell designed for single occupancy—while little care is taken to select compatible cellmates. Numerous prisoners told Human Rights Watch of being celled together with men who were much larger and stronger than them, had a history of violence, were racially antagonistic, openly threatening, or otherwise clearly incompatible. In such circumstances, rape is no surprise.

Understaffing and the Failure to Prevent

> The greatest preventive measure [against rape] is posting staff [to monitor] areas that are high risk for assault. The reality however, is that funding for prison administration doesn't provide for adequate patrolling. . . . Prisoners are pretty much left on their own.
>
> —A Virginia prisoner[15]

> You know, when you look at the low numbers of staff around—who really owns this prison?
>
> —High-level state prison administrator who insisted upon anonymity[16]

Another casualty of the enormous growth of the country's prison population is adequate staffing and supervision of prisoners. Texas, one of the largest prison systems in the country—and one in which rape is widespread—is known to be seriously understaffed. It is short an estimated 2,500 guards, what a high official in the prison guards' union characterizes as a staffing crisis.[17] Prison attrition statistics reportedly show that about one in five guards quit over the course of 2000.

Paradoxically, lower numbers of correctional staff can lead to more ineffective monitoring by existing staff. Instead of redoubling their efforts to make up for their insufficient numbers, they are more likely to remain as much as possible outside of prisoners' living areas, because fewer staff makes close monitoring more dangerous to those employees who do make the rounds of housing units. Being at a disadvantage, they also have a stronger incentive to pacify—rather than challenge—the more dangerous prisoners who may be exploiting others.

Poor design, especially common in older prisons, exacerbates the problem of understaffing and may provide opportunities for assaults. Explained one Florida prisoner: "Rapes occur because the lack of observation make it possible. Prisons have too few guards and too many blind spots."[18]

Inadequate Response to Complaints of Rape

An absolutely central problem with regard to sexual abuse in prison, emphasized by prisoner after prisoner, is the inadequate—and, in many instances, callous and irresponsible—response of correctional staff to complaints of rape. When a prisoner informs a guard that he has either been threatened with rape or actually assaulted, it is crucial that his complaint be met with a rapid and effective response. At the least, he should be immediately removed from the unsafe area and perpetrator, so his complaint may be made in a confidential manner. If the rape has already occurred, he should receive any necessary medical care, and physical evidence of rape should be collected.

It is much more common, however, for prison staff to dismiss complaints of rape, or even take steps that further endanger the victimized prisoner. This prisoner's account is typical of many received by Human Rights Watch:

> Lt. B.W. had me identify the assailant in front of approximately "20" other prisoners . . . which immediately put my safty [sic] & life in danger as a "snitch" for telling on the other prisoner who sexually assaulted me. . . . the Prison officials trying to Place Me Back in Population after I identified the assailant in front of 20 prisoners clearly placed my life in danger Because of the "snitch" concept.[19]

Another prisoner who claimed to have been raped several times said that officers refused to take his complaints serious, telling him, "No way— you're not that good of a catch." A Texas prisoner said that after he reported that he had been raped, "I was pulled out and seen by Mrs. P, Capt. R, and Major H. I told my complaint and Mrs. P said that I was never raped that I just gave it up."[20] Significantly, consensual sex is a rules violation in all prison systems, leaving the complaining prisoner with the possibility of facing disciplinary sanctions.

Prison staff may also dismiss the victimized prisoner as merely engaging in "gay" behavior (the implication being that gay men cannot be raped because they always consent to sex). A Texas prisoner who was raped by numerous other prisoners over a long period of time received the following response when he complained to staff:

> Defendant J.M, a security officer with the rank of sergeant, came to investigate the series of latest allegations. Defendant J.M. refused to interview the prisoner witnesses and told plaintiff that he was lying about being sexually abused. After plaintiff vehemently protested that he was being truthful, defendant J.M. made comments that plaintiff "must be gay" for "letting them make you suck dick."[21]

Some guards do respond to reports of sexual abuse, typically by moving the prisoner to a place of safety, often to a holding cell or what is called the "transit" area of the prison. Sometimes a medical examination is conducted and sometimes an investigation into the incident is opened. The problem is that these steps rarely lead to adequate measures being taken against the perpetrator of abuse. Rather than internal disciplinary proceedings or external criminal prosecution, the solution is typically found in isolating the two parties. Either the rapist or, more commonly, the complaining prisoner may be transferred to another prison.

Serious investigation of abuses is all too rare. The basic procedures followed when a crime is committed outside of prison—involving collection of physical evidence, interviews with witnesses, interrogation of suspects— are much less likely to be employed when the crime involves prisoners.

Failure to Prosecute

> As of this time I have almost 14 years in prison and have never heard of a
> prison rape case being prosecuted in court. . . . I'm quite sure if a man com-
> mitted a rape in prison and got 5 or 10 years time, prison rape would
> decline.
>
> —An Ohio prisoner[22]

Human Rights Watch surveyed both correctional departments and prisoners as to whether rapists faced criminal prosecution. The response (or
lack of response) was instructive. Although corrections authorities generally stated that they referred all or some cases for prosecution by outside authorities, they had little information regarding the results of such
referrals.[23] Prisoners were much more blunt: they uniformly agreed that
criminal prosecution of rapists rarely occurs.

Judging solely by the direct accounts of rape we have received, criminal prosecution of prisoner-on-prisoner rape is extremely rare. Of the
well over 100 rapes reported to Human Rights Watch, not a single one
led to the criminal prosecution of the perpetrators. Even the most violent
rapes, and those in which the victim pushed strongly for outside intervention, were ignored by the criminal justice system. Unlike rape in the
outside community, rape in prison is a crime the perpetrator can usually
commit without fear of spending additional time in prison.

The following letter, from an official with the Minnesota Department
of Corrections, suggests just how rare such prosecutions are. Questioned
in 1997 as to specific instances in which prisoners had been prosecuted
for raping other prisoners, he cited a case that occurred twelve years
previously:

> You also asked if I was aware of any cases in which perpetrators of pris-
> oner-on-prisoner sexual assault have been criminally prosecuted. I spoke
> with staff in our Office of Special Investigations and they informed me of
> one such case in September 1985. A prisoner was charged and pled guilty
> to criminal sexual conduct in the third degree. He received a sentence of 1
> year and 1 day to be served consecutively to his original incarceration
> offense.[24]

Although this response clearly indicates that rape prosecutions are rare in
Minnesota, it is worth noting that almost all other state corrections
department did not bring up *any* cases in which a perpetrator of rape in
prison was prosecuted for the crime. Several said that they simply did not
follow the progress of such cases.[25] The Missouri correctional authorities
told Human Rights Watch in mid-1998 that three cases in the category
"Forcible Sexual Misconduct" were submitted for prosecution in 1996,

two of which had been refused by the prosecutor and one of which was still pending. They noted, in addition, that there were no criminal convictions stemming from prisoner-on-prisoner rape or sexual abuse during the past two years.

The case of M.R., a Texas prisoner, is a particularly egregious example of the failure to criminally prosecute rape in prison. Not only was M.R. raped repeatedly, the last time in full view of other prisoners, but he was nearly killed by the rapist, receiving a severe concussion, broken bones, and scalp lacerations. Desperate to see the man prosecuted, M.R. wrote both the local district attorney and sheriff explaining his strong desire to press charges. He even filed a grievance against the Texas correctional authorities requesting their help in securing the criminal prosecution of the rapist. None of his efforts made a difference: the prosecution was never instituted.

Why are criminal prosecutions of prisoner-on-prisoner rape so rare? First, it is obvious that the severe underreporting of cases of abuse means that only a small minority of rapes are known to prison authorities, let alone to anyone outside the prison. Second, the failure of prison authorities to react appropriately to complaints of sexual abuse—including collecting physical evidence of rape—and to properly investigate such complaints means that the necessary fact-finding to support a criminal prosecution is lacking. Since local police do not patrol prisons, they rely on correctional authorities to gather the proof of crime. But another crucial problem is the low priority that local prosecutors place on prosecuting prison abuses. Although local prosecutors are nominally responsible for prosecuting criminal acts that occur in prisons, they are unlikely to consider prisoners part of their real constituency. Prisoners have no political power of their own, and impunity for abuses against prisoners does not directly threaten the public outside of prison. Since many state prosecutors are elected officials, these factors may be decisive in leading them to ignore prison abuses.

Internal Administrative Penalties

M.R., the Texas prisoner who was nearly killed by his rapist, received another shock when he found out that the man was punished for the attack by spending a total of fifteen days in disciplinary segregation. Judging by the reports received by Human Rights Watch, however, the punishment meted out against M.R.'s rapist is only unusual in that it was meted out at all, not in that it was lenient. Since it is rare for prison authorities to conduct the investigation necessary to make a finding of rape, perpetrators of rape facing disciplinary proceedings are usually charged with a lesser offense such as disorderly conduct. The following account is typical:

[While I was in a temporary cell], officers allowed another prisoner who was not assigned to my cell to enter and stay in my cell for two days with me. This was two days of living hell in which he raped and abused my body. He threatened to kill me if I let officials know. However, I began kicking the cell door anyway after the second day and officials came to my aid. I informed officials of what had transpired the previous two days, but it was logged that I merely "alleged" that I had been sexually assaulted and raped. The prisoner was charged only with the disciplinary offense of threatening me, he got away with the sexual assaults—a much more serious offense—unpunished.[26]

Perpetrators may spend a week or two, or even a month, in "the hole," rarely longer. Needless to say, when they return to the general prison population they may be primed for revenge.

The Lack of Legal Redress

[L]awyers are, and with reason, terribly skeptical about the merits of prisoners' civil rights suits, most of which are indeed hoked up and frivolous.

—Chief Judge Richard Posner,
U.S. Court of Appeals for the Seventh Circuit[27]

Prisons are necessarily dangerous places; they house society's most antisocial and violent people in close proximity with one another. Regrettably, "[s]ome level of brutality and sexual aggression among [prisoners] is inevitable no matter what the guards do ... unless all prisoners are locked in their cells 24 hours a day and sedated."

—Justice Clarence Thomas, U.S. Supreme Court[28]

Like the public, many federal judges appear to view prisoners' legal claims with an extremely cynical eye. Either they disbelieve prisoners' complaints of abuse, preferring to focus their concern on the constraints under which correctional authorities operate, or they seem resigned to tolerating prison violence and exploitation. Not all federal judges are so insensitive to prison abuses—indeed, a few worthy efforts have been made to put a stop to prisoner-on-prisoner sexual abuse, including the rulings in *LaMarca v. Turner* and *Redman v. County of San Diego*—but it is fair to say that the courts have not proven to be an effective champion of the sexually abused prisoner.[29]

In theory, prisoners seeking recourse for violations of their constitutional rights may file a civil action in federal court. However, as described in chapter 7 of the present book, the obstacles presented by legislation like the Prison Litigation Reform Act (PLRA) impede most of these suits from ever getting to court, and lower the prospects for a successful outcome once they get there.

Yet, despite the small number of lawyers willing to litigate such cases, and the formidable obstacles of legislation like the PLRA, some prisoners do manage to file suit against prison authorities in the aftermath of rape. They typically assert that the authorities' failure to take steps to protect them from abuse violates the prohibition on "cruel and usual punishments" contained in the Eighth Amendment to the U.S. Constitution. But too often, such cases are dismissed in the early stages of litigation, with some judges going out of their way to excuse the actions of prison officials.

The reasoning expressed by the court in *Chandler v. Jones* is typical. The case involved a prisoner who was sexually harassed after being transferred to a dangerous housing unit. In dismissing the case, the court reasoned that "sexual harassment of prisoners in prisons would appear to be a fact of life."[30] Even while acknowledging the widespread nature of the problem, courts have been extremely reluctant to hold prison officials responsible for it. Their caution may, to some extent, reflect their belief that crucial policy and budgetary decisions affecting prison conditions are made elsewhere, and that guards and other officials should not be blamed for the predictable abuses that result.[31] By such reasoning, however, the courts have ensured near-complete impunity for prisoner-on-prisoner sexual abuse.

Finally, the rare case that does survive to reach a jury typically finds the prisoner plaintiff before an unreceptive audience. Consider, for example, the case of *Butler v. Dowd*, in which the jury found that three young prisoners had been brutally raped due to prison officials' deliberate indifference, but only awarded the plaintiffs the sum of one dollar each in nominal damages.[32] Or *James v. Tilghman*, in which the jury found that the prisoner plaintiff had been raped due to the defendants' negligence, but awarded him nothing—neither compensatory nor punitive damages.[33] In many other cases, moreover, juries have found in favor of the defendants despite compelling evidence to the contrary. Even the well-known case of *Farmer v. Brennan*, in which the transsexual victim of prisoner-on-prisoner rape prevailed before the U.S. Supreme Court, resulted in an unfavorable decision on remand to the district court.

The Need for Reform

Too many U.S. prisons reflect a wholesale disregard for prisoners' right to be free of violent rape and other forms of unwanted sexual contact. Reform is urgently needed. As many have noted, the state of a country's prisons is a telling indicator of its level of civilization. The barbarity of sexual assault in U.S. prisons reflects poorly on prison officials, on the courts, and on our society.

Notes

1. In this excerpt, as in other excerpts from prisoners' letters included in this chapter, the author's idiosyncrasies of spelling and grammar have been retained. In addition, prisoners' names and other identifying facts have been withheld to protect their privacy.
2. E-mail communication to Human Rights Watch, July 28, 1997.
3. Struckman-Johnson, "Sexual Coercion," p. 67. The survey had a 30 percent return rate, so it is possible that overall rates of victimization were lower than 22 percent. But for several reasons, including the fact that staff and prisoner estimates of the incidence of these abuses correlated closely with the actual numbers found, the researchers believe that the 22 percent figure is reasonably accurate. Ibid., p. 74.
4. Ibid., p. 71.
5. Stephen Donaldson, the late president of Stop Prisoner Rape, made a similar estimate in 1995 on the basis of previous academic studies. He concluded that 119,900 male prison prisoners—as well as many thousands of jail prisoners—had been anally raped. Stephen Donaldson, "Rape of Incarcerated Americans: A Preliminary Statistical Look," *Stop Prison Rape*, 7th ed., July 1995.
6. Although few past studies have specifically examined correctional authorities' response to prisoner-on-prisoner rape, most commentators agree that little has been done to address the problem. See, for example, Robert W. Dumond, "Prisoner Sexual Assault: The Plague That Persists," *The Prison Journal*, vol. 80, no. 4 (2000). Dumond notes: "Although the problem of prisoner sexual assault has been known and examined for the past 30 years, the body of evidence has failed to be translated into effective intervention strategies for treating prisoner victims and ensuring improved correctional practices and management." p. 407.
7. Arkansas corrections authorities give a course "designed to train correctional personnel to recognize and prevent potential sexual abuse among the prisoner population and to intervene quickly and efficiently in instances of suspected, actual, or on-going abuse." The staff training manual on the topic is clear, detailed, and includes extremely useful guidelines as to how prison employees should react to instances of known or suspected sexual abuse. Arkansas Department of Correction, "Sexual Aggression in Prisons and Jails: Awareness, Prevention, and Intervention," (undated manuscript). The manual itself says the course is eight hours long, although the training academy manual says it lasts four hours.

   The Nebraska correctional authorities, in their response to our 1997 survey, stated that they were "in the process of defining and implementing a formal sexual assault prevention program for both prisoners and staff." Letter to Human Rights Watch from Harold W. Clarke, Director, Nebraska Department of Correctional Services, July 10, 1997. The department did not respond to any of our subsequent requests for information.
8. Massachusetts is one of the few states that provided such a protocol, titled the "Prisoner Sexual Assault Response Plan," which came into effect in October 1998. It covers the appropriate staff reaction to incidents of sexual assault, evidence collection, prisoner medical care, reporting procedures, witness interviewing, seeking of criminal charges, and psychological evaluation and counseling. Massachusetts Department of Correction, "Prisoner Sexual Response Plan," 103 DOC 520 (October 1998). In a welcome step, the department trains certain staff members to be Certified Sexual Assault Investigators.

   The Federal Bureau of Prisons, charged with the management of one of the largest prison populations in the country, has also established a comprehensive protocol of this sort. It is designed to "provide guidelines to help prevent sexual assaults on prisoners, to address the safety and treatment needs of prisoners who have been sexually assaulted, and to discipline and prosecute those who sexually assault prisoners." Federal Bureau of Prisons, "Program Statement: Sexual Abuse/Assault Prevention and Intervention Programs," PS 5324.04, December 31, 1997.

   Connecticut has a sexual assault response protocol that was drafted in December 1996. The protocol covers staff response, evidence collection, medical treatment, mental health treatment, and prisoner housing placement. It is aimed at prison medical practitioners, however, rather than the correctional officers who are generally responsible for the initial response to claims of sexual abuse. "Health Services: Prisoner Sexual Assault/Rape Protocol," December 11, 1996.

9. Arkansas Department of Correction, "Sexual Aggression in Prisons and Jails: Awareness, Prevention, and Intervention" (undated manuscript), p. 4.

10. *Farmer v. Brennan*, 511 U.S. 825, 841 (1994).

11. See, for example, *Ginn v. Gallagher*, 1994 U.S. Dist. LEXIS 16669 (1994) (summary judgment for defendants granted); *Dreher v. Roth*, 1993 U.S. Dist. LEXIS 209 (1993) (summary judgment for defendants granted).

12. North Carolina General Statutes, Chapter 143B-262.2.

13. Human Rights Watch has previously documented abuses that occur in supermax prison units, including the fact that a lack of due process in assignment to such units means that prisoners may wrongly end up in them. See Human Rights Watch, *Cold Storage: Super-Maximum Security Confinement in Indiana* (New York: Human Rights Watch, 1997). In other words, not all prisoners housed in supermax units are actually the "worst of the worst," as proponents of such units like to claim. Indeed, Human Rights Watch has even found rape victims taking refuge in such units, having purposefully broken prison rules in order to escape to a highly regulated and secure environment.

14. Letter to Human Rights Watch from B.J., Connecticut, September 23, 1996.

15. Letter to Human Rights Watch, November 7, 1996.

16. Human Rights Watch telephone interview, August 6, 1997.

17. Jim Yardley, "Escape Prompts Scrutiny of Texas Prison System," *New York Times*, January 11, 2001 (quoting Brian Olsen, deputy director of the American Federation of State, County and Municipal Employees, which represents roughly one-sixth of the state's correctional officers).

18. Letter to Human Rights Watch from K.M., Florida, June 18, 1999.

19. Letter to Human Rights Watch from D.A., Texas, September 18, 1998.

20. Letter to Human Rights Watch from L.T., Texas, February 19, 1997.

21. Letter to Human Rights Watch from S.H., Texas, September 10, 1996 (excerpt from legal pleadings).

22. Letter to Human Rights Watch from L.L., Ohio, August 10, 1997.

23. Texas was the only state that provided precise numbers regarding criminal prosecutions. In 1997, the Texas correctional department stated: "Since 1984, Internal Affairs has investigated a total of 519 cases [of prisoner-on-prisoner sexual assault]. Four cases have resulted in prosecution, with the guilty party receiving an additional prison sentence." Letter to Human Rights Watch from Debby Miller, executive services, Texas Department of Criminal Justice, May 19, 1997. The department did not provide specific numbers in response to our 1998 and 1999 queries. In 1998, for example, Human Rights Watch was told that "our Internal Affairs Division is not always notified by the prosecuting attorneys as to the outcome of these cases, [so] we do not have the precise number of cases that are prosecuted and result in an additional prison sentence." Letter from Debby Miller, executive services, Texas Department of Criminal Justice, July 29, 1998.

24. Letter to Human Rights Watch from Terry Carlson, Adult Facilities Support Unit Director, Minnesota Department of Corrections, August 26, 1997.

25. Typical is the response of Oklahoma correctional authorities: "Our reports do not list the felony charges filed in district court so we cannot confirm whether charges have been filed, but it does not appear to be routine." Letter to Human Rights Watch from James L. Saffle, Oklahoma Department of Corrections, June 5, 1997. Similarly, Rhode Island correctional authorities told us that they had no statistics on actual convictions. Letter to Human Rights Watch from Ashbel T. Wall, II, Director, Rhode Island Department of Corrections, April 25, 2000.

26. Letter to Human Rights Watch from J.C., Texas, December 16, 1998.

27. *Billman v. Indiana Department of Corrections*, 56 F.3d 785, 790 (1995). For an instructive shock, change the word "prisoners" in that sentence to denote any other group—women, Native Americans, or homeowners, for example.

28. *Farmer v. Brennan*, 511 U.S. 825, 839 (1994) (Thomas, J., concurring in the judgment) (quoting *McGill v. Duckworth*, 944 F.2d 344, 348 (7th Cir. 1991)).

29. See *LaMarca v. Turner*, 662 F.Supp. 647 (S.D. Fla. 1987) (granting $201,500 in

damages, as well as injunctive relief, in class action brought by prisoners who were gang raped at the Glades Correctional Institution), affirmed in part and vacated in part, 995 F.2d 1526 (11th Cir. 1993), cert. denied, 510 U.S. 1164 (1994); *Redman v. County of San Diego*, 896 F.2d 362 (9th Cir. 1990) (affirming district court direct verdict that a small, eighteen-year-old prisoner who was raped by his cellmate and others did not prove that he had been treated with deliberate indifference), affirmed in part, revised in part, 942 F.2d 1435 (1991) (en banc) (reversing district court, finding that a reasonable jury could have concluded that jail officials had acted with deliberate indifference), cert. denied, 502 U.S. 1074 (1992).

30. *Chandler v. Jones*, 1988 U.S. Dist. LEXIS 693, *3 (E.D. Mo. 1988). It thus absolved the prison officials of responsibility, stating that the officials "made the best of a bad situation."

31. See, for example, *McGill v. Duckworth*, 944 F.2d 344 (7th Cir. 1991) (reversing verdict in favor of raped prisoner, reasoning that legislatures, architects, taxpayers and judges all bear a share of the blame for prison abuses). Ruling against two prisoners who were sexually assaulted, the court suggested that sexual assault was extremely common in the overcrowded jail under consideration, but that prison officials could not be blamed for the problem. It explained: "The assaults were a result of the physical layout and overcrowding of the jail, both matters beyond the control of the defendant." *Kish v. County of Milwaukee*, 441 F.2d 901, 905 (7th Cir. 1971).

32. *Butler v. Dowd*, 979 F.2d 661 (8th Cir. 1992).

33. *James v. Tilghman*, 194 F.R.D. 408 (D. Conn. 1999). At the suggestion of defense counsel, the court revised the award, giving the plaintiff one dollar in nominal damages.

Corcoran

Sex, Lies, and Videotapes

WILLIE WISELY

"I heard yelling and screaming. I heard batons hitting," Connie Foster told California lawmakers in July 1998, at a joint legislative hearing regarding guard brutality at Corcoran prison. Foster, who worked at the prison from 1987 to 1996, recalled watching guards beat a prisoner lying defenseless and prone, his face pressed into the ground, hands cuffed behind his back. The hearings, which lasted five days, revealed a system out of control. "The [guards] were just thrashing him. I walked away. It made me sick," Foster told the *Sacramento Bee*.

Between 1989 and 1995, 50 Corcoran Security Housing Unit (SHU) prisoners were shot by guards, seven fatally. The number of prisoners brutalized in other ways is yet undetermined. The widely publicized killing of a prisoner, Preston Tate, gave rise to state and federal investigations of a prison where institutional violence was commonplace and killings of prisoners were routinely organized by guards for their macabre entertainment.

On April 4, 1994, Preston Tate was shot dead by a Corcoran guard at close range with a nine-millimeter assault rifle. Tate, serving a term for robbery, was intentionally put on the tiny SHU exercise yard with a rival street gang member. A guard later revealed in testimony that prison staff routinely staged "cockfights" between prisoners, then falsified reports to cover up the brutality. After the Tate killing, the horrified guard went to federal authorities with the story. A prison videotape caught Tate's murder in the yard; the tape made its way to television news shows across the nation, causing public outcry for an investigation.

Seven years after the first unarmed prisoner was killed by a guard for fighting, and amid probes by the FBI and a local prosecutor, the Department of Corrections and Attorney General's office launched their own investigations into the shootings, violence, and cover-ups at

This article was written in October 1998.

Corcoran. Not surprisingly, both concluded there was no widespread staff misconduct.

"It's clear investigations for the department are not adequate," Senator Ruben Ayala, D-Chino, chairman of the hearing told the *Bee*. "We must take a closer look at how they investigate problems and where that information goes." Even the Department's own investigators were unhappy.

"The [guards] union and the governor's office ran the investigation," Jim Connor, a parole agent who supervised the Department's team, told the *Los Angeles Times*. "We would try to question a witness, and the union was there blocking us. The [union] even told us how many interviews we could do, and our bosses in Sacramento backed them. This was no independent inquiry. It was just a sham."

Investigators for the state called the probe an exercise in futility. "I've been an investigator for 10 years, and no one has ever told me before that I couldn't talk to certain important people and couldn't pursue certain key leads," said Ben Eason, a supervisor with the Department's investigation team. "If this was a search for the truth, how can you establish those parameters?" Governor Pete Wilson and Attorney General Dan Lungren denied that the investigations were hamstrung.

Lungren called the complaints regarding the sham investigation a "bunch of crap." Lungren insists that the state investigation was purposefully "limited" so it wouldn't obstruct ongoing federal probes. "We weren't going to duplicate or interfere with what the feds were engaged in. It's a matter of not screwing up another investigation," he told the *Times*. Federal authorities refute Lungren's contention. They say their only mandate was to investigate the Preston Tate killing, and point out that there were plenty of other allegations of misconduct to occupy state investigators.

During the hearings in July 1998, Connor denied saying that the Department's investigation was a sham in interviews with the *Times*. But the *Times* explained that the reporter read the quote to Connor twice before publication, and Connor had agreed it was correct. Other investigators said they were afraid of losing their jobs if they testified truthfully. "I was told to be careful of my opinions," one confided to the *Times*. "No doubt about it, if I spoke my mind, there would be retaliation. That's the way it is. That's the nature of the beast."

After spending 500,000 tax dollars on the state probe, only one person was singled out for discipline by the Department's investigation. Richard Caruso, a former Corcoran guard who had provided key evidence about staged fights, shootings, beatings, and cover-ups to the FBI, was docked pay for 90 days for firing wooden blocks at prisoners.

The FBI told the *Times* they believe Caruso's punishment was an attempt to discredit Caruso and sabotage his relationship with the Bureau. Considering that Caruso was the central figure in the continuing federal investigation into Corcoran, prison officials had ample reason to be angry with him.

Caruso, along with former Facility Captain Ralph Mineau and former Lieutenant Steve Rigg, turned to the FBI in 1994 because their supervisors and corrections officials refused to listen. Their information led to the indictment February 26, 1998, of eight Corcoran guards for violating the civil rights of prisoners. The eight guards were charged with staging fights between gang rivals, falsifying official reports in an attempt to cover up those fights, and using a staged fight to kill Preston Tate.

"I'm a whistle-blower. I'm not sorry for the action I took," Rigg testified at the hearing. "I'm sorry I put my family through the horrors of the reprisals and harassment we've been subjected to. My career came to an abrupt end. I'm sorry I've been threatened with death or harm. I'm sorry my wife is frightened to sleep in our home at night and often sleeps on the bathroom floor fearing ambush."

Brutality at Corcoran was common knowledge to those of us who spent time at the prison. In December of 1988, I left New Folsom's B Facility on one of the first five buses bound for Corcoran. With a one-year SHU term for assaulting two guards, I had reason to worry. We'd heard rumors of what could be expected for prisoners accused of assaulting a guard. It was hot that day. The air in the bus was stagnant, without circulation. We had no drinking water and sat crammed together, wearing dirty transportation jumpsuits without underwear or socks. Our hands were tightly cuffed to waist chains. Steel ankle restraints bit into bare flesh with every step.

Located on a flat stretch of burned out farmland laden with toxic chemicals in California's Central Valley, Corcoran was the first prison in the state to open a modern "supermax" SHU. The prison loomed at the end of a narrow highway in the distance, dancing in the heat. Most of the surrounding fields were barren, a few scraggly patches of cotton sprinkle the rock-hard, parched earth. By the time the bus rolled into the prison, we'd been chained in the bus fourteen hours.

A group of SHU baton-wielding guards stood in full riot gear next to the bus. They ran through marching drills before taking us off the bus. One by one, they grabbed us and tossed us from the bus. The guards screamed, "Don't look at us! Look straight up at the sun! We'll kill you if you look at us! This is Corcoran SHU!"

The guards separated and surrounded us. One jerked my head back, another leaned menacingly toward me, and another screamed into my face showering me with his spittle: "You like hitting officers, huh, asshole?" he bellowed. "We've got something for you!" I was hoping to make it to a cell alive, so when they peppered my kidneys and solar plexus with blows, I struggled to keep looking up.

Corcoran's welcome wagon was composed of a group of rogue guards who called themselves The Sharks. According to the *Los Angeles Times*, in 1995 a busload of black prisoners transferred from nearby Calipatria prison was greeted by the Corcoran welcome wagon with the requisite pummeling. As the bus arrived, dozens of guards jumped to attention, performed a half-hour of warm-ups and cheers, then proceeded to beat the prisoners senseless.

With tape obscuring name tags, the guards grabbed the shackled prisoners, jerked them off the bus one at a time, and ran them through a gauntlet of fists, batons, and combat boots. Prisoners with braids were held down while a guard cut their hair off. The abuse lasted over thirty minutes.

One prisoner was thrown headfirst through a window, another smashed into a concrete wall. Some of the guards weren't scheduled to work that day, but nevertheless came to join the activities. A lieutenant helped cover up the incident, faking time sheets so it appeared many of the guards weren't at the prison that day. "I've seen guards beat [prisoners], but nothing ever like that," Connie Foster would recount to legislators in 1998. "I couldn't watch it all. After it was over, I went to my car and threw up."

When I arrived in 1988, only one of the two SHU facilities was open. It was dark before I got to a cell. I spent a few hours standing naked in a telephone booth-size holding cage, hands cuffed behind my back. The cells were concrete, save for the stainless steel toilet/sink combination. There was no mirror, locker, or electrical outlet.

Two concrete slabs for bunks lay side by side. No more than 18 inches separated them. Crude spaces carved out of the side of the concrete bunks served as shelves. I put my belongings, a half-toothbrush, a small envelope of tooth powder, and pen filler in one of the spaces.

When the door opened for yard, I went. In California, racial politics require you to go to yard in segregation or SHU. It's mandatory. It doesn't matter if you're scared or don't want to go. You go, or you're marked as a coward and subject to assault or stabbing.

Corcoran's SHU yards are narrow triangles with high walls some twenty feet across at the wide end, eight feet across at the narrow end, and maybe thirty feet long. The floors are unfinished concrete, slanted, and uneven. There's one combination toilet/sink, and one shower nozzle. Sometimes they worked, most of the time they didn't.

The high walls reflected the burning sun onto the SHU yards, making them several degrees hotter than the outside air. You only go to the yard with your tier. Each building has two sides, three sections, and two tiers per section.

Prisoners group by race in segregation unit yards. New arrivals are quickly told the rules, "This is our area here. That's theirs. Cross the line and it's on. Sometimes the guards shoot the [wooden] blocks first. Sometimes the line," explained an older con my first day in the yard. Prisoners exercise separately according to racial group. Handball, the one game available, is sometimes played between races, sometimes not, depending on the yard.

Corcoran was a place of extremes. It was either extremely hot, extremely cold, or extremely wet. When the cold came, a thin layer of ice formed on the SHU yard floors and the toilet water froze. Hot, cold, wet, or dry, I went to the yard, exercised and played handball. A few weeks after I arrived, William Martinez, 30, was the first prisoner shot to death. He'd finished fighting with another prisoner and was walking away when a guard shot him in the back. I heard the shot, then the alarm.

You never got too comfortable in one cell because guards moved you constantly. They stacked tiers with enemies, letting the fighters out first for yard. Everyone knew what was expected. If it happened to you, you had to fight. You might get shot either way. Southern Mexicans and whites stuck together. Northern Mexicans and blacks stuck together. Others picked sides when they hit the yard.

I was lucky. I never got shot. Occasionally, bullet fragments and splinters of wood blocks hit me as they ricocheted off the concrete, but nothing serious. On one rainy morning, guards shot their 37 millimeter guns 19 times on my yard.

After a couple of months, the SHU yard walls showed pockmarks from bullets. Dark stains blotched the yard floors, some with long smears where a body was dragged away. When my SHU term was up, I was given an indeterminate term in newly opened Pelican Bay without charges, notice, or a hearing. They needed bodies to fill the new prison. My wife made a few calls, and I was on the next bus to a mainline. I felt sorry for those with no one to help. Those like Eddie Dillard.

Eddie Dillard was a 120-pound, 23-year-old first termer. He came to Corcoran SHU for kicking a female guard at Calipatria prison. Roscoe Pondexter, a 6-foot-7-inch former pro-basketball player turned guard, knew Dillard was a marked man when he read the order to cell him up with Wayne Robertson. Robertson beat and raped black prisoners as a favor for the guards according to the *Times*, and prison records clearly indicated that he was a known enemy of Dillard.

Serving life for murder, Robertson was known in the prison as the "Booty Bandit." He told state corrections investigators that when SHU guards wanted another prisoner "checked," they used him. He said he got extra food and tennis shoes in payment.

"I didn't know what wrong Dillard had done, but my superiors obviously wanted him punished," Pondexter told the *Times*. "Everyone knew about Robertson. He had raped [prisoners] before and he's raped [prisoners] since.... The Booty Bandit was just one of the tools of punishment that we used."

Now out on parole, Dillard told the *Times*, "They took something away from me that I can never replace. I've tried so many nights to forget about it, but the feeling just doesn't go away. Every time I'm with my wife, it comes back what he did to me. I want a close to the story. I want some salvation. But it keeps going on and on."

Dillard has sued four Corcoran guards over the incident. Pondexter corroborates Dillard's claim that he was repeatedly raped by Robertson, as do multiple corrections investigative reports, and admissions by Robertson himself.

Although they were from the same neighborhood outside, when Dillard arrived in prison Robertson propositioned him. Dillard turned Robertson down and they fought, according to the *Times*. Under Department policy, the fact that they were listed as enemies should have prevented them from being placed in the same yard, let alone the same cell.

At Corcoran, when Dillard was ordered to move to Robertson's cell, he told Pondexter, Sergeant Alan Decker, and Anthony Sylva, another guard, that he and Robertson were enemies. Sylva said, "It's happening. Since you like hitting women, we've got somebody for you," Dillard told the *Times*.

The lights went out and Robertson grabbed Dillard. They struggled, Dillard pounded on the cell door, but no one came. Eventually, Robertson overpowered and raped him. Guards walked by two hours later, but just laughed at Dillard. Over the next two days, he was repeatedly raped. Finally, when the cell door opened, Dillard ran out and refused to go back in.

A prison medical technician examined Dillard for sexual assault, but Dillard refused to snitch Robertson out. Robertson, however, openly bragged to a guard, "Yeah, I punked him," according to the *Times*. The guard reported the incident to Sergeant Jeff Jones and was told, "What do you want me to do with this? Nobody wants to do anything about it."

An order to transfer Dillard to an outside hospital for a full rape examination was mysteriously canceled. Dillard was moved to a different cell and warned by Decker not to make noise or they'd put him back with Robertson, Dillard told the *Times*.

Pondexter later told FBI investigators he was routinely used by staff and administrators as an "enforcer" to intimidate and keep prisoners in line with terror. Seven guards and supervisors were investigated by the state, but no action was taken against them or the prison.

State prosecutor James Jahn told the *Fresno Bee* that a Corcoran medical technician first tipped off state investigators about the canceled rape exam for Dillard in 1997. The technician said the cancellation came from the prison's "security squad," according to the *Bee*. Corrections records indicate the same squad covered up at least 13 other cases of excessive force at Corcoran.

Corrections investigators told the *Times* their investigation of the Dillard case was stymied when the guards' union posted fliers all over Corcoran prison telling guards they did not have to answer any questions without a union representative present. Even during the joint legislative hearings, State Senators were met with a wall of silence.

Guards refused to testify on advice of their attorneys, citing the so-called "Peace Officers Bill of Rights." Those civil statutes provide that anyone with the designation "peace officer," like a prison guard, has the right to refuse to answer questions which might expose him to civil or criminal liability. Frustrated lawmakers promised to take a closer look at the statute for possible revision.

Efforts to thwart investigation didn't end at the prison walls. In the town of Corcoran, guards went door to door distributing fliers, pleading for support for their indicted colleagues. During recent demonstrations inflamed by the brutality at the prison, guards staked out local parking lots and took down license numbers from protestors' cars. The union drew crowds of hundreds of guards and several Republican legislators at various gatherings organized to garner support.

In the aftermath, information surfaced that the guards union spent over $27,000 for fliers denouncing Kings County District Attorney Donald Strickland as a friend of prison gangs because he prosecuted a guard for misconduct. Strickland was subsequently voted out of office; his opponent had been heavily financed by the union.

Corrections Director Terhune approved spending more than $1 million of taxpayers' money to defend the guards charged by the federal grand jury, according to the *Bee*. Despite overwhelming evidence of their guilt, Terhune claims use of tax funds is appropriate because he's confident they are innocent. Governor Pete Wilson backed Terhune's decision. In the meantime, six of the guards are back to work at Corcoran, and two took early retirement.

As chilling as the abuse and killings was the lack of any public concern or oversight, oversight that might have precluded the abuse's longevity. "The fact that no one noticed seems to be the worst crime," Fresno attorney Catherine Campbell told the *Times*. Campbell represents the Tate family in their wrongful death suit. "Corcoran was given license to act out the worst impulses of our criminal justice system," Campbell concluded.

With the probability of further action by state legislators—including the introduction of bills aimed at curbing the guards union's resistance to cooperating with investigators in the future, civil judgments against prison staff and the corrections department, the pending federal grand jury indictments, an ongoing FBI probe, and a second state investigation—it seems unlikely the Department's problems will go away anytime soon. And that's a good thing. Unfortunately, it usually takes the loss of life or outrageous examples of brutality before the public and lawmakers take notice or demand changes in prison.

Guarding Their Silence

Corcoran Guards Acquitted of Rape

CHRISTIAN PARENTI

The acquittal in November 1999 of four California prison guards charged with arranging for a young prisoner to be raped by Corcoran State Prison's notorious "Booty Bandit" was the result of a massive legal and political show of force on the part of the state's prison guards union, prisoners' advocates say. The four guards were facing nine years in prison.

State prosecutors alleged that in March 1993, the four Corcoran State Prison Security Housing Unit officers, led by Sgt. Robert Alan Decker, deliberately transferred prisoner Eddie Dillard to the cell of Wayne Robertson, aka the "Booty Bandit," knowing that the younger, smaller prisoner would be raped. At trial, Robertson testified that he had indeed beaten and sodomized Dillard for two days because guards had said that Dillard needed to "learn how to do his time."

But the defense—led by four adroit lawyers and funded by the guards' union—countered that the accused guards had no idea at the time that Robertson was a rapist. "I agree that Wayne Robertson is a rapist and a thug, but that fact was not known to the floor staff," said defense attorney Curtis Sisk in his opening arguments. One of the officers told the jury that the first time he even heard of Wayne Robertson was in an article in the *Los Angeles Times*.

The California Correctional Peace Officers Association—which paid the defendants' legal costs and launched a media campaign to support them—is one of the state's most powerful lobbies. During the last election cycle, the group poured millions of dollars into state races, supporting candidates from both parties and waging a $2 million media campaign on behalf of Governor Gray Davis.

"We are obviously very pleased. The four guards and their families are the real victims here," said union president Don Novey.

This article was written in 2000.

With a pending federal trial and several criminal investigations of prison staff still open, the CCPOA left as little as possible to chance during the state investigation and trial. The union's publication, the *Peace Keeper*, encouraged rank and file members not to trust or speak with the FBI and state investigators. Critics of the union say this and quick intervention by CCPOA lawyers effectively shut down the flow of information at the source.

As the so-called "Booty Bandit" trial approached, the CCPOA also turned to the public relations side of the political equation, targeting Hanford-area residents with a slew of radio and TV ads full of menacing, tattooed convicts and brave guards walking "the toughest beat in the state." (The union says the timing of the ads was mere coincidence, and was not related to the pending case.)

And once arguments in the case opened, the CCPOA's concern was manifest in attendance of a steady stream of local chapter officials and union heavies.

For prisoners' rights activists like Tom Quinn, a private investigator who specializes in researching cases against California jails and prisons, the presence of CCPOA honchos was just another example of how a code of silence is encouraged and enforced by the leadership of both the union and the Department of Corrections.

"Fundamentally, the claim that these guards didn't know that Robertson was a rapist is totally implausible," Quinn said. "The SHU [Security Housing Unit] is a unique social experiment designed to generate information." Along with elaborate records and dossiers kept on all the prisoners, Quinn points out that guards have a relatively clear view into most of the SHU cells, both from the tier and from inside the control booth. "Furthermore," adds Quinn, "the COs [correctional officers] are constantly working snitches. They know who's who. And they knew . . . that Robertson was a rapist."

Quinn's claims were affirmed by Connie Foster, who worked as a staff member at Corcoran in 1993. "I heard about Robertson a week after I arrived," Foster said.

Did Lockyer's Office Botch the Prosecution?

But despite claims like these, the state has had difficulty breaking the guards' silence. Among other things, say the union's critics, the CCPOA's massive campaign war chest has proved a valuable tool in discouraging local district attorneys from prosecuting cases against prison guards.

The Dillard case, for example, was almost filed by the Kings County district attorney, but Greg Strickland, who then held the county post, dropped the charges, citing lack of evidence. Many speculate that

Strickland was also scared of the CCPOA. He had already crossed the group once, by prosecuting Corcoran guards involved in a 1995 beating incident. Sure enough, the union's wrath materialized during the next DA's race, in the form of a massive campaign donation to Strickland's opponent. In testimony before a state legislative committee, Strickland suggested the creation of "an independent prosecution unit" because, as he put it, "My incumbent owes the CCPOA $30,000 worth of campaign contributions." That project was vetoed by Governor Davis, but a compromise was eventually struck, leading to the creation of a new inspector general position, which is filled by gubernatorial appointment.

Lockyer spokesman Nathan Barankin said that getting good investigations from local prosecutors and police forces in the small towns that house many of these prisons continues to be a problem. He said in the Dillard case specifically, there was no investigation after the crime was committed.

Barankin did acknowledge that, in the wake of this case and the federal investigation at Corcoran, a number of changes have been implemented both by the Legislature and the Department of Corrections. Besides the new inspector general position, new shooting policies have been implemented at all state prison facilities.

Still, Barankin conceded, the new policies are not a guarantee that this will never happen again. "You can investigate until you're blue in the face, but you still have the question of who prosecutes it." Barankin said local district attorneys would normally prosecute these cases, but that in the small counties where most state prisons are located, "to accept one of these cases would eat up everybody you have in the place, plus every red cent you've got to get one of these cases to court." The local DA could hand the case off to the attorney general, but Barankin said by the time that happens, usually "the AG's office comes in to pull together the pieces. DAs have their own investigators" who work closely with local police right after the crime is reported. "It remains to be seen if this new inspector general will work the same way."

While prisoners' rights activists sympathized with Barankin, they blamed Lockyer's office—specifically deputy attorney general Vern Pierson—for botching the prosecution. They say the state's strategy failed to make the code of silence and culture of terror at Corcoran central issues in the case.

Based on his research of California jails and prisons, Quinn said the "Booty Bandit" trial was about much more than the fate of four prison guards. "Clearly, part of what was on trial here was the guards' code of silence, the power of the CCPOA, and the culture of terror that defines life in California's maximum security prisons," he said.

Quinn acknowledged that much of that was impossible to pursue in court when Judge Louis Bissig disallowed conspiracy charges brought against the four guards. "Our hands were tied by some of the judge's rulings and the fact that it took five years for this crime to surface and be prosecuted," Pierson told the *Los Angeles Times*. "And it's never easy when your best witnesses of what really happened are felons and officers who have committed [crimes] themselves."

That sentiment was echoed by Barankin. "Having the conspiracy charges thrown out by the judge was gigantic. That can't be quantified," he said. But Barankin conceded that "there were all sorts of places along the way where things fell apart."

The "Bonecrusher"

Activists say much of the blame rests with Pierson, arguing that his most crucial misstep was the handling of star witness Roscoe "Bonecrusher" Pondexter. A former guard and onetime professional basketball player, Pondexter testified against the four accused guards in exchange for immunity from prosecution.

Pondexter testified that he was once a sadistic "search and escort" officer in the Corcoran SHU. He ran with a gang of guards called the Sharks and his specialty was to beat and strangle prisoners. "We would show them 'the Corcoran way' and tell them this was a 'hands on' institution," said Pondexter. He was eventually fired for brutality.

But Pondexter's testimony was later picked apart by defense attorney Katherine Hart, who showed that Pondexter was on vacation the day Dillard was moved into the Booty Bandit's cell. Pondexter had previously testified he was working that day. "You had a faulty memory about that, didn't you?" asked Hart.

"Yes," Pondexter admitted, squandering much of his credibility in the process.

Afterward, a vexed and embarrassed Pondexter was heard complaining to a friend that Pierson hardly prepared him for testimony, briefing and questioning him for only 25 minutes, just before he took the stand.

Barankin refuted that claim, saying prosecutors spent "a considerable amount of time preparing Mr. Pondexter for the trial." When asked about why they did not check records that showed Pondexter was not even working that day, Barankin said, "The defense had access to information we didn't have. We found out the same time [the jury] did."

Also missing from the state's case was much of the detail that had emerged during grand jury testimony and during last year's legislative hearings. According to both these inquiries, the story of the Dillard rape and ensuing cover-up went as follows: Dillard and Robertson—both members of the Piru Bloods, a Los Angeles street gang, though separated by a 20-year age difference—had first come into conflict at Tehachapi State Prison in 1992. There Robertson made sexual advances to Dillard and was rebuffed. Soon thereafter Robertson, already a documented jailhouse rapist, was transferred to the Corcoran SHU.

In 1993, Dillard kicked a female guard and was sent north to Corcoran. In his grand jury deposition, Robertson told how Sgt. Robert Alan Decker showed him a list of four proposed cellmates. Robertson chose Dillard and a few days latter, while lying on his bunk, looked up to see the protesting Dillard being thrust into his cell by two guards.

Dillard explained the rest when he took the stand: "Before I knew it, we were getting into it. We were tussling and he said he was going to rape me. I tried to fight him off but I couldn't. He raped me," said Dillard, his voice breaking. Dillard finally escaped the cell when guards came to take Robertson to an unrelated disciplinary hearing. Desperate, Dillard refused to reenter the cell.

Finally, Dillard told a guard that Robertson had raped him. The guard filed a report and passed it on to a sergeant, but the report was lost. Dillard was then examined by a prison medic, who saw no sign of rape. A doctor examined Dillard and ordered a "rape kit"—a full internal rape examination—but the order was quickly and mysteriously countermanded and Dillard was never properly examined. After getting a new cell, Dillard started sending administrative complaints, known as "602s," about Sgt. Decker and the rape to officials in Sacramento.

Records show that on June 16, 1993, Dillard suddenly withdrew his complaint and stopped his follow-ups. That was the same day that Decker signed in for a visit with Dillard on his new cell block. According to Dillard, Decker gave him a simple choice: Drop the 602, or go "back in the cell with Robertson."

Little of this chronology was spelled out during the trial, though, and none of the defense witnesses seemed to remember much—all of which undermined the prosecution's case.

"We went over everything, covered everything, a lot of documents," the jury foreman, who declined to give his name, told the Los Angeles Times. "In the end, there was just too much reasonable doubt. There just wasn't a lot of evidence that supported what the prosecutor was trying to prove."

That was the fault of the prosecution, said prisoners' rights attorney Catherine Campbell. "My impression was that [Pierson] was on automatic, doing a job that was distasteful to him," she said. "He had no moral passion. The lapses, particularly the one with Pondexter—that sort of thing throws a witness off center."

The attorney general's office stood by Pierson, saying that he had inherited an impossible situation. "The football field is littered with

Monday-morning quarterbacks," said Barankin. He agreed that "most right-thinking people should feel a sense of moral outrage based upon the evidence that we were privy to. Unfortunately, the jury was not allowed to hear all that evidence."

[Editor's note: In March 2000, eight other Corcoran guards were brought to trial on federal charges for shooting Corcoran prisoners. All eight defendant guards were acquitted on all charges.]

Our Sisters' Keepers

DANIEL BURTON-ROSE

While incarcerated in a for-profit prison in Arizona, Christina Foos says she was attacked by a guard, Ernesto Rivas, as she stepped out of the shower in March 1997. Christina told *Prison Legal News* that she was startled by the sight of him, standing there with his exposed erection in hand.

Before she could think of what to do, she says, Rivas ordered her to bend over the bed in her cell and he raped her. She says he returned less than two hours later to repeat the act.

Foos was among 78 women exiled in October 1996, by the Oregon Department of Corrections. Because of overcrowding, the women were shipped to the Corrections Corporation of America's (CCA) Central Arizona Detention Center in Florence.

Predominantly a men's facility, CCA Florence lacked a separate disciplinary segregation unit for women. A medical quarantine room adjacent to the hospital area served as the improvised solution. According to a suit filed in Tucson by five women against CCA and at least fifteen former or current CCA Florence employees, the all-male guard staff that watched over the improvised seg unit perpetrated sexual abuses with impunity for months.

At least five of the women were returned to Oregon in August 1997, in an apparent attempt by the Oregon DOC to hush the matter. That's when Barrilee Bannister first contacted *PLN*.

Barrilee, one of the prisoners transferred back to Oregon, explains that the abuse started when a guard captain Newton (full names could not be confirmed because CCA refused to speak to *PLN* for this article) gave six or so women a marijuana joint. Hours later he returned with several other guards and notified the women their cells would be searched. Barrilee says the captain told them that they could avoid charges for

---

This article was written in February 1999.

possession of contraband by performing a strip tease for him and the other guards. Barrilee said several of the women obliged, fearing additional time added to their sentences if they refused, or worse.

The dancing, Barrilee says, led to more aggressive behavior, from groping to oral sex and intercourse.

A number of CCA Florence guards were eventually placed on administrative leave as a result of an internal CCA investigation of the abuse allegations. Foos told *PLN* that shortly before she departed for Oregon, a CCA guard told her there were currently 27 such complaints filed. Bannister estimates that up to 50 CCA Florence guards were involved in all—with offenses ranging from perpetrating the abuse to covering it up.

In U.S. prisons, such degradation is not uncommon. A July 20, 1995, incident in one of Washington, D.C.'s jails offers another glimpse of this seamier side of "corrections."

As D.C.'s soul station WHUR-FM was piped over the jail's public address system, several female prisoners began to dance and strip on tables in the common area of the block called "Southeast One." A crowd of prisoners and guards gathered to watch. Among them was Sunday Daskalea, a naturalized Greek immigrant and exotic dancer from New York City who was in the jail facing cocaine charges.

Daskalea later described to the *Washington Post* how, swept away by the "festival" atmosphere, another prisoner exclaimed, "Sunday's a dancer too!" But Daskalea says she wanted nothing to do with the exhibition and retreated to her cell.

According to Daskalea, the captain in charge of the block, Yvonne C. Walker, instructed a crew of prisoners to force Daskalea back to the exhibition. "You're going to make [Walker] mad," one of the prisoners warned. Daskalea relented.

"I didn't want any trouble," she recalled. She did the strip tease, in which another prisoner also undressed and poured baby oil on a nude Daskalea.

Although jail staff were present, none reported the incident. D.C. jail officials eventually heard about it through a prisoner. And this incident occurred just three months after a federal jury found the D.C. Department of Corrections liable in a sexual harassment suit in which the department eventually settled for $8 million.

Sexual abuse of prisoners by guards is not particularly new. What is striking today is the extent of the abuse, in both men's and women's prisons, and the near-total lack of interest among prison administrators in stopping it. No state or federal government entity collects reports of prison rape, so exact numbers are difficult to gauge. But with a barrage of high-profile individual and class action suits, and the stunning exposé of rampant sexual abuse in American prisons as disseminated by a 1996 Human Rights Watch report on the topic, sexual abuse appears to be endemic to prisons across the nation.

Susan Fiester, an expert witness on sexual abuse who has testified for prisoner plaintiffs in five states, estimates that 70 to 80 percent of the general female prison population has experienced sexual abuse during and/or previous to incarceration.

The effects of sexual abuse on victims can be debilitating, resulting in depression, frequent headaches, insomnia, trouble concentrating, low confidence and self-esteem, and isolation from others. These symptoms can be especially acute when the rapist is a guard and the victim is forced to live each day with the fear that the abuser will violate them again.

Few such cases are reported. And if they ever come to trial, they are often framed as "he said/she said" in which the issue central to the case is the credibility of the aggrieved prisoner.

According to court testimony, Tanya Giron was raped by a guard named Danny Torrez while she was incarcerated in the disciplinary seg unit of another CCA prison, the Western New Mexico Correctional Facility in Grants. Giron, who had been incarcerated for shoplifting, said the seg unit was isolated and poorly monitored. She testified that Torrez (who no longer works for CCA) took advantage of the isolation, raping her when he came to deliver a meal tray to her cell.

In a civil trial in the summer of 1997, Giron demanded more than a million dollars in damages from Torrez and CCA. Torrez acknowledges only that he and Giron had sex; he claims Giron wanted it. The defense strategy was to elicit testimony from Giron that she had been raped before—more than once—and then twist that into a seed of doubt to plant in jurors' minds.

The defense strategy worked. Though no one disputed that sex took place, the eight-woman federal jury awarded Giron nothing. Paul Kennedy, Giron's attorney, recounted, "There was a lot of hostility from the jury because [Giron] was a prisoner."

Former Michigan prisoner Sadia Zoe Ali asks in a November 1996 *Prison Life* article, "Will somebody please tell me why the fuck it's so hard to believe these women?" As Sadia explains, any prisoner who steps forward to report abuse risks retaliation from the DOC and personal vengeance from the "Blue Gang" (the baddest gang in any prison: the guards). Because of that, says Sadia, reporting rape to prison officials is a choice fraught with negative consequences.

Bannister, for example, says that soon after she spoke to CCA's investigators at Florence, she was attacked by three guards, led by a female guard named Collens, who beat her. The guards accused Bannister of being responsible for their friends being fired. And, assuming that Bannister had been raped (despite her protestations that she "didn't go that far"), the guards aimed their kicks at Bannister's stomach, saying they would force her to abort if she was pregnant.

Later that same day, according to a statement Bannister made after her return to Oregon, Collens sprayed mace under her cell door.

Sexual assaults against male prisoners by male guards similarly receive little, or no attention. In these cases, homophobia can be an extra strike against the victim. According to a June, 1997, finding against the District of Colombia's Department of Corrections, for example, prison administrator L.C. Jones expressed disbelief when presented with a charge that one of his male guards sexually harassed a male prisoner.

Jones, who had charges of sexual harassment pending against him as alleged by both female guards and women prisoners, cited the accused guard's age of 60 and testified in court, "I'll give you the fact that maybe he might be turned on by that fag, I don't know. I just do not. I find it hard to believe."

Jones was promoted to Deputy Warden soon after the incident took place.

Prison administrators may simply ignore (or attempt to cover up) allegations of sexual abuse. Several women who allege abuse at CCA Florence report that they sent numerous letters complaining of the abuse to both warden Crandel and assistant warden Alford Scott.

"They put blinders on. They didn't care," says Jackie Scott, who claims she was sexually harassed by a male nurse at CCA Florence.

When CCA was eventually forced by media attention in Oregon to investigate the claims of sexual abuse at CCA Florence, the women prisoners report that investigators were insulting and abusive. Bannister additionally states that she was offered $100 by several CCA administrators (including the chief of security) if she would keep quiet.

Quida Graham, a guard who witnessed the July '95 strip tease in D.C.'s jail, told the *Washington Post* that she knew she should have reported the incident to prison officials but was afraid of other guards labeling her a snitch. "Nobody wants to work with you once you break the code of silence," Graham explained. She added, "If an inmate is attacking you, you might be waiting for assistance for a very long time."

[Editors' Note: Daskalea and several other women filed suit over the 1995 strip tease incident. A D.C. jury awarded $350,000 in compensatory damages and $5 million in punitive damages. An appeals court upheld the compensatory damages award, but ruled that the Dictrict of Columbia could not be held liable for punitive damages. See Daskalea v. D.C., 227 F.3d 433 (D.C. Cir. 2000).]

Not Part of My Sentence

SILJA J. A. TALVI

Annette Guzman-White, a 32-year-old minimum security prisoner incarcerated on a second-degree burglary charge at the Washington Correction Center for Women (WCCW), is eager to get out of prison.

It's something that could probably be said of most of Washington state's 15,000 prisoners, just slightly over 1,000 of whom are women.

But Guzman-White says that her time at WCCW has put her through a kind of emotional hardship she says she wouldn't wish on anyone. She alleges that a male prison guard, Joseph Solaita, preyed on her vulnerabilities and coerced her into a sexual relationship.

Solaita, who was fired in 2000 but not charged with a crime, has been accused by at least two other women of rape or sexual assault.

One of those women, Rosie Hamann, alleges that Solaita forcibly raped her in September 2000, information, which only emerged after prison investigators approached each of the women separately to confirm an anonymous report that Solaita was having sex with prisoners. Even then, the women were not eager to share the information, and Guzman-White initially insisted she had no sexual contact with Solaita whatsoever. "I denied everything. I was scared of what would happen," she now admits.

Guzman-White told of the rape in September 2000, after prison investigators repeatedly reassured her that she would not be punished for telling the truth.

Since then, Susan Luna, a former prisoner at WCCW, has alleged that she was sexually harassed and molested by Solaita.

And when those allegations came to light, another prisoner came forward in November 2000, with a confidential written statement to the DOC that Solaita had repeatedly sexually harassed her when he first

A shorter version of this article first appeared in *In These Times*, October 2001.

began working at WCCW. While she has not filed claims for damages, she alleges that Solaita told her: "I'm in hog heaven up here," in reference to his job at the women's prison.

On one occasion, she writes in her sworn declaration, he pulled his penis from his pants and said, "You want this, you know it." Solaita did not return calls for comment.

And WCCW prisoner Tamara Smith has alleged sexual harassment and physical contact of a sexual nature involving various other male guards while she was showering in the prison. A fifth prisoner, Danielle Revis, says she was coerced into having sex numerous times with a cook at WCCW.

All five women filed claims for damages against the state.

Consensual Sex is "OK"

Tim Tesh, an attorney with the Seattle law firm Browne & Ressler representing the prisoners, says that a mediation between him and the DOC in July 2001, "was a joke," and that in the meantime, Guzman-White endured punishments at WCCW, including placement in isolation for a minor infraction.

His office now plans to team with nonprofit legal agencies to file a class-action lawsuit. Tesh hopes that the lawsuit will result in monetary payment to the prisoners and improvements in the "prison culture" at WCCW to prevent similar incidents from happening in the future.

"What is perceived to be consensual sex between correctional officers and prisoners is 'OK' and continues to be tolerated in the prison," says Tesh. "It's part of the code of silence."

But prison officials say nothing could be further from the truth.

"As an agency, we have a no-tolerance policy for this type of behavior by DOC personnel, volunteers, or contractors," answers WCCW Superintendent Belinda Stewart. "I take the time to tell new employees, very bluntly, that I absolutely have a no-tolerance policy for this kind of behavior. We have a job to do as professionals to keep the environment safe for the people that are incarcerated within our system, and when staff overstep boundaries, it can make this kind of environment unsafe and dangerous to be in.

"As a woman myself," she adds, "I don't want people overstepping boundaries with me, and so it's important that we keep this environment safe."

Indeed, the DOC's official zero-tolerance stance on sexual relations between guards and prisoners helped to usher in legislation which went into effect two years ago, criminalizing rape and other forms of sexual contact—consensual or not—between guards and inmates.

At the urging of the DOC, Washington's Sexual Offenses chapter of the criminal code was revised to find a person guilty of a felony when that person—whether employee or contract personnel—was proven to have had sexual intercourse with a person under correctional supervision. Sexual misconduct of any other kind is classified as a gross misdemeanor.

Provisions in the law also specifically ensure that prisoners will not be penalized for disclosing information about sexual contact or abuse. Under revised state regulations, prison guards (or other employees of the state) would immediately be suspended, investigated, terminated from employment in the case of a preponderance of evidence of sexual misconduct.

"That is the process that is intended under the law," explains State Senator Jeanine Long (Republican-Mill Creek), who sponsored the Senate bill to criminalize sexual relations between guards and prisoners. "If [the DOC] is following it, everything should work out in the proper way."

"It's a two-way street," adds Senator Long. "The officers have authority and ability to influence where a person is held and how long they're held, and prisoners have the ability to cause a correctional officer to be investigated and possibly lose their job. We attempted . . . to balance those two areas."

Quiet Firings and Resignations

In the two years since the law went into effect, investigations of sexual misconduct and terminations of employment have occurred. In these most recent cases, WCCW confirms that the DOC no longer employs Solaita, but Stewart indicates that there have been no other employment terminations related to sexual misconduct allegations.

And in the interim, the state has paid out hefty sums of taxpayer dollars by way of settlements to some prisoners who alleged sexual abuse in various prisons before and since the law was passed.

In total, according to information obtained from the Office of Risk Management, nearly a half-million dollars has been paid out in settlements since 1998, including a $150,000 settlement to Heather Wells, a WCCW prisoner who alleged she was raped by guard Michael Stevens. She endured punitive segregation when she came forward with her allegations, and became impregnated by the rape.

Stevens, who initially denied any sexual contact with Wells, was proven to be the father through paternity testing. He later tried, unsuccessfully, to gain custody of the child. Stevens was never charged with a crime, although he did resign from his position.

And while some prison guards may be losing their jobs, or are being pushed toward resignation, they have not faced criminal charges.

The two recent exceptions involve female guards. Sergeant Monika Sukert, who had worked at the Clallam Bay Corrections Center for 14 years, resigned from her position in December 2000, for having relations with a male prisoner. Sukert entered a guilty plea to custodial sexual misconduct in February 2000, and was sentenced to one year in jail, with all but 10 days suspended. In October 2001, Flora Pellechio pleaded guilty to one count of custodial sexual misconduct. Pellechio, a librarian at the Washington Corrections Center in Shelton, was caught by guards having sex with Lowrie Campbell, a convicted rapist, in the library storeroom.

"What we need to see are aggressive prosecutions, and the people who actually perpetrate these crimes brought to justice," emphasizes Trine Christensen, a research associate at Amnesty International USA (AIUSA) who helped to write *Abuse of Women in Custody*, a state-by-state survey released by AIUSA in March 2001.

"It's a terrible sign to send to other correctional officers who work within these systems that you can do these things and go unpunished, or get a slap on the wrist, or get let out through the back door."

Superintendent Stewart forwarded Solaita's file in November 2000 to the Pierce County Prosecutor's Office in Tacoma. Despite the investigation that resulted in his firing, the local prosecutor's office opted not to file charges in late June, when Deputy Prosecutor Mary Robnett cited a lack of "corroborating evidence" to ensure conviction.

Senator Long criticized the decision not to prosecute, telling the *Seattle Times* on June 21, that "[t]he guards, in these cases, have tremendous power and authority over the inmates."

Tesh expressed outrage at the reasoning of the prosecutor's office, and promptly filed a civil rights complaint with the FBI and the U.S. Attorney's Office. No significant action has yet been taken on those complaints.

The Coercion Game

To Guzman-White, the memories of the encounters in August and September 2000, still haunt her. She explains, in halting terms, how she was coerced into a sexual relationship with the guard on her second day in the minimum custody unit where he worked.

After approaching Guzman-White earlier in the day, Solaita asked to talk to her after midnight—when most prisoners are asleep—to "ask her a few questions."

Then, after midnight, Solaita began a several-hour-long game of seduction and insistent sexual behavior, asking her if she had ever "been" with women while in prison, and asking her what her "nationality" was.

"'I've never been with a Hispanic woman before,'" Guzman-White remembers Solaita saying.

Frightened and confused, Guzman-White recounts that she tried to fend off his advances and requests for oral sex several times in those early morning hours. Eventually, Solaita took her to a staff break room where, she says, she finally gave in to his insistence to have sex.

"I was feeling vulnerable ... I felt like he had something over me," she says. "I knew he could make my time harder [in prison]."

When Solaita returned after a vacation, he resumed sexual contact with Guzman-White. It was a situation, she says, which left her feeling guilty, confused, scared. She says that he warned her not to say anything about the situation lest she jeopardize his job.

Other situations over the past few years involving the sexual abuse and rape of female prisoners by male guards have involved more overt threats, including a case in 1998 where, according to internal DOC documents, prison guard Robert Perry had sex with a mentally ill prisoner at WCCW. Perry told her that if she ever said anything about the sexual contact that she would be "taken care of." Perry, who was subsequently dismissed, also threatened the prisoner that he would kill anyone who said anything about the incidents.

Seattle attorney Rebecca Roe also won a $50,000 settlement for Valerie Stone in April 1999, for a 1994 rape alleged against now-deceased prison gynecologist Dr. Dale Huber. Stone alleged that Huber raped her during a pelvic exam. Dr. Huber resigned, but he was not charged with a crime.

There were a number of other similar incidents at McNeil Island Corrections Center, says attorney David Gerhke, of the Seattle law firm Gerhke and Tizzano. Gerhke represented Brenda Pierce, who won a $50,000 settlement in 1998 involving a rape allegation against guard Jeffrey Donaldson. Gerhke says that Donaldson threatened to get Pierce transferred back to WCCW if she refused sex, where she would serve more time than at MICC. She was on a special six-month work program at MICC, called the Work Ethic Camp (WEC), and the threat apparently terrified her into having coerced sex with Donaldson.

"Most correctional officers are good and dedicated people, although they're underpaid and get no respect," stresses Gerhke. "But part of what's going on is the power and control issue. When you want to dominate and rape women . . . what better [job] than being a prison guard?"

The problem of recognizing and addressing the prevalence of sex behind prison walls is compounded, Gerhke says, by the "upper echelons" of the DOC, where an "Us vs. Them" mentality rules.

"They've got this real attitude that they're above the law. They've got a tough job, they know how to do it . . . and outsiders shouldn't try to make suggestions or tell them how to do it. They're resistant to change."

Donaldson maintained his innocence and was never charged with a crime, despite a settlement for $22,500 involving another female prisoner, Trisha Mechtley, who made similar allegations against him.

In a sworn declaration filed in Thurston County Superior Court in 1997, Donaldson provides a rare glimpse into the prison milieu, and provides a clue as to why such sexual misconduct is possible in this environment: "There was a great deal of prisoner sex," wrote Donaldson in his declaration. "Sexual activity occurred regularly behind the gym, behind the kitchen, and in the bathrooms. I recall a case where one prisoner was 'sold' to another for stamps ... Drug smuggling and drugs-for-sex exchanges were major problems."

Donaldson mentions investigating sexual contact between a cook and a female prisoner, and names two guards, Sergeant Long and Officer Ralph Wilkins, whom he knew to be engaging in sex with prisoners. He also refers to a widespread rumor regarding a physician's assistant who serviced the work camp at MICC (WEC), and who was "doing more than gynecological examinations ... [H]e wasn't wearing gloves ... he was feeling prisoners up [and] women were being called in for exams without explanation."

"The state has that declaration," Gerhke points out. "As far as I know, there's been no official investigation of that." Records procured via a public disclosure request show that the DOC disciplined at least 15 employees for sexual harassment or assault from January 1995–January 2001 at McNeil Island Corrections Center.

The kind of environment described by Donaldson's declaration at McNeil's WEC over the past several years may have contributed to a recent DOC decision to transfer the remaining women—who numbered no more than a dozen—from the WEC to WCCW. It is unclear if the women, who were transferred on April 6, 2001, will still be eligible for the shorter sentence granted to eligible prisoners who were to participate in the kind of job and life skills training touted by the WEC program, as the DOC would not comment on the subject. Roughly 40 men remain enrolled in the program.

Gerhke considers the transfer of the women to the prison from WEC to be "utterly outrageous."

"They can't control their own staffing and personnel problems, so they have to punish the women that otherwise would be qualified and deserving of something like this," Gerhke says emphatically.

Protecting Women Prisoners

Statewide, the DOC employs 2,755 prison guards, 78 percent of whom are male. At WCCW, says Superintendent Stewart, 57 percent of guards are men and 43 percent are women. The national average of male guards working in female prisons is around 41 percent, according to a 1997 survey.

Some human rights organizations and many prisoners' advocates call for women's prisons to be predominantly or entirely staffed by women; and where that is not possible, for male guards to be disallowed from unsupervised access to women's living quarters.

The Standard Minimum Rules for the Treatment of Prisoners, a provision in the First United Nations Congress on the Prevention of Crime and the Treatment of Offenders states: "[W]omen prisoners shall be attended and supervised only by women officers." This international law, also called Rule 53(3), was adopted on August 30, 1955, and has been accepted by all European Union countries. Moreover, says Trine Christensen of Amnesty International USA, male guards were rare in U.S. women's prisons until the 1970s, when employment antidiscrimination laws were applied to prisons.

But the call for exclusively female-staffed prisons or for increased supervision doesn't go over well with state officials and prison administrators. "How many layers of supervision do you impose? It isn't workable," says Senator Long. "We have women guarding men in other [prisons], so are we going to say that we can only have men guarding men? I think we'd get into some discrimination issues if we did that."

Guzman-White argues that more careful supervision of all prison guards would make the lives of female prisoners better and safer than an all-female-staffed prison. She cites multiple instances of female guards who sexually and/or physically harass female prisoners.

"I think we have a nice female complement at this institution, and it's about people acting professional in the workplace," answers WCCW Superintendent Stewart. "There's no scientific study to say that if we had more females here that [sexual assaults] wouldn't happen."

The bottom line, says Tesh, is the fact that no prisoner—regardless of their crime or gender—deserves to be subjected to violations of basic human rights.

"Rape is cruelty. Sexual assault is cruelty," he stresses. "A 'zero-tolerance' policy doesn't mean anything if you have no enforcement of that policy."

"Make It Hard for Them"

A Hunger Strike Against the INS

MARK DOW

Nabil Soliman believes that "accepting a tray of food" from his jailers means accepting what he calls his "illegal detention" by the Immigration and Naturalization Service (INS). Soliman has argued that it is a violation of his First Amendment right to expression and his Fourteenth Amendment right to privacy for jail officials to force-feed him. The INS responds that while Soliman "may have constitutional protections," these are limited when weighed against the government's interest "in preventing hunger strikes and preserving the life of INS detainees." Soliman is just one hunger striker, but his case has national implications for the INS's management of its ever increasing, and increasingly frustrated, population of detainees.

The INS currently holds over 20,000 detainees nationwide in its own Service Processing Centers, in privatized contract facilities, and in hundreds of local and county jails. The federal mandatory detention laws of 1996, which resulted in lengthy detention for thousands of legal residents convicted of often minor crimes, have transformed the agency into "a mini-BOP," according to one INS official, referring to the Federal Bureau of Prisons. The average daily population of INS detainees just before the 1996 laws was about 8,000; local politicians around the country have been more than willing to help ease what that INS official calls "significant growing pains."

In early March 2001, for example, the Etowah County Detention Center in Gadsden, Alabama—where Nabil Soliman is in custody—announced an $8.4 million dollar expansion. The jail currently has 376 "fixed beds," and, with the use of plastic "stackable bunks" or "boats," its population is usually "in the 400-range," according to Chief of Corrections Wes Williamson. Between 70 and 100 of those beds are contracted by the INS. Once construction has been completed, Etowah

---

This article was written in August 2001.

County will house 324 INS detainees at a rate of $30–33 per detainee per day, well below the $55 per "man-day" national average. Etowah County Sheriff James Hayes told the *Gadsden Times* that the old INS contract has already helped the county pay for new vehicles, training, and equipment. The new 15-year contract, he says, should raise $120 million in revenue.

As for the INS, the agency seems poised to hold out Etowah County as one of its flagship facilities. Even INS detainees like Soliman who are frustrated by their detention have few complaints about conditions per se at Etowah County. The jail opened in 1994 to replace its outdated predecessor across the street. The new jail's conditions are the direct result of a consent decree that followed a 1988 class-action suit against the old jail (*Rogers et al. v. Etowah County*), according to attorney Tamara Serwer of Atlanta's Southern Center for Human Rights.

This is no small matter for the INS, which holds over 60 percent of its detainees in county jails. After years of criticism, the INS recently announced that its long-awaited (but legally unenforceable) detention standards would apply to all of those contracted jails. According to one Justice Department official, only three of forty local facilities audited last year actually complied with all of the national standards. Etowah County complied, and Chief Williamson, known for his respectful attitude toward prisoners, says his jail is ready to handle some of the INS's more difficult cases, including hunger strikers as well as long-term or "post-order" detainees, whose deportation cannot be carried out easily, if at all. (The American Bar Association has unsuccessfully argued for a detention standard that would prohibit the involuntary transfer of detainees to areas with no *pro bono* resources, and in Etowah County there is "a complete dearth," according to the ABA's Chris Nugent.)

Soliman, a 40-year-old Egyptian, qualifies as one of the INS's difficult cases. He entered the United States legally and lived in New Jersey for nine years before being detained, having married and later divorced a U.S. citizen. He drove an eighteen-wheeler for a living, and he has five children, two of them U.S. citizens as well. The INS eventually labeled Soliman's marriage fraudulent. He has been detained now for almost four years, including one year in Gadsden. His case is complicated, but it illustrates the kind of frustration that leads so many INS detainees to protest.

According to the U.S. government, Soliman "is wanted by the Egyptian authorities" for his alleged connection to a group which is held to be responsible for the 1981 assassination of President Anwar Sadat. Soliman argues that he is a victim of mistaken identity, based on a confusion of names. (The *New York Times* has cited documents reportedly showing that Soliman had no criminal record in Egypt [January 31, 2000].) In May 2000, the Board of Immigration Appeals (BIA) granted Soliman "deferral of removal" under the Convention against Torture;

this means that, based on the likelihood that he would be tortured if returned to Egypt, the United States cannot return him there, regardless of the truth of his identity.

Soliman remains detained, however, because the INS maintains that he is a danger to the community and unlikely to appear for proceedings. This decision appears to stem from earlier U.S. government allegations that Soliman had connections to persons involved in the 1993 World Trade Center bombing. An immigration judge called these allegations "not sustainable" and "unconvincing." The government itself admitted back in 1997 that it had "abandoned that line of inquiry" and, more recently, that Soliman was "never charged with any terrorist activity in the United States." Soliman has never been charged with any crime in this country. Nevertheless, the government continues to use those allegations against him in its most recent court pleadings. Atlanta District INS officials, who have jurisdiction in Soliman's case, did not return calls seeking their explanation for continuing to hold Soliman as a "danger."

While Soliman himself did not raise the possibility of anti-Arab bias within the INS, when I asked him about that possibility, he told me that after the World Trade Center bombing convictions, many in New Jersey's Arab community said the evidence must have been fabricated. Soliman defended the integrity of the American justice system to them. "But after I got in INS [detention] and I see how the system work[s]," he says, and how "they make me a terrorist," his faith has been shaken.

Although Soliman has agreed to be deported to any available third country, and to pay the expenses himself, a Justice Department official familiar with the case acknowledges that "we can't find anywhere else to deport him." These are the circumstances which have led to what even the District Court judge who would rule against Soliman called his "prolonged, *and potentially indefinite*, detention" (italics added).

Soliman has protested with hunger strikes before, including more than a month without food while detained in an INS facility in Batavia, New York, in 1999. He was soon moved to the Columbia Care Center, a private hospital run by Just Care in South Carolina to hold federal prisoners. Then he was transferred to Etowah County. He began a new hunger strike there, and was moved to Columbia again. INS officials tried to win a force-feed order from a District Court in South Carolina, and when a judge ruled against the agency, it moved Soliman back to Alabama, where a previous force-feed order was still in effect.

On one occasion late last year, Soliman resisted by biting through the force-feed tube. Then jail officials forcibly sedated him. Because the medication caused him to sleep for some thirteen hours, complains Soliman, he was unable to comply with the Muslim tradition of praying five times each day. Another time, a jail guard pulled him off his prayer mat without warning, Soliman alleges, "disrespect[ing] Ramadan." He adds, however, that officials performed subsequent force-feedings at night in order to respect Ramadan, during which Muslims fast during the day. After he challenged the force-feeding order in federal court in December 2000, Soliman agreed to allow officials to feed him Ensure, a nutritional supplement, until the judge ruled.

Meanwhile, high-level INS officials had gotten involved. In the internal newsletter of the INS's Office for Immigration Litigation (OIL), an article about strategies for litigating such force-feeding cases had focused on Soliman. According to its author, OIL attorney Paul Kovac (who did not return calls for this article), that article was prompted by the "increasing number of cases involving detained aliens who conduct hunger strikes." Many of these cases involve the "post-order" detainees (that is, those with final orders of deportation who nevertheless remain detained). Spread around the country, these protests "have left INS officials and Assistant United States Attorneys scrambling for the appropriate response." Kovac continues, "Detention officials are confronted with a dilemma—do they respect the alien's choice to starve to death or do they abide with their obligation to render medical treatment and prevent suicide by starvation?"

On February 15, 2001, Judge Lynwood Smith of the Northern District of Alabama, ruled that the INS has "legitimate peneological interests" in force-feeding Nabil Soliman. Smith wrote that Soliman has been "an onerous administrative burden," and also (citing the government) that the Chief of Corrections at Etowah County Jail "overheard that other INS detainees plan to engage in a mass hunger strike if Soliman wins his case." In an interview in mid-February, while awaiting the judge's decision, Soliman said that the hunger strike is "only for myself." He noted that since he is being held in the high-security unit, he has no contact with the other INS detainees.

The government was thus successful in obtaining what might be called double deference from the court. First, the court should be asked to grant "substantial deference to the decisions of prison administrators," Kovac suggested. Second, "arguments in the immigration context are further strengthened by the deference courts afford to the Executive Branch in the area of immigration law." Kovac adds, somewhat ominously for the innumerable INS detainees who have been complaining in detail of the harsh conditions under which they are held, "An alien's status in this country may also dictate the degree of constitutional protections he or she may be afforded . . . Perhaps some of these same constitutional principles can be applied to aliens challenging their treatment while in INS detention."

At this writing (mid-March), Soliman remains in the high-security unit of the Etowah County Detention Center. He is brought to the infirmary each day for "oral-gastric" force-feeding, according to Chief Williamson. Soliman has filed a *pro se*, handwritten appeal of the District Court order affirming his detention and force-feeding to the Eleventh Circuit. In the meantime, he is demanding that he not be handcuffed and shackled each day when taken to the clinic, and he is trying to obtain a reasonably priced phone card so that he can make calls to Egypt in an effort to continue fighting his case. Chief Williamson points out that he does not control the price of phone cards sold to the prisoners (the jail has a contract with Global Tel-Link). Williamson also says that while he is sympathetic to Soliman's frustrating situation, Soliman "likes to use the 'don't-eat' issue for anything he wants . . . I can't let him hold me hostage."

"I am not making my detention easy for them," Soliman said in our February interview at the jail in Gadsden, before the District Court had ruled on force feeding. "I have to make it hard for them." When I asked if he might starve himself to death, he compared himself to a soldier who fights "for his right and his people," saying that while it is "not my intention to die," that that could be the result. "This is the legal way to fight them," he says.

[Editor's Note: In June 2002 Soliman was deported to Egypt. See In Re Soliman, 134 F.Supp.2d 1238 (ND AL 2001). According to Amnesty International, he was detained at a secret location by Egyptian authorities for over three months. In September 2002 he was moved to the Tora Prison in Cairo—where he has received visits from family members, his lawyer, and U.S. Embassy officials—to await trial before a secrecy court for membership in an illegal organization.]

Anatomy of a Whitewash

MUMIA ABU-JAMAL

Authority is never without hate.
—Euripides

In a decision that was as remarkable as it was predictable, the Greene County DA, David Pollock, announced his office would take no criminal action against prison guards who were viewed on videotape, "roughing up" men in the Restrictive Housing Unit (RHU) of the State Correctional Institution located in Pennsylvania's Southwest. He reportedly uttered a sentence that was to the effect that his office "would not tolerate" violence against prisoners.

Yeah right.

For several years now, men imprisoned at SCI Greene have written to the local DA's office, charging any number of violent acts against them, to no avail. Most have received no answer at all. Some were told to file institutional grievances. Others had their letters Xeroxed and forwarded to Greene prison officers, virtually insuring a negative and vengeful retaliation for daring to seek "legal redress." And still others had their letters intercepted, opened, read, and undelivered.

This DA initially announced his "probe" after a series of articles came out in Pittsburgh and regional newspapers detailing violence against prisoners and threats of violence against staffers at the prison who questioned, or reported on, the violence. It was a politically savvy thing to do, as it obtained broad coverage. Several video tapes were turned over, and some (limited) interviews were taken.

As politics dictated the probe, so too did it dictate that no prosecution results, for to do so would be an act of political suicide.

Let us look at the matter clearly: The DA found, in his politically-influenced opinion, that the "shoves," "pushes," and intentionally violent

This article was written in October 1998.

physical contact against naked men (some of whom may have been hand-cuffed!) does not constitute a crime. In the "common" law, for one to threaten to do another bodily harm constitutes an assault; to touch another in an offensive way constitutes a battery. These same acts, taken up a few degrees, could cross the line to terrorist threats, or official oppression, both statutory crimes.

Critical legal scholar David Kairys put it aptly when he wrote, "Law is simply politics by other means."

Essentially then, the DA did what politicians do every day; he counted votes.

Prisoners don't vote. Guards do.

The nice speech about "not tolerating" violence against prisoners obscures the grim and bitter truth. It has been tolerated; it is tolerated; it will be in the future.

Law, in its very heart, is profoundly conservative, and as applied to men's lives works to restrain and restrict. Over a century ago, American writer Henry David Thoreau wrote disparagingly of the pro-slavery "courts of justice—so called" that sided with the slave owners and were "merely the inspectors of a pick-lock and murderer's tools, to tell him whether they are in working order or not."

In his *Civil Disobedience* he wrote, "The law will never make men free; it is men who have got to make the law free."

Sentenced to the Backwaters of Greene County, PA

Mumia Abu-Jamal

> There's an atmosphere created by [prison officials] in which this kind of thing has been going on for years. The attitude is, "You're in Greene County now, boy."
>
> —Randy Gauger, Pennsylvania Prison Society,
> Fayette-Greene Chapter (*Pittsburgh Post-Gazette*, April 26, 1998)

A handcuffed man is bludgeoned and a nightstick is jammed into his mouth, knocking out a tooth. A prison guard dips his fingers into the bloody spittle and traces the letters KKK. Welcome to Greene County's State Correctional Institution (SCI) at Waynesburg, Southwestern Pennsylvania.

The prisoner savagely beaten by SCI guards, Antonio Noguerol, brought a lawsuit against the prison in 1996. In response to SCI guards' insistence that the beating was in self-defense, attorney Rita Murillo wrote that this beating was instead a "calculated, systemic and sadistic assaults, administered for the purpose of summarily punishing Mr. Noguerol for perceived insolence ... to make an example of a 'problem' inmate in order to maintain discipline" (*Pittsburgh Post-Gazette*, April 26, 1998).

Anticipating the release of a series of articles exposing a campaign of brutality and torture at Greene, the Pennsylvania DOC (PA DOC) beat the media pack in announcing an "investigation" of an estimated forty guards at the high-tech hell. The PA DOC offered a selection of routinely recorded prison videotapes to the public as proof of their innocence: not surprisingly, the incident of Noguerol's beating was not among these tapes.

According to locally published reports, several former SCI Greene staffers, who questioned the beatings and false institutional misconduct

This article was written in September 1998.

filings, were ushered out of the joint and fired. Linda Welling, a former unit manager of the prison, and Bob DeBord, a former counselor, charged they were threatened with violence for daring to question the repressive status quo. After their charges hit the airwaves, Greene's warden was demoted and transferred to a smaller, medium security prison.

According to set theory, if one determines the perimeters of a set (or the elements which it will include), one can determine the outcome. The State Corrections Department, by virtually ignoring the most serious cases of brutality, has already determined the outcome of the investigation. There will be a few sacrifices, a few transfers, a few examples of departmental discipline, but nothing substantive will change; or if it changes; it will be for the worse.

The prison will remain a place of approved brutality, and staffers, terrified of the loss of jobs and pensions (not to mention threats of violence), will see and not see, hear and not hear, and engage in the chilling crime of silent acquiescence.

For Greene was, and is, a creation of the state's political will, with terrorism merely a tool of state policy. Here, judges dare not rule against the repressive status quo, for judges, too, must bow to the dictates of state policy.

THE BARS TO PRISON LITIGATION

In recent years, non-white, poor Americans have seen the continuous stripping away of their civil liberties and other fundamental rights via various federal legislation. From the Reagan-Bush-Clinton-baby Bush eras came several pieces of legislation that took direct aim at prisoners' meager rights: both at entry points to the system and post-conviction. Now the poor, drug-addicted, and swarthy-skinned of this country can expect a variety of ways to be incarcerated for a long list of nonviolent offenses, like drug crimes; longer sentences than in any other industrialized country; lifetime incarceration under "Three Strikes" legislation (for crimes including, for example, theft of a pizza); indefinite detention for immigrants with no due process or even charges filed for trivial, or nonexistent offenses; and few remedies against arbitrary, dangerous, or illegal imprisonment.

For prisoners, sanctified constitutional concepts like due process, freedom from unjust imprisonment, the prohibition against cruel and unusual punishment, or even the most basic of human rights often do not apply; in large part because of legislation like the Prison Litigation Reform Act and the Anti-Terrorism and Effective Death Penalty Acts. The PLRA and AEDPA, in combination, present a nearly impenetrable wall against prisoners' redress for violations of fundamental human rights. Under the mandates of AEDPA, for example, it is not enough for a death row prisoner to be actually innocent of the crime to win a grant of habeas corpus (the last-chance legal remedy available to prisoners). And the PLRA bars any federal funding from going to legal aid groups that represent prisoners on any civil matter.

Without access to competent representation the basic means of legal redress are barred to prisoners. Prisoners now scramble to learn esoteric law as they are forced to become their own counsel. Even those prison lawyers who are capable have little to work with, as avenues of redress have been entirely closed off to them by the promulgation of a spate of antiprisoner legislation and, in many states, the elimination of prison law libraries.

The following section examines the history of prison law, its progression and regression.

—TH

Prison Litigation 1950–2000

Hands Off, Hands On, Gloves On

JOHN MIDGLEY

Before the middle of the Twentieth Century, there was very little federal recognition or enforcement of prisoners' rights, as courts used the so-called "hands off" doctrine to ignore prison conditions. Gradually, beginning at mid-century, rising political activism coupled with increased public awareness of atrocious prison conditions and agitation by prisoners, changed judicial attitudes toward prison issues. At the same time, advocates and courts refined the legal vehicles needed to raise prisoner issues, and so some prisoner claims started to be successful.

Then, in the late 1960s through the '70s, after recognition that the Eighth Amendment's "cruel and unusual punishments" clause applied to the states, the movement to bring the Constitution into prisons was ablaze with hope and inventiveness as many entire prison systems were found unconstitutionally cruel. I became involved in prisoners' rights work in 1975, at a time when my colleagues and I thought that fundamental changes in prisons could be brought about through the legal system.

But we were too optimistic. Starting in the mid-'70s and continuing through the rest of the century, the Supreme Court and the federal circuit courts began to limit how federal district courts could intervene to remedy the ills of prison systems. As the century drew to a close, those of us fighting for the legal rights of prisoners could be both justifiably proud of many accomplishments and apprehensive about how Congress' and the courts' trimming of the gains would play out in the long run.[1]

Dark Ages End: Federal Courts Begin to Take Notice of Prison Conditions

For a very long time, federal courts refused to review claims by prisoners. In the nineteenth century, prisoners were commonly viewed as slaves of

This article was written in February 2002.

the state. In the early twentieth century, the courts refused to deal with prison issues by creating the "hands off doctrine," which basically set fourth that prison conditions were not the courts' business.[2]

By the 1950s, the wall of refusal erected by the "hands off doctrine" started to crack. The Supreme Court had not yet held that most of the provisions of the Bill of Rights were enforceable against the states. Among the few federal constitutional rights that did apply to the states were the First Amendment and the Due Process and Equal Protection Clauses of the Fourteenth Amendment.[3] And federal courts began, slowly, to address abuses of prisoners under these limited legal theories.[4]

In the 1960s, several developments would create a platform for prisoners to raise a much broader array of claims in federal court. Heightened political activism of the time moved into the prisons, as prisoners and free people started to question what was happening behind the walls. At the same time, the Civil Rights Movement revived use of 42 U.S.C. § 1983 to vindicate federal constitutional rights in federal court.[5] In addition, the Supreme Court began to hold that many more provisions of the Bill of Rights were "incorporated" into the Due Process Clause of the Fourteenth Amendment, and so were enforceable against the states. For prisoners, a crucial moment came in 1962, when the Supreme Court applied to the states the Eighth Amendment's requirement that "nor cruel nor unusual punishments [shall be] inflicted."[6]

Although the incorporation of the cruel and unusual punishments clause came in a case in which a sentence and not a condition of imprisonment, was challenged, prisoners' advocates and thoughtful judges soon grasped what this meant for punishments carried out *within* prisons. In 1968, Harry Blackmun (before he became a Supreme Court Justice) wrote for the Eighth Circuit one of the leading early statements of the Eighth Amendment's application to prison life.

In a challenge to the use of "the strap" (the whipping of prisoners) in Arkansas, Blackmun concluded that the history of the Eighth Amendment embodies "broad and idealistic concepts of dignity, civilized standards, humanity, and decency...."[7] Application of these principles led to his conclusion that:

> ... [T]he use of the strap in the penitentiaries of Arkansas is punishment which, in this last third of the 20th century, runs afoul of the Eighth Amendment; ... the strap's use, irrespective of any precautionary conditions which may be imposed, offends contemporary concepts of decency and human dignity and precepts of civilization which we profess to possess; and ... it also violates ... standards of good conscience and fundamental fairness....[8]

At the same time, during 1968–1971, prison riots broke out all over the country, dramatically increasing public awareness of the horrors inside many prisons. The most dramatic and famous was, of course, New York's Attica Rebellion in September, 1971.

Prisoners at Attica rebelled against a multitude of poor conditions, including rampant and widespread brutality by guards, irrational limits of one shower per week and one roll of toilet paper every eight weeks, and prison staff's refusal to allow the rising number of African-Americans who converted to Islam to practice their religion. 1,300 of the 2,000 prisoners at Attica participated in the rebellion, which began as a strike and eventually ended in prisoners holding 50 guards and civilians hostage. The rebellion ended, after many attempts at negotiation, in a bloody retaking of the yard by state officials. Twenty-nine prisoners and 10 hostages died, and many were wounded. The state initially claimed that prisoners had slit the hostages' throats, but it was later revealed that they had been killed by the gunfire of the troops retaking the yard.[9]

Prison riots, like the urban riots of the same time, placed the otherwise obscure experience of prison directly under a national media spotlight. The resulting public outcry over such graphic examples of overt abuse by both state actors and prison staff forced a change that would wind its way, eventually, into the courts.

A New (and Brief) Era: Successful Challenges to Entire Prison Systems

In the early 1970s, federal court scrutiny of prison conditions exploded, as prisoners and their advocates claimed that entire prison systems were cruel and unusual. In many cases, often beginning with *pro se* complaints, federal courts declared that whole jails and prisons, and even whole state prison systems, inflicted "cruel and unusual punishment" that is forbidden under the Eighth Amendment. Some of the leading early cases came out of the truly horrible conditions in the prisons of the Southeastern United States,[10] but brutal conditions and broad reforms were the norm in other parts of the country as well, including New England.[11]

In these cases and many others that followed, federal courts looked at the overall conditions (in legal parlance, the "totality of the conditions") in the prisons and often declared that an entire system failed to provide adequate medical care, protection from harm, and other needed services, and therefore imposed unconstitutional punishment.[12] In case after case, the federal district courts appointed special masters, or court monitors to oversee implementation of detailed orders requiring massive changes in the way prisons did business. Perhaps the peak of this kind of federal involvement in an entire prison system came when Judge Justice in the Southern District of Texas ruled that the huge Texas prison system was riddled with unconstitutional conditions throughout, and did so under the "totality" standard:

Many courts confronted by prison cases have determined the issues, not by looking at each individual area of prison life separately, but by viewing them collectively and deciding whether the totality of prison conditions is such as to violate the constitution. The ambient circumstances affecting inmates, considered as a whole, were found unconstitutional in [previous cases] . . .

Based on a review of the exhaustive evidence and the applicable law, separate constitutional violations have been found in the areas of over-crowding, security and supervision, health care delivery, discipline, and access to the courts at TDC [Texas Dept. of Corrections]. Basically, these violations exist independently of each other, although the harms caused by each have been exacerbated by the others. However, even if the conditions in any one of these areas were considered not sufficiently egregious to con-stitute an independent violation, their aggregate effects upon TDC inmates undeniably contravene the constitution. The grave consequences of ram-pant overcrowding, inadequate security, substandard health care, inappro-priate disciplinary practices, and substantially impeded access to the courts manifestly dictate this result. [13]

Undergirding many of the challenges to entire state prison systems was a vision and the hope that the brutal way of imprisonment being used—the very nature of imprisonment as many of these states practiced it—could itself be made humane. A few federal district courts, who took seriously that the Eighth Amendment embodies "broad and idealistic concepts of humanity," required major changes, for example going so far as to order the establishment of rehabilitative and work programs where there was little for prisoners to do.[14] Some adopted an Eighth Amend-ment theory that any prison that threatens prisoners with deterioration due to lack of opportunities for betterment is unconstitutional:

The basic import of these cases is that prison authorities have a duty to provide sufficient time, opportunities, and encouragement to overcome the degenerative aspects of the prison in question so that at least the state takes no part in the promotion of future crime.[15]

My own early experiences were with the Washington State Peniten-tiary in Walla Walla, Washington. I first encountered the prison in late 1975 and conditions there were a bizarre mix. The prison was then known for being very open, with many prisoners milling around in a huge recreation area called the "big yard." Some prisoner "clubs" were even given their own spaces that guards usually did not enter. Although this gave many prisoners, especially those running the clubs, some free-doms not enjoyed in other prisons, this arrangement often placed vulner-able prisoners in jeopardy. There were many deaths and injuries of prisoners and guards in this largely uncontrolled environment.

At the same time, health and safety conditions were atrocious. Prisoners held in administrative segregation, sometimes for many months or even years, were not allowed outdoor exercise. Some guards routinely brutalized prisoners. Medical care was awful, and guards often decided whether prisoners should be allowed to go to the medical unit.

Mental health treatment, however, was the strangest of all the programs at Walla Walla. A psychologist named Dr. Hunter ran a mental health unit on the third floor of the prison hospital. Prisoners feared being sent to "The Third Floor," and for good reason. Many prisoners reported that the floor was run by "inmate attendants" who were allowed to assault other prisoners, and perhaps even to administer psychotropic medication. Program staff verbally assaulted prisoners and intentionally confiscated mattresses and blankets and used other means as well to deprive them of sleep.

At the helm was Dr. Hunter, who devised a kind of aversion therapy based on performing deliberate acts of humiliation upon "noncompliant" or "problem" prisoners, including putting some prisoners in diapers and trying to humiliate gay prisoners into becoming straight.

Dr. Hunter's program was eventually closed, but only after the prison was sued several times. Finally, in 1977, a state court judge held that the program violated the constitutional rights of the prisoners subjected to such "therapy." A federal district court and the Ninth Circuit later found that many other conditions at Walla Walla—including medical care, segregation, and guard brutality—were unconstitutionally cruel.[16]

Although it is hard to imagine now (given the current political and legal climate), in the heady days of these early victories many people thought that the federal courts would be the catalyst for a major change of not just a few awful conditions of confinement, but of an entire way of confinement.[17] But it was not to be.

New Legal Hurdles Erected; The Supreme Court Jumps In

The federal judiciary became more conservative beginning in about 1969.[18] One result was that some of the federal courts of appeals began to trim the most ambitious of the federal district courts' attempts to reform prisons. The appeals courts found that while awful medical care and gross lack of safety may be remedied through constitutional litigation, other important components of prison life—such as a lack of rehabilitative programs and even prisoner classification systems (designating what housing and work programs prisoners were assigned to, and impacting prisoner safety)—were not of constitutional concern.[19] Under particular attack in some federal circuits was the "totality of the circumstances" test used to find entire prisons or systems unconstitutional in some jurisdictions; the Ninth Circuit strongly disapproved of the "totality" standard and reversed district court opinions employing the standard.[20] Many of these same decisions also started to place stricter limits on what forms of relief could be ordered to remedy constitutional violations.

These developments provide the background for the Supreme Court's involvement in the development of the law of prisoners' constitutional rights. The Court had decided only a few scattered prisoners' rights cases over the years. But starting in the mid-1970s, the Court became very active and, while making clear that the Constitution does reach into state prisons, also began to set limits on what federal courts could do to remedy bad prison conditions.

First, the Supreme Court made clear that the "hands off doctrine" was long dead. Though some state officials continued to insist that federal courts should leave the issue of prisoners' constitutional rights alone, the Court emphatically disagreed in the early 1970s. To underscore this recognition of prisoners' claims, the Court pointed to areas where prisoners' constitutional rights had already been articulated in the law.[21]

But to say, as the Supreme Court did, that the Constitution has some reach behind prison walls does not answer exactly what constitutional rights prisoners have in specific situations. And the increasingly conservative Court, with a few exceptions, has acted to limit prisoners' rights in many important ways. This is shown in the following, which is a brief survey of Supreme Court developments in four selected areas of the law of prisoners' rights that are analytically distinct: general prison conditions and practices, procedural due process, personal rights, and access to courts.

Conditions of Confinement and the "State of Mind" Requirement

The Supreme Court's first venture into conditions issues involved a claim by one prisoner that he was denied necessary medical care and that this was a violation of the Eighth Amendment. *Estelle v. Gamble*, 429 U.S. 97 (1976). Justice Marshall, in writing for the Court majority, affirmed the general Eighth Amendment analysis that many of the lower federal courts had been applying to conditions issues, embodying "broad and idealistic concepts of dignity, civilized standards, humanity, and decency" and "the evolving standards of decency that mark the progress of a maturing society. . . ." (429 U.S. at 102).

The Court, however, also decided that while the Eighth Amendment requires prison officials to provide medical attention for those they incarcerate, not every failure to provide adequate care would be a constitutional violation. The Court therefore articulated a standard that prisoners must meet in order to state a claim for the unconstitutional denial of medical care: a prisoner must show that defendant prison officials demonstrated "deliberate indifference to serious medical needs."[22] This has proven a difficult standard to meet, and most medical abuse cases fail because of it.

In the lone dissenting opinion in *Estelle*, Justice Stevens prophetically questioned the newly-coined "deliberate indifference" standard, noting that it focused on the defendant's state of mind instead of the impact on the prisoner:

> ... [W]hether the constitutional standard has been violated should turn on the character of the punishment rather than the motivation of the individual who inflicted it. Whether the conditions in Andersonville were the product of design, negligence, or mere poverty, they were cruel and inhuman.[23]

In 1978, the Supreme Court first reviewed one of the class-action cases in which a federal district judge was trying to reform a truly awful prison regime.[24] The Arkansas prison system, was described as "a dark and evil world alien to the free world ... " in which the court noted that supervision at night in the large barracks was so lax that some prisoners "dared not sleep; instead they would leave their beds and spend the night clinging to the bars nearest the guards' station." Other prisoners were out in punitive isolation, where an "average of 4, and sometimes as many as 10 or 11 prisoners were crowded into windowless 8' x 10' cells [sic]" and were fed "fewer than 1,000 calories a day" in the form of a thing called "grue." In the Arkansas system it was also routine to arm prisoners with guns, and employ them as guards. And prisoners were frequently whipped with "a wooden-handled leather strap five feet long and four inches wide."[25]

The Court was asked to decide whether the district court properly limited stays in disciplinary isolation to 30 days. The Court found that although the Eighth Amendment did not, in the abstract, require a limit of 30 days in isolation, given the horrors that had been proven about isolation the district judge was within his powers to impose this limit.[26]

A few years later, the Court took up the legal standard to be applied in deciding whether prison conditions were bad enough to be cruel and unusual. Perhaps unfortunately, this consideration came in a case where prison conditions were not nearly as bad as the conditions in the nightmare that prevailed in Arkansas. In *Rhodes v. Chapman*, 452 U.S. 337, 346–347 (1981), prisoners in a relatively new Ohio prison claimed that forcing two people to live in a 63-square-foot cell designed for only one violated the Eighth Amendment. The Court held, as it had earlier in a jail case that involved a slightly different Constitutional standard,[27] that the Constitution, through the Eighth Amendment, does not require a certain amount of living space for a prisoner or mandate only one prisoner per cell, even a small cell designed to house only one person. The Court did make passing reference to idealism and "the evolving standards of decency that mark the progress of a maturing society," but nevertheless declared that the Eighth Amendment is violated only if conditions amount to at least one of the following: "the wanton and unnecessary infliction of pain," "pain without any penological purpose," "serious deprivation of basic human needs," or deprivation of "the minimal civilized measure of life's necessities."[28]

In defining these standards, the Court also gave lower courts a contradictory set of instructions that makes it harder for prisoners to prevail in Eighth Amendment cases. The Court said that whether conditions are cruel must be determined "objectively," but also said that the lower courts could not use expert opinions and published professional standards (such as American Correctional Association standards) to determine constitutional minimums for prisoner living conditions.[29] In lieu of using published standards, *Rhodes* says that federal judges should, in making Eighth Amendment judgments, decide whether a prison condition "is viewed generally as violating decency."[30] Thus the Court took from prisoners a powerful objective measure of what is reasonable treatment and replaced it with an obviously quite subjective inquiry into "general" views of decent standards for prisoners.

The Supreme Court thus set difficult standards for prisoners to meet before a federal court could declare conditions unconstitutional, but nevertheless prison litigation continued all over the country. However, federal courts found that conditions in plenty of jails and prisons were poor enough even to meet the new standard.[31]

In 1986, the Court again considered whether a prisoner claiming an Eighth Amendment violation must in some cases show that a defendant has a particular "state of mind." In a case in which a guard wielding a shotgun had shot a prisoner in connection with a prison disturbance, the Court held 5–4 that there could be no Eighth Amendment violation in the shooting unless the prisoner could demonstrate a very difficult to prove "state of mind," that is, that the guard acted "maliciously and sadistically for the very purpose of causing harm."[32]

In a major development five years later, the Court held that there is a "state of mind" element in all claims that the Eighth Amendment has been violated, even claims made by large groups of prisoners that conditions of confinement for all of them are unconstitutional. In *Wilson v. Seiter*, 501 U.S. 294 (1991), the Court held 5–4 that bad conditions alone are never enough to make out an Eighth Amendment violation. Instead, in addition to an "objective" component (are the conditions bad enough?), all Eighth Amendment claims also have a "subjective" component (are the defendants' intentions bad enough?). The Court then said that for most claims, individuals or groups of prisoners claiming that conditions of confinement violate the Eighth Amendment must prove that the defendant acted with "deliberate indifference" to the bad conditions.

The "deliberate indifference" standard had of course been coined in *Estelle v. Gamble* as a way to determine whether a single prisoner's complaint about medical care amounted to more than an accusation of ordinary medical negligence. The dissent in *Wilson* echoed the original lone dissent of Justice Stevens in *Estelle*, pointing out that the Eighth Amendment focus should be on the unnecessary pain inflicted by bad conditions, and that what is in the mind of the prison officials is irrelevant to whether those conditions are "cruel and unusual." But the *Wilson* majority ignored this and extended the "deliberate indifference" standard far beyond its original purpose, to a requirement that all prisoners claiming an Eighth Amendment violation show not only how bad living conditions are but also that prison officials ignored the conditions.

Wilson also addressed the still lingering "totality of conditions" question: Can a combination of several bad conditions not each unconstitutional in itself add up to an Eighth Amendment violation? In *Rhodes*, the Court had said that conditions, "alone or in combination" could be cruel and unusual punishment.[33] But *Wilson* read "in combination" very narrowly and said that the Eighth Amendment can be violated only in terms of discrete conditions that must be analyzed separately:

> *Some* conditions of confinement may establish an Eighth Amendment violation "in combination" when each would not do so alone, but only when they have a mutually enforcing effect that produces the deprivation of a single, identifiable human need such as food, warmth, or exercise—for example, a low cell temperature at night combined with a failure to issue blankets. . . . Nothing so amorphous as "overall conditions" can rise to the level of cruel and unusual punishment when no specific deprivation of a single human need exists.[34]

Wilson signaled the Court majority's abandonment of the "broad and idealistic concepts of dignity, civilized standards, humanity, and decency" that had animated Eighth Amendment analysis of prison conditions since Harry Blackmun's groundbreaking analysis for the Eighth Circuit in 1968. Instead of invoking these important ideals of our civilization that could spark real change in prisons, *Wilson* requires a much narrower focus: Federal courts should look at one distinct prison condition at a time, and may intervene only if the condition is a severe deprivation of basic human needs that prison officials have deliberately left to fester.

Details Filled In

The Supreme Court's later prison conditions cases in the 1990s elaborated upon the objective and subjective components of Eighth Amendment doctrine. In the most significant case on this issue, the Court held that when a prisoner makes any claims that a guard used excessive force, the prisoner must prove that the guard acted "maliciously and sadistically for the very purpose of causing harm."[35] However, the Court also said prisoners claiming excessive force do not have to also show that they received a serious injury. The Court said it would be enough to show that there was an unnecessary infliction of pain and the defendant acted maliciously and sadistically. The Court also affirmed for the first time a principle of Eighth Amendment law that many lower courts had been applying for some time: that prisoners may obtain an injunction (that is, to force the defendant to immediately end a questionable practice) against a condition that poses an unreasonable risk of harm to prisoners before the likely harm occurs.[36]

The Court's final major foray in prison law in the 1990s addressed the meaning of the strange legal phrase "deliberate indifference," which had become the crucial issue in many cases. Most everyone agreed that "deliberate indifference" must be more than negligence (because *Estelle v. Gamble* said so), but less than the "malicious and sadistic" standard that the Court applied to officials' use of force on prisoners. The available mental states between these two poles are so-called "civil recklessness" (the defendant disregards a substantial harm that he *should* have known about) and "criminal recklessness" (the defendant disregards a substantial harm that she *did* know about). In *Farmer v. Brennan*, 511 U.S. 825 (1994), the Court adopted the criminal recklessness standard and held that to be "deliberately indifferent," a prison official must know of a substantial risk of serious harm and fail to remedy it.[37]

The "deliberate indifference" requirement of Eighth Amendment analysis has not served as a complete barrier to federal court intervention where prison conditions are poor enough and the harm to prisoners is obvious. But the "deliberate indifference" requirement poses an unnecessary hurdle in many cases, where very bad conditions or obviously unnecessary inflictions of pain should be plenty for a prisoner to show that the Eighth Amendment's prohibition against "cruel and unusual punishment" has been violated.

Procedural Due Process

The Due Process Clause of the Fourteenth Amendment prohibits states from depriving "any person of life, liberty, or property, without due process of law. . . ." Thus if the state proposes to take a citizen's liberty or property, the state must do so by process of law. Prisoners often claim that the state is taking their liberty or property without legal justification.

In order to claim that the state is unconstitutionally taking liberty without due process, a prisoner must first establish that there is a "liberty interest" that is protected against arbitrary state action. "Liberty interests" that are subject to due process can come from two sources: Directly from the idea of physical liberty that is inherent in the Due Process Clause itself, or from state-created "liberty interests." A state creates a liberty interest when it makes a rule that it cannot do something to a citizen unless certain things are proven, for example that prison officials cannot take a prisoner's "good time" sentence reductions away unless the prisoner is proven to have misbehaved.[38] With respect to prisoners, the Court has found inherent liberty in very few instances, and usually requires prisoners to show a state-created liberty interest. And recently the Court erected barriers to prisoners' due process claims, even where there are state-created liberty interests.

Wolff v. McDonnell, 418 U.S. 539 (1974), a "state-created liberty interest" case, brought procedural due process into prisons. In *Wolff,* Nebraska prisoners were entitled by law to "good time" sentence reductions unless the state proved a prisoner had engaged in serious misconduct. The Court found that the state-created good time entitlement triggered federal procedural due process protections. The Court held that the process due was advance notice of specific charges, a hearing at which the prisoner had the right to testify and present witnesses and evidence, and a statement of evidence and reasons for any finding of guilt.

In "inherent liberty" cases, by contrast, the Court has found that prisoners have inherent liberty protected by the Due Process Clause in matters that are significantly outside the bounds of the criminal sentence that has been imposed on the prisoner. For example, prisoners are protected by the Due Process Clause against involuntary transfer to a mental hospital, or involuntary administration of psychotropic drugs without procedural due process, because these deprivations of physical and mental liberty are not generally seen as within the bounds of a prison sentence.[39]

But within what the Supreme Court majority has seen as the broad bounds of the sentence imposed, the Court has refused to find inherent physical liberty. In *Meachum v. Fano,* 427 U.S. 215 (1976), the Court majority refused to find inherent liberty implicated in transfer from one prison to a more restrictive one, because transfer to another prison was "within the normal limits or range of custody which the conviction has authorized the State to impose."[40]

Justice Stevens, writing for three dissenters, foresaw, just as he had at the birth of the "deliberate indifference" standard, the constitutional mischief that the Court's new analysis would create:

> If the inmate's protected liberty interests are no greater than the State chooses to allow, he is really little more than the slave described in the 19th century cases. I think it clear that even the inmate retains an unalienable interest in liberty—at the very minimum the right to be treated with dignity—which the Constitution may never ignore.[41]

Stevens' worst fears were realized when the Court later held that a prisoner in Hawaii had no inherent liberty interest to prevent a transfer to a prison thousands of miles away on the mainland.[42] The Court majority, quoting *Meachum*, found that "[c]onfinement in another State, unlike confinement in a mental institution, is 'within the normal limits or range of custody which the conviction has authorized the State to impose.'"

The Court consistently refused to find that federal due process was involved in prison operations unless there was a "state-created liberty interest" in the form of facts the state had to prove under its own laws or regulations before it could impose discipline or more restrictive conditions. The Court held that prospective parolees had no federal constitutional right to a parole hearing in the absence of a state-created liberty interest.[43] Similarly, when state prison regulations allowed placement of a prisoner in administrative (nondisciplinary) segregation only if the state could prove certain facts (such as danger to self or others), the Court found a state-created liberty interest and required procedures (although they were minimal).[44]

Then the Court completely changed the "state-created liberty interest" analysis to make it even harder for prisoners to invoke the protections of procedural due process. In *Sandin v. Conner*, 515 U.S. 472 (1995), the Court held that liberty interests for federal due process purposes can be created only when the state imposes an "atypical and significant hardship" compared to what the Court views as the "ordinary incidents of prison life." In *Sandin*, 30 days of disciplinary segregation was held not to present such a hardship and so due process protections did not apply to the procedure that resulted in the segregation even though the state regulations *did* stipulate that there would be no disciplinary segregation unless the state could prove that the prisoner had committed particular acts.[45]

Under longstanding Due Process analysis (which prevailed until the Court altered it just for prisoners in *Meachum v. Fano) either* a "grievous loss" *or* a "state-created liberty interest" would suffice to invoke due process protections. After *Sandin*, it now appears that in order to invoke procedural protections of the Due Process clause prisoners must show both that the state has bound itself to prove certain facts before taking action, and that there is an "atypical and significant hardship" as to actions by the state that do not relate to the length of incarceration.[46]

Personal Rights—First, Fourth, and Fourteenth Amendments

The Supreme Court's entry into the area of personal rights retained by prisoners started off fairly well for prisoners. The Court held early on that overt racial discrimination and segregation is unconstitutional.[47] The Court also found that a Buddhist prisoner who was not afforded the same right to worship as members of other religions stated a violation of his Equal Protection rights.[48] And in a very significant case, *Procunier v. Martinez*, the Court held that while prison officials could censor prisoners' mail in some circumstances, the First Amendment required that they only censor mail to the extent that they could show that the regulation "further[s] an important or substantial governmental interest unrelated to the suppression of expression" and is "no greater than is necessary or essential to the protection of the particular governmental interest involved."[49] Using this test, the Court invalidated California's mail censorship regulations because they allowed censorship of criticism of prison conditions and management.

However, as the Court became more conservative, some of these early openings were soon isolated and then reversed. In *Jones v. North Carolina Prisoners' Labor Union, Inc.*, 433 U.S. 119 (1977), the Court endorsed a state prison system's ban on meetings of a "prisoner's labor union" formed to improve working and living conditions for prisoners, and also allowed prison officials to prohibit prisoners from asking each other to join the union, and from using bulk mailings on union business (even though other groups, such as the Boy Scouts, were allowed to use bulk mailings). In dissent, Justices Marshall and Brennan strongly disagreed with the Court's extreme deference to the preferences of prison administrators who clearly intended to suppress prisoners' organizations.[50]

Jones is a crucially important case in the development of the rights of prisoners. The majority determined that rather than prison administration having to show good reasons for its drastic restrictions, the prisoner must show that there is no plausible basis:

> [P]rison officials concluded that the presence, perhaps even the objectives, of a prisoners' labor union would be detrimental to order and security in the prisons.... It is enough to say that they have not been conclusively shown to be wrong in this view.[51]

Thus the Court laid the theoretical groundwork for a new "hands off" doctrine in the area of personal rights.

After *Jones*, the Court increasingly restricted prisoners' intellectual freedoms. In *Bell v. Wolfish*, the case involving the rights of pretrial detainees who have not yet been convicted, the Court relied heavily on *Jones* to hold that detainees could not receive books except from publishers, book clubs, and bookstores, and could not receive any packages from outside. Then, several years later, in *Turner v. Safley* and its progeny, the Court explicitly overruled the *Procunier* test requiring a substantial relationship to a legitimate governmental interest, and replaced it with a standard that is exceedingly deferential to those who run the prisons: Any regulation that a court finds "reasonably related to legitimate penological objectives" will be upheld.[52] Crucially, the burden is now on the prisoner to show that the regulation is irrational rather than being on the prison administration to show why the regulation is reasonable. This changes the result in many cases. For example, the Supreme Court upheld a prison rule that prohibited Muslim prisoners from attending their sacred Friday service, and did so without requiring the prison to show that there were not other ways in which legitimate security interests could be accommodated while still allowing the Muslims to worship on their holy day.[53]

Prisoners have never fared well in the Supreme Court regarding Fourth Amendment rights against unreasonable searches and invasions of privacy. Prisoners have no right of privacy in their cells, which are completely subject to search.[54] Personal privacy is very limited: The Court has even allowed pretrial detainees to be strip-searched without probable cause.[55]

The Court has relented slightly in areas involving family and the right to association with people outside prison. The Court has held that prisoners are entitled to some visitation, at least with family members, but not "contact" visitation (that is, prisoners can be required to "visit" through glass barriers or the like).[56] And the Supreme Court has found that prisoners retain the right to marry subject to relatively minimal restriction by prison authorities.[57]

Access to courts is a crucial issue for prisoners. After *Jones v. North Carolina Prisoners' Union*, prisoners have no right to organize, or even to assemble to speak on subjects of clear public and political concern, rights upon which the rest of us rely in making our voices heard on important public policy questions. This enforced powerlessness necessarily increases prisoners' reliance on the courts to address awful conditions and other terrible problems. In light of *Jones,* and the ability of the political system to completely ignore prisoners, prisoners' reliance on the courts is not excessive, it is necessary: Since courts are the only powerful institution that must at least consider prisoners' petitions for redress of grievances, court is naturally where prisoners go to seek relief.

Even before the modern era of prisoners' rights litigation, the Supreme Court recognized a right of prisoners' access to the courts, at least to file habeas corpus petitions challenging whether they should be imprisoned at all, and held that prison officials cannot obstruct exercise of this right.[58] And after courts began to hear cases regarding conditions inside prisons, the Court extended the right of access to include the filing of complaints regarding conditions.[59] It was understood that prisoners are entitled to unobstructed and confidential communications with courts, attorneys, and their assistants.[60]

Beginning in the 1970s, prisoners began to assert that in order to put flesh on the right of access, they needed tools to help them put together court papers. In 1977 the Supreme Court seemed to agree, suggesting that in order to make real the right of access, prisoners are entitled either to adequate law library facilities or persons trained in law to help them exercise that right.[61] After this ruling, law libraries were established in many prisons throughout the country and for many years there was litigation regarding the adequacy of systems of providing either law libraries or legal assistance.

However, in *Lewis v. Casey*, 518 U.S. 343 (1996), the Court "clarified" its earlier pronouncements, holding that this constitutional right of access encompasses less than the provision of tools so that prisoners may adequately litigate cases. Instead, the Court found that the right of access is merely the ability to file adequate initial papers in criminal appeals, conditions, and habeas cases; and that prisoners cannot sue for denial of access just because the prison law library is allegedly inadequate, but rather must show actual injury. To be entitled to relief, a prisoner must show that "the alleged shortcomings . . . hindered his efforts to pursue a legal claim." 518 U.S. at 351.

Casey involved prison officials' affirmative obligation to provide access to the courts, and it certainly raises questions about whether something other than full law libraries will suffice to meet constitutional requirements. However, *Casey* did not disturb the early cases holding that prison officials cannot interfere with access to courts and counsel.

Full Backlash by the End of the Century

By the century's end, Congress weighed in with a series of measures designed to limit prisoners' access to the courts: access that had for thirty years provided at least a measure of relief from the worst prison conditions. As is detailed in the following chapter of the present book, through the Prison Litigation Reform Act (PLRA) and the Antiterrorism and Effective Death Penalty Act (AEDPA), Congress sought to limit when and how prisoners could seek court redress; how much and for how long federal courts can be involved in trying to eradicate bad conditions; and even how much prisoners' lawyers can be compensated by the perpetrators of the conditions being remedied.[62] In another blow to prisoner access, especially those in local jails, Congress also prohibited any lawyers receiving federal civil legal services funds for poor people from representing any prisoner *on any matter*.[63]

The Supreme Court majority, as chronicled above, also had done its part by century's end; while giving lip service to the continued existence of constitutional rights, the Court limited as much as possible the day-to-day realization of the rights prisoners supposedly retain. Personal rights, especially under the First Amendment, were scuttled in the late '80s with the rise of the extremely deferential *Turner v. Safley* doctrine. In the '90s, more damage was done. The Scalia opinions in *Wilson v. Seiter* (at least deliberate indifference must be shown in all Eighth Amendment cases, conditions must be viewed separately) and *Lewis v. Casey* (drastically limiting implementation of the right of access to courts) along with the Rehnquist opinion in *Sandin v. Conner* (no due process except in very extreme circumstances) all make it much harder for prisoners to obtain relief from oppressive conditions and practices.

Qualified Success: What Has Been Accomplished, What Has Not

Viewed in historical perspective, prison litigation has accomplished much. The very idea that people in prisons have basic, enforceable human rights has become accepted at a level that could not have been anticipated even fifty years ago. For example, today the United States Supreme Court, as destructive as it has been to the rights of ordinary people, takes as a given that the United States Constitution stipulates that certain basic human rights are to be provided to people the state holds in institutions.[64] Because of this recognition of constitutional protection for prisoners, many of the very worst conditions that prevailed in prisons throughout the country into the 1970s have been eradicated. This is not enough or where it should end, but it is a great victory.

In addition, prison litigation has been a major catalyst in the incredible increase in at least the expectation of professionalism in two areas: medical care and personal safety of prisoners. When I started doing prison law in 1975 at the Washington State Penitentiary in Walla Walla, the "medical" staff consisted mostly of men who had been medics in the military; these unlicensed people were prescribing medications and were virtually unsupervised; there were no serious standards or procedures by which the medical staff was governed; no official expectation that custody staff must report medical complaints to the medical department rather than conduct on-the-tier diagnosis themselves. Medical care in prisons today is far from ideal, but there now are standards, expectations, licensure and training, and even professional organizations dedicated to adequate care for prisoners. These developments, if they had happened at all, would have been much slower without the many federal cases condemning inadequate care and staffing in prisons and jails across the country.

Similarly, largely as an outgrowth of cases such as *Jackson v. Bishop*, 404 F.2d 571 (4th Cir. 1968) (guards cannot use corporal punishment); *Holt v. Sarver*, 309 F.Supp. 362 (D.Ark. 1970) (prisoners cannot supervise other prisoners); and *Woodhous v. Virginia*, 487 F.2d 889 (4th Cir. 1973) (excessive prisoner-to-prisoner violence violates Eighth Amendment) and their progeny, the official *expectation* that prisoners should not be abused has become the norm. This has resulted in higher standards of conduct for guards, better training, and closer supervision of prisoners for protection.

I do not suggest that bad prison medical care and brutality against prisoners has been eliminated. Obviously, they have not. But I also believe that this litigation-spurred establishment of professional standards and expectations has saved the life and limb of many prisoners who would otherwise have been brutalized.

But there is also much to be unhappy about (in addition to the obvious, such as the enactment of the PLRA). As the discussion above shows, the true essence of the constitutional provisions prisoners invoke is human dignity, and a crucial focus on this has been lost. The early cases focused on this core value and so naturally looked at the conditions of incarceration as a whole. But the Supreme Court has turned away from these higher values and what they imply for the way we treat prisoners, and has delivered a most destructive blow in the area of conditions by requiring that conditions must be looked at in a discrete, disconnected way—in effect, requiring that only one condition at a time may be viewed and determined to be either constitutional or not.[65]

One fairly recent case illustrates this approach. In *Madrid v. Gomez,* 889 F.Supp. 1146 (N.D. Cal. 1995), a conscientious federal judge looked at the horrific conditions and practices at the infamous Pelican Bay "supermax" prison in California. The judge found that there was a "practice of permitting and condoning a pattern of excessive force by subordinates, as reflected by defendants' management of the prison over an extended period of time." This pattern consisted of "assaults, beatings, and naked cagings in inclement weather."[66] In addition, as to medical and mental health care, conditions were objectively awful and the defendants had exhibited deliberate indifference. Therefore, the court had little trouble finding Eighth Amendment violations and issued an injunction against these practices.

But on the subject of whether the confinement in the Security Housing Unit (SHU) at Pelican Bay was, in and of itself, cruel and unusual punishment, this conscientious judge found his hands tied. The judge noted that prevailing Eighth Amendment law is that while some degeneration of prisoners in certain conditions is not necessarily a constitutional violation, evidence that serious deterioration is caused by certain conditions might be a violation. The Court then said:

> What plaintiffs object to is not merely an absence of programs, but a more universal deprivation of human contact and stimulation . . . including the stark physical environment, the lack of any window to the outside world, the geographically remote location of Pelican Bay, and the extreme degree of social isolation . . . [S]ome of these conditions appear, at best, tenuously related to legitimate [penological] concerns.
>
> [T]he conditions of extreme social isolation and reduced environmental stimulation . . . will likely inflict some degree of psychological trauma upon most inmates confined there for more than brief periods . . . however, for many inmates, it does not appear that the degree of mental injury suffered significantly exceeds the kind of generalized psychological pain that courts have found compatible with Eighth Amendment standards.[67]

The judge in *Madrid* then found that the SHU was unconstitutional housing only for people who already had serious mental health issues, as "putting them in SHU is the mental equivalent of putting an asthmatic in a place with little air to breathe."[68] But for other prisoners, housing in this same place was not unconstitutional. It is sad, indeed, that Eighth Amendment law now apparently allows prison officials to place an asthmatic in a place with little air to breathe, or, more to the point, put a sane person in a place that necessarily makes people prone to insanity more insane. Eighth Amendment analysis for prisons started with the ideals of basic decency and humanity; it has surely strayed from these ideals if it permits this kind of obviously inhumane incarceration.

Finally, while courts must look at bad physical conditions and medical care, or the very worst of them anyway, the spiritual and political rights of prisoners are very severely restricted, and under the prevailing *Turner* standard of extreme deference to authority, there is often little prisoners can do about this. Something very close to "hands off" prevails in areas of rights that free people take for granted: Privacy, speech, assembly, exercise of religion.

Even if prisoners must have more restrictions on these rights than free people, many of the restrictions that the federal courts have allowed in the name of holy deference are not necessary. The people we incarcerate can be killed in spirit even if we keep their bodies alive. The federal courts are not powerless to address crucial issues of the spirit for prisoners: Much of the Bill of Rights addresses exactly these vital matters. Perhaps someday the courts will begin to grant prisoners a greater measure of these important rights.

Notes

1. Because of space limitations, what follows is an extremely condensed overview of the large body of federal constitutional prison law over the period I discuss.
2. See Mushlin, *Rights of Prisoners* (2d Ed.) (Shepard's/McGraw-Hill, 1993), Vol. 1 at 7–9.
3. *Gitlow v. New York*, 268 U.S. 652 (1925) (First Amendment applies to the states). The Fourteenth Amendment, of course, explicitly applies to the states.
4. See, for example, *McCollum v. Mayfield*, 130 F.Supp. 112, 115 (N.D.Cal. 1955) (denial of serious need for medical care "could well result in the deprivation of life itself" without due process of law); *Sewell v. Pegelow*, 291 F.2d 196 (4th cir. 1961) (Muslim prisoners entitled to reasonable opportunity to worship).
5. Matthew T. Clarke, "Barring the Federal Courthouse to Prisoners," (see the following chpate in this book, pp. 301–14).
6. *Robinson v. California*, 370 U.S. 660 (1962).
7. *Jackson v. Bishop*, 404 F.2d 571, 579 (8th Cir. 1968).
8. Id.
9. A good short account of the Attica Rebellion is Coughlin, "Attica: The Prison Revolt of 1971," http://home.earthlink.net/-dwsgsht/attica.html.
10. See, for example, *Gates v. Collier*, 501 F.2d 1291 (5th Cir. 1974) (Mississippi); *Pugh v. Locke*, 406 F.Supp. 318 (M.D.Ala. 1976) (Alabama).
11. *Lamaan v. Helgemoe*, 437 F.Supp. 269 (D.N.H. 1977) (New Hampshire).
12. See the listing of cases in Justice Brennan's concurring opinion in *Rhodes v. Chapman*, 452 U.S. 337, 353–54 (1981).
13. *Ruiz v. Estelle*, 503 F.Supp. 1265, 1383–84 (S.D.Tex. 1980) (citations and subsequent history omitted).
14. E.g., *Pugh*, 406 F.Supp. at 335.
15. *Laaman*, 437 F.Supp. at 317.

16. *Hoptowit v. Ray*, 682 F.2d 1237 (9th Cir. 1982).
17. See Yackle, *Reform and Regret: The Story of Federal Judicial Involvement in the Alabama Prison System* (Oxford University Press, 1989).
18. For twenty of the twenty-four years beginning on Inauguration Day in 1969 and ending Inauguration Day in 1993, Republican Presidents Nixon, Ford, Reagan, and the elder Bush were appointing all federal judges.
19. *Newman v. Alabama*, 559 F.2d 283, 290–92 (5th Cir. 1977); *Hoptowit*, 682 F.2d at 1253–55.
20. *Wright v. Rushen*, 642 F.2d 1129 (9th Cir. 1981); *Hoptowit*, 682 F.2d at 1246–47.
21. *Wolff v. McDonnell*, 418 U.S. 539, 555–56 (1974) (citing earlier Supreme Court cases regarding the First Amendment, due process, access to courts, and equal protection).
22. 429 U.S. at 104.
23. Id. at 96–97.
24. *Hutto v. Finney*, 437 U.S. 678 (1978).
25. Id. at 681–83.
26. Id. at 687.
27. *Bell v. Wolfish*, 441 U.S. 520 (1979), applying a Due Process standard to people detained pending trial but not yet convicted.
28. 452 U.S. at 345–47. *Compare Bell*, 441 U.S. at 542: For prisoners being held in lieu of bail but not yet convicted of a crime, absent a showing of intent to punish, only conditions that are not "reasonably related to a legitimate governmental objective" or inflict "genuine privations and hardship over an extended period of time" would violate the Due Process Clause.
29. *Rhodes*, 452 U.S. at 346–47, citing *Bell*.
30. Id. at 348.
31. E.g., *Hoptowit*; *Fisher v. Koehler*, 692 F.Supp. 1519 (S.D.N.Y. 1988).
32. *Whitley v. Albers*, 475 U.S. 312 (1986).
33. *Rhodes*, 452 U.S. at 347.
34. 501 U.S. 304–305 (emphasis by the Court).
35. *Hudson v. McMillian*, 503 U.S. 1, 5–7 (1992).
36. *Helling v. McKinney*, 509 U.S. 31 (1993).
37. In practical terms, whether the defendant had actual knowledge depends upon how obvious and how longstanding the bad conditions are, and a defendant who avoids on purpose "knowing" the obvious may be found to be deliberately indifferent. See generally Boston et al., *Farmer v. Brennan: Defining Deliberate Indifference Under the Eighth Amendment*, 14 St. Louis U. Pub. L. Rev. 83 (1994).

    Farmer also made clear what lower courts had assumed for many years: Prisoners are protected by the Eighth Amendment against a serious and pervasive risk of harm through assault by other prisoners.
38. *Vitek v. Jones*, 445 U.S. 480 (1980).
39. *Vitek* (transfer to mental hospital); *Washington v. Harper*, 494 U.S. 210 (1990) (psychotropic medication).
40. *Meachum*, 427 U.S. at 225.
41. 427 U.S. at 233–34.
42. *Olim v. Wakinekona*, 461 U.S. 242 (1983).
43. *Greenholtz v. Nebraska Inmates* 442 U.S. 1 (1979); *Board of Pardons v. Allen*, 482 U.S. 369 (1987).
44. *Hewitt v. Helms*, 459 U.S. 460 (1983).
45. A revealing aspect of the Court's transparent shifting about to avoid due process results favorable to prisoners is Chief Justice Rehnquist's sharp criticism in the *Sandin* majority opinion of the "state-created liberty interest" analysis in *Hewitt v. Helms*—an opinion Rehnquist also authored! Faced with the fact that *Hewitt* would actually provide expanded rights in some cases, the Chief Justice, with a more conservative majority in place, decided *Hewitt's* purpose had been served, and abandoned it as though it had been misguided from the beginning.
46. The court in Sandin suggested that the results in both *Wolff v. McDonnell* and *Board of Pardons v. Allen*, did still demonstrate a liberty interest sufficient to invoke the Due Process Clause. Both of those cases involved length of incarceration issues.
47. *Lee v. Washington*, 390 U.S. 333 (1968).
48. *Cruz v. Beto*, 405 U.S. 319 (1972).

49. *Procunier v. Martinez*, 416 U.S. 396, 413 (1974).
50. 433 U.S. at 139–147.
51. 433 U.S. at 132.
52. *Turner v. Safley*, 482 U.S. 78 (1987); *O'Lone v. Estate of Shabazz*, 482 U.S. 342 (1987); *Thornburgh v. Abbott*, 490 U.S. 401 (1989).
53. *O'Lone v. Estate of Shabazz*. (See note 52 supra.)
54. *Hudson v. Palmer*, 468 U.S. 517 (1984).
55. *Bell v. Wolfish*, 441 U.S. at 558–560.
56. *Block v. Rutherford*, 468 U.S. 576 (1984).
57. *Turner v. Safley*. (See note 52 supra.)
58. *Ex parte Hull*, 312 U.S. 546 (1941).
59. *Wolff v. McDonnel*. (See note 21 supra.)
60. *Procunier v. Martinez*, 416 U.S. 396, 419 (1974).
61. *Bounds v. Smith*, 430 U.S. 817 (1977).
62. Matthew T. Clarke, "Barring the Federal Courthouse to Prisoners," (see the following chapter in this book, pp. 301–14).
63. See 45 Code of Federal Regulations, Section 1637.
64. Thus Chief Justice Rehnquist, no friend of prisoners' rights, can write matter-of-factly in an opinion he penned for the Court that "[w]hen the State by the affirmative exercise of its power so restrains an individual's liberty that it renders him unable to care for himself, and at the same time fails to provide for his basic human needs—e. g., food, clothing, shelter, medical care, and reasonable safety—it transgresses the substantive limits on state action set by the Eighth Amendment and the Due Process Clause." *DeShaney v. Winnebago Cty. Soc. Services Dept.*, 489 U.S. 189, 200 (1989).
65. See discussion above of *Rhodes v. Chapman* and *Wilson v. Seiter*.
66. 889 F.Supp. at 1250, 1252.
67. *Madrid*, 889 F.Supp. at 1264–65.
68. *Id.* at 1265.

Barring the Federal Courthouses to Prisoners

MATTHEW T. CLARKE

If someone assaults you, or illegally holds you against your will, you would likely report it to the police. In theory, the police and prosecutors take over from there. If someone at work calls you by a racial slur, or sexually harasses you, you might go to the relevant civil rights enforcement agency (such as the EEOC) for redress. If your landlord refuses to keep up your building, you could file a grievance with the housing commission. If you are injured on the job due to unsafe workplace conditions, you might head to your local workman's compensation office, and perhaps you might hire a personal injury lawyer.

But what would you do if you were a prisoner who experienced any of these conditions? Who would you turn to if the people who assaulted you, subjected you to the unsafe conditions, sexually harassed, or even raped you were the very people responsible for your safety? What would you do if your incarceration was unjust—the result of police and prosecutors willing to "bend the rules" to secure convictions?

Until recently, there were two groups of laws that acted as the guardians of prisoners' rights: the federal civil rights laws (42 United States Code (U.S.C.) §§ 1983 and 1985), and the federal habeas corpus laws (28 U.S.C. §§ 2241, 2254, 2255 and Article I, Section 9, Subsection 2 of the United States Constitution). The civil rights laws were the historic vehicle for a prisoner to enforce his or her right to decent prison conditions and medical treatment, and to sue for abuse suffered at the hands of prison staff. Habeas corpus laws were used by prisoners to get another day in court if illegal prosecution and police actions eclipsed justice during their criminal trial.

Passage of two fairly recent pieces of legislation, the Antiterrorism and Effective Death Penalty Act (AEDPA) and the Prison Litigation Reform Act (PLRA) of 1996 radically emasculated these historic vehicles for legal

This article was published in 2001.

redress, and just for one class of people: prisoners. With recent amendments to these two groups of laws, it is now much more difficult for prisoners to get into court, and nearly impossible for them to win once they get there.

The Civil Rights Laws and §1983

Of the civil rights statutes available, the statute most commonly utilized by prisoners in vindicating their civil rights is 42 U.S.C. §1983, generally referred to as §1983, which states the following:

> Every person who, under color of any statute, ordinance, regulation, custom, or usage, of any State or Territory, subjects, or causes to be subjected, any citizen of the United States or other persons within the jurisdiction thereof to the deprivation of any rights, privileges, or immunities secured by the Constitution and laws, shall be liable to the person injured in an action of law, suit in equity, or other proper proceedings for redress.

Essentially, §1983 allows people whose civil rights have been violated to sue the people who violated them. Under §1983, the illegal action must be performed "under color" of state law, which limits possible defendants to government employees and those performing traditionally recognized government acts. Thus, it is one of the most useful statutes for state prisoners whose civil rights have been violated by prison employees. This primary tool was retracted—for prisoners only—with the passage of the PLRA.

The Prison Litigation Reform Act

On April 26, 1996, President Clinton signed the Prison Litigation Reform Act (PLRA) into law. The express purpose of the PLRA was to impede prisoner litigation and it has been enormously successful in this respect. Because of key provisions discussed below, prisoners now cannot secure representation for most civil rights complaints.

To create an effective bar to prisoners' suits, the PLRA addressed several central aspects of such litigation, including: 1) the right to file a lawsuit without pre-paying filing fees; 2) the right to have attorney fees awarded upon winning the suit; 3) the requirement of exhausting all administrative remedies available prior to filing the lawsuit; and 3) the scope of relief the court may grant a prisoner.[1]

Attorney Fees Limitations

The stereotype of prison litigation is that prisoners entertain themselves by mounting one frivolous, often ridiculous civil rights lawsuit after another.

With nothing to do, they while away the hours acting as a thorn in the government's side as often as possible. Suits, like the one brought by a prisoner for slipping on a pillow, help confirm this idea of prison litigation. Capitalizing on this perception, drafters of the PLRA ensured that prisoners are now likely to be the only ones who will bring their case. The mandates of the PLRA effectively cut most prisoners' attorneys out of the field.

The drafters of the PLRA separated the interests of prisoners and their attorneys significantly by changing the way attorney's fees are awarded. Prior to the PLRA, any prevailing party in a civil rights action could be awarded attorney's fees at the lawyer's standard billing rate, which means that the prevailing party could require the losing party to pay for the winning party's attorney. The amount awarded was then determined by the court, subject to a challenge and/or appeal if found to be unreasonable.

With the enactment of the PLRA, attorneys' fees may not be awarded at an hourly rate greater than 150 percent of what court-appointed counsel are paid in criminal cases.[2] Another provision mandates that a total attorney fee may not exceed 150 percent of the final judgment.[3] For example, a First Circuit court recently interpreted this provision as such: a prisoner who prevails and wins a nominal damage award of $1.00 may not recover more than $1.50 in attorneys fees.[4] Additionally, the attorney fees award first comes out of up to 25 percent of the damage award won by the prisoners: this requirement essentially means prevailing parties must pay themselves from monies in the damages award.[5]

At first blush, 150 percent of the court-appointed criminal defense attorneys' rate may not seem so bad. However, there are three factors that make this arrangement unacceptable to most attorneys. Court-appointed criminal defense attorneys are paid whether they win or lose, whereas attorneys representing indigent prisoners in civil rights cases only get paid if they win (and winning is tremendously difficult in this type of litigation, for reasons detailed below). Also, court–appointed criminal defense attorneys are notoriously underpaid. One hundred and fifty percent of an underpaid attorney's fee may still be only a fraction of the average fee charged by private attorneys. And private attorneys have large overhead costs. Therefore, very few attorneys can afford to represent prisoners, regardless of how meritorious their claims are.

The impact is devastating for prisoners' claims. Most prisoners are barely literate, much less skilled in the complex workings of the law. Prisoners are dependent on the assistance of attorneys to help them vindicate their civil rights, but they are fundamentally discouraged by the PLRA from doing so.

Limitations on Awards

The PLRA eliminated mental and emotional injuries without an accompanying physical injury from the list of recoverable injuries.[6] In other words, prisoners could suffer extreme mental injury—including mental cruelty and torture—yet they are barred from suing their tormenters. Non-prisoner litigants continue to enjoy the right to sue for mental and emotional injuries without the requirement of proving physical injuries, too.

Limitations on Types of Relief

The PLRA limits the relief granted in a civil action, allowing it to "extend no further than necessary to correct the violation of the Federal right of a particular plaintiff or plaintiffs," requiring the relief to be as narrowly drawn as possible. Additionally, the court granting relief must "give substantial weight to any adverse impact on public safety or the operation of a criminal justice system caused by the relief."[7] The provision therefore forbids an order that will result in the release of a prisoner, unless other remedies have been attempted and rejected, and a three-judge panel issues the order.

The tone of this provision is clear: make it extra difficult for prisoners to get relief, but if they are granted relief, don't make it too much, and grease the path for prison, law enforcement, and legislative personnel to hamstring the ultimate grant of any relief.

Termination of Relief

Any relief granted by a court in a prison conditions suit, including those granted before the passage of the PLRA, is immediately and automatically terminated two years after its grant, unless the court makes a written finding that the relief remains necessary to correct the ongoing violation of a federal right and is the least intrusive and most narrowly drawn relief possible to correct the violation.[8]

The prison and jail officials may move for termination of any relief in a prison conditions suit two years after it was granted, and may renew the motion annually. The mere filing of the termination motion results in an automatic stay of the relief previously granted by the court from 30 days after the motion is filed until the court rules on the motion.[9]

This provision of the PLRA streamlines the ability of prison officials to file motions to dismiss previously litigated suits they have lost on the merits; it also predisposes the federal courts to dismiss suits in which the prisoners prevailed. This is especially onerous in cases previously settled by a consent decree (an agreement by the parties endorsed by the court), in which prisoner plaintiffs may have settled for less than the minimum constitutionally required relief to gain additional relief over the minimum in other areas. Under the PLRA, the additional relief is simply discontinued.

Exhaustion of Administrative Remedies

PLRA provides that a prisoner may not bring a lawsuit challenging prison conditions under federal law unless he or she has first exhausted "such administrative remedies as are available."[10] This means that the prisoner must file a grievance and then appeal all the way through the prison or jail grievance system before he or she may bring suit. Exhaustion is mandatory even if the prisoner's suit seeks a remedy, such as money damages, that the grievance system will not provide.[11]

This provision impedes prisoners' access to the courts in several important respects. First, many prison grievance systems are complex, with several levels of appeal and very short deadlines (as short as 24 hours) for filing a grievance or an appeal. A prisoner who fails to meet these deadlines and navigate this procedural maze may find his or her lawsuit barred from court. Second, many prison systems require the prisoner to attempt "informal resolution" with the staff member whose conduct is at issue before filing a grievance. Thus, for example, a prisoner who was sexually assaulted by a staff member may have to attempt "informal resolution" with her rapist before she is even allowed to start the grievance process.

Finally, the grievance process is completely under the control of prison officials, who can make it as complicated and onerous as they like in an attempt to frustrate litigation. Before 1996, prisoners could be required to exhaust only grievance systems that had been certified by the United States Attorney General or found by the court to be "fair and effective."[12] The PLRA abolished this fairness requirement, and now requires prisoners to exhaust whatever grievance system prison officials establish.

Prison officials do not hesitate to wield the power given them by PLRA's exhaustion requirement. In 2001, prisoners housed at Wallens Ridge State Prison, a "supermax" prison in a remote corner of Virginia, filed suit in federal court, alleging a pervasive climate of excessive force. At the time the prisoners successfully exhausted the grievance system, it had three steps. Three weeks after the prisoners filed suit, the warden issued a directive stating that henceforth, the grievance system would have *six* steps.[13]

In Forma Pauperis Reforms

Prior to the enactment of the PLRA, a prisoner with little or no money could file a lawsuit without prepayment of filing or other court fees (called filing *in forma pauperis*). Post-PLRA, prisoners have no such option. Scrutiny of prisoner trust fund accounts is strict and, even in jurisdictions where prisoners are not paid for their labor, even near-destitute prisoners are required to pay a portion of the fees and the remainder by installments reckoned as a percentage of their trust fund balances.[14]

Indigent nonprisoner litigants, of course, continue to enjoy their right to affordable and free (if necessary) access to the federal courts.

With the enactment of the PLRA came the "three strikes" rule, disallowing a prisoner from filing a lawsuit as a pauper if, while he was a prisoner at any time in the past, three lawsuits were dismissed as "frivolous," "malicious," or for "failing to state a claim upon which relief may be granted."[15]

While this might not seem particularly onerous (after all, prisoners shouldn't file frivolous or malicious lawsuits, and thus waste valuable court time), keep in mind that most prisoners now act as their own lawyers, and may easily make out what is seen by the courts as a "frivolous" claim, or fail to state a viable claim for lack of knowledge of the subtleties of the law and the complexities of legal pleadings. A prisoner who is unskilled in the law knows only that a wrong has been committed, and how to describe the facts related to that wrong. Under the PLRA scheme, the *pro se* prisoner can easily gain a strike for failing to state a claim upon which relief might be granted—even with a legitimate claim. If not initially frustrated by the morass of procedural barriers to litigation, the average indigent prisoner will eventually be trapped by procedural errors to come. Then, as quick as one-two-three strikes, the prisoner is permanently barred from court. But that is the purpose of the PLRA.

The Writ of Habeas Corpus

The writ of habeas corpus (Latin for "you have the body") has existed in English common law since the 1300s. By the mid-seventeenth century, the writ of habeas corpus was established as the premier mode for attacking illegal confinement, having become codified in England's first Habeas Corpus Act in 1641, and refined in a second Habeas Corpus act in 1679. By the time the United States Constitution incorporated the writ of habeas corpus, it had existed as a common law right for four centuries and enjoyed a 130-year history as statutory law.

Immediately upon passage of the Bill of Rights in 1789, Congress enacted a habeas corpus statute providing for habeas corpus review of the constitutionality of all arrests made under the color of federal law.[16] Because the federal constitutional right to habeas corpus did not extend to state actions, state prisoners initially had no federal right to challenge their state convictions. In 1867, the Judiciary Act granted jurisdiction to the federal courts to review all habeas actions, whether pursuant to state or federal law. [17]

The statute remained largely unchanged until the enactment of the Antiterrorism and Effective Death Penalty Act (AEDPA) in 1996. Until AEDPA, it was the primary vehicle for state and federal prisoners to challenge unconstitutional actions of police and prosecutors that led to the prisoner's confinement.

Hobbling Habeas

State and federal prisoners, including those with capital cases awaiting execution, historically have used federal habeas corpus to regain their freedom, or at least another day in court.

Eager to shut down a prisoners' last effort at appeal, and undaunted by stakes that may include death, Congress enacted AEDPA with little real dissent over its radical provisions. In the wake of the Oklahoma City bombing of 1995, conservatives who had been struggling for years to hobble the writ saw their opportunity and took it.[18]

Then, after the Oklahoma City bombing in 1995, conservative forces saw an opportunity to finally force passage of radical reforms to the habeas corpus statute. Cynically packaging the proposed reforms as a necessary tool in the fight against domestic terrorism and banking on the public fury following the bombing of the federal building in Oklahoma City, habeas corpus detractors cobbled together a new bill. Entitled the Antiterrorism and Effective Death Penalty Act, the bill dramatically over-hauled the availability of habeas corpus review for *state* prisoners— reforms that had little or nothing to do with combating acts of domestic terrorism, which are generally prosecuted in federal courts. Notwith-standing the lack of a logical connection between the ostensible objec-tives of the legislation and the proposed reforms, the conservatives had a sure winner. The bill passed by an overwhelming margin.

Detractors of habeas corpus claimed that the scattered successes of some prisoners was a gross expansion of the right to habeas corpus, and therefore called for massive diminishment in its scope. The Supreme Court, however, had already erected many barriers to prisoners' relief via habeas corpus prior to enactment of AEDPA. Prisoners' successes were so limited that "in the twelve month period ending September 30, 1995, a total of 1,062 [habeas corpus] petitions were filed in federal courts in the Seventh Circuit ... Of that number, the district courts disposed of 986 petitions, granting only 14. A grant rate of 1.5 percent hardly indi-cates a federal judiciary that routinely secondguesses the results reached in state courts."[19] Nonetheless, the detractors prevailed, and on April 24, 1996, AEDPA was enacted, significantly curtailing the rights of federal habeas corpus litigants. Now a win rate of 1.5 percent in habeas corpus litigation seems astronomical.

The Impact of AEDPA

The AEDPA is a multi-pronged attack on American federal habeas corpus rights. It requires that federal courts defer to state court interpre-tations of fact and federal constitutional laws; substantially increases the burden of proving entitlement to relief; imposes an unprecedented statute of limitations on the filing of a petition for federal habeas corpus review;

and curtails the federal courts' ability to grant evidentiary hearings. AEDPA also severely reduces the availability of habeas corpus review of INS decisions to deport noncitizens, and increases the difficulty of appealing an adverse habeas corpus decision as it imposes new, severe procedures and requirements for filing a successive petition for writ of habeas corpus. AEDPA's supporters made their intentions quite clear: the purpose of AEDPA was to shift primary (but not exclusive) responsibility for habeas corpus review to the state courts.[20]

Consider the following examples of wrongly-accused prisoners who would not have received relief from execution under AEDPA's requirements. Rubin "Hurricane" Carter, the famous former boxer, was sentenced to death for the murder of a police officer. He was eventually found innocent of the crime and released from prison. Carter was vindicated via federal habeas corpus over 20 years after his imprisonment, when a court determined that prosecutorial misconduct, police misconduct, and extreme local racial prejudice led to the erroneous conviction. If his motion for habeas were brought now, it would likely have been thrown out of court without a ruling on the merits under AEDPA's time limitations and state remedies exhaustion provision.[21]

In another high-profile case in Illinois, thirteen death row prisoners were recently released by Illinois Governor George Ryan when DNA evidence conclusively proved they were innocent of the crimes for which they were convicted. Governor Ryan immediately announced a moratorium on executions. In announcing the moratorium, Ryan said, "What is unique about Illinois is there has been better reporting and uncovering of problems that also exist elsewhere, often to a greater extent."

The exoneration of the Illinois prisoners was due to a robust process of habeas corpus review. A less searching review will inevitably lead to innocent persons remaining in prison, or being executed, as occurs in more careless jurisdictions.

The primary instrument to forestall the execution of innocent citizens—the federal writ of habeas corpus—has been so gutted by AEDPA that we can expect more, not fewer, innocent lives to be snuffed out by government.

Deference to State Court Determinations of Fact

The AEDPA requires the federal courts to defer to state court determinations of fact.[22] This represents a codification of existing federal statutory and common law except that prior law required deference to state factual determinations only if the prisoner had been given a "full and fair opportunity" to develop and present the factual issues in state court.[23] Now the requirement of a "full and fair opportunity" falls away and the only check on the state's factual findings is whether they are unreasonable in light of the record. This places the ability of a state prisoner to pursue federal habeas corpus in the hands of the party the prisoner is litigating against—the state.

Deference to State Court Determinations of Federal Law

Under AEDPA, the federal courts are also required to defer to the state court's interpretation of federal law, even if it was clearly wrong, so long as it did not directly contravene a Supreme Court decision.[24] Thus, the state courts (generally, the very court the prisoner was convicted in) become the primary arbiters of the prisoner's federal habeas corpus rights.

Prior to the enactment of AEDPA, a prisoner could use the published final opinions of the United States District Court and United States Court of Appeals for the federal circuit in which he was convicted or incarcerated as a valid basis for his petition for a writ of habeas corpus. Under the AEDPA, only the opinions of the Supreme Court count and then only if the state court's decision was "contrary to or an unreasonable interpretation of" the Supreme Court's decision.[25] This means that, even if lower federal courts strongly disagree with the state court's interpretation of the Supreme Court's opinion, or if there is no controlling Supreme Court authority, the state court's decision stands, as long as it was not "unreasonable."

Statute of Limitations

Imagine a teenager with nothing but medical textbooks and an eighth-grade education to guide him as he rapidly performs brain surgery on himself, and you have an idea of the obstacles facing the typical prisoner who wishes to challenge his capital conviction. AEDPA set a statute of limitations on the use of federal habeas corpus bringing life to this scenario.[26]

Prior to the enactment of AEDPA, there was no statute of limitations on the right to federal habeas corpus; the Supreme Court had only allowed a time limitation on habeas if a prisoner's unjustified delay effectively prejudiced the state's case.[27] Now prisoners must file their habeas corpus actions in federal court within one year of their state convictions becoming final, or the ability to use habeas is lost forever.

Consider the one-year clock in this light: Because the state is not required to appoint an attorney for a prisoner filing a habeas petition in noncapital cases, prisoners are on their own to secure counsel for their post-conviction appeals. And now many prisoners must act as their own counsel, hamstrung by the complex barriers presented by AEDPA that actively discourage and limit the availability of professional legal assistance in this area of litigation. It is more typical that prisoners must craft their own habeas actions, rather than find the rare attorney who will do it for them. Consider, too, that habeas law is one of the most complicated, difficult areas of the law: the implications are clear for prisoners who typically possess less than even a high school education and are unable to afford counsel (even if there were counsel to choose from). Thus, prisoners are at a significant disadvantage for navigation of the tangled web of legal procedure that faces them upon conviction.

But the prisoner has only time on his hands and well-stocked law libraries to spend it in—or that's what many people erroneously believe. However, law libraries are currently being dismantled across the country under a Supreme Court case holding that prisons are not required to maintain law libraries.[28] Taking the cue, prisons in Utah, South Dakota, North Carolina, Idaho, and Arizona have done away with their law libraries, leaving a vastly indigent prisoner population to their own, very limited devices. Even assuming the best-case scenario—where a prisoner is "lucky" enough to be in a prison with a law library, and finds an experienced prison lawyer (or even a real attorney) to help with the procedural hurdles—there are many more obstacles to overcome.

To effectively litigate a habeas corpus action, the prisoner must have a copy of the state trial court's records. Most states charge a small fortune (for a prisoner) for these trial transcriptions. What ensues is a battle to get the records in some other way to fight the conviction. This battle for transcripts may take up most, or all, of a year's time: a potentially fatal loss of time considering AEDPA's one year statute of limitations.

Then, under AEDPA, a prisoner must first exhaust all state remedies before petitioning for federal habeas corpus relief. This means that a prisoner must work his or her way through all available state remedies and courts before bringing a habeas petition in federal court. Most states have some form of post-conviction remedy, and the prisoner must first learn their procedure and pursue them. The time after the state remedy is filed does not count toward the one-year limitations period, but the time spent obtaining the record, finding the errors in the record, marshaling the facts, researching the law, drafting the pleadings, and learning the state court's procedures does.

Once the state courts deny the post-conviction relief, the clock starts ticking again, and the prisoner is faced with another round of fact-gathering, legal research, and drafting of the habeas petition. If, by this time, the one-year clock still has some time on it, the prisoner may actually file the petition for a writ of habeas corpus in federal court.

Because much of how the federal petition will be drafted depends upon what the state court's findings of facts and conclusions of law are, little of the work necessary to produce the federal petition can be performed while the state remedy is pending in state court. Suddenly, one year doesn't seem like such a long time after all. Certainly college-educated law school students need more than a year to learn the theoretical aspects of the law. Unrepresented prisoners must then learn and practice one of the most complex areas of law in their own cases in a mere 365 days.

Successive Petitions and Procedural Default

Prior to the passage of AEDPA, a prisoner could file a successive federal habeas corpus petition only upon the showing of a reasonable explanation of why the error was not addressed in the previous petition, and with proof that the error actually prejudiced the prisoner. This was called the "cause and prejudice" standard. The "cause" generally had to be something outside of the prisoner's control, such as a new change in the law or the state's withholding of evidence of innocence.[29]

Now, before a successive petition may be filed, the prisoner must first get permission from the appropriate federal circuit court of appeals. The only reasons for granting permission to file a successive petition are either: 1) the claim rests on a new rule of constitutional law made retroactive to habeas corpus cases by the Supreme Court; or 2) the facts underlying the claim could not have been reasonably discovered by the prisoner prior to the filing of the first petition and are so compelling that no rational jury would have returned a guilty verdict.[30] This change makes it much more difficult to get federal court review of the merits of a successive petition. The claim must not only be based on new retroactive law, or previously undiscoverable facts, but also must be accompanied by a "colorable" showing of actual innocence. In other words, even if one can present a claim of a substantial constitutional violation that could not have been previously presented, there is no federal review of the claim unless the prisoner can also make a colorable showing of innocence. In short, prisoners who can show only that their convictions were unconstitutionally obtained—but not that they are possibly innocent—are categorically barred review.

Prior to AEDPA, a prisoner was required to first exhaust available state remedies by presenting his federal claims to the highest court in the state hearing criminal matters.[31] If the prisoner failed to exhaust state remedies, the same "cause and prejudice" test applied in determining whether to excuse the failure. Additionally, the failure could be excused if the prisoner showed compelling proof of actual innocence.[32] Now a prisoner must still exhaust state remedies; however, courts' recent interpretations have weakened the "cause and prejudice" test, and there is not even an exception to procedural default based on actual innocence. Essentially, a prisoner may procedurally default on his or her claim because of a technicality, rendering the claim forever barred from being heard by the courts—*even if that prisoner is actually innocent.*[33]

Deportation

The passage of AEDPA marked Congress' successful attempt to eliminate habeas corpus relief for aliens under an order of deportation due to a criminal conviction. It eliminated the language in the Immigration and

Naturalization Act (INA) that "any alien held in custody pursuant to an order of deportation may obtain judicial review thereof by habeas corpus proceedings,"[34] replacing it with: "Notwithstanding any other provisions of law, no court shall have jurisdiction to review any final order of removal against an alien who is removable by reason of having committed a criminal offense. . . ."[35]

Even though the obvious intention of this language is to deny aliens convicted of criminal offenses their right to habeas corpus review of the legality of their detention, most of the courts that have reviewed the law have interpreted it to allow a limited review for purely statutory questions under the general habeas corpus statutes.[36] If interpreted otherwise, the law might run afoul of the habeas corpus suspension clause, which forbids the peacetime suspension of the right to habeas corpus.[37]

AEDPA also modified the INA by adding a provision that limits the ability of aliens to apply for a waiver of deportation, where those aliens have been convicted of the statute's interpretation of "criminal" offenses.[38] (But under the INA, some "aggravated felonies" defined as crimes for which a noncitizen may suffer deportation are not even felonies in some jurisdictions.) Aliens who are deportable because they have been convicted of an INA-specified criminal offense have almost no legal recourse.

Conclusion

The AEDPA and PLRA strike at the heart of federal civil rights vehicles like §1983 and federal habeas corpus, imposing on prisoner litigants arduous restrictions, many of which are the antithesis of the laws' historical precedence. Both were passed into law with minimal debate, steamrollered into law as addendums to a large federal budget bill.

Some might believe that it is good to hound prisoners out of the courts; but this belief is a grave and costly error. One of the central complaints of the rioting Attica prisoners was a lack of an impartial court forum to hear their grievances regarding inhumane treatment and illegal irregularities in their convictions. The courts first began paying attention to prisoners' complaints after Attica's large body count, after which prisoners' demands for humane treatment made the issue one of national shame.

One need look no further than the recent events of Cuban prisoners taking hostages in Louisiana to see that AEDPA is having an unintended, though totally foreseeable effect: when prisoners are allowed no legal recourse to have their grievances addressed, they are forced to resort to whatever means available. It is in society's interest to allow prisoners their day in court, rather than to so limit the rights of all prisoners in reaction to the perceived abuses of a few.

Notes

1. 42 U.S.C. § 1997e(a).
2. 42 U.S.C. § 1997e(d)(3).
3. 42 U.S.C. § 1997e(d)(2).
4. *Boivin v. Black*, 225 F.3d 36 (1st Cir. 2000).
5. 42 U.S.C. § 1997e(d)(2).
6. 42 U.S.C. § 1997e(e); 28 U.S.C. § 1346(b)(2).
7. 18 U.S.C. § 3626(a)(1).
8. 18 U.S.C. § 3626(b)(2).
9. 18 U.S.C. § 3626(e)(2).
10. 42 U.S.C. § 1997e(a).
11. *Booth v. Churner*, 532 U.S. 731 (2001).
12. 42 U.S.C. § 1997e(a) (1994).
13. Wallens Ridge State Prison, Warden's Directive #4, February 28, 2001.
14. 28 U.S.C. § 1915(b).
15. 28 U.S.C. § 1915(g).
16. Judiciary Act of 1789, ch. 20, 14 Stat., 1 Stat. 81–82.
17. Judiciary Act of 1867, ch. 28, 14 Stat., 385; see R. Stephen Painter, Jr., "*O'Sullivan v. Boerckel* and the Default of State Prisoners' Federal Claims: Comity or Tragedy?" 78 North Carolina Law Review 1604 (2000).
18. For thirteen years, conservative forces (led by U.S. Supreme Court Chief Justice Rehnquist), had attempted to revise habeas corpus laws to eliminate prisoners' "abuse" of the writ. In 1988, Rehnquist, acting in his capacity as CEO of the Judicial Conference of the United States, appointed an ad hoc committee that was chaired by retired Supreme Court Justice Lewis Powell, to examine the post-conviction process in capitol cases. The conservatives deferred action until the Powell Committee could present its report. The reports of the Powell Committee and an ABA Task Force on Death Penalty Habeas Corpus were released in 1989 and habeas corpus reform bills immediately followed. Each year from 1989 until 1994, bills proposing draconian restrictions on the availability of federal habeas corpus review were introduced into Congress; each year, however, they were defeated.
19. *Moleterno v. Nelson*, 114 F.3d 629, 630 (7th Cir. 1997). The estimation noted ("1.5 percent") pertains solely to the Seventh Circuit; the reversal rate in other circuits was higher than 1.5 percent and lower in others.
20. 28 U.S.C. § 2254(d)(2); 28 U.S.C. § 2254(d)(1); *Lindh v. Murphy*, 521 U.S. 320 (1997); 28 U.S.C. § 2244(d); 28 U.S.C. § 2254(e); *Keeney v. Tamayo-Reyes*, 504 U.S. 1, 11 (1992); 8 U.S.C. § 1105a(a)(10); 28 U.S.C. § 2253(c); FRAP 22(b); 28 U.S.C. § 2244(b); *Thompson v. Calderon*, 523 U.S. 538 (1998); *Hohn v. United States*, 524 U.S. 236, 254 (1998).
21. Under AEDPA, 28 USC § 2244(d)(1), the statute of limitations (SOL) would have begun to run from the date that Carter's conviction was affirmed on direct appeal, i.e., 20 years before habeas relief was finally granted, with relief precluded by the SOL. He may have alternatively invoked 28 § U.SC. 2244(d)(1)(D), which provides that the SOL begins to run from "the date on which the factual predicate of the claim or claims presented could have been discovered through the exercise of due diligence." This provision allows that if the factual basis for Carter's challenge could not have been discovered through due diligence until many years after his conviction, the SOL would not preclude federal review—unless he waited more than a year from the date that he discovered the factual basis to file his federal petition. Whether this provision is applicable depends upon when the factual basis for Carter's challenge was discovered, whether it could have previously been discovered through the "exercise of due diligence," and how much time lapsed between the discovery of the factual basis and the filing of the petition in federal court. Though this provision possibly could have been invoked, it is unknown whether it would have applied, and demonstrates yet another obstacle to relief—no matter the circumstances—under AEDPA.
22. 28 U.S.C. § 2254(d)(2).
23. 28 U.S.C. § 2254(d) (prior to April 24, 1996).
24. 28 U.S.C. § 2254(d)(1).
25. 28 U.S.C. § 2254(d)(2).

26. 28 U.S.C. § 2244(d).
27. Rule 9(a), Rules Governing Section 2254 Cases; *Lonchar v. Thomas*, 517 U.S. 314 (1996).
28. *Lewis v. Casey*, 518 U.S. 343 (1996).
29. *McCleskey v. Zant*, 499 U.S. 467, 493–94 (1991).
30. 28 U.S.C. § 2244(b); *Thompson v. Calderon*, 523 U.S. 538 (1998).
31. *Ex parte Royall*, 117 U.S. 241 (1886); *Ex parte Fonda*, 117 U.S. 516 (1886); 28 U.S.C. §§ 2254(b) and (c) (prior to April 24, 1996).
32. *McCleskey v. Zant*, 499 U.S. 467, 493–94 (1991).
33. 28 U.S.C. § 2254(b).
34. 8 U.S.C. § 1105(a)(10) (repealed April 24, 1996).
35. INA § 242(a)(2)(c), 8 U.S.C. § 1252(a)(2)(C) (after Sept. 30, 1996).
36. 28 U.S.C. § 2241; *Goncalves v. Reno*, 144 F.3d 110, 125–26 (1st Cir. 1998); *Tuckhan v. INS*, 123 F.3d 487, 489–90 (7th Cir. 1997); *Mansour v. INS*, 123 F.3d 423, 426 (6th Cir. 1997); *Auguste v. Attorney General*, 118 F.3d 723, 726 n. 7 (11th Cir. 1997); *Romallo v. Reno*, 114 F.3d 1210, 1214 & n. 1 (D.C. Cir. 1997); *Fernandez v. INS*, 113 F.3d 1151, 1154–55 (10th Cir. 1997); *Williams v. INS*, 114 F.3d 82, 83–84 (5th Cir. 1997); *Salazar-Haro v. INS*, 95 F.3d 309–311 (3d Cir. 1996); *Hincapie-Nieto v. INS*, 92 F.3d 27, 30–31 (2d Cir. 1996); *Duldulao v. INS*, 90 F.3d 396, 400 n. 4 (9th Cir. 1996).
37. "The Privilege of the Writ of Habeas corpus shall not be suspended, unless when in Cases of Rebellion or Invasion the public Safety may require it." Article I, section 9, clause 2 or the United States Constitution.
38. INA § 212(c).

The Limits of Law

MUMIA ABU-JAMAL

Human law is law only by virtue of its accordance with right reason, and by this means it is clear that it flows from eternal law. In so far as it deviates from right reason it is called an unjust law; and in such a case, it is no law at all, but rather an assertion of violence.
—St. Thomas Aquinas, *Summa Theologiae* (c. 1260)

It is tempting for many to regard the law as a thing that is almost sacred, as an expression of the highest secular thought. Courts of law bear a striking resemblance to churches of religion. Both are often situated in large, imposing, intimidating buildings. Both feature large center aisles to accommodate large masses of people. Both have raised places in the front; an altar in church, a bench in court. Both priests and judges wear large, flowing black robes.

Where one places a deity at the altar, the other places a being upon an elevated bench, who is said to possess god-like powers over life, liberty, and property.

A church administrator is called "Reverend" or "Your Eminence"; a judge is addressed as "Your Honor." Yet while one may opt for faith in a church, faith is surely misplaced in a court. For the law is not a religion, but a set of ideas designed to protect the dominance and the maintenance of those who rule.

Under all the robes, the architecture, the books, and other such artifacts, lie the interests of those in power. As such, the law is inherently conservative, as shown by the extreme rarity of the grant of temporary restraining orders (TRO) or preliminary injunctions, thereby preserving, in most instances, the status quo.

What's wrong with preserving the status quo?

This article was written in 1998.

If the status quo is an oppressive one, with white supremacy as the guiding principle, to preserve such a regime is wrong indeed. If the status quo is on the side of wealth and class, with the poor in a position where their interests are trampled on, then such a system cannot be called a fair one.

Black law professor Derrick Bell explains the law functions under what he calls "interest convergence," which means:

> The interest of Blacks in achieving racial equality will be accommodated only when it converges with the interest of whites. However, the Fourteenth Amendment, standing alone, will not authorize a judicial remedy providing effective racial equality for Blacks where the remedy sought threatens the superior societal status of middle- and upper-class whites. (Bell, *Critical Race Theory*, 22).

If this is so in law as generally practiced, what of prisoners' law, brought to bear by legions of jailhouse lawyers in every state of the union?

Many jailhouse lawyers know, only too well, of good, solid suits tossed out of court on the whim of a conservative judge, preening for his next judicial appointment. They know, from their own experience, that they are damned at the doorway of the courthouse, and it will be the rarest piece of luck if they can prevail in court (or even get in!).

Seen from Bell's perspective, the law protects white class interests, above all else.

That's what they are in business for. *Weiss über alles* (white over all) is the ruling, unwritten law.

Sources

Derrick Bell, *Critical Race Theory: The Key Writings that Formed the Movement*, eds. Kimberle Crenshaw, Neil Gotanda, Gary Peller, and Kendall Thomas. (New York: The New Press, 1995).

Contributors

Mumia Abu-Jamal is a journalist and activist on death row in Pennsylvania. He has authored *Live From Death Row* (1995) and *Death Blossoms* (1996) and he is also a *Prison Legal News* columnist.

Nell Bernstein is a media fellow with the Center on Crime, Communities and Culture of the Open Society Institute in New York. Her fellowship work focuses on the impact of parental incarceration on children and families, and has appeared in *Salon.com*, *Redbook*, and *The Industry Standard*. She garnered the PASS Award from the National Center on Crime and Delinquency for her fellowship work. Her writing on child welfare and criminal justice has appeared in numerous national publications, including *Glamour, Health, Mother Jones, Newsday, O: The Oprah Magazine*, and *The Washington Post*.

Stephen B. Bright is the director of the Southern Center for Human Rights in Atlanta, and teaches courses on criminal law and capital punishment at the Harvard and Yale law schools. As director of the Center since 1982, he has defended people facing the death penalty and represented people suffering human rights abuses in prisons and jails in the South. He was a public defender from 1976 to 1979, a legal services lawyer from 1975 to 1976, and directed a legal clinic for five law schools in Washington, D.C., from 1979 to 1982. His work and that of the Center have been featured in two books, *Proximity to Death* by William McFeely (1999) and *Finding Life on Death Row* by Kayta Lezin (1999).

Daniel Burton-Rose is a freelance journalist whose writing has appeared in *Z Magazine, Vibe, San Francisco Bay Guardian, Middle Eastern Report, Dollars & Sense*, and *The Multinational Reporter*. He is a co-editor of *Battle of Seattle: The New Challenge to Capitalist Globalization* (2001), and *The Celling of America* (1998) with Paul Wright and Dan Pens. He also assisted with research for Ken Silverstein's *Private Warrior* (2000).

Noam Chomsky is a world-renowned political activist, writer, and professor of linguistics at Massachusetts Institute of Technology, where he has taught since 1955. He has authored over 35 books on political philosophy and linguistics.

Matthew T. Clarke earned an M.S. in Chemistry from the Johnann-Wolfgang Goethe University in Frankfurt, Germany, and an M.A. in the Humanities from the University of Houston-Clear Lake, the latter earned while serving time in the Texas prison system. His publications include articles in scientific journals, legal and news articles in *Prison Legal News* and other legal journals, and short stories. He is currently serving a 174-year sentence in Texas.

Anne-Marie Cusac is the Managing Editor of *The Progressive*. In 1996 her investigative report on the stun belt won the George Polk Award for magazine reporting. Her investigative reporting has also won two Project Censored Awards, in 1997 and 1998. Cusac also writes about politics and culture, and is a poet. Her first book of poems was published in 2001.

Mark Dow is a Brooklyn-based writer. His work on immigration detention has won a Project Censored Award, and has appeared in *PLN, Index on Censorship, The Texas Observer,* and *The Miami Herald.* He is co-editor, with David R. Dow, of *Machinery of Death: The Reality of America's Death Penalty Regime* (Routledge, 2002) and is currently working on a book about the Immigration and Naturalization Service.

Joelle Fraser is the author of *The Territory of Men: A Memoir,* published by Random House in summer, 2002. A MacDowell Fellow, Fraser has an MFA from the University of Iowa. She has received several fellowships and awards and has been nominated for a Pushcart Prize. Her essays, stories, and interviews have appeared or are forthcoming in *The Iowa Review, Michigan Quarterly Review, Fourth Genre, Nerve.com, Tin House,* and *Zyzzyva.* She teaches writing, serves on the Review Panel for Caldera Artists Colony, and writes book reviews for the *San Francisco Chronicle.*

Alex Friedman is a former Tennessee state prisoner. A frequent *PLN* contributor, Alex focuses his activism on the private prison industry.

Judith Greene is a criminal justice policy analyst and a Soros Senior Justice Fellow. She is a consultant to Families Against Mandatory Minimums, the Justice Policy Institute, the RAND Corporation, and Human Rights Watch. Over the past decade she served as a Senior Research Fellow at the University of Minnesota Law School, and directed the State-Centered Program for the Edna McConnell Clark Foundation. From 1985 to 1993 she served as the Director of Court Programs at the Vera Institute of Justice. Ms. Greene's articles on criminal sentencing issues, police practices, and correctional policy have appeared in numerous publications, including *The American Prospect, The Index on Censorship, Crime and Delinquency,*

Current Issues in Criminal Justice, Prison Legal News (PLN), Over-crowded Times, The Wake Forest Law Review, The Rutgers Law Journal, The Justice Systems Journal, and *Judicature.*

Gordon Lafer is an assistant professor at the University of Oregon's Labor Education and Research Center, and is the author of *The Job Training Charade* (2002). He has worked as a union organizer for hotel workers, construction workers, and university teachers, and is a member of the national steering committee of Scholars, Artists and Writers for Social Justice. His articles have been published by *The American Prospect, Dissent, New Politics,* and *Politics & Society,* among others.

Adrian Lomax is a Wisconsin prisoner, jailhouse lawyer, activist, and writer.

John Midgley is a prisoners' rights attorney who has represented Washington state prisoners both individually and in class actions for the past 25 years. He has worked with the Institutions Project at Columbia Legal Services in Seattle, where he is currently the Regional Coordinator. He writes a quarterly column for *PLN* entitled *Pro Se Tips and Tactics.*

Robert Owen is a former federal public defender now in private practice in Austin, Texas, with a practice focused on death penalty defense.

Christian Parenti is the author of *Lockdown America* (1998). His writing has appeared in *The Nation, The Progressive, In These Times,* and *The Christian Science Monitor.*

Bob Posey is a Florida prisoner and activist. He is also the founder and editor of *Florida Prison Perspectives,* a bimonthly prisoners' rights magazine.

Kevin Pranis is the campaign organizer for Not With Our Money!, a grassroots campaign to end U.S. universities' financial alliances with private prison industries. He is also a Soros Justice Fellow and organizer with Grassroots Leadership, and a board member of the Prison Moratorium Project in New York.

Ken Silverstein is a contributing writer to *Harper's* and *Mother Jones.* He also writes for publications such as *The Nation, American Prospect, Salon,* and *Slate.* Several of his articles have been nominated for national magazine awards. Silverstein is the author of four books, most recently *Private Warriors* (2000), a look at the privatization of national security during the past decade. He is currently at work on a book about the post–Cold War arms trade.

Jeffrey St. Clair is an investigative journalist based in Oregon and the co-editor of *CounterPunch,* a bimonthly investigative newsletter.

Paul Street is the director of research at the Chicago Urban League. His articles, essays, and reviews have appeared in *In these Times, Z Magazine,*

Monthly Review, the *Journal of Social History*, and the *Journal of American Ethnic History*.

Silja J. A. Talvi is a full-time freelance journalist who focuses on issues pertaining to prisons, women's issues, and criminal justice. Silja writes frequently for publications ranging from *The Christian Science Monitor* to *In These Times*. She is also a co-editor of *LiP Magazine* and a frequent contributor to *Prison Legal News*.

Kelly Virella is a graduate student in journalism at U.C. Berkeley. She wrote her piece while working at AlterNet, the news service of the alternative press.

George Winslow is an editor and business journalist who has specialized in international business, the global entertainment industry, the drug trade, money laundering, financial fraud, and global crime groups. He has been covering corporate crime for the last 16 years and is the author of *Capital Crimes* (1999). His work has appeared in the *Columbia Encyclopedia, The Encyclopedia of New York City History, In These Times, The New York Times Book Review,* and many business publications. He currently oversees all the editorial operations at Reed International Television Group, which publishes such magazines as *Television International*. He can be reached at gpwin@aol.com.

Willie Wisely is an activist and journalist, a California prisoner, and frequent *PLN* contributor.

Ronald Young is a former Texas prisoner, an anarchist, and an activist. He is also the founder of *Chain Reaction* magazine, and a frequent *PLN* contributor.

Editors

Tara Herivel is a prisoners' rights activist and attorney who has written for *Prison Legal News* and other progressive periodicals in the Seattle area.

Paul Wright is a Washington state prisoner, jailhouse lawyer, political activist, and journalist. Paul is the co-founder of *Prison Legal News*, a monthly magazine published since 1990, that is prisoner written and edited. He also coedited *The Celling of America* with Daniel Burton Rose and Dan Pens (1998).

About *Prison Legal News*

Prison Legal News (PLN) is an independent, monthly magazine edited by Prison Nation co-editor Paul Wright. Published since 1990, *PLN* is the longest-running independent, prisoner-produced magazine in U.S. history. With a national circulation of more than 4,000 subscribers, *PLN* focuses on reporting news and legal developments involving prisons, jails, and the criminal justice system. Each issue is packed with news, analysis, book reviews, and legal information. *PLN's* content is uncensored.

PLN is a § 501 (c)(3) nonprofit and is almost entirely reader supported. If you believe in the concept of an independent media that reports on prison and jail issues from a perspective other than that of the government, the private prison industry, or the "lock 'em up" crowd, subscribe to *PLN* today.

If you would like to support *PLN's* work, you may do so by sending a tax-deductible donation to the address below. Those who subscribe at the $60 level or make donations allow us to subsidize subscriptions for prisoners in lockdown control units and on death row.

A *PLN* subscription for 12 issues is $25 ($18 for prisoners) and $60 for high income, institutional, and professional subscribers. A sample copy can be viewed at *PLN's* website or obtained for $1 from:

Prison Legal News
2400 NW 80th St. PMB 148
Seattle, WA 98117
(206) 781–6524
PLN@prisonlegalnews.org
www.prisonlegalnews.org

For more information about *PLN,* our back issues, and other related information please go to PLN's website: www.prisonlegalnews.org.

The staff of *Prison Legal News* thank you for reading this book. We hope your interest in this important topic does not end here. To continue receiving regular updates and articles about the U.S. prison system, prisoner struggle, organizing, and legal and political developments found nowhere else, subscribe to *Prison Legal News* today!

Paul Wright
Tara Herivel

Index